New Directions in Question Answering

New Directions in Question Answering

Edited by

Mark T. Maybury

AAAI Press / The MIT Press
Menlo Park, California   Cambridge, Massachusetts   London, England

Copublished and distributed by The MIT Press, Massachusetts Institute of Technology, Cambridge, Massachusetts, and London, England.

ISBN 0-262-63304-3

Manufactured on acid-free paper in the United States of America.

10 9 8 7 6 5 4 3 2 1

Contents

Section Six: Advanced Methods for Question Processing and Answering

Section Seven: Knowledge and Inference-Enabled Question Answering

Preface

New Directions in Question Answering arose from the AAAI Spring Symposium on New Directions in Question Answering held at Stanford University March 24-26, 2003. The symposium was organized by David Day (MITRE), Mark Maybury (MITRE), John Prange (ARDA), James Pustejovsky (Brandeis Univ.), and Janyce Wiebe (Univ. of Pittsburgh) and brought together forty-seven practicing question answering scientists who reported on advances in question answering methods and technologies, and together charted a roadmap for the future. Based on 25 submissions from the U.S., Europe, Japan, and Egypt, 13 papers, 8 posters, and one panel were selected. Three invited speakers-one each from government, academia, and industry-augmented the program. The work of this international group covered presentations of new findings in areas including temporal question answering, multiple perspective question answering, multimedia question answering, multilingual question answering, usability and habitability of question answering systems, reuse in question answering, interactive and/or dialogue based question answering, question analysis, information integration, and answer presentation generation, methods and systems for question answering on the web, and evaluation of question answering. The entire group engaged in two sessions to create a roadmap of the future of question answering, identifying prior work and articulating necessary resources for, impediments to, and planned or possible future capabilities. A summary of the result can be found at the end of the introduction to this collection.

Full chapters of the original submissions, together with an open call for new submissions, were submitted to a highly selective peer review process. From forty excellent submissions, an intensive peer review and highly competitive selection process yielded *New Directions in Question Answering*, the first book to capture the current state and principal trends and influences in this exciting and vital field. *New Directions in Question Answering* is especially timely given the explosion of new research directions, as well as commercial systems (e.g., Ask Jeeves, AskEric).

New Directions in Question Answering is intended to serve multiple purposes. First, it is intended to motivate and define the field of question answering. Second, it is intended to serve as a standard reference for new developments in this field. Third, it can be used for continued research into many remaining problems and as a catalyst for new applications. The book can be used as a reference for students, researchers and practitioners, or a collection of papers for use in undergraduate and graduate seminars. To facilitate multiple uses, the introduction includes a content overview as well as a list of resources including Web links to bibliographic databases, workshops, and commercial products.

New Directions in Question Answering is organized into seven sections, representing key areas of research and development:

Section One: Foundations and History
Section Two: Definitional, Biographical, and Terminology QA
Section Three: Multiperspective, Temporal, and Multimedia QA
Section Four: Interactive and Scenario-Based Question Answering
Section Five: Question Answering Reuse
Section Six: Advanced Methods for Question Processing and Answering
Section Seven: Knowledge and Inference Enabled Question Answering

The book begins with an introduction that defines key terminology, describes a question answering abstract architecture, summarizes a future roadmap, and provides an overview and content index of the collection. This is followed by a chapter by Eric Nyberg (CMU), John Burger (MITRE), David Ferrucci (IBM), and Scott Mardis (MITRE) describing software architectures for advanced question answering. Finally, Brian Ulicny (AskJeeves) discusses question answering patent history and experiences commercializing question answering on the web.

Each remaining section contains an editorial introduction that offers concise summaries of the chapters, placing them in the perspective of the fundamental framework for question answering, along with a discussion of relationships to other chapters in the book and to the literature at large. In addition, each section introduction offers a critical assessment of the remaining problems and challenges in that particular area.

This book articulates a collective vision of the future. We hope it will help promote the development of further advances in question answering making it possible for all of us to more effectively and efficiently exploit the billions of pages of materials we are faced with each day.

Acknowledgments

I thank my secretary, Paula MacDonald for administrative support during the AAAI symposium and Bev Nunan and especially Madge Harrison for detailed proofreading of the final collection. I thank Dr. Inderjeet Mani and Ken Samuel, whose concept extraction software served as a basic source for our conceptual hierarchy behind the index. I am indebted to Dr. John Prange at ARDA for encouraging the collection and the authors—80% of the contributions have some association with John's AQUAINT program. I also thank those in the collection and those that initially submitted, for their interest, energy, and excellence in peer review to create what we hope will become a landmark collection in question answering. Finally, I thank all the brave men and women serving in Operational Iraqi Freedom who kept me safe while I was serving on a special assignment there where late one evening I completed this collection.

I am also indebted to my wife, Michelle, not only for her encouragement and selfless support, but for her creation of the graphic on the back cover. The design derives from a question mark, where the bottommost dot is replaced by an equal sign (representing the "answer" portion of a "question"), and the dot of an eye in the top represents the human, the focus and an integral element of the process of question answering.

– Mark Maybury
Baghdad, Iraq

New Directions in Question Answering

Chapter 1

Question Answering: An Introduction

Mark Maybury

1.1 Question Answering Defined

A dream since the first investigations into artificial intelligence has been to converse with a machine in natural language to get answers to questions. Simply defined, question answering aims to provide natural language responses to natural language queries. More comprehensively:

> *Question answering (QA)* is an interactive human computer process that encompasses understanding a user information need, typically expressed in a natural language query; retrieving relevant documents, data, or knowledge from selected sources; extracting, qualifying and prioritizing available answers from these sources; and presenting and explaining responses in an effective manner.

As is evident from the above definition, QA relies upon many component technologies, including but not limited to natural language processing, information retrieval, and explanation generation. QA promises an important new way of information access for all, a natural step beyond the keyword query and document retrieval characteristic of today's web search.

Several significant question answering activities include the Text Retrieval Evaluation Conference (TREC) QA track, ARDA Advanced Question Answering for Intelligence (AQUAINT) Program, the ARDA Northeast Regional Research Center (nrrc.mitre.org) summer workshops on question answering, several question answering roadmapping activities (ARDA, LREC 2002 workshop, AAAI Spring Symposium), and of course a range of emerging commercial question answering systems (e.g., Ask Jeeves, AskEric). It has been argued that the TREC annual QA competition, which traditionally focused on short, fact-based, general domain questions, answers to which often can be found exploiting answer redundancy on the web, results largely in homogenous QA system approaches (Hirschman and Gaizauskas, 2001). However, it has also been ob-

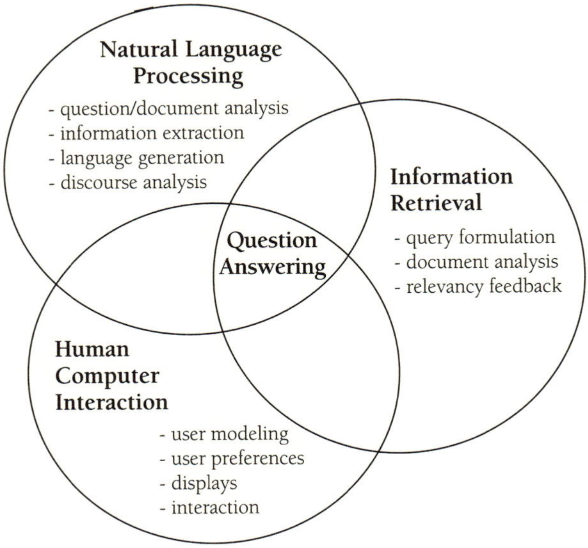

Figure 1.1. Relationship of Question Answering to Other Disciplines

served that TREC QA systems have increased in complexity and have distinct question taxonomies, different ways of exploiting the web (e.g., data source, answer verifier) and both shallow and deep language processing algorithms (Voorhees 2002). This collection aims to explore nonfactoid questions, new application contexts, and new, interactive forms of responses.

The need has never been greater. Not only does the web and technical documentation continue to grow, but a survey this year found that 57 leading e-commerce sites responded only one quarter of the time with relevant answers to three simple questions. Microsoft supports an *English Query* feature of its SQL Server technology and intends to build a QA facility into its upcoming operating system underscoring the importance of this nascent technology.

1.2 Scope and Focus

Question answering is challenging, in part, because it lies at the intersection of several scientific fields including natural language processing (understanding and generating natural language text), information retrieval (query formulation, document analysis, relevancy feedback), and human computer interaction (interface design, user modeling). Figure 1.1 illustrates the relation of the three areas and their intersection in systems that support question answering. Several additional scientific disciplines that may support question answering are not shown, for example knowledge representation and reasoning for question and answer analysis, or recommended technology to find preferred answers, or multimodal information processing to help extract answers from audio or video sources, or information visualization for results display.

This collection focuses on bringing together results from a range of government, industrial, and academic initiatives in question answering with the aim of disseminating accomplishments and fostering new research directions. The work presented in this collection aims to go beyond the factoid questions of conventional QA systems such as who, what, when, and where questions. The collection addresses many exciting new dimensions of question answering such as the following:

Temporal question answering: The automated interpretation of questions with temporal elements such as absolute or relative times, points, durations and extraction of answers with temporal aspects.

Spatial question answering: Providing answers to questions involving spatial objects (e.g., locations, regions), attributes (e.g., size, shape), and relations (e.g., above/below, inside/outside, near/far), possibly requiring spatial inference.

Definitional and descriptional question answering: The automated creation of definitions or descriptions of objects or terms.

Biographical question answering: The automated creation of answers regarding questions about the most significant characteristics and events in the life span of a person, group, or organization.

Opinionoid question answering: The automated detection of opinions (of individuals, groups, or institutions) and response to questions about viewpoints and perspectives oftentimes regarding subjective content.

Multimedia/multimodal question answering: Processing queries that might be expressed a range of media (text, audio, imagery, video) and/or modalities (i.e., auditory, visual senses) and extracting responses from sources that may equally be in a range of media and/or modalities.

Multilingual question answering: Answering questions either for users with varying languages or from multilingual sources requiring translingual retrieval, foreign language content extraction, and language specific response generation.

Additional areas of research addressed by this collection are advances in specific components of question answering systems such as question analysis, source retrieval, answer extraction (e.g., from structured, semi-structured, or unstructured sources), information integration, and answer presentation generation. There are also a number of important system properties or issues explored such as usability, interactivity, and question and answer reuse. Finally, while the TREC QA track provides community evaluations of systems, methods and metrics for evaluation of QA systems remain an active research area.

1.3 The Past

Question answering has an extended legacy. With roots in the Socratic method, automated question answering marked the advent of computers with the creation of systems for question answering from databases as early as the 1950s. As figure 1.2 illustrates, an important initial application of question answering was natural language access to databases. For example, Green et al.'s (1961) BASEBALL system provided answers to factoid questions about the American League from a database using syntactic and semantic processing. Analogously, Bill Woods' (1972) LUNAR system provided answers to questions regarding lunar samples from the Apollo mission. Natural language access to databases became commercially popular in the late 80s and early 90s with systems such as Mercado (for heterogeneous sources), Intellect, and EasyAsk with brand name adopting companies such as Macy's, Sears, and Petco for Mercado. In the early 90s, Broad Daylight's Broad Mind provided natural language access to frequently asked questions (FAQ) for commercial corporations such as Kodak, NASD, and SEC.

Early on scientists explored important dimensions of question answering. For example, deductive question answering has roots in work in deductive question answering and program synthesis (Green 1969). MYCIN (Shortliffe et al. 1976) was able to provide explanations of medical expert system reasoning. Some began exploring the use of natural language processing for story comprehension and question answering (Boris 1972). Lehnert (1977) explored story comprehension using Schankian scripts in her system QUALM. Others began to explore the use of dialogue to enhance QA. For example Winograd's (1972) SHRDLU provided interactive discourse with the blocks world. Bobrow et al.'s (1977) GUS provided simulated question answering from a travel database. By 1999, iPhrase, based on the Galaxy interactive spoken discourse system, had been applied to commercial systems such as Charles Schwab and Staples.

The first Web-based QA system, MIT's START, appeared in 1993 followed shortly by Ask Jeeves in 1996. Ask Jeeves supported NL Query and the Teoma search engine both on the web, as well as for organizations such as Ford, Nike, Nestle, Purina, and the U.S. Navy. The Ask Jeeves capability transitioned into the Kanisa Site Search QA Shell.

The U.S. government's Text Retrieval and Evaluation Conference (TREC) Question Answering track (Voorhees 2002), initiated at TREC-8 in 1999 with 20 participants, is a competition-based systems evaluation of question answering in unrestricted domains. NIST provides a document collection and a set of test questions and participants build QA systems and return ranked responses (a document number and an answer string). One common comparative metric is the mean reciprocal rank (MRR). The MRR of each query is the reciprocal of the rank at which the first correct answer was re-

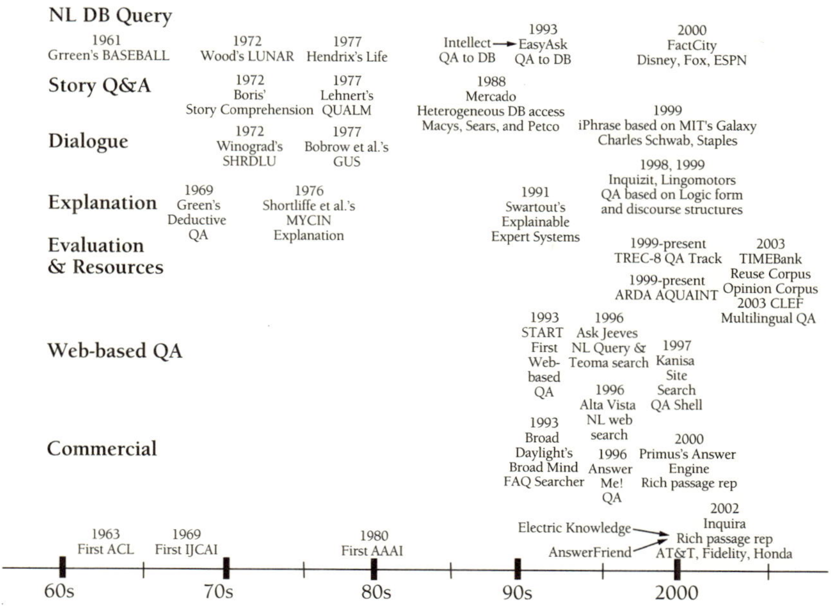

Figure 1.2. History of Question Answering

turned or 0 if none of the first *N* queries included a correct answer. The MRR of a series of queries is the mean of the individual MRRs. Thus a system that gives a correct answer as the first answer gets a 1/1 = 100% but only a 1/5 = 20% if the correct answer is in fifth slot. This gives weight to systems that get the correct answer closest to the top of the list. Over the years the numbers of TREC QA questions has grown (from 200 to 500), news sources have expanded to include AP newswire and WSJ text, and the types of questions have evolved from only factoid questions to include list questions, which require multiple answers. Question sources have ranged from FAQ Finder Logs and assessors (TREC-8), to Encarta and Excite logs (TREC-9), to MSN Search and AskJeeves logs (TREC-10). Of TREC-10's 500 questions, 135 were definitional questions. Early results have been very promising. The top performing systems in TREC 8, 9, and 10 achieved, respectively, 67% MRR (Cymfony), 76% MRR, (Language Computer Corporation – SMU), and 69% MRR (InsightSoft-M). The former two were on the short answer category (50-byte answers). TREC-11 added the confidence weighted score to measure a system's ability to know when it has found a correct answer. It also required exact answers, not just a string containing the answer and only one response per question. The top performing system from Language Computer Corporation achieved a confidence weighted score of 0.856, returning 415 of 500 or 83% correct answers.

The TREC QA track commenced the same time as the ARDA AQUAINT program which, together with additional commercial investments, helped fuel a number of innovations. Developed capabilities included QA based on extracted logic form and discourse processing (e.g., Inquizit 1998, Lingomotors 1999), domain independent passage processing (e.g., Inquira 2002) for companies such as AT&T, Fidelity, Honda, dialogue based QAs (e.g., iPhrase based on MIT's Galaxy spoken dialogue system), and systems providing question answering access to tabular data for companies such as Disney, Fox, and ESPN (FactCity 2000).

A number of these commercial systems and their underlying innovations are overviewed in Chapter 3. In short, QA is no longer an academic effort but a vibrant business with many applications/new services as illustrated throughout the collection.

1.4 Abstract Architecture

As illustrated in figure 1.3, question answering systems typically address some range of questions (e.g., who, what, when, where, how, why), process a range of sources (e.g., documents, web pages, databases), in order to produce answers for users. A question answering system typically contains modules or components for question analysis, source retrieval, answer extraction, and answer presentation, with the possibility for feedback to improve the process over time. In the future we might expect systems which can be tuned in terms of answers being generic for a stereotypical user or tailored to a specific user, providing the best or all answers, providing answers along with their justification or explanation, and presenting a selectable range of answers such as entities (e.g., people, locations, or time for who, where, and when questions), fragments or passages of the source of the answer, or the full source along with the answer. The chapters in the book address various parts of this generic architecture which serves as a common reference throughout the book.

1.5 Overview of the Collection

This book is organized into seven sections. Following a general overview, each section addresses a particular class of questions, system property, or theoretical challenge in the field of question answering.

1.5.1 Foundations

The first section addresses the foundations of the field of question answering. The first chapter articulates software architecture requirements for advanced question answering and characterizes several approaches such as distributed

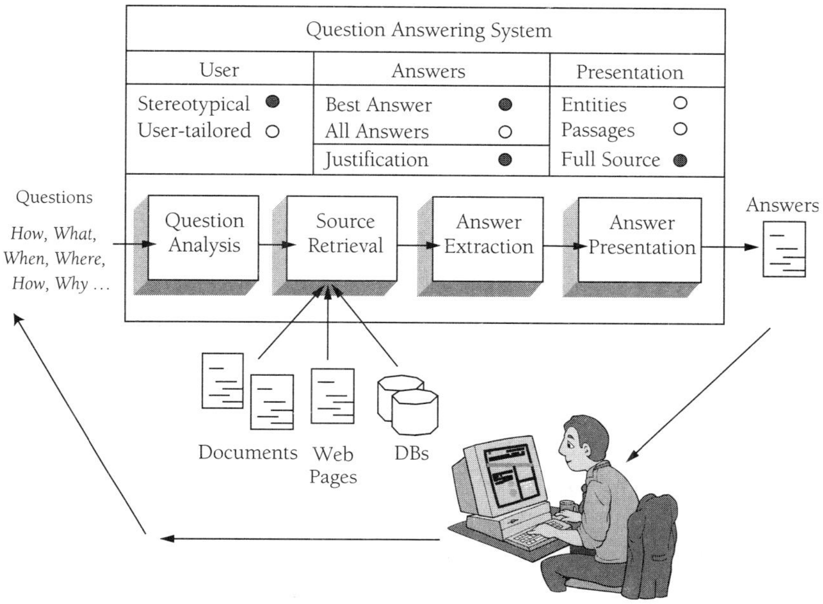

Figure 13. Question Answering Architecture

data flow models or open, modular architectures with explicit support for central planning and coordination that support reuse and ease of integration of a variety of language processing modules in a variety of problem-solving contexts. A second chapter reviews the history of question answering on the web as a commercial service since the early 1990s, reporting the need for lighter weight query and document processing methods and simple interfaces, the use of user analytics to understand customer behavior, and the importance of addressing popular questions well, i.e., not all questions are equal.

1.5.2 Definitions, Terminology and Biography

Whereas question answering systems initially addressed primarily factoid questions (i.e., who, what, when, where kinds of questions), the chapters in the second section focus on systems to address new question types requiring definitions, biographies, and terminology definitions. The first chapter in this section considers a hybrid approach to answer questions about definitions. The second chapter reports on a system that can automatically generate biographies of individuals from web documents. The third chapter explores question answering in terminology-rich technical domains.

1.5.3 Opinions, Time, and Multimedia

The third section considers additional questions types, namely answering questions about opinions, time, and multiple media. The first chapter describes a language for annotating opinions to support answering questions about perspectives held by individuals or groups. The second chapter addresses temporal question answering, including reporting a temporal markup language (TimeML) and an associated gold standard of temporally annotated documents (TIMEBANK). A third chapter in this section considers responding to questions about moving objects in video.

1.5.4 Dialogue and Interactivity

Often the clarification of user questions or answers demands an interactive approach to question answering, the focus of the fourth section of the book. The first chapter explores the utilization of information extraction, clustering, and visualization and includes exploring narrowing, broadening, and fact seeking dialogues to enhance interaction around event frames which are used to bridge the query to document. The second chapter reports on answering complex questions about space exploration in a virtual collaborative environment, and describes a question clarification method motivated by library science. The final chapter explores the use of information extraction together with dialogue management to support question answering sessions for a Swedish public television bird program. This includes the use of models of context (e.g., anaphora, ellipsis) and query clarification/refinement.

1.5.5 Reuse

The fifth section focuses on reuse of answers to previously asked questions. Moving beyond simply identifying redundant questions or reusing context to interpret questions, the first chapter reports on a collaborative analysis and construction of a corpus of reuse and a classification scheme of a dozen types of reuse in questions, answers, and the relation between the two. Motivated by an analysis of several thousand frequently asked questions (FAQs) on the internet, the second chapter explores methods for matching user questions to existing questions or answers in FAQs in order to retrieve pre-existing answers.

1.5.6 Advanced Methods

The sixth section considers a range of special topics related to question answering. The first chapter describes a method for responding to questions about the relationship of two terms, in part by expanding the original query with terms that connect the two. The second chapter reports on the START QA system available on the web since 1993, which exploits information represented in an object-property-value model populated by common web sources such as World Factbook on countries; Biography.com (25,000 biographies of famous people) and the Internet Movie Database of 100,000+ movies. The third chapter reports a system which analyzes question types to provide better proximity-based, answer-focused summaries used to complement existing search engines and other document retrieval systems. Experiments demonstrate better performance than Google's summarizer. A final chapter explores a multi-agent approach to exploit redundancy and reinforcement and, by using a range of agents with differing competencies, the approach is able to enhance performance by 12-16%.

1.5.7 Knowledge and Inference

The seventh and final section of the book explores the issues involving knowledge representation and reasoning in support of question answering. The first chapter explores the use of automated deduction to infer answers from information extracted from multiple sources (databases, Web, programs, and unstructured text). Inspired by a corpora of French question answer pairs regarding traveling, the authors in the second chapter use advanced reasoning to detect and explain user misconceptions or false presuppositions as well as to relax queries to provide cooperative responses to possibly ill formed or unanswerable questions. A final chapter reports on Inference Web, which can provide both inferential and explanation services to enhance the perspicuity of answers to increase user trust in question answering systems.

1.6 Content Index

To facilitate access to relevant content in this collection, each chapter is classified according to its architectural focus, technical approach, question type, and type of sources processed as shown in table 1.1. Using the principal architectural elements defined in figure 1.2, table 1.1 indicates the primary architectural focus of each chapter. That is, we specify whether the research explores the analysis of questions, retrieval of sources, extraction of answers, or presentation to the end user. Table 1.1 further classifies each chapter in terms of the technical approach explored, such as the use of statistical or machine learning methods, linguistic processing, knowledge sources (e.g., linguistic knowledge bases such as electronic dictionaries or thesauri as in WordNet, ontologies and inference machinery such as found in CYC, and domain knowledge bases such as the CIA fact book), agent architectures, or interactive or dialogue methods. We further distinguish the class of questions addressed by each chapter, such as if the chapter addresses traditional factoid questions (e.g., who, what, when, where), definition (e.g., "what is X"?) or biographical questions (e.g., "Who is Y"?), explanations (e.g., why) or relations (e.g., "Compare X and Y."), opinionoid questions, and temporal questions (e.g., "When"). Finally, we characterize each chapter in terms of the (unstructured, semistruc-

Chapter Number	Architectural Emphasis				Technical Approach					Question Focus					Sources				
	Question Analysis	Source Retrieval	Answer Extraction	Presentation	Statistical	Linguistic	Knowledge Based	Agent Based	Interactive/Dialogue	Factoid	Definition/Bio	Explanations/Relations	Opinion	Temporal	Web	Special Collection	Data/Knowledge bases	Multimedia	Multilingual
2	X	X	X	X	X	X	X	X	X	X									
3	X	X	X	X	X	X				X					X	X	X		
4		X	X	X	X	X					X				X	X			
5	X	X	X	X	X	X					X				X	X			
6	X		X	X		X	X			X		E				X			
7			X	X	X	X							X			X			
8	X		X			X				X				X		X			
9	X	X	X	X	X	X				X				X		X	X	X	
10	X	X	X	X	X	X			X	X		X				X			
11	X	X		X	X	X			X		X	E				X	X		
12	X	X	X	X		X	X		X	X		R			X		X		
13	X	X	X		X	X				X	X				X	X			
14	X	X		X	X	X													
15	X	X	X	X	X							R				X			
16	X	X	X	X	X	X				X					X				
17	X	X	X	X	X	X				X					X	X			
18	X	X	X	X	X	X	X	X		X	X				X	X	X		
19	X	X	X	X		X	X	X		X					X	X	X		
20	X	X	X	X		X	X		X	X		E			X				
21			X	X			X		X	X	X	E			X	X	X		

Table 1.1. Content Index of Articles in the Book

tured and/or structured) sources investigated such as the world wide web, special collections (e.g., TREC data), data and/or knowledge bases, multimedia (e.g., text, audio, video), and multilinguality. One area not directly reported on in this collection is multilingual question answering, a recent focus of the Cross-Language Evaluation Forum (CLEF) question answering track (Magnini et al. 2003), which has created a Dutch Italian Spanish English Questions and Answers (DISEQuA) corpus.

1.7 The Future: A Question Answering Roadmap

Motivated by an earlier roadmap (ARDA), Figure 1.4 is a roadmap jointly created by participants of the LREC 2002 Q and A workshop (Maybury et al.,

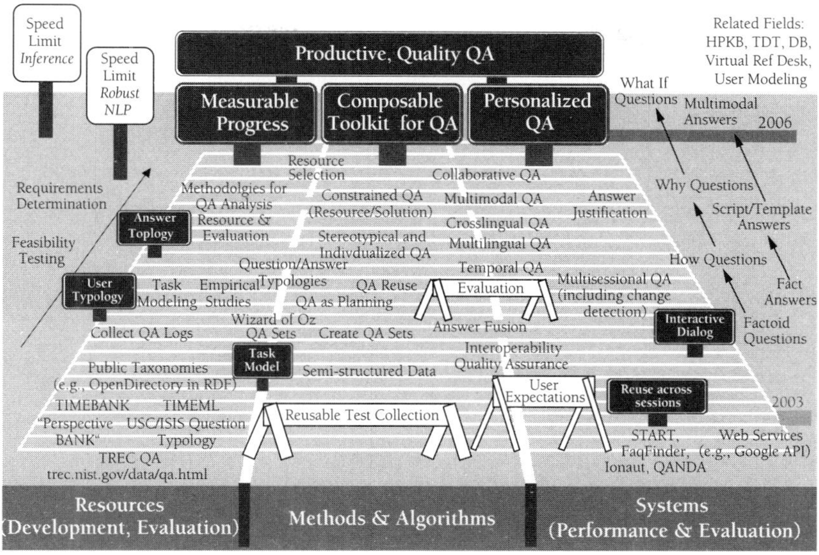

Figure 1.4. Question Answering Roadmap

2002) and further refined at the AAAI Spring Symposium (Maybury et al. 2003). The roadmap is divided into three lanes dealing with resources necessary to develop or evaluate QA systems, methods and algorithms, and systems (including their performance and evaluation). The roadmap starts now and runs until 2006. Each lane leads to outcomes (indicated by sign posts) such as measurable progress from having shared resources, a composable QA toolkit, personalized QA, and an overall, long-term outcome of QA systems that become high quality and enhance productivity.

Sign posts along the road indicate intermediate outcomes, such as a typology of users, a topology of answers, a model of QA tasks (from both a system and user perspective), QA reuse across sessions, and interactive dialogue. Roadblocks along the way include the need to manage and possibly retrain user expectations, the need for reusable test collections, and the need for evaluation methods. Overall workshop participants felt that general natural language processing and inference were limiters to progress, and so these were represented as speed limits signs on the left hand side of the road map. Here also we can see an arrow that indicates that feasibility testing and requirements determination are continuous processes along the road to productive, quality QA.

On the right hand side of the road map we can see the progression of question and answer types. Questions progress from simple factoid questions to how to why then to what-if questions, whereas answers start out as simple facts but move to scripted or templated answers and then progress further to include multimodal answers.

Related fields such as high performance knowledge bases (HPKB), topic detection and tracking (TDT), databases, virtual reference desks, and user modeling were noted as having particular importance for solving the general QA problem which will require cross community fertilization. Individual activities within the lanes are either currently planned or future desired events progressing toward longer term objectives.

Mark Maybury is executive director of MITRE's Information Technology Division and also serves as the executive director of ARDA's Northeast Regional Research Center. His interests are in language generation, multimedia generation, intelligent interfaces, text summarization, and information retrieval. He can be reached at maybury@mitre.org. (Maybury's affiliation with The MITRE Corporation is provided for identification purposes only, and is not intended to convey or imply MITRE's concurrence with, or support for, the positions, opinions, or viewpoints expressed by him.)

Section One

Foundations and History

This section addresses the architectural foundations and commercial history of question answering. The first chapter, authored by Eric Nyberg (CMU), John Burger (MITRE), David Ferrucci (IBM), and Scott Mardis (MITRE), considers software architectures necessary for advanced question answering. These include the need to support multiple engines, flexible data/control flow, long and short term memory, and semantic interpretation and reasoning. The authors describe some of the common approaches as emphasizing information retrieval, information extraction or natural language processing in general, or a hybrid of several methods (e.g., Harabagiu et al.'s 2000 Falcon system). The authors describe functional requirements that are user driven, community-driven, or engineering driven. Some trends include increasing user and task sophistication (e.g., information-gathering dialogs requiring background information, related and ranges of questions), a multiplicity of sources, unrestricted domains, output sophistication, multiple integrated strategies, data persistence, and answer validation. The authors specify key design criteria as including modular and flexible data/control flow, distributed/heterogeneous sources, media and format independence, language and encoding independence, inferential reasoning, and user-accessible data repository. They then illustrate a range of architectural approaches using three exemplar systems: the Catalyst architecture, which incorporates a distributed data flow model for integrating a variety of language processing modules; the JAVELIN system, which emphasizes an open, modular architecture with explicit support for central planning and coordination; and the Unstructured Information Management Architecture (UIMA) approach, which treats QA as an example of an unstructured information management problem, and presents a generalized architecture that supports the reuse of modules in a variety of problem-solving contexts.They conclude by outlining future research areas, including query management, outcomes analysis, linguistic reasoning, interactive answer synthesis, and situated awareness.

In the final chapter in this section, Brian Ulicny (Kanisa) considers the commercialization of QA, with particular emphasis on the hundreds of QA systems on the web. The table that follows outlines several of these. MIT's START

QA system (See Katz and Lin, this volume, Boris Katz and Patrick Winston's U.S. Patents 5,309,359 and 5,404,295) is based on semantic annotation, which matches semantic triples computed from natural language queries to recursive semantic triple structures assigned to documents and passages. In contrast, Xerox PARC's MURAX QA (Julien Kupiec's U.S. Patent 5,519,608; see Ulicny, this volume, for references in this section) ranks noun phrases as answers based on the co-occurrence of the phrases in articles with phrases found in the original query and secondary (derived) queries. MURAX provides an NL interface to encyclopedia content, developed against a corpus of factoid questions from the board game Trivial Pursuit. By 1996, WWW search engines (e.g., Alta Vista) encouraged users to input NL questions as queries. In 1996, Quarterdeck Corporation announced the Web QA system AnswerMe! as part of its client-side metasearch product, WebCompass. Inquizit (Dahlgren and Stabler 1998) and, later, LingoMotors (Pustejovsky et al. 1999) developed question-answering systems relying on large-scale computation of logical forms and discourse structures for unrestricted text. IPLearn was granted a very general patent (U.S. Patent 5,884,302) for transforming user questions into an internal command format. Challenges with many of the early systems include their knowledge/linguistic engineering intensity, lack of modularity, NLP dependency, and inability to address FAQs.

Common assumptions are that users expect a single interface for querying structured and unstructured question sources. System performance should be evaluated in terms of the most common queries, and that precision matters more than recall. A 2003 survey of 57 leading e-commerce sites revealed that only 25% could provide relevant answers to 3 simple questions. Motivated in part to fill this gap, many question answering interfaces have been created to address structured data. For example, FactCity (Traub et al. 2000) offers question answering for tabular data for well known corporate web sites (e.g., ESPN, iWon, Disney's Movies, and FOXSports). EasyAsk, provides QA access to product catalogs for online retail Web sites (e.g., clothiers Talbots, Land's End, and Coach) and Mercado provides the same (e.g., for Macys, Sears, and Petco) but also combines data from disparate data sources (rows of relational database tables, synonyms, text blobs). Inquira (2002), formed by the merger of two Web QA companies (Electric Knowledge and AnswerFriend) provides commercial solutions (e.g., to BEA, Net App, AT&T, Fidelity Investments, Bank of America, Yahoo! and Honda) by indexing a rich representation of passages at a conceptual level, using sentence-, discourse- and document structure, but avoids computing each sentence's logical form. A spin-off of MIT's Spoken Language System Group, iPhrase Technologies (1999), leverages WebGalaxy and Galaxy-II spoken language systems (Seneff et al. 1997) for interactive dialogue with sites such as Charles Schwab, Yahoo! Finance, Staples, and Neiman Marcus. As with EasyAsk, queries that are not translatable to SQL queries are transformed to Boolean queries for keyword search. Primus's An-

Year	Company/ System	Method	Users/Corporations
1993	MIT's START (See chapter 16)	NL interface to web. Semantic annotation: matching semantic triples computed from natural language queries to recursive semantic triple structures assigned to documents and passages. U.S. Patents 5,309,359 and 5,404,295.	web
1993	EasyAsk	QA access to product catalogs	Talbots, Land's End, and Coach
1994	Broad Daylight's Broad Mind	FAQ searching. (Acquired by Primus in 2003)	Kodak, SBC Comms, NASD, SEC
1996	Xerox PARC's MURAX QA	NL interface to encyclopaedia. Ranks noun phrases as answers based on co-occurrence of the phrases in articles with phrases found in the original query and secondary (derived) queries. Julien Kupiec U.S. Patent 5,519,608.	web
1996	Ask Jeeves	Matches natural language questions against precompiled question patterns which can contain pull-down lists and textboxes, else invokes Teoma search	web
1996	Kanisa Site Search (JeevesOne)	QA shell or toolkit using a *question templates* and answer actions.	Ford, Nike, Washington State, Novartis, Roche Pharma., U.S. Navy, Nestle Purina PetCare
1996	Quarterdeck's AnswerMe!	Client-side metasearch product, WebCompass	
1998	Inquizit (Dahlgren and Stabler)	Logical forms and discourse structures for unrestricted text	
1999	LingoMotors	Logical forms and discourse structures for unrestricted text (Pustejovsky et al.)	
1999	iPhrase Technologies	Based on MIT's Spoken Language System Group's WebGalaxy and Galaxy-II systems based on spoken language dialogue (Seneff et al. 1997)	Yahoo! Finance, Staples, Neiman Marcus
2000	FactCity (Traub et al.)	QA from tabular data	ESPN, iWon, Disney's Movies, and FOXSports
1999	IPLearn	Transforming user questions into an internal command format. U.S. Patent 5,884,302.	
1998	Mercado	QA access to product catalogs - combines data from disparate data sources (rows of relational database tables, synonyms, text blobs)	Macys, Sears and Petco
2002	Inquira	Merger of Electric Knowledge and AnswerFriend. indexes rich representation of passages at a conceptual level, using sentence-, discourse- and document structure, but avoids computing each sentence's logical form.	BEA, Net App, AT&T, Fidelity Investments, Bank of America, Yahoo! and Honda
2000	Primus's	Enhanced token-level representation of each sentence, using sense discrimination and some surface semantic roles (subject/object, potential/actual)	
2002	Inquira	Indexes a rich representation of passages at a conceptual level, using sentence-, discourse- and document structure, but avoids computing each sentence's logical form	BEA, Net App, AT&T, Fidelity Investments, Bank of America, Yahoo!,Honda

The Commercialization of Question Answering.

swer Engine by AnswerLogic (Hamilton 2000), like Inquira, indexes an enhanced token-level representation of each sentence, using sense discrimination and some surface semantic roles (subject/object, potential/actual) rather than computing a full logical form. In contrast, Broad Daylight's Broad Mind is an FAQ searching system which returns the most similar question-answer pair(s) to user questions (they also support natural language search and distributed FAQ search) for customers such as Kodak, SBC Communications, NASD, and the SEC. Ask Jeeves matches natural language questions against precompiled question patterns (learned by monitoring user queries), which can contain pull-down lists and textboxes. If a query fails, the Teoma search engine is invoked. Notably, only 20% of queries are stated as interrogatives, and of those 7% are where questions, 4% how; 3.5% definitional and 2% identity statement questions (e.g., "What is the speed of light?").

In July 2003, Kanisa acquired JeevesOne and renamed it Kanisa Site Search (KSS), a QA shell or toolkit used by customers such as Ford Motors, Nike, the State of Washington, Novartis, Roche Pharmaceuticals, the U.S. Navy, and Nestle Purina PetCare. Indicative of the commercial maturation of question answering, Kanisa computes the cost of getting a particular query type correct as the query frequency multiplied by the sum of increased sales and decreased customer service representative costs and minus the incremental development cost. Finally, Microsoft has announced that it intends to build a QA facility into its upcoming operating system, codenamed Longhorn, possibly also supporting web document search and using a redundancy-based approach to QA for encyclopedic knowledge questions.

Ulicny summarizes a number of lessons learned from these commercial systems including the need for light weight methods, content control/adaption by non-expert system administrators, user analytics to understand customer behavior, disproportionate question focus (address popular ones well), a single interface to structured and unstructured data, and a range of answer types (text, document, image, structured data, or combination)

Chapter 2

Software Architectures for Advanced QA

Eric Nyberg, John Burger, Scott Mardis & David Ferrucci

1.1 Introduction

As question-answering (QA) research moves beyond single-answer, factoid-style questions, the architectural requirements for QA systems become more complex. Session-based QA, wherein the user provides a detailed context and asks several questions in the course of an ongoing dialog, requires more than just a simple passage retrieval and ranking pipeline. While it may be desirable to build systems targeted at specific domains or problems, any QA system will nonetheless benefit by treating architecture from a broad perspective. Architectures for advanced QA should consider the following:

Integration of multiple engines. Research shows that a variety of approaches are required for best performance on a variety of question types. List questions, for example, require a different strategy than date questions. Advanced QA systems should support multiple algorithms and/or modules where appropriate.

Support for flexible control flow and data flow. It should be possible to adapt or modify the flow of data through the basic QA steps (question analysis, document retrieval, etc.) to support specific strategies, error recovery, and clarification with the user.

Long-term and short-term memory. Advanced architectures must provide an accessible database of past and current sessions that can be directly accessed by the QA system as part of its knowledge base. The memory should also store the decisions made by the system during processing, which provide the foundation for answer justification and system adaptation via machine learning.

Semantic interpretation and reasoning. Effective answers to complex questions sometimes require a deeper understanding of the question and potential answer passages. Future systems will compare the meanings of passages to detect contradictions, different opinions, implied relationships, etc. Architectural design should support the integration of language understanding and reasoning components for more complex question answering strategies.

In section 2.2, we provide a brief summary of past approaches to architecture in QA systems. Section 2.3 presents an emerging set of architectural requirements for advanced QA, and the associated design criteria for QA systems. In section 2.4, we highlight some of the newer approaches to QA architecture that attempt to address these requirements. We conclude in section 2.5 with a discussion of remaining open research questions for QA architecture.

2.2 Past and Present Approaches

A survey of past publications on question answering reveals a variety of fundamental approaches:

> *QA as Information Retrieval.* Systems that rely primarily on traditional IR techniques attempt to find the most relevant documents for a query. If shorter answers are required, some method is used to identify the most relevant passage in the document, typically via some passage-ranking scheme based on query terms (e.g., Kwok 2000).
>
> *QA as Information Extraction.* Systems that rely primarily on traditional IE techniques use a template-based approach widely explored by participants in the TIPSTER and MUC competitions. Questions and answers are associated with slot-filler structures, which are fully or partially matched by the contents of searched documents. Extracting the contents of filled templates provides answers (Srihari 2000, Prager et al. 2000).
>
> *QA as Natural Language Processing.* More recent systems have begun to improve on the performance of purely IR or IE based system through the use of NLP techniques that include deeper semantic analysis (Clarke 2000, Ferret et al. 2002, Hovy et al. 2000, and Harabagiu et al. 2000).

More recent QA systems, such as the Falcon system developed at SMU (Harabagiu et al. 2000), acknowledge that a hybrid approach, with several levels of sophistication, can produce better results than systems that rely purely on IR or IE approaches with a bit of parsing thrown in. Where traditional IE- or IR-based systems relied on a simple pipeline architecture, future systems will require more sophisticated architectures that integrate multiple agents, data sources, etc.

2.3 Requirements for Advanced QA

In this section, we describe the emerging functional characteristics that are desired for advanced QA. Then we analyze the associated design criteria that must be considered when building an advanced QA system.

2.3.1 Functional Characteristics of Advanced QA Systems

There are three different perspectives on QA systems that provide differing (yet complementary) sets of functional requirements:

User-Driven Requirements. Requirements influenced by the needs of the users; in particular, those that are generated as a result of supporting scenario-based QA. Examples might include: the need to support interactive QA sessions; specific task support; and real-time performance.

Community-Driven Requirements. Requirements whose genesis is the need for QA research to be a community endeavor that integrates increasingly complex systems in interdisciplinary efforts. Examples include component modularity, transparency for "glass box" evaluation, and standard data formats.

Engineering-Driven Requirements. Requirements necessitated simply by good engineering practice and the need to migrate maturing technologies into operational prototypes and test deployments. Relevant issues include programming language neutrality, ease of application development and integration, as well as support for debugging (logging, trace facilities, etc.).

Current research trends (as captured in recent roadmap exercises) (Burger et al. 2002, Maybury 2002) tend to focus on increasing algorithmic complexity as systems attempt to solve problems with practical performance and scale for real-world information analysts. Requirements that are driven more by community and engineering perspectives tend to emerge as the practical consequences of specific research programs and projects (e.g., the use of metadata markup in text corpora). A more central focus is given to the variety of user-oriented requirements that drive the evolving complexity of QA systems design.

Increasing User Sophistication. The user of the system is an "information professional." Their task is typically more complex, and their understanding of the data sources and the technology more sophisticated than for the average Web searcher. In some cases, an experienced user may be able to take advantage of a flexible architecture that permits them to manipulate some of the internal parameters and structures of the system.

Increasing Task Sophistication. To support information-gathering dialogs with a professional information analyst, a QA system must accept a variety of interactive inputs that go beyond isolated factoid questions. An advanced QA scenario may include background information (both from the present scenario and past scenarios with this user) and a range of questions, each building on the results of the previous question as more information is uncovered. Analysis of the question will require solving challenges in NL dialog understanding (turn-taking, interruptions, reference resolution, user guidance, etc.), along with an explicit representation of the individual interactions within a dialog.

A Multiplicity of Sources. The system may search multiple, heterogeneous sources of information, such as text corpora, relational databases, ontologies, video/audio signals, and transcripts. Sources may cut across different human languages, language styles, encoding formats, and application domains. Providing a clear understanding of an answer's provenance (sources searched, methods applied, inferences performed, verification steps taken) may be as important as the answer itself.

Unrestricted Domain. Questions will require answers that fall into an unrestricted set of semantic types. In contrast with current factoid QA systems, advanced QA systems will answer questions about complex phenomena such as causes of events, relationships between entities, and comparisons between the attributes and relationships of particular entities.

Increasing Output Sophistication. Questions will require answers in different surface forms. In addition to short answers and single sentences drawn directly from the sources searched, QA systems will provide composed answers in the form of lists, biographical sketches, event narratives, and other paragraph-length responses. Answers may also include the results of inferences based on facts reported in the sources plus world knowledge possessed by the QA system.

Support for Multiple Strategies. It should be possible for the system to utilize different algorithms for individual question answering steps, combining the results in a way that maximizes the overall utility of the system. Advanced QA systems will also allow the user to tailor the system's behavior according to various utility parameters (e.g., speed of response, thoroughness of search, veracity of sources, completeness of answer, etc.).

Data Persistence. All of the questions, answers, and intermediate data structures produced by a system will be stored in a long-term memory or data repository. The repository will support not only subsequent examination and verification on the part of the user, but also direct access by the system itself during future question answering scenarios.

Answer Validation. The system provides a means of verifying its answers based on a range of techniques, including: (a) checking knowledge bases; and (b) posing questions to sub-QA systems. We believe that the ability of systems to answer verification questions will be important as the community begins to construct large-scale integrated QA systems.

The following subsection discusses some design criteria associated with these requirements, and how QA systems must evolve in order to meet them.

2.3.2 Design Criteria for Advanced QA Systems

To satisfy the functional requirements listed in section 2.3.1, advanced QA developers should consider the following design points:

Modularity. The system design should encapsulate the individual steps in the QA process (question analysis, retrieval, extraction, answer formulation, answer selection) as separate, swappable modules to support comparative evaluation, reuse, etc. This modularity may be achieved via common linguistic representations (Katz et al., chapter 16), multiple data views (Small et al., chapter 10), and abstract interfaces for external data (Katz et al., chapter 16).

Flexible/Multiple Control Flows. The system should support a variety of control strategies, as appropriate to the particular problem (question type, answer type, sources to be searched, etc.). Advanced systems will go beyond selecting from a hard-wired set of alternatives to full-blown AI-style planning and execution in the space of possible solutions. Possible approaches include multi-agent, multi-question QA (Prager et al., chapter 18), hybrid algorithms (Weischedel, Xu, and Licuanan, chapter 5).

Flexible/Multiple Data Flows. The system should support a variety of interconnections between components, as appropriate to the problem at hand. If necessary, the system should distribute work to multiple agents and rank/merge the results of individual agents at a particular step in the QA process.

Distributed, Heterogeneous Sources. Advanced QA systems should incorporate appropriate abstractions to support straightforward access to data sources with multiple domains and genres. Adding a new data source should be a matter of implementing a pre-specified interface for data sources.

Media and Format Independence. To the extent that it is possible, the system should incorporate appropriate abstractions to support multiple media (text, audio, video) and desired formats for each medium (raw ASCII, XML, etc.).

Language and Encoding Independence. Where appropriate, the system should incorporate abstractions to support sources in multiple human languages (English, Japanese, Chinese, etc.) and encodings (e.g., UTF-8, Big-5, etc.).

Support for Inferential Reasoning. Advanced QA systems will produce answers that cannot be found by direct search, but must be inferred from the available sources using spatial, temporal, or linguistic reasoning. For example, questions such as "What is the occupation of Bill Clinton's wife?" will require decomposition into subquestions by reasoning about the linguistic properties of the question (e.g., by recognizing an indirect reference like Bill Clinton's wife and attempting to resolve the reference by finding a specific named entity that satisfies the references). Deeper reasoning will require support in the form of markup standards and annotation programs that recognize various entities of interest and relationships between them (Pustejovsky et al., chapter 8), as well as more global text features such as perspective and opinionated language (Cardie et al., chapter 7). See chapter 19 for a possible approach to deductive reasoning in QA.

User-Accessible Data Repository. All of the data artifacts created during a QA session (questions, answers, clarifications, passages, reasoning chains, verifications, etc.) must be stored in a linked archive that preserves the processing history for each question. The data repository will support direct examination by the user, as well as introspective search and reuse on the part of the system itself (e.g., in response to queries such as, "What questions have been asked about X in the last two weeks?"). The question of answer provenance is addressed in chapter 21; see Light et al., chapter 13, for an approach to reuse in QA systems.

This set of design criteria has certain implications for the low-level design of algorithms, control structures, data representation, and data storage for advanced QA systems. In the following section, we summarize some recent work that attempts to advance QA architectural design along these dimensions.

2.4 New Approaches to QA Architecture

In this section, we highlight a few of the recent approaches to QA architecture that attempt to address the emerging requirements for advanced QA in different ways. The Catalyst Architecture focuses on a distributed data flow model for integrating a variety of language processing modules. The JAVELIN system emphasizes an open, modular architecture with explicit support for central planning and coordination. The UIMA approach treats QA as an example of an unstructured information management problem, and presents a generalized architecture that supports the reuse of modules in a variety of problem-solving contexts.

2.4.1 The Catalyst Architecture

The Catalyst Architecture (Mardis and Burger 2002) represents a unique approach to QA system organization. It has a highly modular structure, composed of separate language processes joined by a distributed dataflow network. It displays some of the required design elements that future systems will need:

Flexible Data and Control Flow. A declarative system specification allows a system designer to succinctly specify which modules are needed and how they will communicate. Process inputs and outputs can be connected in arbitrary ways, making it simple to connect modules that were built with very different nomenclatures and thus permitting novel uses of standard components.

Persistent Storage. Catalyst supports the creation of a user-accessible data repository as the communication link between all modules using a simple standoff annotation model similar to that used in ATLAS (Laprun et al. 2002). This common data format permits all inter-module communication to be stored, indexed and retrieved for use by other system components and system users.

Modularity and System Performance. Catalyst's simple dataflow architecture strongly supports technology evolution as systems are scaled up to perform on larger data sets or operate under tight real-time performance requirements. Slow components can be easily replicated on distributed hardware. Output from prior components in a process can be fanned out to a group of subsequent processes, and the results combined for maximum performance.

2.4.2 PIQUANT

The PIQUANT system (Chu-Carroll et al. 2002, 2003) is a multi-agent, multi-strategy architecture for QA that incorporates several of the architectural elements expressed in Section 2.3. PIQUANT incorporates a modular abstraction (abstract interfaces) for the main activities in a QA architecture. Some of the principal component types defined by the PIQUANT include:

Question Analysis components, using parsing and named entity detection techniques, identify, among other things, the answer type, focus, and type of the question. The results are represented in an XMLdata structure named the QFrame.

Answering Agent components take a QFrame as input and produce a set of triples, each including an answer, a confidence, and a justification. PIQUANT's planning elements decide which available answering agents to apply to which QFrames. This decision is predicated on elements of the QFrame and available meta-data associated with the answering agents. Answering agents have access to multiple sources from which to derive their answers, including semantic search engines and structured knowledge sources (data bases and knowledge bases).

Answer Resolution components take the output of a set of answering agents and employ a variety of techniques to combine the results into a single ranking.

Knowledge Source Adapter components provide uniform access to structured knowledge sources, insulating the other components from the implementation-level details of particular knowledge sources (such as data formats, access mechanisms, etc.).

Modular abstraction in the PIQUANT architecture supports the construction of hybrid QA systems—for example, systems that combine statistical answering agents with knowledge-based answering agents. Recent work by Chu-Carroll et al. (2002) has shown that performance in a hybrid system is substantially better than that of individual agents working in isolation. PIQUANT also incorporates a form of answer verification. As part of the answer resolution process, answers are checked for validity (using the Cyc knowledge base); for example, numeric answers are judged for validity by checking to see if they fall in an acceptable range for the quantity being queried.

2.4.3 JAVELIN

The JAVELIN system (Nyberg et al. 2002) is a distributed architecture that integrates individual QA components with an explicit planning module and a long-term repository of results. JAVELIN attempts to address the following dimensions of advanced QA design:

Modularity. JAVELIN components are distributed on a local network and utilize XMLinput and output specifications transmitted over TCP/IP sockets. By combining highly structured ASCII data with a simple low-level transmission protocol, it is possible to integrate components developed rapidly in a variety of languages (PERL, Java, C, etc.).

Multiple Strategies. The planner module in JAVELIN selects a strategy based on the current state of computation, and can adjust its strategy after each execution step (question analysis, document retrieval, etc.). To carry out a particular step in processing (for example, answer extraction), the planner may select from a set of suitable modules the one that has the best-known performance in the current context.

Language and Encoding Independence. JAVELIN is designed to work with multiple human languages; the XML objects passed between components are language-independent, and are used to represent cross-lingual queries in Japanese and Chinese. A single encoding (UTF-8) is used as a standard within the system; components that import data from external sources (e.g., search engines) must provide their results in the standardized encoding.

User-Accessible Data Repository. The JAVELIN system stores all of its intermediate and final results in a persistent data store, which a user may search and view using a standard web browser. The system can present a structured summary of the repository contents for any given input question, which affords the user the ability to examine the individual steps taken in answering the question, the sources searched, documents retrieved, etc.

2.4.4 UIMA

Many of the requirements and design criteria for QA systems are shared by the general class of unstructured information systems—systems that must analyze and process large-scale sources of information that is inherently unstructured (such as natural language text). The UIMA (Ferrucci and Lally 2002) captures this level of abstraction in a set of component interfaces and architectural patterns:

Text Analysis Engine (TAE). A single component interface is used to encapsulate a variety of language processing components (e.g., translators, summarizers, classifiers, taggers, etc.).

Common Analysis System (CAS). Each TAE produces an analysis represented in a general structure called the CAS, analogous to the "annotations" used in other architectures such as TIPSTER (Grishman 1996). The CAS is general and extensible, and supports multiple metadata types under single inheritance.

Collection Analysis Engine (CAE). A CAE produces aggregate inferences over all or a subset of the documents in the collection. For example, a search engine indexer might be integrated implementing the CAE interface.

Collection Processing Manager (CPM). A CPM applies a particular TAE to each document in the collection to be processed. A CPM can be configured to provide a variety of functions, such as filtering, indexing, and external storage of results. The CPM can also support parallel execution of multiple TAEs for better performance.

Knowledge Source Adapter (KSA). KSA objects provide a uniform interface to disparate knowledge sources containing structured data (databases, dictionaries, ontologies, etc.). The output from a KSA is represented as a set of instantiated predicates, using knowledge interchange format (KIF) and XML.

Analysis Engine. An analysis engine is a general component interface that accepts a CAS as input and produces a (possibly modified) CAS as output. This interface is intended for developers who are focusing on specific phases in information processing, and insulates the developer from system-level details (such as control flow) and lower-level implementation details. Analysis engines are primarily data-driven, and are designed to operate on their input independently of the framework application in which they are deployed. Analysis engines are also recursive; it is possible to build an aggregate analyzer from several low-level analyzers. Finally, each analysis engine is also self-descriptive—its data model is formally declared in XML, making it possible for humans and/or automated brokers to examine an analysis engine to understand its data requirements, output, etc. All of these features are intended to promote ease of implementation and a higher degree of component reuse across applications.

2.5 The Future for QA Architecture Research

The systems described in the previous section represent some recent attempts to address the list of design criteria listed in section 2.3. It is clear that some current architectures are already addressing issues such as modularity, flexible control flow and data flow, multiple heterogeneous sources, language/media/format independence, and a long-term data repository. There has been less work, perhaps, on generalized architectural design for: (a) scenario-based QA in a dialog context (vs. a single factoid question); (b) the role of linguistic reasoning and reasoning about the QA process itself; and (c) support for user management of questions, answers, and output products that are synthesized from multiple questions and answers. Clearly more work is required in these areas. While by no means an exhaustive list, the following set of advanced research topics emerged during our discussions of current and future QA architectures.

Query Management. Although systems like JAVELIN provide a persistent storage of questions, answers, and intermediate results, more work is needed on mechanisms that will allow the end user to effectively manage these resources. Under the broad rubric of query management, we might include support for functions such as: (a) meta-questions ("What questions have been asked about Iraq?"); (b) standing queries that are rerun at predetermined intervals to find new potential answers; (c) new question instances that are essentially "copy and edit" clones of earlier queries, where some parameters affecting the outcome (e.g., sources, languages searched, time bounds, confidence threshold, etc.) are deliberately varied by the user; and (d) support for sharing of questions, answers, and intermediate results among users.

Outcomes Analysis. Why does one question get a different answer than a slight rewording of the same question? Why does a system succeed when some of its internal parameters are set a certain way, but fail otherwise? The answer lies in a solution to the credit/blame assignment problem, which is a classic challenge in the field of machine learning; before we can modify the system's behavior, we must understand where it went wrong, and what contributed to the erroneous decision or action. An initial goal might be a QA system that can reflect on its own behavior, and provide explanations or justifications for wrong answers as well as right answers. In the long term, it should be possible for QA systems to learn from their mistakes, by combining reflection with direct feedback from the user in a supervised learning scenario.

Linguistic Reasoning. Most of the early and current QA systems that utilize semantic knowledge about natural language incorporate pre-existing knowledge bases and ontologies (e.g., WordNet, OpenCYC, etc.). Semantic processing has been used primarily in question analysis (to identify the semantic type of the answer being sought) and in answer verification (to confirm that the answer retrieved matches the type sought). Although some systems attempt to incorporate a full logical derivation or proof to link the question with the answer, this approach is susceptible to brittleness in unrestricted domains where ontological coverage may be spotty. Nevertheless, it is a commonly held belief that QA systems require deeper semantic understanding to answer complex questions about phenomena such as cause-and-effect, relationships between entities, etc. To provide deeper understanding in unrestricted domains without pre-building a vast ontology, remains a challenge.

Interactive Answer Synthesis. The current set of answer formats produced by QA systems is limited primarily to textual output. Future QA systems should provide more meaningful answer formats, for example, time lines for answers to when questions. Each answer format should support a simple algebra of operations, such as "intersection," "union," etc. For example, if two different time lines are produced by two different answering agents, it should be possible for the system to merge them into a single time line, while maintaining references back to the agents that originally produced the data (as well as a pointer to the original data sources). It should be possible for the user to incorporate these results into a variety of intelligence products in required formats (e.g., HTML, Word, etc.). In a more visionary scenario, answers that have been incorporated into synthesized output products might be checked for continuing validity, and updated dynamically as desired.

Situated Awareness. Today's intelligence analysts use a variety of separate tools to do their job. Current QA systems have no awareness of those tools, or how the analyst is using those tools on a current information task. Future QA systems should exhibit situated awareness of the global context (e.g., analyst's desktop), and use contextual information to improve system performance. A simple example would be the use of a Google proxy that stores queries sent and documents retrieved; this information could be directly accessed by a QA system running on the same desktop. A more futuristic example would capture all of the relevant information events (email, newswires, etc.) and make them available to a variety of QA answering agents working together on a task.

In this chapter, we have attempted to summarize both areas of active research and topics for future research on QA software architectures. What is certain is that the evolving sophistication of QA system functionality will require a corresponding evolution in the complexity and sophistication of QA software design. While recent work has advanced the state of the art in the design of flexible control structures, data flows, and useful modular abstractions, more research is needed on what is broadly referred to as scenario-based QA—tasks that involve a sustained dialog between system and user, and include by reference the results of previous QA tasks. Future QA systems will represent dialogs as part of a persistent, long-term memory of user tasks, and will incorporate ever more sophisticated levels of reasoning as the intelligence of QA systems improves.

Acknowledgments

This work was supported in part by the Advanced Research and Development Activity (ARDA)'s Advanced Question Answering for Intelligence (AQUAINT) Program under contracts MDA904-01-C-0988, F19628-99-C-0001, and MDA908-02-C-0009.

Eric Nyberg is an associate professor at the School of Computer Science and the Heinz School, Carnegie Mellon University.

John Burger is principal scientist at The MITRE Corporation.

Scott Mardis is a scientist and engineer at The MITRE Corporation. He can be reached at mardis@mitre.org.

David Ferrucci is the senior manager of the Semantic Analysis and Integration department at the IBM T.J. Watson Research Center, Hawthorne, NY. He specializes in architectures for unstructured information analysis and knowledge integration. He can be reached at ferrucci@us.ibm.com.

Chapter 3

Bringing Commercial Question Answering to the Web

Brian Ulicny

3.1 Purpose and Scope

Nearly as soon as the world wide web first boomed, it was followed by attempts to provide commercial question-answering (QA) systems on the web. These attempts left a trail of patent applications, vendor materials, and industry analyst literature often neglected by the research community.[1] Commercial implementations of QA on the web now number at least one hundred or so.

Just prior to the web explosion, important noncommercial QA systems were patented. Boris Katz and Patrick Winston patented the START QA system at MIT.[2] Julien Kupiec patented the MURAX QA system at Xerox PARC.[3] On the web, several early attempts to develop commercial QA systems fizzled for reasons explored below. Going forward, contemporary commercial QA ventures have learned to steer between requiring too much knowledge engineering to be cost efficient and providing "just search." Second-generation commercial QA are beginning to develop sustainable models to meet evolving customer expectations and are poised to become even more widespread soon.

3.2 Early Web QA Systems

As early as 1996, then state-of-the-art web-wide search engines such as Alta Vista encouraged users to input natural language questions as queries. Such systems are more properly seen as *natural language search* rather than question-answering, since only links to whole documents (with abstracts) were returned. Internally, the search engine removed stop words and ranked documents with a preference for leftmost query terms and term proximity.

Innovations such as these were immediately followed by the commercial release of QA technologies on the web by a variety of early players. Most of these players focused on answering limited-domain questions from the general public by web-enabling QA interfaces to particular document sets. At least one offered an open-domain QA interface to the entire web.

Both Inquizit[4] and, later, LingoMotors[5] developed question-answering systems relying on large-scale computation of logical forms and discourse structures for unrestricted text. In addition to simple truth-conditions, the systems relied, respectively, on Inquizit cofounder Kathleen Dahlgren's Naïve Semantics taxonomy of events and things (Dahlgren 1998) and LingoMotors' cofounder James Pustejovsky's Qualia Structure (Pustejovsky 1995) to support inferencing. Both systems provided interfaces for knowledge engineers to specify lexical properties and rules.

Inquizit listed three commercial implementations of its technology on its website. LingoMotors demonstrated a natural language query system developed for a "large online bookseller" at Demo 2001 in Arizona.[6] No customers for the natural language query system were listed on LingoMotors' website.

At the same time as Inquizit, Quarterdeck Corporation was developing web QA as part of its client-side metasearch product, WebCompass. WebCompass 3.0 was announced in 1996[7] and was to include client-side QA, returning ranked sentences as answers to user-supplied questions. The QA functionality was described in Ulicny et al. 1996 as the AnswerMe! system.

AnswerMe! was perhaps the earliest system specifically designed to use the entire web as the source of sub-document answers. AnswerMe! submitted user questions to multiple search engines (AltaVista and InfoSeek's FAQ Search, others could be added). Returned documents were scanned sentence-by-sentence in order of document relevance. Sentences containing question keywords were then parsed into a neo-Davidsonian representation using a finite-state chunker and a set of thematic role grids derived from Beth Levin's verb taxonomy.[8] Candidate sentences were ranked as answers to the user query to the extent that they represented similar events. No attempt at anaphora resolution or other discourse-level analysis was made.

AnswerMe! performed reasonably well for questions such as "When was Pluto discovered?" As a client-side application, it took on the order of minutes to process an entire document set. Answers were presented as they were found. A phenomenon that became apparent from interacting with the system was that the redundancy of the web allowed one to spot consensus answers, even if individual erroneous answers scored highly. WebCompass 3.0 was finished but never released. However, Kristina Lerman (now at USC's ISI) went on to incorporate a simpler sentence-ranking algorithm based on word order alone into a web-based QA service for Quarterdeck's PC help desk product, RealHelp. RealHelp's Find-A-Fix function allowed users to pose questions to internal document knowledge bases.[9] If no satisfactory answer was found, a metasearch QA functionality like that of WebCompass was used to find answers by querying first known support-site search engines, then general web search engines.

IAskWeb's QA system grew out of technology developed by Boris Galitsky at Rutgers.[10] IAskWeb's QA technology, like Inquizit's, was Prolog-based and used inferencing to match queries interpreted into a set of first-order Prolog predicates against Katz-like semantic annotations called semantic headers. IAskWeb's commercial implementations included Perot Systems, CBS Marketwatch, H&R Block, Netgravity, ISN, First Auction and BenefitStreet.

FactCity (Traub et al. 2000) emphasized tabular data for its online QA system. Their patent application detailed a system for matching user queries to one or more 'Searchable Data Objects' (SDOs) of tabular data, based on the detection of query terms known to be (synonymous with) a particular table's column names or data values. For example, "When was *Gone with the Wind* published?" would be determined to have both a book and movie title *Gone with the Wind* but a book-specific term *published,* so the relevant values would be formulated into an SQL query to return the relevant book information. SDOs might require the presence of certain fields before a query could be issued. FactCity provided implementations for ESPN.com, iWon.com, Disney's Movies.com, and FOXSports. Aggregate functions like "average score" were not supported.

It is not clear precisely what combination of business or technical issues caused these attempts at web QA to fizzle. For the most part, these technologies relied on large-scale semantic interpretation and discourse representation. It is likely that the knowledge engineering cost to support large-scale, unconstrained semantic interpretation was just too high to maintain a sustainable business while delivering accurate results. Automatic interpretation of unconstrained text is still too brittle. Secondly, for the most part, these systems treated all queries equally, so it would be hard to make localized improvements to the system behavior. The systems did not focus on the most frequently asked questions. Finally, updating the system's grammars and data structures required scarce expert knowledge.[11]

3.3 Current Web QA Systems

Recently, the Allen Bonde Group (ABG) surveyed how well fifty-seven leading e-commerce sites handled common customer questions using three test queries: "What is your return policy?" "How do I contact customer service?" and "Do you sell gift certificates for less than $50?"

Sites were graded on the number of correct responses, average number of returned links and overall user experience. Overall, ABG concluded that companies had largely failed to provide adequate online customer self-service, despite the cost advantage of automatically answering questions on the web. ABG found that about 75% of site searches were ineffective in answering these simple questions.[12]

It is interesting to note that assumptions made by the ABG study are widely shared: that users expect a single interface for querying structured and unstructured data sources, that system performance should be evaluated in terms of the most common queries, and that precision matters more than recall.[13] Clearly, there is a need for QA capabilities on outward-facing sites. Several companies have begun to create such cost-effective QA solutions on the web.

One such company is EasyAsk, founded in 1993 by Larry Harris, another of the 1980s AI "Gang of Four" (Phillips 1999). Harris's previous company developed Intellect, an application that allowed executives to query data warehouses without having to learn SQL. EasyAsk builds on Harris's long experience in this area. EasyAsk primarily targets online retail web sites such as clothiers Talbots, Land's End, and Coach, providing a web QA interface to their product catalogs.

EasyAsk's SQL translation searches both individual data product attributes and textual descriptions. An EasyAsk dictionary represents all potential values for data cells, as well as their equivalences (*bl* = blue). It also represents the vocabulary of the column headings and their relationships. The dictionary informs a generic English-to-SQL translation engine about the particularities of this catalog's vocabulary. The dictionary is populated by a process that '"surveys" the underlying database's cells and column headings. For standard e-commerce databases, the survey process already understands the schema of the data and the product hierarchy that it represents and so produces a dictionary that is ready for use without any further customization.

If an EasyAsk system can't adequately formulate an SQL query for a question, EasyAsk reformulates the question into a Boolean query and submits it to an associated keyword search engine. Additionally, EasyAsk can associate certain question patterns with a canned response for questions with a fixed answer, such as "What is your return address?" It also handles anaphoric follow-up questions, like "Does it come in blue?"

Harris 2001 describes a system for federating search to multiple online catalogs with disparate vocabularies and schemas. A central engine represents in its dictionaries the types of queries that each federated dictionary can answer. The user question is then routed to those federated engines that can answer it. Each broadcast engine then translates the query into appropriate SQL for its underlying data.

EasyAsk can translate English queries into SQL in sophisticated ways, handling operators such as AVERAGE and negation. EasyAsk can also present results not only in tabular form but within OLAP objects such as pie charts or bar graphs, useful for ad hoc site usage analytics.

Mercado, founded by Eran Palmon as DTL Data Technologies Ltd, provides similar functionality but via a considerably different methodology. Instead of querying data in situ, Mercado extracts and combines data from disparate data sources (rows of relational database tables, synonyms, text passages) into a schema-free graph structure called a hyperbase. (See Palmon 1998 and Dar et al 1998 for details.) Querying the hyperbase returns a subgraph of data elements based on matching the individual query tokens as leaves of hyperbase elements. It is not clear if operators like negation or aggregation operators like AVERAGE can be handled. Mercado currently has eleven customers, including Macys.com, Sears.com and Petco.com.

In early 2002, Inquira was formed by merging two web QA companies: Electric Knowledge and AnswerFriend. Mekikian and Yuret 2001 (see also Cooper and Hammond 1997) describes a system for sentence-level semantic indexing. Sentences are indexed according to their explicit content as well as the extra-sentential content represented by anaphoric antecedents and document structure such as section headings and datelines. By making use of sentence-, discourse- and document structure, Inquira indexes a rich representation of passages at a conceptual level, while avoiding computing each sentence's logical form. This type of conceptual indexing is used for rows of structured data as well. Current Inquira customers include BEA, Net App, AT&T, Fidelity Investments, Bank of America, Yahoo! and Honda.

iPhrase Technologies, founded in 1999, is a venture-backed spin-out of technology developed at MIT's Spoken Language System Group in the 1990s. iPhrase has launched about 20 implementations since September 2001, including Charles Schwab, Yahoo! Finance, Staples, and Neiman Marcus. Like EasyAsk and Mercado, iPhrase's major focus is providing a natural language interface to structured data.

iPhrase's OneStep QA platform, as described in Chang et al. 2000, seems to be an evolution of the WebGalaxy and Galaxy-II systems described in Seneff et al. 1997 originally developed for a voice dialogue system. The iPhrase system incorporates a novel parsing strategy, combining both context free grammars and regular expressions. The output of the parser is a frame representation of clauses, topics, and predicates related to that described in Seneff 1992. The parser looks for instances of key/value pairs (e.g., airline: United) previously discovered in the customer's structured data sources. A table of equivalences mediates between the user's query and the formation of SQL queries to produce the answer. OneStep also echoes the intention of the user's query in a generated prose caption for the table of results, rather than exposing the SQL that produced it. As with EasyAsk, queries that are deemed not translatable to SQL are transformed into Boolean queries for keyword search.

Primus's Answer Engine is the second generation of the technology developed by AnswerLogic (Hamilton 2000), a startup cofounded by Paul Jacobs. Like Inquira, AnswerEngine indexes an enhanced token-level representation of each sentence, using sense discrimination and some surface semantic roles (subject/object, potential/actual) rather than computing a full logical form.

Broad Daylight's Broad Mind is an FAQ searching system. The system returns the most similar question-answer pair(s) in a collection to a user question Broad Mind does not search a site's documents directly. Click-through popularity is monitored to raise or lower an answer's relevance. The software manages the workflow of routing and approving new question-answer pairs and publishing them on the website.[14] The company lists about fourteen customers, including Kodak, SBC Communications, NASD, and the SEC.

Ask Jeeves was founded in 1996 by former CTO David Warthen, and venture capitalist Garrett Gruener. Ask Jeeves has emphasized natural language questions on its advertising-supported sites from the start. As detailed in Warthen 2000, Ask Jeeves matches user queries against precompiled question patterns for which Ask Jeeves editors have found an answer. These questions can contain pull-down lists, textboxes, and other features allowing users to focus their question without typing another query. In some cases, called *editorially selected answers,* Ask Jeeves questions map directly to snippets of text hyperlinked to their source that provide an exact answer to the question posed, such as "How old is [pop star] John Mayer?" Ask Jeeves monitors user queries to learn popular question patterns. Additionally, it automatically interprets queries using expressions like *pictures of* or *the weather in* to return appropriate pictures and weather reports, respectively. When a query fails to match an Ask Jeeves question pattern, or additional results are needed, Ask Jeeves submits the user's query to the Teoma search engine, a citation-based search engine acquired by Ask Jeeves in 2001.[15] Only about 20% of queries on Ask Jeeves are interrogative sentences in form. Of these, about 7% are *where* questions; 4% are *how* questions; 3.5% are *definitional* questions ("What is X?" or "What does X mean?") and 2% are *identity statement* questions ("What is the speed of light?").

Kanisa was founded in 1997 by Mark Angel, its current CTO. Kanisa indexes both the textual content and the conceptual content of documents according to multiple taxonomies such as activities, symptoms, products, and objects, where each concept has associated evidence patterns of terms and their relationships (Angel et al. 1997). By returning not only matching documents but sub- or supernodes of concepts found in the query, suggestions for making the user's query more specific or more general can be echoed to the user.

In July 2003, Kanisa acquired the enterprise software division of Ask Jeeves and its enterprise QA software called JeevesOne (now called Kanisa Site Search). Kanisa Site Search (KSS) is a product designed to enable companies to construct and maintain QA functionalities on their own web sites.[16] KSS provides answers in the form of text snippets and structured data elements as well as entire documents. Initially released in September, 2001, KSS has over 40 implementations, including Ford Motors, Nike, the State of Washington, Novartis, Roche Pharmaceuticals, the U.S. Navy, and Nestle Purina PetCare, among others representing a variety of vertical markets.

KSS provides customizable semantic indexing of site content, indexing synonym and hyponym sets, character-level patterns (e.g., part numbers or error message numbers), token-level patterns (like addresses), and custom stem groups. By default, an end-user query is transformed into a search over that index.

By design, most KSS user queries will match a KSS *question template*. Essentially a KSS question template is a finite-state transducer for transforming user questions into commands submitted to one or more command services. Custom-made question templates are feasible here because outward-facing search sites such as KSS's have a query distribution in the form of a Zipf curve: a small number of query types account, through repetition, for the great majority of queries.[17] The default natural-language search strategy is applied to the "tail" of the query distribution: query types that are issued only very rarely. It is important to handle the most frequent queries in an optimal way, because these are the queries that are most important to the site's users and, thus, to the site itself. Put in terms of cost, the overall cost of getting a particular query type correct is the query frequency multiplied by the sum of increased sales and customer service representative savings and minus the incremental development cost. Rationalizing incremental development in this way provides a metric for calculating the return on investment for getting any particular query right.

Each KSS template consists of one or more left-hand side patterns to match user queries. Values from this match are then dynamically inserted into a guidance question pattern that echoes the system's understanding of the user's intention. More importantly, matched elements are used to fill slots in commands to be executed by the command services. KSS command services include search commands; dynamic URL commands for redirection to a particular page; exact answer commands for finding short answers in text,[18] or enterprise information system (EIS) commands[19] that pass and/or transform query parameters into SQL for structured data search. Follow-up question functionality allows the system to prompt the user for additional parameters. On the right-hand side, synonyms and hyponyms are expanded as appropriate. KSS's online processing of user queries is context-sensitive in several ways: templates make use of where the query was issued, stored profile information, and previous query context to interpret anaphoric and elliptical follow-on questions.

KSS Analytics allows companies to measure the performance of the KSS application and gather actionable feedback from customers to continuously improve their web site and online business initiatives.

3.4 Conclusions and Future Directions

The current generation of web-based QA applications has learned several lessons from the earlier generation. First, this generation of applications largely forgoes full-scale semantic interpretation in favor of lighter-weight methods.

Second, because customers want to control their own content and update the system as necessary for themselves, these systems provide functionality enabling nonexpert system administrators to perform at least some of the knowledge engineering construction and maintenance. Third, buyers of these applications want to understand their end-users better by understanding their queries, so sophisticated user analytics capabilities are a necessity. Fourth, current systems recognize that not all user queries are equal; outward-facing query distributions tend to be Zipflike, so it is more important to handle frequent question types well than unique user queries for which back-off methods can be provided. It is crucial to understand a site's query-type distribution in order to forecast development costs. Fifth, end users want to be able to query structured and unstructured data from a single user interface, so engines must be able to decide which data source to query. Structured data back-ends help to constrain query interpretations. Finally, the optimal answer to a user question may be any number of things—a text snippet, a document, a picture or multimedia file, a set of structured data elements, or any combination thereof—therefore, the QA application must be flexible enough to provide different sorts of answers to different sorts of questions in contrast to the verification-oriented paradigm of the TREC competitions, where every answer is in a set format.

In the near future, QA interfaces are only likely to become more ubiquitous. Microsoft has announced that it intends to build a QA facility into its upcoming operating system, codenamed Longhorn.[20] There is some indication that the proposed system will be used to search documents both locally and on the web. Secondly, there is some indication that the system will employ the redundancy-based approach to QA for encyclopedic knowledge questions outlined in Dumais et al. 2002. When QA interfaces become embedded in the world's dominant operating system, this can only encourage user expectations in this area.

Notes

1. In part this neglect is understandable because patents are awarded on novelty of method alone. The patent must be detailed enough for a third party to implement the same method, but inventors need not say how well a system performed or provide other metrics. Research papers focus on presenting results more than details of method. All awarded U.S. Patents (from 1790) and recent pending applications are searchable at www.uspto.gov. World-wide patent applications are searchable at the World Intellectual Property Organization, www.wipo.org, a world-wide clearinghouse for patent applications. It should be noted that this survey makes no claim to being exhaustive but only to be representative of systems for which patent applications have been filed.

2. START is based on semantic annotation, matching semantic triples computed from natural language queries to recursive semantic triple structures assigned to documents and passages. See Katz and Winston's U.S. Patents 5,309,359 and 5,404,295. See also chapter 9 in this volume.

3. Kupiec's MURAX was a natural language interface to encyclopedia content, devel-

oped against a corpus of factoid questions from the board game *Trivial Pursuit*. MURAX involved ranking noun phrases as answers based on the co-occurrence of the phrases in articles with phrases found in the original query and secondary (derived) queries. See Kupiec's U.S. Patent 5,519,608.

4. See Dahlgren and Stabler 1998. Work based on U.S. Army Contract No. DAAA15-92-C-0025.

5. Pustejovsky et al. 1999. Pustejovsky, Clippinger and Ingria 2000. Pustejovsky and Ingria 1999.

6. Mark Hachman, "Once Bitten, VCs Shy from New Dot-Coms," *TechWeb Finance*. Feb 13, 2001.

7. C|Net News, "WebCompass to Get New Direction." http://news.com.com/2100-1001-215535.html. Quarterdeck acquired the WebCompass technology from Limbex Corporation founded by Alex Jacobson and Brad Allen. Jacobson was one of the original commercial AI "Gang of Four" in the 1980s. See Phillips 1999.

8. For "neo-Davidsonian," see Parsons 1990. The index of Levin 1993 was licensed in electronic format from the University of Chicago Press and transformed into a suitable format.

9. See Scot Finnie. "Smart Utilities Diagnose and Repair Your PC." *Windows Magazine*. March 1998, page 142. http://content.techweb.com/winmag/library/1998/0301/other081.htm

10. See Galitsky and Grudin 2001; Galitsky 2003.

11. The previous survey is not exhaustive. There were several other patents filed for natural language question answering during this period. IPLearn, for example, was awarded a very general U.S. Patent 5,884,302 for transforming user questions into an internal command format.

12. Allen Bonde Group, The State of Web Self-Service: Search Effectiveness and the Customer Experience of the Leading Retail Sites, Jan. 2003. A correct answer was judged to be a result containing a relevant answer or a link to relevant information presented in a "reasonable" number of overall links. Of the 47 sites with a search capability, 17 (36.2%) provided a relevant response to at least one of the test queries, 11 sites (23.4%) correctly answered at least two out of three questions, and only three sites (6.4%) provided relevant answers to all three questions. Poor precision was often a problem. One site returned over 607,000 irrelevant links for the gift certificate query. Another leading site returned an average of 72,000 documents per query.

13. See, for example, Susan Feldman and Henry D. Morris, Content and Data Technologies Converge. IDC Technology Assessment, IDC #28678. January, 2003.

14. Founder Louise Kirkbride is listed as a coinventor on Gifford et al. 1994. Broad Daylight also offers a natural language search product and a distributed FAQ search product. Primus acquired Broad Daylight in August 2003.

15. According to Ask Jeeves' 2001 Annual Report: "[In 1999] Patrick H. Winston and Boris Katz filed a complaint against [Ask Jeeves] ... alleging infringement ... of United States Patent Nos. 5,309,359 and 5,404,295 ... [Ask Jeeves] settled this lawsuit in July 2001. ...Under the terms of the settlement agreement, the Company...receive[d] a license to certain intellectual property owned by [Winston and Katz]." See http://www.sec.gov/Archives/edgar/data/ 1054298/000091205702008214/ a2071701 z10-k.htm.

16. See Harrison et al. 2003.

17. See Lowe 2000. Question templates are easily customizable in KSS by means of a programming-by-example user interface that doesn't require any pattern-matching expertise.

18. Exact Answer commands take parameters for the question target type, elements that must be in the same sentence, elements that must be on the same page and elements that should be boosted or discounted. For example, "What mileage does the Ford Taurus get?" would target a *numeric expression* that must be in the same sentence as *miles per gallon* (or its synonyms), in a page containing *Ford Taurus*, where containing *EPA*, *city* and/or *highway* would be a bonus. Special highlighting is used to present the exact answer.

19. The EIS command service incorporates technology acquired from Octopus Inc. in 2001. EIS includes connectors to Siebel, RDBMS databases, public web sites such as Yahoo Finance, UPS Tracking, WebMethods, and SAP by default. There is an API to create additional connectors.

20. Rashid 2003. Foley & Rothenberg 2003. Microsoft earlier provided a customizable interface to structured data as the English Query feature of its SQL Server technology. Customers specified the relationships between columns by providing natural language sentences expressing their relationships. Oracle's interMedia Text add-ons also provide functionality for natural language passage retrieval for text stored in Oracle databases.

Brian Ulicny is a senior scientist in the Advance Development Group at Kanisa, Inc., Natick, Massachusetts. He has been working on commercial question answering applications since 1995. Ulicny can be reached at brian.ulicny@kanisa.com.

Section Two

Definitional, Biographical, and Terminology QA

Whereas classical question answering focused on factoid questions, more recent research has explored answering new classes of questions such as definitions and biographies. In the most trivial of cases, this would be a lookup in an electronic dictionary or biography web site. In more complicated cases, this might require analysis of multiple, possibly conflicting sources, verification of the pedigree of the associated sources, redundancy removal and summarization, and validation that the response is satisfactory to the user's need.

The first chapter in this section by Sasha Blair-Goldensohn, Kathleen McKeown, and Andrew Schlaikjer (Columbia University) presents a hybrid approach to answering definitional questions of the form, "What is X?" The authors' DefScriber system combines goal-driven (knowledge-based) and data-driven (statistical) methods to produce coherent, multi-sentence, encyclopedia-style definitions. The goal-driven methods exploit knowledge of the task by explicitly seeking out types of information typically found in definitions. These types are modeled by a set of "definitional predicates" including genus (i.e., class), species (distinctive properties), target partition (subclasses), history, and nonspecific definitional (NSD) content. After goal-driven methods identify sentences of interest, data-driven methods use statistical techniques adapted from summarization to select a subset of these sentences into a cohesive definitional answer. (The use of summarization techniques in the context of short-answer QA is discussed in chapter 17.)

The authors' current implementation of goal-driven methods in DefScriber automatically identifies three predicate types: genus, species, and NSD. Their methodology starts with the manual annotation of texts followed by machine learning of features and manual pattern extraction to create predicate identifiers. Using term concentration and positional features, identification achieved 81% precision and recall. Using 18 manually extracted patterns, identification of sentences containing genus and species information for 19 evaluation terms was 96% (recall is unknown).

The data-driven techniques used in DefScriber include centroid-based ranking, clustering, local IDF weighting, and cohesion ordering. The authors define a definitional centroid (a method which approximates centroid-based summarization) by creating a stemmed-word vector of all the NSD sentences and sorting individual sentences in terms of cosine proximity. They then perform nonhierarchical clustering on these sentences. The first answer sentence is then chosen as the top genus-species sentence in the centroid-based ranking, and remaining sentences are chosen to maximize a combination of centroid ranking, cohesion with previous sentences, and cluster coverage.

The authors evaluated two versions of their DefScriber system (data-driven and data- plus goal-driven) against a centroid-based baseline, measuring relevance (precision), redundancy, structure, breadth of coverage, and term understanding for answers that were 10 sentences long. They selected 24 terms, choosing 12 randomly from the TREC AQUAINT pilot evaluation (Voorhees 2003) and 12 by hand. The combined results of 38 judges showed that data-plus-goal-driven DefScriber achieves the best scores in structure, redundancy, term understanding, and relevance, with statistically significant margins in the first two categories. Regarding coverage, data-driven performed the best, and DefScriber the worst, though the differences were not statistically significant. According to the authors "the leading genus-species sentence significantly improves the answer definition's structure by giving readers solid orientation and context."

The next chapter by Ralph Weischedel, Jinxi Xu, and Ana Licuanan (BBN Technologies) explores providing extended answers from multiple documents to biographical questions. While similar to definitional questions, biography of course focuses on people and is also related to group and organizational profiles. This chapter utilizes hybrid complementary components, in particular IR, linguistic analysis (parsing & proposition recognition), information extraction, and sentence compression. As in the previous chapter, the authors analyzed example biographies to model what should be in a good biography compared to what is in a general document collection. Their system first performs question classification to identify the question type (e.g., a biography, an organizational profile, or an extended definition) and also the target (e.g., person, organization, term). BBN's HMM IR system retrieves relevant documents. Next BBN's HMM NE tagger IdentiFinderTM detects 29 types of NEs and parses the sentences into UPenn TREEBANK standard trees. Rules create predicates from these parse trees. The Sherif IE engine performs name and pronominal co-reference and extracts 24 binary relations based on relation extraction as defined in the ACE guidelines. Sentences are ranked based on a statistical model of example "training" biographies from two web sites (www.s9.com and www.wikipedia. org), the portion of sentence containing linguistic features and semantic features is selected, and redundant facts are eliminated, namely if the predicate (relation) in each is the same and if the head of the noun phrase of the corresponding argument of each fact is the same. Kernel facts are used for three different output forms: tables, lists of concisely stated facts, or graphs showing associations to other entities.

The authors performed both a subjective evaluation and an automated evaluation using the BLEU scorer, previously used in machine translation evaluations. BLEU measures the precision of word n-gram overlap between the system output and an answer key. The authors selected 8 biography questions from a pilot study published by NIST (Voorhees, 2003) and 18 from TREC9&10 questions. Three independent individuals wrote these 26 biographies following the answer keys of the NIST pilot study. They truncated system output to the length of the answer key and compared one to four n-grams. They contrasted two baselines (documents retrieved and top ranked IR sentences) to four system configurations looking at linguistic features, linguistic features plus IE, linguistic features plus IE plus redundancy removal, and phrases generated by the reduction process, respectively.

What they found was that sentence selection via IR and name finding is surprisingly good according to BLEU. Linguistic features and redundancy removal seem promising; however, according to the BLEU metric, relation extraction hurts scores slightly. They then compared results using one, two, and three human-generated reference answers. Scores increased with the number of reference answers but they found no change in ranking. Including relations in the processing helped for two assessors, but hurt for the third. The authors concluded that 24 relation types is too small and, although subjective evaluation and BLEU do not always agree, they found the two were positively correlated. A 2002 pilot study on extended definitions, biographies, and organizational profiles included BBN, Columbia University, Cycorp, IBM, LCC, and U.S.C/ISI and these were evaluated in TREC 2003, distinguishing required facts (termed "nuggets") and a set of optional facts.

In summary, these authors concluded that an IR model of biographies improves sentence selection, apparently selecting sentences like those seen in human-generated biographies. Also, they found syntactic and semantic linguistic analysis promising and that the IR model could be improved as well, if effective heuristics for redundancy removal can be found. Relation extraction may improve on the IR model of sentence selection if extended beyond the 24 current relations. They found the BLEU measure stable with respect to length of n-grams and a promising method for automatic evaluation of progress in single system development although BLEU may not be accurate enough for cross-system evaluation. In short, further research is required to verify the utility of automatic scoring versus subjective evaluations.

The final chapter in this section by Fabio Rinaldi, Michael Hess, and James Dowdall from the University of Zürich together with Diego Mollá and Rolf Schwitter from Macquarie University in Australia addresses a related class of questions, namely addressing complex, terminological questions, possibly requiring inference, in terminology-rich technical domains. The authors point out that while many conventional TREC QA systems exploit the redundancy of the web to select among many possible answers to questions, this approach fails for technical document QA because of the non-redundant nature of most technical documentation and the domain specific sublanguage and terminology they contain (e.g., the maintenance manual of a commercial aircraft such as an Airbus A230/330). Manual content is unlikely to be published on web because of copyright and because questions tend to be procedural (how to) as opposed to factoid.

Terminology plays a central role in technical domains, analogous to the role of named entities in the previous two chapters. To further complicate things, unfamiliarity with domain terminology often results in imprecise or even faulty questions. A useful QA system must try to fix this by detecting terminological variants and exploiting the relations between terms (like synonymy, meronymy, antonymy). Furthermore, the document collections containing answers have important properties. In contrast to newswire, for example, technical documentation has a high-value over time and thus properties of correctness, completeness, and consistency increase in importance with the complexity of the system. Unlike the web or TREC collections, they are limited in size/volume. For example, the UNIX manual has 500 pages; the Airbus A320 manual is about 120 MB (vs. a gigabyte of TREC data). There are few NEs but typically many component/part types and numbers. The materials tend to be highly structured, highly formatted, and concise. Because of specialized terminology, terms are unlikely to be found in electronic dictionaries such as WordNet, but possibly defined in a glossary.

Whereas the first chapter in this section focuses on generating multi-sentence answers to definitional questions and the second on biographical answers aggregated across multiple documents, technical domains require terminology processing. Terminology challenges include identifying phrasal boundaries when presented with compound nominals and multiword terms and challenges with paraphrases (Woods, 1997). In building ExtrAns, a real-world answer extraction system, the authors needed to focus on parts of the aircraft, tool, and procedures, which together account for a large part of the source text (manuals). ExtrAns consists of three key processes: (1) extraction of the document collection's terminology as glossaries of abbreviations, markup, and recurring lexical patterns (e.g., "Power Transfer Unit (PTU)"), (2) analysis to uncover any semantically related terms, and (3) exploitation of this knowledge during the QA process.

Terminology extraction starts with a stop-phrase method that chunks certain SGML-zones (titles, paragraphs) using a list of generic (non-terminological) phrases. This is followed by an automatic statistical method based on n-grams but allowing for non-contiguous holes. The authors report that a terminology list obtained by the statistical methods of Mutual Expectation and

LocalMax produced a recall of 44% and precision of 15%. In contrast, the list obtained by the stop-phrase method resulted in recall of 66% and precision of 12%. Combining these methods, recall increased to 78%, but precision dropped to 10%.

Analysis includes processing of synonymy and hyponomy. This work considers both "lexical hyponymy" and "WordNet hyponymy." ExtrAns automatically discovers these relations. For example, from 6,032 terms in the Airbus A320 maintenance manuals, ExtrAns produces 2,770 synsets with 1,176 lexical hyponymy links and 643 WordNet hyponymy links. Through manual validation of 500 synsets, 1.2% were determined to contain an inappropriate term. A similar examination of 500 lexical hyponymy links identified them all as valid. However, out of 500 WordNet hyponymy links more than 35% were invalid.

The authors evaluated ExtrAns both for the UNIX and Airbus A320 maintenance domain, comparing performance to a baseline IR system. A logical form is produced for each sentence. Logical forms are simplified to verbs and their arguments, plus modifier and adjunct relations, called Minimal Logical forms (MLF) and are easily converted to prolog queries. MultiWord Terms (MWT) are replaced with their synset identifier from the Thesaurus, which reduces the number of parses per sentence by 46%. The authors argue their approach is easily portable since it requires, apart from terminological knowledge, no additional domain knowledge.

Taken as a whole, these chapters illustrate the expansion of the field beyond factoid questions to answer new classes of questions such as definitions, and biographies and to specific domains not previously addressed by standard TREC approaches. They also illustrate the value of standing on the shoulders of prior capabilities such as lexica, IR, IE, and explanation generation.

Chapter 4

Answering Definitional Questions

A Hybrid Approach

Sasha Blair-Goldensohn, Kathleen R. McKeown, & Andrew Hazen Schlaikjer

4.1 Introduction

In recent years, question answering (QA) systems such as those in the yearly TREC conferences have reached a remarkably high level of performance. These systems are premised on the *short-answer model,* in which the goal is to answer questions for which the correct response is a number, short phrase, or sentence fragment.

However, many questions that occur in real-life tasks are not in this class. Consider a student asked to prepare a report on the Hajj, an Islamic religious duty. In the context of short-answer QA, both patience and prescience will be required to elicit the core facts. First, a relatively long list of questions would be required (e.g., "Where is the Hajj carried out?" "How long does it last?" "Who undertakes a Hajj?" etc.). Second, knowing which questions to ask requires knowledge that the questioner likely does not have. That is, the questions that best elicit a description of one thing (e.g., the Hajj) can be quite different than those best suited for finding out about something else (e.g., the Caspian Sea).

Producing rich, multi-sentence responses to open-ended questions—such as those requiring definitions, biographies, or opinions as answers—is the focus of *long-answer* QA. This area is still in early stages of development, but already the subject of several pilot studies and much active research (Voorhees 2003). In this chapter, we will concentrate on *definitional* QA, the task of providing long answers to "What is X?" type questions.

Definitional QA systems are not only interesting as a research challenge. They also have the potential to be a valuable complement to static knowledge sources like encyclopedias. This is because they create definitions dynamically, and thus answer definitional questions about terms which are new or emerging. They also can tailor an answer to a user's needs, for instance by creating a longer or shorter definition, or one which is drawn from specified knowledge sources.

We will focus our discussion around DefScriber (Blair-Goldensohn et al. 2003), a definitional QA system that implements a hybrid of goal-driven (knowledge-based) and data-driven (statistical) methods. The *goal-driven techniques* (section 4.4) shape the answer in a top-down manner, using a set of definitional predicates modeled on typical elements of a definition. *Data-driven techniques* (section 4.5) operate in a bottom-up way, using statistical measures to identify themes in the data. An overview of DefScriber's operation is given in section 4.3. We conclude the chapter by presenting results of a recent evaluation which show DefScriber's hybrid approach achieving significant improvement over a competitive baseline.

4.2 Related Work

Our hybrid approach to definitional QA builds on research in summarization and generation. Previous work in multi-document summarization has developed solutions that identify similarities across documents as the basis for summary content (Mani and Bloedorn 1997, Carbonell and Goldstein 1998, Hatzivassiloglou et al. 1999, Barzilay et al. 1999, Radev et al. 2000, Lin and Hovy 2002). (The use of summarization techniques in the context of short-answer QA is discussed in chapter 17.) Whether similarities are included through sentence extraction or information fusion (Barzilay et al. 1999), all of these approaches are data-driven because similarities in the data determine content.

Goal-driven, or top-down, approaches are more often found in generation. Schemas (McKeown 1985), rhetorical structure theory (Mann and Thompson 1988, Moore and Paris 1992, Hovy 1993, Marcu 1997) and plan-based approaches (Reiter and Dale 2000) are examples of goal-driven approaches, where the schema or plan specifies the kind of information to include in a generated text. In early work, schemas were used to generate definitions (McKeown 1985), but the information for the definitional text was found in a knowledge base. In more recent work, information extraction is used to create a top-down approach to summarization (Radev and McKeown 1998) by searching for specific types of information which can be extracted from the input texts (e.g., perpetrator in a news article on terrorism). Here, the summary briefs the user on domain-specific information assumed a priori to be of interest.

Other long-answer QA systems are currently under development as part of the AQUAINT program (Voorhees 2003). Some of these share attributes with DefScriber. In chapter 5, Weischedel et al. explores biographical questions using a combination of methods that are largely complementary to those used in DefScriber—namely, identification of key linguistic constructions and information extraction (IE) to identify specific types of semantic data.

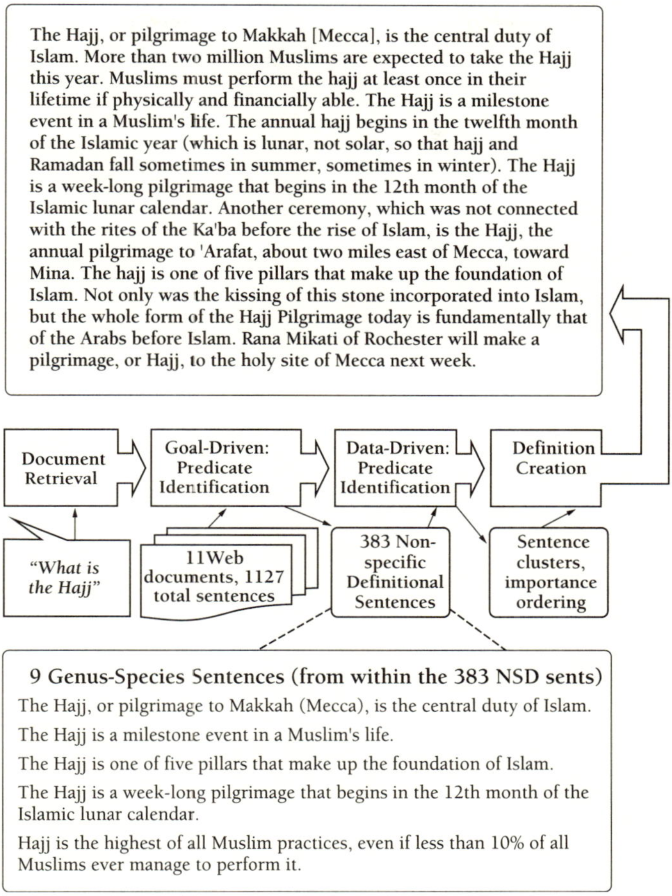

Figure 4.1. DefScriber's Operation on the Question "What is the Hajj?"

Another important contrast between DefScriber and most of the long-answer systems developed under the AQUAINT program has to do with answer format. While these systems (including the one presented in chapter 5) mostly produce answers as a ranked list of descriptive phrases or sentences, DefScriber uses summarization methods to produce a coherent, multi-sentence, encyclopedia-style definition.

4.3 DefScriber: Architecture Overview

Before turning to the development of our goal- and data-driven methods, a brief overview of DefScriber is useful to understanding where these pieces fit. Figure 4.1 gives a high-level view of DefScriber's operation, illustrating input

Predicate	Description	Instance Example
Non-specific Definitional	Any type of information relevant in a detailed definition of the term. NSD are a superset of the below predicates.	Costs: Pilgrims pay substantial tariffs to the occupiers of Makkah and the rulers of …
Genus	Category to which term belongs.	The hajj is a type of ritual.
Species	Describes properties other than or in addition to Genus. Species are a superset of the below predicates.	The annual hajj begins in the twelfth month of the Islamic year.
Target Partition	Divides the term into two or more conceptual or physical parts.	Qiran, Tammatu' and Ifrad are three different types of Hajj.
Cause (effect)	States explicitly that the term is the cause (effect) of something.	The pilgrimage causes the past sins of a Muslim to be forgiven.
History	Gives historical information relating to the term.	Mohammed, founder of Islam, started the tradition in 632 C.E.
Etymology	Information on the term's genesis, e.g., adaptation from another language.	In Arabic, the word Hajj means a resolve of magnificent duty.

Table 4.1. Definitional Predicates: Descriptions and Examples

and output of each stage. This example traces an actual answer generated for the question "What is the Hajj?" during our evaluation (section 4.6).

The input is specified as a question, which feeds into the document retrieval phase. The user can also specify which databases to search, a maximum number of documents to retrieve, and the desired answer length.[1]

The information retrieval (IR) module uses a fixed set of patterns to identify the term to be defined in the question, and then generates a set of search queries in order of decreasing expected precision with respect to that term. Queries are sent to a search engine until a threshold number of documents has been retrieved.[2]

Once documents are retrieved, the primary goal-driven step is performed, with the system examining documents for instances of definitional predicates. Next, data-driven analysis is performed to produce sentence clustering and ordering information. In the last step, a definitional answer is created via sentence extraction, guided by the analysis done in the goal- and data-driven stages.

4.4 Definitional Predicates: A Goal-Driven Approach

Answering a "What is X?" definitional question and creating a summary of query results for the search term X are strongly related problems. Yet, as readers, we have more specific expectations for a definition than for a general-use summary. The idea of definitional predicates is to model these special properties of a definition so the system can use them to create better answers.

4.4.1 The Predicate Set

Our set of definitional predicates is shown in table 4.1. Currently, the system automatically identifies instances of three of these types in text: genus, species and nonspecific definitional (NSD). Active research on identifying target partition and cause-effect instances is ongoing.

An important distinction is that NSD subsumes all of the other more specific predicate types that appear underneath it in table 4.1. Thus, identifying NSD text is crucial because it is a cue to the presence of other predicates; it also removes noise and provides a set of useful definitional text which is given as input to data-driven methods even when the text cannot be further classified with a more specific predicate. We choose genus and species as the first specific predicates to implement because they are at the core of what definitions are. Related work (Sager and L'Homme 1994, Swartz 1997, Sarner and Carberry 1988) consistently identifies these two concepts as key parts of defining a term.

We build on work such as (Klavans and Muresan 2000), who acquire dictionary-type definitions, and (Sarner and Carberry 1988), who propose three "strategic predicates," including identification and properties predicates which are analogous to our genus and species, respectively. Research in terminological theory (Sager and L'Homme 1994) and philosophy (Swartz 1997) also theorizes that the type of information modeled by many of our predicates (including genus, species, synonym and target partition) is crucial to descriptive-type definitions.

Our definitional predicates contrast with those from rhetorical structure theory (RST) (Mann and Thompson 1988, Moore and Paris 1992, Hovy 1993, Marcu 1997) in that our predicates do not represent the intent or overall structure of a document in their definition. That is, each unit of text in a source document can be evaluated intrinsically as to whether it instantiates a definitional predicate.

To use these predicates in our system, we must identify units of text which contain them. To do this, we first did a manual examination of documents to create sample data annotated with predicates. Using this data, we explored two approaches to identifying predicates. The first uses machine learning to learn a feature-based classification that predicts when a predicate occurs. The second uses pattern recognition over patterns extracted from the annotated data.

4.4.2 Creating a Training Set

To produce the training data for DefScriber, coders marked 81 total documents for instances of the predicates in table 4.1. The data included 55 documents marked by one coder and 13 marked by two coders. To gather documents, 14 terms were first selected for broad coverage from several diverse categories: geopolitical, science, health, and miscellaneous. Then we retrieved approximately 5 web documents for each term using a process similar to our system's IR component.

4.4.3 Rule Extraction: Statistical Techniques

Using this set of annotated documents, we applied machine learning techniques and tools to extract rules for predicate identification. These approaches allow us to efficiently discover relationships between text features and the presence of definitional predicate instances. The text unit we use here is the sentence; that is, we wish to discover rules that will take the features of a source sentence as input, and output those (if any) definitional predicates that are predicted to be in the sentence.[3]

Feature selection was done in part using observations from document markup. For instance, we include several features measuring a sentence's "term concentration," i.e., the term's frequency within a sentence and/or nearby sentences, based on the observation that appearance of the term appears to be a predictor of definitional material. We also include features for relative and absolute position of a sentence in a document, based on the observation that key information tends to concentrate toward the top of documents. Other features, such as presence of punctuation, are added to detect full-sentence text (as opposed to headings or other fragments), since most predicates other than NSD seem to occur mainly in full sentences. Some "blind" features such as bag-of-words are also used.

We applied two machine learning tools to the learning problem: the rule-learning tool Ripper (Cohen 1995) and the boosting-based categorization system BoosTexter (Schapire and Singer 2000). Both algorithms performed similarly in terms of the accuracy of their predictions on test data; Ripper's rules are used in DefScriber since they were somewhat simpler to implement.

The nonspecific definitional (NSD) predicate, which indicates a sentence's relevance to any aspect of defining the term, fares well using rules that consider term concentration and position in document. Using cross-validation, accuracy of 81 percent was obtained with Ripper (76 percent using BoosTexter). This is sufficient for DefScriber since this predicate is not used to place sentences directly into the definition, but rather to pare down noisy and voluminous input by pulling out sentences which merit further examination.

4.4.3 Rule Extraction: Syntactic and Lexical Patterns

Using lexicosyntactic patterns manually extracted from the predicate-annotated documents, we create a set of high-precision patterns for the two predicates most core to definitions: genus and species. We currently model sentences containing both genus and species information, as these "G-S" sentences provide a strong grounding context for understanding the term. G-S sentences situate a term in a higher level category (its "genus"), and the "species" information in such sentences tends to give key features that distinguish a term within that category.

Rather than modeling the patterns at the word level, i.e., as flat templates with slots to fill, we model them as partially specified syntax trees (figure 4.2).

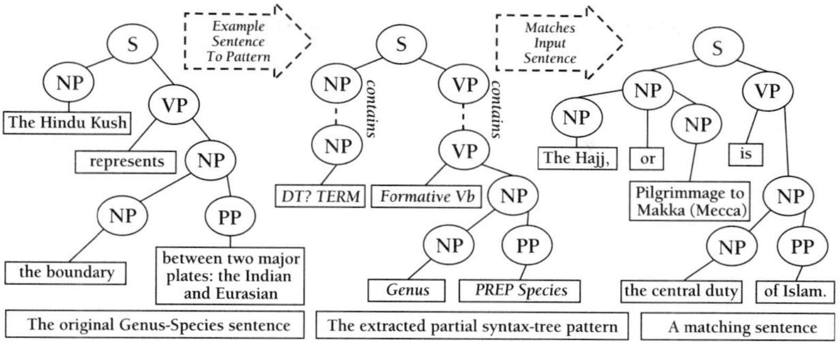

Figure 4.2. Pattern Extraction and Matching for a Genus-Species Sentence.

One such pattern can match a large class of semantically similar sentences without having to model every type of possible lexical variation. This approach derives from techniques used in information extraction (Grishman 1997), where partial *sub*trees for matching domain-specific concepts and named entities are used because automatic derivation of full parse trees is not always reliable. However, data-driven techniques (section 4.5) offer additional protection from false or extraneous matches by lowering the importance ranking of information not corroborated elsewhere in the data.[4]

Figure 4.2 illustrates the transformation from example sentence to pattern, and then shows a matching sentence. Our patterns are flexible—note that the example and matched sentences have somewhat different trees. Another point of flexibility is the verb itself; FormativeVb will match various forms of verbs in a set which our matching algorithm considers expressive of "belonging" to a category (e.g., "be," "exemplify").

Using our predicate-annotated data set, we manually extracted 18 distinct patterns which match G-S sentences. These 18 patterns provide sufficient recall to reliably find at least one instance in modestly sized document sets; over our evaluation test set (see section 4.6), at least one G-S sentence was identified for 16 of 19 terms, with a mean of 3.5 G-S sentences per term (culled from a mean of 15 documents retrieved). Precision was 96%, recall unknown.

4.5 Data-Driven Techniques: Applying Summarization

While our set of predicates, including genus and species, are domain-neutral, they are not meant to model all possible important information for a given term definition. Some information types may be hard to define computationally a priori. Also, a given sentence may instantiate a definitional predicate but include only peripheral content. We address these issues in the data-driven stage of DefScriber's pipeline (refer to figure 4.1), applying statistical tech-

Source	Term
Pilot Evaluation	asceticism, Aum Shinrikyo, battery, fibromyalgia, *gluons*, goth, Hajj, Mobilization for Global Justice, nanoparticles, religious right, *Shining Path*, Yahoo!
Hand-picked	autism, Booker Prize, Caspian Sea, East Timor, *hemophilia*, *MIRV*, orchid, pancreas, passive sonar, skin cancer, tachyons, *tsunami*

Table 4.2. Evaluation Terms (in Italics Were Used for Training, the Rest for Testing)

niques adapted from multi-document summarization to the nonspecific definitional sentences identified in the goal-driven stage.

First, a *definition centroid* is computed by creating a stemmed-word vector of all the NSD sentences. Then the individual sentences are sorted in order of decreasing "centrality," as approximated by IDF-weighted cosine distance from the definition centroid. This method creates a definition of length *N* by taking the first *N* unique sentences out of this sorted order, and serves as the TopN baseline method in our evaluation. Note that this method approximates centroid-based summarization, a competitive summarization technique (Radev et al. 2000).

After ordering sentences with TopN, we perform a non-hierarchical clustering that we use to decrease redundancy by avoiding same-cluster sentences in the answer. Since our clustering similarity measure uses IDF computed over a large collection, it can suffer from overweighting of specialized terms; to account for this, we augment the cosine distance calculation, using local IDF values calculated dynamically from the pool of NSD sentences.

The final data-driven technique improves cohesion by considering the content of the previous answer sentence when choosing a sentence to add to the answer. After choosing the first sentence as in TopN, we choose each remaining sentence as the top-ranking sentence from the cluster that minimizes cosine distance from the definition centroid and the previously chosen sentence's cluster.

DefScriber's default configuration integrates all the above data-driven techniques—TopN, clustering, local IDF weighting, and cohesion ordering—combining them with the goal-driven method of genus-species predicate identification. We place the top-ranking (in terms of TopN) G-S sentence first in the definition, and use the cohesion-based ordering to add the remaining sentences. We call this integrated goal- and data-driven method *DefScriber*.

4.6 Evaluation

Our evaluation used human judgments to measure the performance of DefScriber's definitions over a set of varied terms. By surveying users on definitions generated by different configurations of DefScriber, we are able to measure the improvement of DefScriber over the baseline (TopN) method. We address five main qualities in our survey: relevance (precision), redundancy, structure, breadth of coverage, and term understanding.

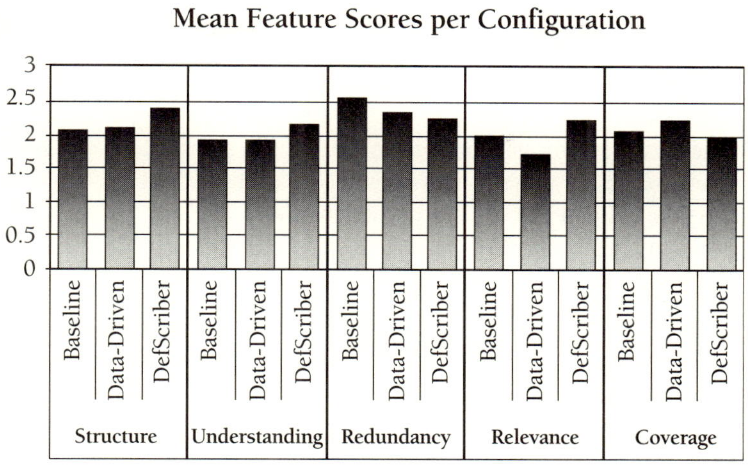

Figure 4.3. Evaluation Results

We chose a set of 24 terms[5] (table 4.2) for which to create answer definitions using the Internet as our knowledge source. We picked half of the terms ourselves, aiming for varied domain coverage; the other half were randomly chosen from among the definitional questions in the AQUAINT pilot evaluation (Voorhees 2003). For each of the test terms, we evaluate three different system configurations: baseline (TopN only), data-driven (all data-driven methods from section 4.5), and full DefScriber (data- plus goal-sriven; described at end of section 4.5). Each answer was ten sentences long.

38 judges participated in the evaluation, and each was asked to rate definitions for 6 different test terms. This resulted in an average of four rated samples for each of the 57 answer definitions (19 test terms, three system configurations). Figure 4.3 shows the resulting mean feature scores for each system configuration.

DefScriber achieves the best scores in structure, redundancy, term understanding, and relevance, with statistically significant margins in the first two categories ($P < .10$) using RIDIT analysis.[6] In coverage, data-driven does best, and DefScriber worst, but none of the differences are significant.

With the best performance in four of five categories, DefScriber is clearly the best configuration. The leading genus-species sentence significantly improves the answer definition's structure by giving readers solid orientation and context. DefScriber's top score in term understanding, while not statistically superior, suggests that this context helps readers to understand the more detailed information that may follow.

4.7 Future Work

Future work on DefScriber will concentrate on increasing the number of definitional predicates automatically identified by the system, as well as on improving identification performance on such predicates.

We are currently working to improve our feature-based predicate identification methods by growing our annotated data set while also extracting more and richer features to input into our machine learning methods. To improve the pattern-based methods, we are actively working with IE bootstrapping techniques developed in Snowball (Agichtein and Gravano 2000) to automatically learn predicate patterns from manually extracted "seed" examples. Such techniques would allow us to supplement our manually-generated patterns and bring new predicates online more quickly.

4.8 Conclusion

Definitional question answering is an emerging research area that goes beyond traditional short-answer questions. In this chapter, we examined the approach of DefScriber, a system that answers definitional questions with dynamically created paragraph-style responses, and uses a combination of goal-driven and data-driven methods to make its definitions fluent and informative. These methods include goal-driven techniques that screen relevant material from voluminous search results, and identify sentences containing types of information typically used in definitions. DefScriber complements these techniques with a set of data-driven methods which guide answer content in a bottom-up manner, using statistical analyses of the data. Our evaluation results demonstrate that the system significantly outperforms competitive summarization baselines. While our ongoing work will continue to improve the system, these results show the promise of DefScriber's hybrid approach for definitional question answering.

Acknowledgments

The authors wish to acknowledge the support of ARDA through AQUAINT contract MDA908-02-C-0008. We are also thankful for the generous and thoughtful contributions of colleagues at Columbia University and at the University of Colorado-Boulder.

Notes

1. Currently, DefScriber can run its search against the Internet as well as several local document collections. Although we currently consider the web as a set of flat documents, chapter 17 considers more rich representations of web pages for QA.

2. The current system recognizes only questions of the form, "What is/are a/the ...," and queries generated for IR are similarly limited. As question recognition and query generation are not an innovative aspect of DefScriber, they are not discussed further in this chapter.

3. This prevents the learning of rules for a predicate instance that spans sentences. However, with our current predicate taxonomy, our document markup found such instances exceedingly rare.

4. For instance, in our "Hajj" example, the system matches the G-S sentence: "The Hajj was Muhammad's compromise with Arabian Paganism." This sentence is in principle a correct match, but the genus and species given here are extraneous and metaphorical. The fact that this information is less central to the definition will be detected statistically by our data-driven methods (section 4.5), and the sentence will thus be ranked below more central G-S sentences.

5. DefScriber is a robust system that produces a definition for virtually any term contained in the document collection; we limited the size of our evaluation for practical purposes.

6. Since the rating scales used by judges are ordered metrics, we analyze the results with RIDIT (Fleiss 1981) analysis, a technique that accounts for the natural ordering information in these measures, i.e., the fact that poor and so-so are both below good, not simply separate categories.

Sasha Blair-Goldensohn is a PhD student in computer science at Columbia University. His research interests include question answering and text summarization. He can be reached via www.cs.columbia.edu/~sashabg.

Kathleen R. McKeown (PhD, University of Pennsylvania) has been a professor of computer science at Columbia University since 1982, serving as department chair from 1997 to 2003. Her interests include summarization,natural language generation, multimedia explanation, and digital libraries.

Andrew H. Schlaikjer is a researcher and programmer in Columbia University's Natural Language Processing Group, focusing on question answering systems. He can be reached at hazen@cs.columbia.edu.

Chapter 5

A Hybrid Approach to Answering Biographical Questions

Ralph Weischedel, Jinxi Xu, & Ana Licuanan

5.1 Introduction

Our point of departure is the recent open-domain question answering evaluations (Voorhees 2002), where the focus has been on "factoid questions" which have "short" answers, e.g., 250 bytes, 50 bytes, or an "exact answer." None of those evaluations have explored extended answers composed from multiple documents. A new direction for us is such answers, e.g., brief biographies ("Who is Joseph Pilates?"), organizational profiles ("What is the World Health Organization?"), or definitions ("What is naproxen?").

Our approach is to synthesize answers from multiple documents using several complementary technologies: information retrieval to find relevant documents; linguistic analysis and information extraction to find sentences mentioning the entity by name, description, or pronoun; and to extract features, e.g., facts, general relations involving the entity to be defined, and syntactic forms typically used to state definitions. These serve as features of the text and its meaning; comparing statistical similarity measures between the features of the candidate sentences and the features of sentences in example biographies or definitions with the similarities between the candidate sentences and the background collection; and syntactic compression to reduce the information to kernel facts, for example to support detection of repeated information.

A subjective evaluation scheme has been proposed for this class of questions (Voorhees 2003). Another aspect of our approach has been to apply BLEU, an automatic evaluation scheme previously applied to evaluate machine translations.

Though our approach will be applied to generate not only biographies but also organizational profiles and extended definitions of terms, in this chapter we describe the techniques and evaluate them in the context of biographical questions.

5.2 Component Technologies

In this section, we first describe the overall system structure, and then describe the contribution of each component technology. Throughout this section, we will use the example question "Who is Gunter Blobel?" for illustration.

5.2.1 Overall System Structure

The structure of the system is shown in figure 5.1. First, question classification identifies (1) the question type, e.g., a biography, an organizational profile, or an extended definition, and (2) the target, i.e., the person for a biography, the organization for an organizational profile, or the term for an extended definition.

Second, information retrieval pulls relevant documents about the target from the collection. This is achieved by treating the target as an IR query. BBN's HMM IR system (Miller et al. 1999) is used for this purpose.

Third, each sentence mentioning the target term from the 20 most relevant documents (as ranked by document retrieval) is processed to identify linguistic and semantic features in the sentence. An example linguistic feature is the presence of an appositive involving the target. An example semantic feature is who the target's spouse is.

Fourth, each sentence is reduced to a list of phrases corresponding to the features identified. This reduction is a heuristic attempt to reduce the sentence to kernel facts encapsulating important information about the target.

Fifth, based on the features, each sentence is ranked for relevance in a biography based on a simple statistical model of example "training" biographies compared with the statistical model of the collection as a whole.

Sixth, starting from the highest ranked kernel fact, each kernel fact is compared against the set of facts already in the biography to eliminate redundant facts.

The kernel facts with high relevance are the material for our biography. These kernel facts can be the basis for alternative output forms, such as tables, lists of concisely stated facts, graphs showing associations to other entities, or prose summaries. Thus far, we have explored only the first three of those output forms.

5.2.2 Document Retrieval

The first step in our approach is to retrieve relevant documents. Our document retrieval system uses the statistical language model of Miller et al. (1999).

Though the collection for our experiments is news (see section 5.3), oftentimes significant biographical material is contained within a single news article. Therefore, one of the baselines that our approach must improve upon is document retrieval. Results will be reported for this baseline in section 3.

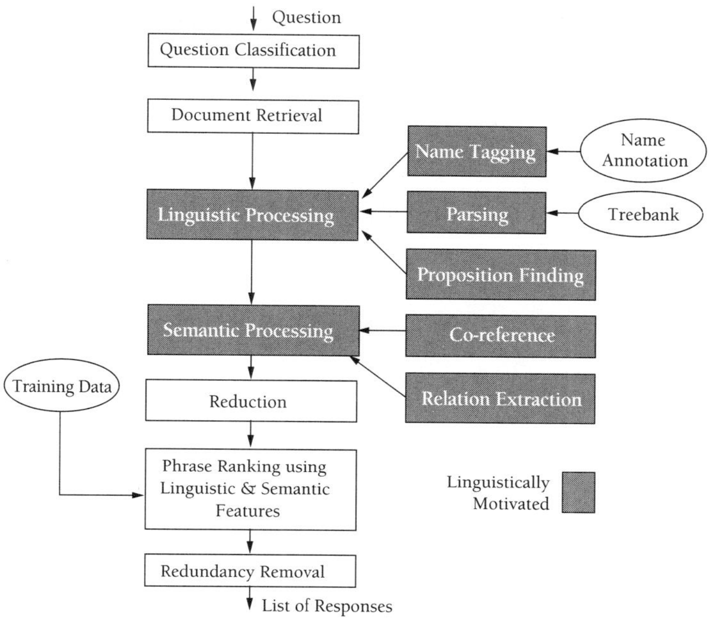

Figure 5.1. System Structure

5.2.3 Linguistic Processing

Linguistic processing produces three kinds of results: names, parse trees, and propositions. Name tagging is performed by IdentiFinder™, a trainable system based on a hidden Markov model (Bikel et al. 1999). The version we are using is trained to identify 29 types.

Parsing produces trees according to the UPenn TREEBANK standard (Marcus et al. 1993). The parser was described in Miller et al. (2000), and uses a model based on Collins (1997). Given a parse, rules create a set of propositions for the sentence. These propositions correspond to the basic predications about the entities mentioned in the sentence.

Propositions represent an approximation of predicate-argument structure and take the form: predicate ($role_1$: arg_1, … , $role_n$: arg_n). The predicate is typically a verb or noun. Arguments can be either an entity or another proposition. The most common roles include logical subject, logical object, premodifier (for noun predicates), and object of a prepositional phrase modifying the predicate. For example, "Smith went to Spain" is represented as went (logical subject: Smith, PP-to: Spain), and "the U.S. president" is represented as president (premodifier: U.S.).

To illustrate this phase, figure 5.2 shows sentences that would be selected

-- Dr. Gunter Blobel, a cellular and molecular biologist at Rockefeller University in New York City , won the 1999 Nobel Prize in medicine on Monday for discovering that proteins carry signals that act as ZIP codes, helping them find their correct locations within the cell . (*APPOSITIVE*=biologist)

-- -LRB - Angel Franco/New York Times Photo - RRB - - LRB- NYT10 - RRB - NEW YORK -- Oct. 11, 1999 -- SCI - NOBEL - MEDICINE, 10-11 -- Dr. Guenter Blobel, a cellular and molecular biologist at Rockefeller University on Monday. (*APPOSITIVE*=biologist)

-- Guenter Blobel, a cell biologist at Rockefeller University in New York , was awarded the Nobel Prize in Physiology or Medicine Monday for discovering how proteins get shipped to their proper destinations within the body after being manufactured by tiny molecular factories inside cells. (*APPOSITIVE*=biologist)

-- Reefers: SCI-NOBEL - MEDICINE - LRB-Undated -RRB- --Dr. Guenter Blobel, a cellular and molecular biologist at Rockefeller University in New York City , is awarded the 1999 Nobel Prize in Physiology of Medicine for discovering that proteins carry signals that act as ZIP codes , helping them find their correct locations within the cell. (*APPOSITIVE*=biologist)

-- Blobel was born in 1936 in Waltersdorf, Silesia, Germany, now part of Poland. (verb=born object=*TERM* in=Germany)

-- Young Gunter graduated from high school "with highest grades , although he never studied very much," his oldest brother , Dr. Hans Blobel, said in a telephone interview from his home in Geissen, Germany. (verb=graduated, subject=*TERM*)

Figure 5.2. Sentences That Would Be Selected for "Who is Gunter Blobel?" Based on Linguistic Features

for the example question if only linguistic features (i.e., propositions, appositives and copulas) are used. In parentheses after each sentence, the parenthetical material shows the feature, e.g., appositive or proposition, that was the basis for selecting the sentence.

5.2.4 Semantic Processing Via Information Extraction

The propositions mentioned in the previous section simply consist of lexical predicates. Since different lexical predicates can represent the same underlying concept or relation, normalizing these propositions into relations that are commonly found in an ontology, where possible, can provide additional, potentially valuable features. Furthermore, the mentions of an entity have not been connected by co-reference. These two issues are handled by deeper processing using the statistical entity and relation information finding (Serif) information extraction engine. Serif uses statistical learning algorithms for name co-reference and for pronominal co-reference (Ramshaw et al. 2001). For definite description co-reference, a set of heuristic rules is applied. This connects the propositional arguments within and across sentences.

Additionally, Serif extracts 24 binary relations based on relation extraction

-- a cellular and molecular biologist at Rockefeller University in New York City,

-- a cellular and molecular biologist at Rockefeller University in New York City,

-- a cell biologist at Rockefeller University in New York

-- a cellular and molecular biologist at Rockefeller University in New York City

-- Dr. Guenter Blobel of The Rockefeller University in New York

-- Blobel was born in 1936 in Waltersdorf, Silesia, Germany, now part of Poland .

-- Young Gunter graduated from high school with highest grades, although he never studied very much

Figure 5.3. An Example Resulting From Reduction

as defined in the ACE guidelines (Linguistic Data Consortium, 2002). Using lexicalized patterns, Serif extracts those relations from the propositions. For the example question, the relation role/general-staff ("Gunter Blobel," "Rockefeller University") will be extracted from the sentence "Dr. Gunter Blobel of The Rockefeller University in New York won the Nobel Prize for medicine today for protein research that shed new light on diseases including cystic fibrosis and early development of kidney stones."

5.2.5 Reduction

Reduction takes as input a sentence and the linguistic features and semantic features identified in the sentence. For each feature corresponding to a relation between the target and another thing, a heuristic is applied to select a portion of the sentence containing the feature. The current heuristic finds the smallest phrase in the parse tree containing a mention of the target and the feature. Note that the selected phrases in general may overlap, but are each part of the sentence. If reduction were the final phrase of processing, our biography of Gunther Blobel would consist of the phrases in figure 5.3.

5.2.6 Phrase Ranking

Our basic hypothesis is that biographies have a character different from normal text, and that we can model that character. We use a very simple statistical model. We order the sentences/phrases based on our estimate of the probability of relevance, given the feature. Equation 1 below is just Bayes' rule, where f is a feature (kernel fact) and $P(R|f)$ is the probability of relevance given f:

$$P(R|f) = P(R)\ P(f|R)\ /\ P(f) \qquad (1)$$

$P(R|f)$ is estimated from training data, i.e, frequencies of features in a set of hu-

-- A cellular and molecular biologist at Rockefeller University in New York City

-- Dr. Guenter Blobel of The Rockefeller University in New York

-- Blobel was born in 1936 in Waltersdorf, Silesia, Germany, now part of Poland

-- Young Gunter graduated from high school "with highest grades, although he never studied very much

Figure 5.4. Final Output

man-generated biographies. *P*(*f*) is estimated from a background corpus, a 10M word sample of the AQUAINT corpus. The prior *P*(*R*) can be ignored for the purpose of ranking.

There are many sources of biographies that can be used for training; in the experiments we report here, we extracted frequency counts of the linguistic and semantic features of biographies from the following two web sites: www.s9.com, and www.wikipedia.org.

5.2.7 Redundancy Removal

The kernel fact which maximizes *P*(*R*|*f*) goes into the biography. Then we process the remaining kernel facts as follows: let f be the kernel fact with the highest *P*(*R*|*f*) not yet processed. If *f* is a feature not included among the kernel facts already in the biography, then it is included in the biography. Otherwise, *f* is considered redundant, since it is already included in the biography. Two kernel facts are considered equivalent if the predicate (relation) in each is the same and if the head of the noun phrase of the corresponding argument of each fact is the same. Figure 5.4 gives the kernel facts selected from the candidates.

5.3 Evaluation

For the experiments reported here, we used 8 biography questions from a pilot study published by NIST (Voorhees 2003) and 18 from TREC9&10 questions. The document collection consists of the two AQUAINT disks used in the TREC 2002 Question Answering track and to be used in the TREC 2003 Question Answering Track. To create the reference biographies, three individuals not familiar with our system or approach drafted biographies for each of the 26 questions. The only instruction was to follow the example of answer keys to 8 questions created by NIST in the pilot study (Voorhees 2003).

5.3.1 Evaluations

In this subsection, we report scores based on subjective evaluation and also based on the BLEU automatic scoring software. Among the many possible measures, we chose to estimate recall given a maximum length answer. That is, the answer keys contained required facts; system output was truncated after the number of words in the human biography of the answer key.

For subjective evaluation, one of the individuals involved in creating the reference biographies was chosen to be the evaluator. For each question, the evaluator assessed which of the required facts (termed "nuggets") in his own answer key were in the system output. The score is the number of "nuggets" found divided by the number of "nuggets" in the answer key. Scores for 26 questions were averaged to produce a single score for a system output.

For automatic evaluation, we applied BLEU (Papineni et al. 2002), which was first developed and applied for automatic evaluation of machine translation. In machine translation the length of the system output is roughly that of the answer key. BLEU measures precision of word n-gram overlap between the system output and answer key. Since there may be many valid translations, typically a few human translations are used in the answer key. To apply BLEU, we truncated system output for each question at the average length of three human generated biographies for that question. One parameter of BLEU scoring is the maximum "*n*" for which *n*-gram matching is scored. Naturally, for a given system output and a given reference, the larger "*n*" is, the lower the degree of matching and the lower the BLEU score.

It is important to know that the BLEU score depends not only on the quality of the system output, but also on factors such as the value of *n* and the number of reference answers used. It does not make sense to interpret the quality of a system output solely based on its BLEU score. What matters is the relative ranking of the BLEU scores of different systems when other factors are fixed. Therefore, we do not report the exact numerical values of the scores, but choose bar charts to present the relative ranking across results.

We should point out that in using BLEU, we made the assumption that the closer a system answer is to manually generated ones in terms of overlapping *n*-grams, the better the system answer is. We will later examine the correlation between subjective evaluation by humans and automatic evaluation by BLEU to verify this assumption.

We employed two simple baselines to calibrate our techniques: retrieval of the most relevant documents based on information retrieval relevance ranking, but not using any model of biographies (this system is labeled "Doc. Ret" in the charts); and ranking the most relevant sentences in the most relevant documents based on information retrieval relevance ranking (labeled "IR Sent." in the charts).

Additionally we evaluated four versions of our current system's output: sentences selected based on linguistic features (labeled "Ling Feats" in the charts); sentences based on both linguistic features and semantic (information extraction) features (labeled "Relations" in the charts); sentences selected by linguistic and semantic features and surviving redundancy removal (labeled "Redundancy" in the charts); and phrases generated by the reduction process (section

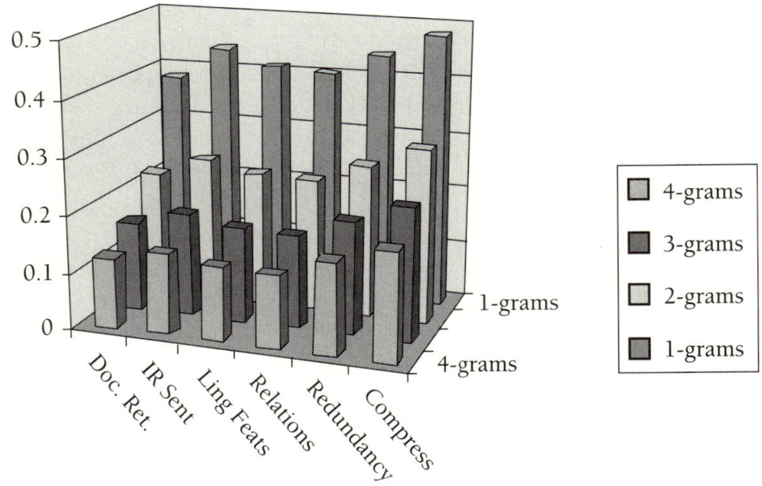

Figure 5.5. BLEU Scores Against the "Nugget" Answer Keys

5.2.5) from the sentences as selected above for relevance and non-redundance (labeled "Compress" in the charts).

Figure 5.5 shows the BLEU scores for the six systems listed above, when measured using 1-gram matching, up to 2-gram matching, up to 3-gram matching, and up to 4-gram matching. The answer keys contain a set of "nuggets," short descriptions of the kind planned for the answer keys of the TREC 2003 evaluation. Several tendencies are evident: sentence selection via IR and name finding is surprisingly good according to BLEU. Linguistic features and redundancy removal seem promising; however, according to the BLEU metric, relation extraction hurts scores slightly. (Subjective evaluation in figure 5.6 shows that these features do contribute.) Sentence compression improves scores on "nugget" answer keys. The relative ranking of the systems is the same for each of the four settings of the maximum number of *n*-grams to be used in matching.

In figure 5.6, we compare results using 1, 2, and 3 human-generated reference answers. Note that scores increase with the number of reference answers. The increase is to be expected since having more human-generated references minimizes the effect of the particular words and phrases used to express a concept. Overall, the relative ranking of different systems is the same regardless of the number of references used. The one exception is on the relation output, where including relations in the processing helped for two assessors, but hurt for three. The differences are small and suggest that the effect of only 24 relation types is too small to have the desired impact.

Figure 5.6 also compares scores for the subjective evaluation and BLEU scores. Since the subjective evaluation and BLEU do not use the same measure, the scores across the measures are not comparable. However, the relative

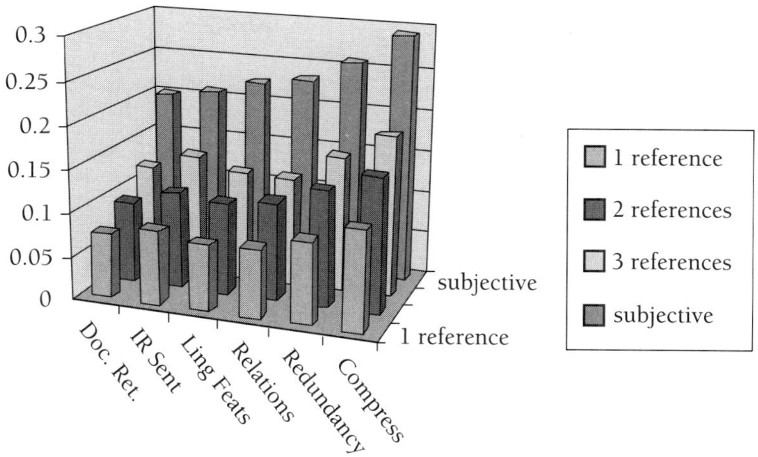

Figure 5.6. Subjective Evaluation and BLEU Scores with Different Number of References

ranking of the systems is the purpose of the comparison. The subjective evaluation shows that each level of processing applied in our research improved performance in the human assessor's view. The results also show that although subjective evaluation and BLEU do not always agree, there is a positive correlation between the two. More work using a larger test set and involving more systems is needed to determine if BLEU can satisfactorily replace subjective evaluation.

5.4 Related Work

Now that extended definitions, biographies, and organizational profiles will be evaluated in TREC 2003, several groups are working in the area. NIST monitored a pilot study on these questions in fall, 2002; the participants were BBN, Columbia University, Cycorp, IBM, LCC, and U.S.C/ISI. This volume represents the first major collection since that pilot study.

Columbia University (McKeown and Blair-Goldensohn 2003, Blair-Goldensohn et al., chapter 4) has had a rather complementary focus to the work reported here. Based on analysis of rules of thumb in rhetoric, they have written patterns to find some key relations, e.g., class-subclass and class-exemplar, in text that supplements the selection of sentences from relevant documents. Their emphasis on ways to compose those sentences into coherent prose complements our work, which has focused more on modeling the kind of kernel facts in biographies and using deeper language understanding techniques to find such facts in a collection.

Lin and Hovy (2003) published a study using a modification of BLEU for automatically evaluating summaries. They took a complementary approach to our use of BLEU. To deal with the bias of BLEU toward answers roughly the same length as the answer key, they modified BLEU to account for length and to measure recall of n-grams, whereas the original BLEU focuses more on precision of n-grams. For tracking our system's performance, we used the original precision-oriented BLEU, but truncated system output to control the length bias. Further work is needed by both groups to determine the best automatic evaluation measure of summarization and of generation of extended answers to questions.

A subjective evaluation of extended answers is proposed for TREC 2003 (Voorhees 2003). People will be asked to generate a set of required facts, termed "nuggets," and a set of optional facts for the answer key for each definitional, biographical, or organization profile question. Systems are to produce a list of responses. Assessors will judge which of the required and optional facts are present in the system output. The score is the harmonic mean of recall and precision, where recall is given five times the weight of precision.

Schiffman, et al. (2001) described a system to generate biographical summaries from multiple documents based on linguistic knowledge and corpus statistics. Similar to our work, descriptive noun phrases such as appositives played an important role in their system. Radev and McKeown (1997) described a system to harvest descriptive noun phrases for entities from online sources (e.g., Internet Newswire). A difference between our work and previous studies is that we used human-created biographies to separate relevant and irrelevant materials, while previous studies typically used unsupervised techniques.

Rinaldi et al. (chapter 6) describes a QA system specifically designed for knowledge-rich technical domains. That system can handle complex questions, such as definitional questions, as well as simple factoid questions. That work complements ours in that our system is primarily designed to deal with unrestricted texts such as newspaper articles. Another difference between their system and ours is that they used a sophisticated inference mechanism while we did not. We believe that incorporating a strong inference mechanism will improve the performance of our system.

5.5 Conclusions

Although 26 questions are not enough to guarantee statistical significance, there are several conclusions from this preliminary study: the IR model of biographies improves sentence selection, apparently selecting sentences like those seen in human-generated biographies; though there are many ideas to try still, linguistic analysis, both syntactic and semantic, seems promising. However, the information retrieval model could be improved as well, if effective heuristics for redundancy removal can be found; relation extraction may improve on the IR model of sentence selection. If information extraction technology were extended to far more than the 24 current relation types, the impact might be greater; the BLEU measure is stable with respect to length of n-grams; regarding automatic (BLEU) versus subjective evaluation, BLEU is promising for automatic evaluation of progress in a single system development. BLEU may not be accurate enough for cross-system evaluation; further testing must be performed to verify the utility of an automatic scoring methodology versus subjective evaluations.

Much work remains. We intend to apply these ideas and evaluate them on organizational profiles and term definitions. The work is just beginning.

Acknowledgments

This work was supported in part by the Advanced Research and Development Activity (ARDA) under contract number MDA904-01-C-1013. We appreciate comments from Donna Harman, John Prange, and Ellen Voorhees on oral presentations of this work in progress.

Ralph Weischedel is a scientist at BBN Technologies, Cambridge, Massachusetts.

Jinxi Xu is a scientist at BBN Technologies, Cambridge, Massachusetts. He can be reached at jxu@bbn.com

Ana Licuanan is a scientist at BBN Technologies, Cambridge, Massachusetts.

Chapter 6

Question Answering in Terminology-Rich Technical Domains

Fabio Rinaldi, Michael Hess, James Dowdall, Diego Mollá, & Rolf Schwitter

6.1 Introduction

Technical documents are very often the only reliable knowledge sources about complex products. Documents are the central repository of information otherwise distributed among numerous experts in an enterprise. To utilize these knowledge sources, methods are needed to answer questions over texts in specific problem situations quickly and with high precision. Research in the area of question answering (QA) over texts has been promoted in the last few years in particular by the QA track of the Text Retrieval Conference (TREC QA) competitions (Voorhees 2001). The TREC QA competitions focus on open-domain systems, i.e., systems that can (potentially) answer any generic question. As these competitions are based on large volumes of text, the competing systems cannot afford to perform resource-consuming tasks, and therefore they usually resort to a relatively shallow text analysis. Very few systems try to do more than skim the surface of the text. In contrast, a question answering system working on technical documents does not have to handle very large volumes of text. It can also take advantage of the formatting and style conventions in the particular text (defined quite strictly in technical documents) and can make use of the specific domain-dependent terminology (Rinaldi et al. 2003b). In other words, technical documentation allows deeper processing strategies which might lead to more accurate results, as we will see in this chapter.

However, technical domains present the additional problem of "domain navigation." Unfamiliarity with domain terminology often results in imprecise or even faulty questions. A useful QA system must try to fix this by detecting terminological variants and exploiting the relations between terms (like synonymy, meronymy, antonymy).

In this chapter we will first explore (in section 2) the peculiarities of technical documentation. The central role that terminology plays in technical domains (parallel to the role of named entities in open-domain question answering) will be explored in section 3. As an example of the practical application of QA in technical domains we then present (in section 4) a real-world system (ExtrAns), specifically designed for technical domains.

6.2 What's Special About Technical Documentation?

Technical documentation is a low-volume/high-value type of text (Hess et al. 2002). In both respects this is the exact opposite of newswire or newspaper texts whose volume is huge but whose value is modest, and declines rapidly after a few days. These differences have a deep impact on the way such texts must be processed, as we will see in this section.

High Value. Technical documentation is a very important type of text. No technical artifact (from equipment, appliance, or tool to hardware and software to complete factory or plant) comes without technical documentation. The more complex a technical artifact is, the more important its documentation becomes. In safety-critical fields (such as aircraft maintenance) a lack in correctness, completeness, or consistency of the relevant technical documentation can have extremely serious legal consequences.

Low Volume. Despite their importance, technical texts are limited in size. The main UNIX commands are explained in slightly more than 500 "man" pages, and many of these pages contain only a few sentences. Similarly, the *Aircraft Maintenance Manual* (AMM) of the Airbus A320 is about 120 megabytes in terms of pure text, which is at least one order of magnitude inferior to the well over a gigabyte of text used in the TREC conferences (Voorhees 2001).

6.2.1 Peculiarities of Technical Documentation

Technical documentation is particular because of its communicative function. Technical texts describe knowledge about concepts and principles and explain how to use this knowledge to do things and to solve problems in a specific domain. They hardly ever refer to facts (events, objects) that are uniquely located in space and time, unlike newspaper texts. Nevertheless, the objects they refer to can normally be identified uniquely (ultimately, by parts numbers). All this makes such texts easier to process in some respects (no need for named entity recognition or for temporal considerations[1]) but more difficult in others (no situational context available to disambiguate).

Conciseness. Concepts are expressed in technical documents once only and in a concise form. There is no room for data redundancy. The user is expected to find the information in one specific part of the manual only. Therefore, if a QA system fails to detect a specific nugget of information in one part of a document, it will hardly be able to find a passage elsewhere containing the same information.

Structuring. Technical documents are typically well-structured. For example, the sections of the AMM are divided into chapters numbered according to a standard coding schema. Each chapter is divided into sections, and the numbering of these sections has been standardized so that, for example, the pageblock number 02 of any section of any chapter is about maintenance practices, and pageblock number 03 is always about servicing. The rigid structuring of such texts facilitates easy access to the specific information that the user is looking for.

Formatting conventions. Technical text also abounds in formatting conventions. For example, cross-references in the AMM and the man pages are standardized, to the extent that browser software for these manuals can readily use the specific format to convert the cross-references into hyperlinks. Unfortunately, such typesetting conventions are extremely idiosyncratic. What is printed in italics in one manual is rendered in boldface in the next. Completely parameterizable high-performance tokenizers and zone identifiers are indispensable in any system that processes such text.

Terminology. Terminology is ubiquitous in technical texts. Every technical domain has its own terminology, and specialized terminology is unlikely to be included in general lexical resources like WordNet (Fellbaum 1998). Since resources like general grammars and lexica may fail to adequately handle expressions containing these different usages of the terms, the terminology needs always to be built up in relation to the technical domain.

Clarity, simplicity, and reduced ambiguity. The very nature of technical text dictates that the sentences should be easy to understand. This is certainly the case in the AMM which is written in a controlled natural language in order to ease the understanding of operational and functional instructions by technical staff. This simplified form of English is not only easier to read by humans but also easier to process by a computer because the sentence structure is less complex and there are fewer word sense ambiguities.

6.2.2 The Aircraft Maintenance Manual (AMM)

The controlled language used in the AMM of the Airbus A320/330 is AECMA's *Simplified English*, a standard for English-language documentation in the aerospace industry (European Association of Aerospace Industries 2001). Simplified English distinguishes two writing styles: declarative writing and procedural writing. Each section in the AMM starts with a declarative description of a unit and then describes operational and functional procedures that are necessary to maintain the unit.

> **LAVATORY SMOKE DETECTORS**
>
> A smoke detection system is installed to detect smoke and/or fire in the lavatories. If smoke is detected, the system gives a visual and aural warning to the flight crew. This system is made-up of:
>
> • One smoke detector for each lavatory,
>
> • The Smoke Detection Control Unit (SDCU).

Figure 6.1. Example of Declarative Writing

From a cognitive point of view this structure makes a lot of sense for the reader of the document since the acquisition of procedural knowledge is always dependent upon the existence of declarative knowledge and the repeated use of procedures or actions.

Declarative writing has a relatively large proportion of text consisting of full sentences. Still, there are a number of lists with incomplete sentences.

In the example in figure 6.1 the list elements are all noun phrases with a parallel structure. The relation between the elements of a list and the preceding paragraph can be ascertained from the last sentence of the paragraph. Thus, the last sentence in the first paragraph determines that the elements of the first list are the main parts that the smoke detection system consists of. As the paragraph also shows, consistent use of terminology is vital to understand the description.

The use of a low-ambiguity Simplified English makes it comparatively simple to find the underlying logical form of each sentence, as the system described later in this chapter will show. Furthermore, the use of a clear structuring of the text enables the use of text coherence and discourse structure techniques. These features, together with the relatively low volumes of text under consideration, make technical texts very good candidates for experimenting with natural language processing techniques.

6.2.3 Why Typical TREC Techniques Will Not Work

The processing of technical text has an enormous practical potential, especially in cases like the AMM where a quick solution to a technical problem can make a difference between departing on time, departing late, or even cancelling the flight. However, techniques geared towards domain-independent question answering over newswire text or web pages cannot take full advantage of the particularities of technical texts. This is certainly the case with most of the main techniques employed in the QA track of TREC:

Data redundancy approaches that rely on the availability of the same information in different formats cannot be used here because there is very little redundant information, and the information that is repeated is typically repeated in exactly the same way.

Web-based approaches that rely on voting systems need the backing of answers found on the world wide web. However, technical information that can be used to supplement a technical manual is very unlikely to ever be published on the web (for reasons of intellectual property), and if related material is found, there is still the issue of technical accuracy. The amount of accurate data that can be used to back a technical manual is very likely to be insufficient for web-based approaches.

Information extraction approaches that rely on the use of named entities are successful only in domains where fact-based questions are dominant (e.g., "Where can I buy a smoke detector?"). However, questions over technical texts are mostly procedural (e.g., "How do I remove the lavatory smoke detector?").

By operating outside the TREC QA model, systems require novel techniques. This applies to generating multi-sentence answers to definitional questions (see chapter 4) as well as biographical answers aggregated across multiple documents (see chapter 5). For technical domains the most obvious novelties are the techniques for processing the terminology of the domain.

6.3 How to Exploit Terminology (and Why)

Where general knowledge ends, terminology provides the means to name concepts and objects specific to the domain at hand. For the AMM, this includes parts of the aircraft, tools, and procedures which account for more than 30% of the running text. Extending everyday language to name a domain's jargon produces terms exhibiting the production rules of canonical phrases (Sager 1990). For example, terms behave like nominal compounds as: (i) the head is the rightmost word, (ii) only the head carries inflectional morphology, and (iii) the compound is a hyponym of its head. However, terms distinguish themselves by excluding extra-linguistic (pragmatic or idiomatic) interpretation.

Just as term formation is modeled as the interaction between tokens with morpho-syntactic and semantic properties (Kageura 2002), so the reference of a term is recovered by examining its context. Where a term fits into the terminology depends on how its constituent tokens interact with each other. In ExtrAns, this interaction identifies taxonomic and synonymous relations.

The high frequency of terms in technical text produces two main problems when locating answers.

The parsing problem is the difficulty of identifying phrasal boundaries when presented with multiword terms (MWTs). The frequency of tokens unknown to a generic lexicon (e.g. "acetic") increases the number of possible parses for a sentence. As lexical categories are 'guessed', the number of possible syntactic parses for the sentence increases as the parser tries odd combinations of the tokens belonging to distinct phrases.

The paraphrase problem (Woods, 1997) resides in the imperfect knowledge of users, who are not completely familiar with the domain terminology. Even experienced users, who can be described as domain experts, will not remember the exact form of a term and use a paraphrase to refer to the underlying domain concept. Besides, even in the documents themselves, various paraphrases of the same compound will appear, and they need to be identified as co-referent. However, it is not enough to identify all paraphrases within the manual; novel paraphrases might be created by the users each time they query the system (Rinaldi et al. 2003a).

Overcoming these problems involves the extraction of the document collection's terminology, its analysis to uncover any semantically related terms and the exploitation of this knowledge during the QA process. These three tasks were performed for our QA system.

6.3.1 Extraction

Different sources of information, both internal and external, were invaluable in the extraction process. First, several kinds of external sources (glossaries of abbreviations used in aircraft industry and different specifications (Air Transport Association 1997)) were used. Internally, different types of structures in AMM can indicate the presence of a term. Some of the terms are already explicitly denoted through the use of markup (e.g., element CONNAME for consumable material, element TOOLNAME for tools etc). Other terms can be detected making use of recurring lexical patterns, such as "Power Transfer Unit (PTU)," where capitalized words are followed by an acronym in parentheses which can be detected and properly processed using simple regular expressions. However, the bulk of terminology is detected using the two separate approaches described below.

The first approach is based on a stop-phrase method that chunks certain SGML-zones (titles, paragraphs) using a list of generic (nonterminological) phrases, that often hint at the presence of an adjacent term. For example, from the task title: "Check of the Electrical Bonding of External Composite Panels with a CORAS Resistivity-Continuity Test Set," we cut the prepositions and determiners to obtain the list of candidate terms: "Check," "Electrical Bonding," "External Composite Panels," and "CORAS Resistivity-Continuity Test Set." Given the high incidence of technical terms in the material we are dealing with, even such crude techniques provide interesting results.

The second approach is a fully automatic statistical method (Dias et al. 1999). This is very general, using no linguistic analysis, allowing *n*-grams to be of any length and allowing them to be non-contiguous (i.e., they can contain "holes"). It uses mutual expectation as an association measure, which evaluates

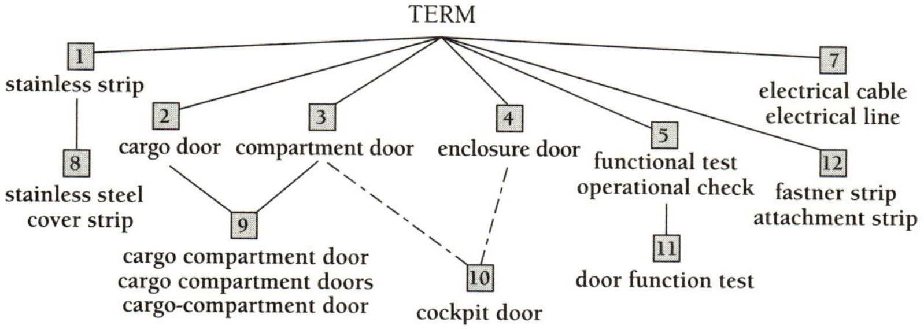

Figure 6.2. The ExtrAns Thesaurus

the cohesiveness of a multi-word unit and a criterion called *LocalMax* to select the candidate terms from the evaluated list. The list obtained by the statistical method of mutual expectation and LocalMax showed the results of recall 44% and precision 15%. For the list obtained by the stop-phrase method the recall was 66% and precision 12%. When combining the methods (the hybrid case), the recall increased to 78% and precision became 10%. After manual validation a 1 million word corpus from the AMM yielded over 13,000 terms.

6.4 Analysis

Once the terminology of a domain is available, it is necessary to detect relations among terms in order to exploit it. We have focused our attention in particular to the relations of synonymy and hyponymy, which are detected as described in this section and gathered in a thesaurus. The organizing unit is a WordNet style synset which includes strict synonymy as well as three weaker synonymy relations. These sets are further organized into an isA hierarchy based on two definitions of hyponymy.

Synonymy detection begins during tokenization to normalize terms that contain punctuation by creating a punctuation free version and recording that the two are strictly synonymous. Further processing is involved in terms containing brackets to determine if the bracketed token is an acronym or simply optional.

In the former case an acronym-free term is created and the acronym is stored as a synonym of the remaining tokens that contain it as a regular expression. Morpho-syntactic processes such as head inversion also identify strict synonymy, like "cargo compartment door" and "door of the cargo compartment." Translating WordNet's synset onto the terminology defines three weaker synonymy relations (Hamon and Nazarenko, 2001) illustrated in figure 6.2: Head synonymy (node 7), modifier synonymy (node 12) and both (node 5). For a description of the frequency and range of types of variation

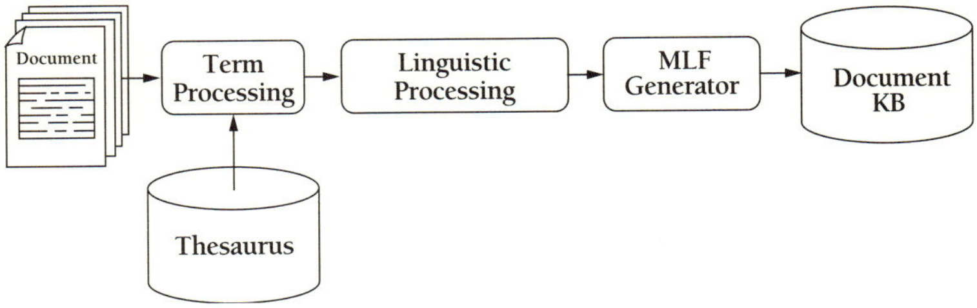

Figure 6.3. Generating the Semantic Representation (Offline Processing)

present in the AMM see Rinaldi et al. (2002).

Hyponymy is defined as two distinct types: modifier addition producing "lexical hyponymy" and "WordNet hyponymy" translated from WordNet onto the term set. As additional modifiers naturally form a more specific term, lexical hyponymy is easily determined. Term *A* is a lexical hyponym of term *B* if: *A* has more tokens than *B*; the tokens of *B* keep their order in *A* and *A* and *B* have the same head.[2] This relation is exemplified in figure 6.2 between nodes 1 and 8. It permits multiple hypernyms, as node 9 is a hyponym of both 2 and 3.

"WordNet hyponymy" is defined between terms linked through WordNet's immediate hypernym relation. The dashed branches in figure 6.2 represent links through modifier hyponymy where the terms share a common head and the modifiers are defined as immediate hypernyms in WordNet. Nodes 3 and 4 are both hypernyms of 10. Similarly, "floor covering" is a kind of "surface protection" as "surface" is an immediate hypernym of "floor" and "protection" is an immediate hypernym of "covering."

Automatically discovering these relations across 6,032 terms from the AMM produces 2,770 synsets with 1,176 lexical hyponymy links and 643 WordNet hyponymy links. Through manual validation of 500 synsets, 1.2% were determined to contain an inappropriate term. A similar examination of 500 lexical hyponymy links identified them all as valid. However, out of 500 WordNet hyponymy links more than 35% were invalid. By excluding the WordNet hyponymy relation we obtain an accurate thesaurus of synsets related through lexical hyponymy which is exploited by our QA system, ExtrAns.

6.5 ExtrAns

ExtrAns answers questions over technical domains exploiting linguistic knowledge from the documents and terminological knowledge about a specific domain. The original ExtrAns system was used to extract answers to arbitrary user queries over Unix documentation files. A set of 500+ unedited UNIX man pages has been used for this application (Mollá et al. 2000). Later, we tackled a different domain, the *Aircraft Maintenance Manuals* (AMM) of the

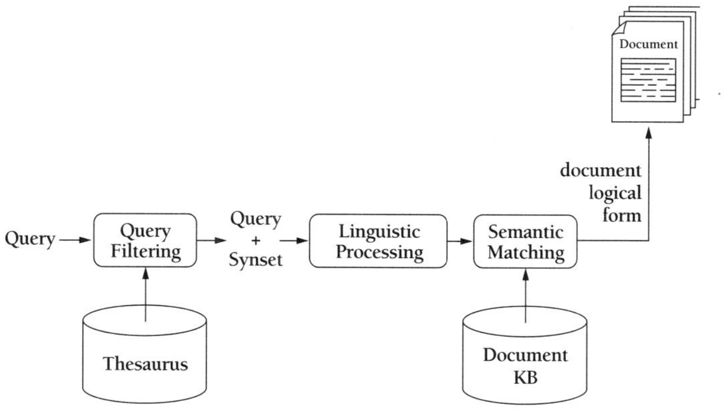

Figure 6.4. Exploiting Thesaurus and KB (Online Processing)

Airbus A320. The highly specific nature of this domain, as well as an SGML-based format and a much larger size (120MB) provided an important test-bed for the scalability and domain independence of the system. An evaluation of the question answering capabilities of ExtrAns against a baseline IR system (based on the MRR measure) is presented in (Rinaldi et al. 2002).

6.5.1 Brief Description of the System

We have chosen a computationally intensive approach to question answering. First, all the documents are analysed in an off-line stage (see figure 6.3) and a semantic representation of their contents is stored in a knowledge base (KB). In an online phase (see figure 6.4), the semantic representation which results from the analysis of the user query is matched in the KB against the stored representations, locating sentences that best answer the query (see figure. 6.5).

The solution to the parsing problem and paraphrase problem (section 6.3) takes place during tokenization of the input stream. Replacing MultiWord Terms (MWT) with their synset identifier from the thesaurus produces two results. First, a MWT is packed into a single lexical token for parsing—reducing the average number of parses per sentence by 46% (Dowdall et al. 2002). Second, any variant of the underlying concept is represented by the same synset identifier producing an implicit "terminological normalization" of the domain.

Documents (in the off-line stage) and queries (in the on-line stage) are first processed by a tokenizer and the terminology-processing module described above. Subsequent linguistic modules include a parser and grammar (an adaptation of Sleator and Temperley 1993), a partial disambiguator (inspired by Brill and Resnik 1994), and a pronominal anaphora solver (inspired by Lappin and Leass 1994). From the output of the above modules ExtrAns derives one logical form per sentence, or more if there are remaining ambiguities.

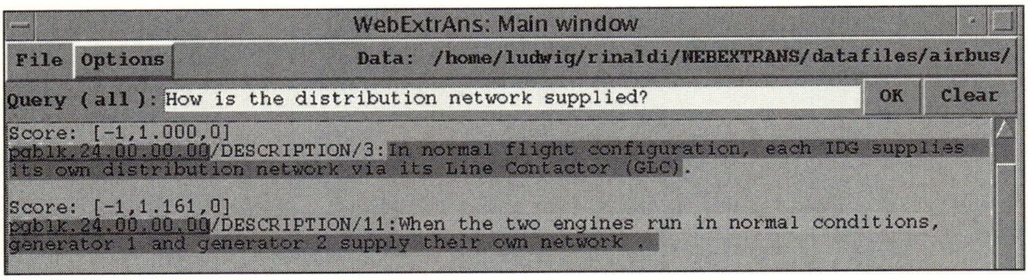

Figure 6.5. Example of Interaction with the System

6.5.2 Minimal Logical Forms

ExtrAns depends heavily on its use of logical forms. The ability of ExtrAns' logical forms to underspecify makes them good candidates for NLP applications, especially when the applications benefit from the semantic comparison of sentences (Copestake et al. 1997). In the case of ExtrAns, the logical forms only encode the dependencies between verbs and their arguments, plus modifier and adjunct relations. Information ignored is, among others, quantification, tense and aspect, temporal relations, plurality, and modality. We have argued elsewhere that overly detailed logical forms may interfere with the answer extraction mechanism and that additional information can be added incrementally (Mollá 2001). This is why ExtrAns' logical forms are called *minimal logical forms* (MLFs).

MLFs use reification to allow different kind of modifications, very much in the line of Hobbs (1985). MLFs do not reify all predicates, as opposed to Copestake et al. (1997). In the current implementation only reification of objects, eventualities (events or states), and properties is used. MLFs are expressed as conjunctions of predicates where all variables are existentially bound and have wide scope. For example, the MLF of the sentence "A coax cable connects the external antenna to the ANT connection" is:

holds(e1), object(coax_cable,o1,[x1]),
object(external_antenna,o2,[x2]), object(ant_connection,o3,[x3]),
evt(connect,e1,[x1,x2]), prop(to,p1,[e1,x3]).

In other words, ExtrAns derives from the sentence three multi-word terms and translates them into objects: *x*1 (a coax cable), *x*2 (an external antenna), and *x*3 (an ANT connection). The entity *e*1 represents an eventuality derived from the verb involving two objects, the coax cable and the external antenna. The entity e1 is used in the property derived from the prepositional phrase to assert that the eventuality happens to *x*3, the ANT connection.

An advantage of ExtrAns' MLFs is that they can be produced with minimal domain knowledge. This makes our technology easily portable to different domains. The only true impact of the domain is during the preprocessing stage of the input text and during creation of a thesaurus that reflects the specific terms used in the chosen domain, their lexical relations and their word senses.

6.5.3 Answer Extraction

User queries are processed on-line and the resulting MLFs are proved by deduction over the MLFs of document sentences stored in the KB. More specifically, the MLFs are translated into Prolog predicates, and Prolog's theorem prover is used to find the answers. For example, the following Prolog goal is generated for the question "How is the external antenna connected?"

```
?- object(external_antenna,O2,[X2]),
   evt(connect,E1,[X1,X2]), object(anon_object,O1,[X1]).
```

If a sentence in the document asserts that the external antenna is connected to or by something, the Prolog query will succeed. This something is the anonymous object in the query. If there are no answers or too few answers, ExtrAns relaxes the proof criteria. First, hyponyms are added to the query terms.

Second, the system will attempt approximate matching, in which the sentence that has the highest overlap of predicates with the query is retrieved.

6.6 Conclusion

Technical domains present an interesting opportunity for the exploration of content-based approaches to question answering. We have illustrated this point using a system (ExtrAns) which uses a combination of robust NLP technology and dedicated terminology processing to create a domain-specific Knowledge Base, containing a semantic representation for the propositional content of the documents. We have discussed why techniques that are typically used in data-intensive open domain question answering systems would not work effectively in technical domains that have less data redundancy. One of the major differences between technical documents and open domain texts is the major role played by domain terminology in the former which compares with the role of named entities in open domain question answering.

Acknowledgments

The work described here was funded by the Swiss National Science Foundation (contracts 1214-45448.95 and 1213-53704.98) and by the Gebert Rüf Foundation (contract GRS-043/98). SR Technics provided us with the Aircraft Maintenance Manual of the Airbus A320 in machine readable format.

Notes

1. In open-domain QA an important problem is that of the temporal validity of the answers which might require all information to be time stamped, see chapter 11.

2. This is simply a reflection of the compounding process involved in creating more specific (longer) terms from more generic (shorter) terms.

James Dowdall is a Research Assistant at the Institute of Computational Linguistics of the University of Zurich. Additional information can be found at www.cl.unizh.ch/dowdall.

Michael Hess is a professor of computational linguistics at the University of Zurich. His interests include computational semantics and logic programming. Additional information can be found at www.cl.unizh.ch/hess

Diego Mollá-Aliod is a lecturer in the Department of Computing and associated with the Centre for Language Technology at Macquarie University in Sydney, Australia. His research interests include question answering and answer extraction. He can be reached at diego@ics.mq.edu.au

Fabio Rinaldi is a project manager at the Institute of Computational Linguistics, University of Zurich. Additional information can be found at www.cl.unizh.ch/rinaldi

Rolf Schwitter is a senior lecturer in the Department of Computing and associated with the Centre for Language Technology at Macquarie University in Sydney, Australia. His research interests include controlled natural languages, answer extraction, and knowledge representation. He can be reached at rolfs@ics.mq.edu.au

Section Three

Multiperspective, Temporal, and Multimedia QA

Just as the second section of this collection introduced new directions in terms of additional types of questions and answers, the chapters in this third section address questions dealing with opinions, time, and multiple media.

The first chapter by Claire Cardie, Janyce Wiebe, Theresa Wilson, and Diane Litman (the first from Cornell University, the others from the University of Pittsburgh) considers the annotation and summarization of opinions in support of multiperspective question answering. The authors describe an annotation scheme developed for the low-level representation of opinions, methods to find and organize opinions in text including the use of opinion-oriented scenario templates, and present results of interannotator agreement studies. Unlike factoid questions, opinionoid questions include examples such as: what is the general opinion from the African press toward the recent presidential election in Zimbabwe?; what was the world-wide reaction to the 2001 annual U.S. report on human rights?; and has there been any change in the official opinion from China toward the 2001 annual U.S. report on human rights since its release?

To answer such questions requires the annotation of the expression of opinion in a text along with its source (i.e., the agent expressing the opinion), its type (e.g., positive, negative, uncertain), and its strength (e.g., low, medium, high, extreme). Opinions can be articulations of private (e.g., unobservable mental or emotional) states expressed using subjective language. This can be done directly (e.g., "western countries were frustrated") or indirectly via subjective expressions (e.g., the anger expressed in lexical choice such as "daylight robbery"). Expressions can capture explicit private state (e.g. "think", "hope," "want") or a private state mixed with speech (e.g., "berate," "praise"). The authors describe a markup language and GATE annotator (http://www.cs.pitt.edu/~wiebe). To assess the quality of the annotation language, interannotator agreement was measured for a particular annotation (called "onlyfactive") that is used to indicate whether the source of the private state or speech event is indeed expressing an emotion, opinion, or other private state. Given 3 annotators and 13 documents with a total of 210 sentences, the pairwise Kappa was 0.81.

Work is in progress to use the defined annotations to create summary representations of opinions, e.g., sources expressing varying strength positive or negative attitudes toward objects (e.g., people, organizations, or things). These relations can be viewed graphically. Opinion summary generation requires a number of steps. These include noun phrase co-reference (for both the opinion source and object of opinion), opinion merging, cross document co-reference, and determining the object of an attitude-towards relation. The authors' approach merges sentences into a segment when there is a single source and clusters evidence and includes the sentence expressing the opinion it supports to support perspective segmentation. This enables the user to query directly regarding individual perspectives, collective perspectives, or user-specified views (e.g., of a source, object). Perspective profiles could be generated to support change detection in agents, groups, and countries, to automatically perform credibility assessment, and to generate gold standard "answer keys."

In addition to opinionoid questions, a relatively unexplored area is temporal and event question answering, addressed in the second chapter by James Pusteyovsky, Roser Saurí, José Castaño, Dragomir Radev, Rob Gaizauskas, Andrea Setzer, Beth Sunheim, and Graham Katz. The authors report TimeML, a rich temporal markup language for event and temporal expressions in natural language text. TimeML provides four primary capabilities including: (a) Time stamping of events (identifying an event and anchoring it in time); (b) Ordering events with respect to one another (lexical versus discourse properties of ordering); (c) Reasoning with contextually underspecified temporal expressions (temporal functions such as last week and two weeks before), supporting delayed interpretation; and (d) Reasoning about the persistence of events (i.e. how long an event or the outcome of an event lasts).

TimeML is sufficiently expressive for aspectual predication and modal subordination. There are four major data structures in TimeML: event, Timex3, signal, and link. Events are classified into a few broads classes including an occurrence (e.g., "die," "crash," "build," "merge," "sell"), a state (e.g., "on board," "kidnapped," "love"), reporting (e.g., "say," "report," "announce"), action (e.g., "attempt," "try," "promise," "offer"), i-state (e.g., "believe," "intend," "want"), aspectual (e.g., "begin," "finish," "stop," "continue"), perception (e.g., "see," "hear," "watch," "feel"), and modal (e.g., "might," "should," "would"). TimeX3 is markup for explicit temporal expressions, such as times, dates, durations, etc. A signal is used to annotate sections of text, typically function words that indicate how temporal objects are to be related to each other. This includes temporal relations such as temporal prepositions (e.g., "on," "during") and other temporal connectives (e.g., "when") and subordinators (e.g. "if"). Finally, one of the major innovations in TimeML, the link tag is used for marking relations among temporal elements. These are: (1) TLINK, a Temporal Link representing the temporal relationship holding between events or between an event and a time; (2) SLINK, a Subordination Link used for contexts introducing relations between two events, or an event and a signal; and (3) ALINK an Aspectual Link representing the relationship between an aspectual event and its argument event.

Using TimeML the authors created TimeBank, a 300 document gold standard as well as a 100 question corpus of time questions. The latter includes both explicit and implicit temporal questions. Where explicit temporal questions reference time directly (e.g., "when?", "what time?", "how often?", "in which century?", etc.), implicit temporal questions use temporal expressions to give non-temporal answers (e.g., "who was president of X in 1990?" or "did world steel output increase in the nineties?").

The authors classify temporal questions using a range of properties that include the type of the answer (e.g., duration, frequency, point, non-temporal, point), number of TEMPEX expressions in the question, if the question is indexical, the number of events mentioned in the question, permissible number of answers to the question, the types of events, how often does the answer change, the subordination type (none, modal, evidential, negative-evidential, factive), whether the question refers to a repetitive event, and what named entity type (if any) is the expected answer to the question (e.g., time, location, person, number).

TimeML is a good starting point for reference to events and times in QA systems because it systematically anchors event predicates to a broad range of temporally denotating expressions; it provides a language for ordering event expressions in text relative to one another, both intrasententially and in discourse; and it provides a semantics for underspecified temporal expressions, thereby allowing for a delayed interpretation.

In the third chapter by Boris Katz, Jimmy Lin, Chris Stauffer, and Eric Grimson (MIT CSAIL), yet another new direction is addressed—answering questions about moving objects in videos. Current video and image retrieval systems rely on low-level features such as color, texture, and shape, but such features severely limit the expressiveness of user queries. The basic thesis of the research is that, in certain domains, it is possible to directly extract the semantic content of videos and provide rich question answering capabilities. The authors have implemented a prototype, Spot, that can answer questions about moving objects in video surveillance footage taken around the Technology Square area in Cambridge, Massachusetts. For example, after a user types "show me all southbound cars." Spot displays a video that consists solely of cars heading south; all other traffic, both pedestrian and vehicular, is omitted. This video QA system is situated within a larger architecture designed to integrate knowledge from multiple domains under a common representation, and supports four major capabilities: event recognition, question answering, event description, and event filtering.

In Spot, a real-time motion tracking system that uses a bottom-up, data-driven framework called *perceptual data mining* (PDM) is combined with the START natural language system. PDM enables robust tracking of multiple moving objects in both indoor and outdoor settings. It is robust to environment effects including weather, wind fluttering objects, lighting, and occlusion. The motion tracker can infer patterns over time, for example, common paths of movement through a site based on the type of object and common patterns of usage as a function of time of day. This enables the discovery of anomalous behavior. To mediate between the linguistic and visual representations, the mapping from symbolic locations (names of place) to on-screen coordinates is accomplished manually: a human must identify the interesting landmarks in a particular scene and associate the screen location of those landmarks to their symbolic names.

The other key subsystem of Spot is START. On December 1993, START (detailed in chapter 16) became the first question answering system available for open question answering on the world wide web. In the last decade, the system has answered questions from hundreds of thousands of users all over the world. START assists the Spot system by translating natural language questions into symbolic queries regarding visual events. For example, the user query "Show me all cars leaving the garage." is translated into:

Query(MOVE(car?, [PATH Source(Garage57)]))

START's syntactic machinery automatically allows Spot to handle variations in language so that all of the following queries receive the same response:

Did any cars leave the garage?
Give me all cars that exited the garage.
Display cars leaving the garage.

While the system already exhibits an impressive integration of motion imagery and question answering, the authors have a number of plans for future extensions. First, they intend to support richer questions such as:

Show me the last delivery truck that stopped in front of the office.
How many people walked out of the building in the last 15 minutes?
Display all blue cars entering the garage from the south this morning.

Second, they intend to address more complex events such as sequences or causal chains, evidence in questions such as "in the last hour, did any car pull up to the curb and let out passengers?" or "have any trucks circled the building more than twice within the last day?" or "show me any instance of a man getting into a car and then getting out of the car within five minutes." The authors plan to explore knowledge representation and inference challenges as well as scaling to larger video archives.

In summary, this third section exhibits some of the rich new types of questions and source classes. Multiperspective, temporal, and multimedia question answering represent important new question-answering challenges.

Chapter 7

Low-Level Annotations and Summary Representations of Opinions for Multiperspective QA

Claire Cardie, Janyce Wiebe, Theresa Wilson, & Diane Litman

7.1 Introduction

Current research in question answering (QA) focuses primarily on the development of methods for finding short answers to factual questions such as, "where is the Susquehanna River?" and "when was Derek Jeter born?" While much progress has been made in recent years in fact-based question answering (e.g., Voorhees 2001), our work aims to extend question-answering methods to handle *multi-perspective question-answering tasks*. We are interested in developing techniques to support the answering of opinion-based questions of the following sort: "What is the general opinion from the African press towards the recent presidential election in Zimbabwe?" "What was the world-wide reaction to the 2001 annual U.S. report on human rights?" "Has there been any change in the official opinion from China toward the 2001 annual U.S. report on human rights since its release?"

It should be clear from these questions that the ability to find and organize opinions in on-line text is of critical importance in building successful multi-perspective question-answering (MPQA) systems. In response, this chapter proposes an approach to multi-perspective question answering that views the task as one of *opinion-oriented information extraction.*

Very generally, an *information extraction* (IE) system takes as input an unrestricted text and "summarizes" the text with respect to a topic or domain of interest: it finds useful information about the domain and encodes that information in a structured form that is suitable for populating databases, e.g., Lehnert and Sundheim (1991), Chinchor et al. (1993). In the domain of natural disasters, for example, an IE system extracts, for each disaster event, the type of disaster, the date and time it occurred, any objects damaged or destroyed, and so on. Event-based IE systems typically operate in two stages. First, the system identifies low-level *template relations* that encode domain-specific facts as expressed in the text (e.g., that the disaster, "a tornado," occurred on a particular day, "today," and so on). Next, the system merges the extracted template relations into a *scenario template* that summarizes the entire event.

In contrast, we hypothesize that an information extraction system for MPQA tasks should rely on a set of opinion-oriented template relations that identify each expression of opinion in a text along with its source (i.e., the agent expressing the opinion), its type (e.g., positive, negative, uncertain), and its strength (e.g., strong, weak). Once identified, these low-level relations can then be combined to create an opinion-based scenario template—a summary representation of the opinions expressed in a document, a group of documents, or an arbitrary text span. This summary representation, in turn, acts as the primary knowledge source that supports a variety of MPQA tasks.

In the sections that follow, we describe the template relation annotation scheme developed for the low-level representation of opinions and present the results of interannotator agreement studies. We then motivate the need for summary representations of opinion and propose a method for their automatic construction using techniques from information extraction with a discourse-based approach to "perspective segmentation." We conclude with a discussion of the potential uses of summary representations of opinions for a variety of MPQA tasks.

7.2 Low-level Opinion Annotations

In this section, we present a detailed scheme for annotating expressions of opinions, beliefs, emotions, speculations, and other private states in newspaper articles. *Private state* is a general term covering mental and emotional states that cannot be directly observed or verified (Quirk et al. 1985). Private states are expressed using *subjective* language (Banfield 1982, Wiebe 1994).

The annotation scheme presented here was developed as part of a U.S. government-sponsored project (ARDA AQUAINT NRRC) to investigate multiple perspectives in question answering (Wiebe et al. 2003). We implemented the scheme in a general architecture for text engineering (GATE) (Cunningham et al. 2002). General instructions for annotating opinions and specific instructions for downloading and using GATE to perform the annotations are available at http://www.cs.pitt.edu/~wiebe.

7.2.1 Expressing Private States in Text

Private States, Speech Events, and Expressive Subjective Elements. There are two main ways that private states are expressed in language. Private states may be explicitly mentioned, or they may be expressed indirectly through the way things are described or the particular wording a speaker or writer uses. An example of an explicitly mentioned private state is "frustrated" in sentence 1.

1. Western countries were left frustrated and impotent after Robert Mugabe formally declared that he had overwhelmingly won Zimbabwe's presidential election.

The second way that private states are expressed is indirectly using *expressive subjective elements* (Banfield 1982). For example, the private states in sentences 2 and 3 are expressed entirely by the wording and the style of language that is used.

2. The time has come, gentlemen, for Sharon, the assassin, to realize that injustice cannot last long.

3. "We foresaw electoral fraud but not daylight robbery," Tsvangirai said.

In sentence 2, the phrases "The time has come," "gentlemen," "the assassin," and "injustice cannot last long" express the negative attitude of the writer. Similarly, in sentence 3, "fraud" and "daylight robbery" reflect the anger of the speaker, Tsvangirai. These phrases are examples of expressive subjective elements.

When looking for opinions and other private states in text, an annotator must consider speech events as well as explicitly mentioned private states. In this work, we use *speech event* to refer to any event of speaking or writing. However, the mere presence of a speech event does not indicate a private state. Both sentences 3 above and 4 below contain speech events indicated by "said." Sentence 3 is opinionated, while in sentence 4 the information is presented as factual. For speech terms such as "said," "added," "told," "announce," and "report," an annotator determines if a private state is present mainly by looking inside the scope of the speech term for expressive subjective elements.

4. Medical Department head Dr. Hamid Saeed said the patient's blood had been sent to the Institute for Virology in Johannesburg for analysis.

Nested Sources The *source* of a speech event is the speaker or writer. The *source* of a private state is the experiencer of the private state, i.e., the person whose opinion or emotion is being expressed. The writer of an article is a source, because he or she wrote the sentences composing the article, but the writer may also write about other people's private states and speech events, resulting in multiple sources in a single sentence. For example, each of the following sentences has two sources: the writer of the sentences, and Sue, who is the source of a speech event in sentence 5 and of private state in sentence 6.

5. Sue said, "The election was fair."

6. Sue thinks that the election was fair.

Note, however, that we don't really know what Sue says or thinks. All we know is what the writer tells us. Sentence 6, for example, does not directly present Sue's speech event but rather Sue's speech event according to the writer. Thus, we have a natural nesting of sources in a sentence. In sentences 5 and

Explicit private states/speech events	Expressive subjective elements
nested-source	nested-source
onlyfactive: *yes, no*	strength: *low, medium, high, extreme*
overall-strength: *low, medium, high, extreme*	attitude-type*: *positive, negative, other*
on-strength: *neutral, low, medium, high, extreme*	
attitude-type*: *positive, negative, both*	
attitude-toward*	
is-implicit	
Minor	

Table 7.1. Attributes for the Two Main Annotation Types

For attributes that take on one of a fixed set of values, the set of possible values are given. The symbol "*" means exploratory attribute.

6, the nested source of "said," and "thinks," is <writer, Sue>. Expressive subjective elements may also have nested sources. In sentence 3, "fraud" and "daylight robbery" are expressive subjective elements, both with nested source <writer, Tsvangirai>.

7.2.2 Annotating Private States in Text

For this work, annotators are asked to mark the word spans in each sentence that indicate speech events or private states. Specifically, there are two main types of annotations: (1) an annotation type for explicit private states and speech events, and (2) an annotation type for expressive subjective elements. An annotator marks a span of a given type, and then sets a number of attributes to characterize the annotation. The attributes for each annotation type, listed in table 7.1, are described in Wilson and Wiebe (2003). The remainder of this section focuses on one particular attribute that is marked on private state and speech event annotations, the *onlyfactive* attribute.

The *onlyfactive* attribute is the core of the annotation scheme. This attribute is used to indicate whether the source of the private state or speech event is indeed expressing an emotion, opinion, or other private state. Any expression that is an explicit private state (e.g., "think", "hope," "want") or a private state mixed with speech (e.g. "berate," "praise") is *onlyfactive* = no; however, *neutral* speech events (e.g., "said," "added") may be either *onlyfactive* = yes or *onlyfactive* = no, depending on their contents. For example, the annotation for "said" in sentence 3 would be marked *onlyfactive* = no, but the annotation for "said" in sentence 4 would be marked *onlyfactive* = yes. Note that, even if *onlyfactive* = no, the sentence may express something the nested source believes is factual. Consider the sentence "John criticized Mary for smoking." John expresses a private state (his negative evaluation of Mary's smoking). However, this does not mean that John does not believe that Mary smokes.

We performed an annotation study to measure agreement for the *onlyfactive* attribute. The data in the study consists of English-language versions of foreign news documents from a variety of publications and countries. Three annotators

	All Expressions		All Sentences	
	Kappa	agree	Kappa	agree
A&M	0.84	0.91	0.75	0.89
A&S	0.84	0.92	0.84	0.94
M&S	0.74	0.87	0.72	0.88

Table7.2 Pairwise Kappa Scores and Overall Percent Agreement for onlyfactive Judgments and Derived Sentence-Level Judgments

(A, M, and S) independently annotated 13 documents with a total of 210 sentences. The articles are from a variety of topics and were selected so that 1/3 of the sentences are from news articles reporting on objective topics (objective articles), 1/3 of the sentences are from news articles reporting on opinionated topics ("hot topic" articles), and 1/3 of the sentences are from editorials.

We measure agreement for the *onlyfactive* attribute by looking at the set of private state/speech event span annotations on which the annotators agree (82%). The Kappa agreement scores for all annotator pairs are given in table 7.2. For the onlyfactive judgments, i.e., whether or not an opinion or other private state is being expressed, the annotators have an average pairwise Kappa of 0.81. Under Krippendorf's (1980) scale, this allows for definite conclusions.

For many applications, it is useful to be able to determine which sentences, not just which expressions, are subjective. We define sentence-level classifications in terms of our lower-level annotations as follows. If an annotator marked one or more *onlyfactive* = no expressions in the sentence, we consider the annotator to have judged the sentence to be subjective. Otherwise, we consider the annotator to have judged the sentence to be objective. The pairwise agreement results for these derived sentence-level annotations are given on the right-hand side of table 7.2. The average pairwise Kappa for sentence-level agreement is 0.77. Note that the agreement is lower than that for onlyfactive judgments because explicit private-state and speech event expressions upon which the annotators did not agree are now included.

7.3 Summary Representation of Opinions

We expect the opinion-based annotation scheme described above to support a wide variety of end-to-end applications in the area of multi-perspective question answering. In addition, we anticipate the need to create *summary representations of opinions* that would provide concise, and ultimately user-tailored summaries of the opinions expressed in an article, in a set of articles, or in any arbitrary segment of text.

We propose to view these summary representations as IE scenario templates. Rather than traditional event-oriented IE scenario templates, ours will instead summarize opinion-oriented scenarios to accommodate the MPQA task. We postulate that methods from IE (see Cardie 1997) will be largely adequate for the automatic creation of opinion-based summary representations. Machine learning methods can be applied to acquire lexico-syntactic patterns for the automatic extraction of low-level opinion relations. The low-level expressions of opinion can then be combined to create the opinion-based scenario template summary representation.

In the subsections below, we first provide a concrete example of an MPQA summary representation for a portion of one opinion-oriented article. We then describe a number of issues in the automatic creation of summary representations. This is work in progress; we do not present empirical results.

7.3.1 An Example

An MPQA scenario template is meant to encode a summary of the opinions expressed throughout one or more texts or text spans. They are summaries in that they merge and make inferences from the low-level opinion annotations that have been identified in the text. As an example, consider the text in figure 7-1, which is the first ten sentences of one document (#20.20.10-3414) from the Human Rights portion of our MPQA annotated corpus. Given the first sentence of the document,

> "The Annual Human Rights Report of the U.S. State Department has been strongly criticized and condemned by many countries,"

our MPQA system should produce the following low-level opinion annotations:

PRIVATE STATE/ SPEECH EVENT: nested-source= <writer>, *onlyfactive*=yes

EXPRESSIVE-SUBJ: nested-source =<writer>, *strength*=medium.

In particular, from the writer's perspective, the sentence can be classified as *onlyfactive* = yes. In addition, the lexical cue "strongly" indicates some (medium) amount of EXPRESSIVE SUBJectivity.

A similar analysis of the remainder of the text fragment would produce the low-level annotations of figure 7-1. It should be clear that the representation of opinions at this level is difficult for humans to absorb. One possible MPQA summary representation for the sample text is shown in figure 7-2. The summary indicates that there are three primary opinion-expressing sources in the text—<writer>; <writer, many countries> and <writer, Chinese information office>. Furthermore, these sources expressed the following opinions: the writer expressed a negative attitude (of medium strength) toward the human rights report; the writer expressed a mildly negative attitude toward the United States; according to the writer, many countries expressed a strongly negative attitude toward the human rights report; according to the writer, the Chinese information office expressed a negative attitude (of medium strength) toward

The Annual Human Rights Report of the US State Department has been strongly criticized and condemned by many countries. Though the report has been made public for 10 days, its contents, which are inaccurate and lacking good will, continue to be commented on by the world media.

Many countries in Asia, Europe, Africa, and Latin America have rejected the content of the US Human Rights Report, calling it a brazen distortion of the situation, a wrongful and illegitimate move, and an interference in the internal affairs of other countries.

Recently, the Information Office of the Chinese People's Congress released a report on human rights in the United States in 2001, criticizing violations of human rights there. The report quoting data from the Christian Science Monitor, points out that the murder rate in the United States is 5.5 per 100,000 people. In the United States, torture and pressure to confess crime is common. Many people have been sentenced to death for crime they did not commit as a result of an unjust legal system. More than 12 million children are living below the poverty line. According to the report, one American woman is beaten every 15 seconds. Evidence show that human rights violations in the United States have been ignored for many years.

<writer>: onlyfactive <writer>: expr-subj (medium)

<writer>: neg-attitude (medium) → <report> <writer>: neg-attitude (medium)
<writer>: neg-attitude (medium)

<writer>: onlyfactive <writer, many-countries>: neg-attitude (medium)
→ <report> <writer, many-countries>: extreme
<writer, many-countries>: neg-attitude (high, high, medium)

<writer>: onlyfactive
<writer, info-office>: neg-attitude (medium) → <US>
<writer>: onlyfactive <writer, chinarep>: onlyfactive
<writer>: ?neg-attitude (medium) → <US> <writer>: expr-subj (low) <writer>: neg-attitude (low)
→ <US> <writer>: expr-subj (low) <writer>: neg-attitude (medium)
<writer>: onlyfactive
<writer>: onlyfactive
<writer>: neg-attitude (low) → <US> <writer>: expr-subj (low)

Figure 7.1 MPQA Sample Text

(First ten sentences from document #20.20.10-3414 from the Human Rights portion of the MPWA collection along with its associated low-level opinion annotations. Annotations are shown in roughly the same position as the original text spans from which they were derived.)

the U.S. Although expressed in graphical form in figure 7.2, the summary representation is equivalent to the relational scenario template representation used in traditional IE systems.

Acquiring portions of the summary representation requires making inferences across related groups of the low-level annotations. One example is the association of a *strength* with scenario template *attitude* relations that cover

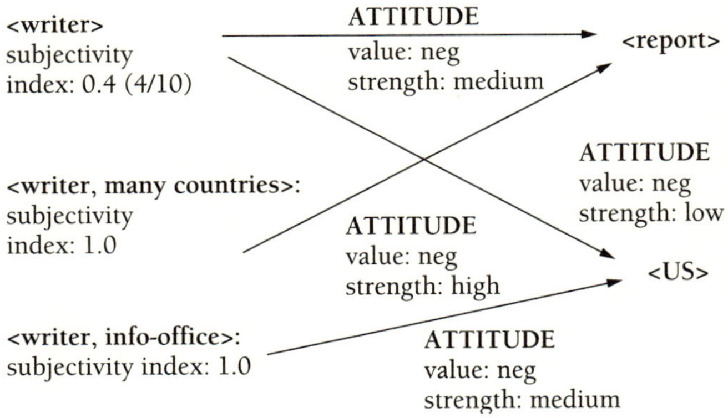

Figure 7.2 MPQA Summary Representation for the Text Sample from Document #20.20.10-3414

multiple low-level attitude-type annotations. In addition, the *subjectivity index* associated with each nested source illustrates the kind of summary statistic that might be inferred from a collection of low-level opinion annotations. Here, the subjectivity index indicates that four out of ten sentences of the writer include subjective language, and that all propositions attributed to many countries and the Chinese information office include subjective content. Summary representations can be encoded as in-line annotations (e.g., XML or SGML), allowing for direct querying by the end-user.

Finally, there are many user-specified options for generation of summary representations. The user might want summaries that focus only on particular agents, particular classes of agents, particular attitude types or attitude strengths. The user might also want to specify a particular level of nested source, e.g., creating the summary from the point of view of only the most nested sources.

7.3.2 Automatic Creation of Summary Representations of Opinion

In the paragraphs below, we discuss some of the issues involved in the automatic creation of MPQA summary representations.

Perfect low-level annotations. Even given a complete and accurate set of low-level opinion annotations, building a summary representation will still be non-trivial. In particular, the MPQA system would need an accurate noun phrase coreference subsystem to identify the various terms and phrases used to refer to each opinion source and each object toward which some opinion was expressed. In particular, the object of an *attitude-toward* relation is often very difficult for even human readers to determine and is often not explicitly expressed in the text. Another issue in creating summary representations from perfect low-level annotations is how to handle the presence of conflicting opinions from the same source.

Imperfect low-level annotations. The situation becomes much harder, of course, when the MPQA summary representation is to be built on top of automatically generated low-level opinion annotations, which are likely to be incomplete and inaccurate. The situation will be akin to the information extraction task of "merging" automatically extracted and errorful template relations into a scenario template. The noun phrase coreference system will continue to be important in this situation — it will need to provide accurate links between coreferent sources as well as coreferent objects. On the other hand, since our goal is to derive a summary representation, we may be able to use redundancy in the expression of opinions to discard incorrect low-level annotations. For example, if the low-level opinion annotations associated with one source indicate that eight out of ten expressions from the source are negative evaluations of object X, then the system might be able to discard the remaining two positive evaluation of X as errors.

Cross-document coreference. Effective MPQA will require collation of information across documents, since the summary representation may span multiple documents. For example, if a user wants to know the range of perspectives on topic X, then the system will need to perform cross-document coreference w.r.t. topic X as well as w.r.t. the various agents that express views on the topic.

Segmentation and perspective coherence. Accurate grouping of the low-level annotations—e.g., according to source, topic, negative or positive attitude — will be critical in deriving usable summary representations of opinion. For this task, we believe that it will be important to develop text segmentation methods based on a new notion of perspective coherence. In the natural language processing literature, the term *segmentation* refers to breaking up a document into smaller chunks—or segments—that are locally coherent. Depending on factors such as corpus type and application need, different notions of coherence have been proposed as the basis of segmentation. In the area of information retrieval, for example, text segmentation has usually been based on semantic coherence. Segmentation is performed by placing segment boundaries at points of semantic discontinuity (Hearst 1997). In the area of discourse analysis, segmentation has instead been based on notions of informational (Hobbs 1979), and/or intentional coherence (Grosz and Sidner 1986, Passonneau and Litman 1993).

To incorporate text segmentation for the derivation of MPQA summary representations, we propose extending our opinion annotation scheme to denote "perspective segments" that will identify sentence spans expressing coherent perspectives. As with other notions of segmentation, perspective segmentation will likely involve merging and performing shallow inferences across sentences.

Consider an example segment produced during an informal manual clustering study we performed as part of the summer workshop. Workshop participants were asked to label opinions, where each opinion could be described by

3-6 Mugabe described the opposition as "donkey being controlled by the British," the former colonial power. (*nested-source=*<**writer**, **Mugabe**>, *onlyfactive=no*)

SEGMENT BEGIN (1 CODER)
3-7 The fledgling MDC won 57 of 120 elected seats in June 2000 parliamentary elections as Mugabe's popularity plunged amid economic devastation and chaos. (*nested-source=*<**writer**>, *onlyfactive=no*)

SEGMENT BEGIN (4 CODERS)
3-8 The U.S. State Department released a human rights report on Zimbabwe Monday that accused the government of extra-judicial killings, undermining the independence of the judiciary and waging a "systematic campaign of violence targeting supporters and potential supporters of the opposition." (*nested-source=*<**writer**, **U.S report**>, *onlyfactive=no*)

3-9 Security forces tortured opponents, ruling party militants abducted people, and police arrested opposition supporters who were themselves the victims of crimes. **3-10** Freedom of the press and freedom of assembly were also severely restricted, the report said." (*nested-source=*<**writer**, **U.S report**>, *onlyfactive=no*)

SEGMENT END (5 CODERS)
3-11 In his speech on Monday, Mugabe thanked African leaders for refusing to buckle to pressure to suspend Zimbabwe from the Commonwealth of Britain and its former territories at a summit of the 54-nation grouping in Australia. (*nested-source=*<**writer**, **Mugabe**>, *onlyfactive=no*) (*nested-source=*<**writer**, **Mugabe**, **African leaders**>, *onlyfactive=no*)

Figure 7.3 An Example Document Excerpt with Human Segmentations and Annotations

a single sentence, or by a segment consisting of a sentence span. The excerpt in figure 7.3 illustrates a sample segmentation from our coding exercise. In particular, four out of seven coders placed sentences 3-8 through 3-10 in the same segment; a fifth coder placed the beginning of this segment one sentence earlier.

The segment consisting of sentences 3-8 through 3-10 seems to illustrate one way in which perspective coherence can be defined in terms of the sentence-level annotations: merge sentences into a segment when from a single source. Linguistic phenomena such as the use of "his" in 3-11 to refer to Mugabe (who was most recently mentioned outside the segment) lends support to this analysis.

Sentence 3-7 provides an interesting borderline case, as one coder also included this sentence in the segment. Sentences 3-8 through 3-10 can be seen as providing evidence for the expressive-subjective element "chaos." A more sophisticated notion of perspective coherence might be to cluster evidence together then include it with the sentence(s) expressing the opinion that the evidence supports (sentence 3-7).

In terms of aiding the creation of higher-level summary representations of opinions, an MPQA system might use segmentation information to ignore the presence of factive sentences that are providing evidence for an opinion when trying to merge a sequence of opinionated sentences into a larger segment.

7.4 Uses for Summary Representation of Opinion on MPQA

In addition to providing a short, optionally tailored summary of the opinions expressed in texts, we anticipate other uses for MPQA summary representations.

Direct querying. When the summary representation is stored as a set of document annotations, it can be directly queried by the end-user using XML "grep" utilities.

Collective perspectives. The summary representations can be used to describe the collective perspective w.r.t., some issue or object presented in an individual article, or across a set of articles.

User-specified views. The summary representations can be tailored to match (some types of) user-specified constraints, e.g., to summarize documents from the perspective of a particular writer, individual, government, ideology, or news service, or to summarize documents w.r.t. a particular issue or object.

Perspective profiles. The MPQA summary representation would be the basis for creating a perspective "profile" for specific sources/agents, groups, news sources, etc. The profiles, in turn, would serve as the basis for detecting changes in the opinion of agents, groups, countries, etc., over time.

Credibility assessment. Credible news reports might be distinguished from less credible reports that are laden with extremely subjective language.

Debugging. Because the summary representation is more readable than the low-level annotations, summary representations can be used to aid debugging of the low-level opinion annotations on which they were based.

Gold Standard "answer keys." Once the gold standard for the low-level opinion annotations has been created for a collection, however, it might be possible to largely automate the creation of gold standards for various MPQA summary representations.

7.5 Conclusions

This chapter proposed an information-extraction approach to finding and organizing opinions in naturally occurring text as a means for supporting multi-perspective question answering. We first presented a low-level annotation scheme for representing opinion-based "template relations," i.e., localized and individual expressions of opinions, and described the results of inter-annotator agreement studies. We next proposed one possible summary representation for concisely encoding the collection of opinions expressed in a document, a set of documents, or an arbitrary text segment. These are akin to the scenario templates produced by event-based information extraction systems. We hypothesize that information extraction techniques can be used to identify the low-level opinion annotations automatically, and that existing methods from information extraction for merging template relations can be extended via perspective segmentation for use in multi-perspective question answering. We concluded with a brief discussion of how opinion-based summary representations might be used to support a variety of multi-perspective question answering tasks.

Acknowledgements

This work was performed in support of the Northeast Regional Research Center (NRRC) which is sponsored by the Advanced Research and Development Activity (ARDA), a U.S. Government entity that sponsors and promotes research of import to the Intelligence Community, which includes but is not limited to the CIA, DIA, NSA, NIMA, and NRO.

Claire Cardie is an associate professor of computer science at Cornell University. For additional information on her research interests and for contact information, please see www.cs.cornell.edu/home/cardie/.

Janyce M. Wiebe is an associate professor in the Department of Computer Science and codirector of the Intelligent Systems Program at the University of Pittsburgh.

Theresa Wilson is a Ph.D. student in the Intelligent Systems program at the University of Pittsburgh.

Diane J. Litman is an associate professor of computer science at the University of Pittsburgh.

Chapter 8

Representing Temporal and Event Knowledge for QA Systems

James Pustejovsky, Roser Saurí, José Castaño, Dragomir R. Radev, Rob Gaizauskas, Andrea Setzer, Beth Sunheim, & Graham Katz

8.1 Introduction

The current question answering technology supports a wide range of query possibilities from text. Any recognizable named entity in a text can be targeted and queried over. At best, however, this set of named entity types rarely includes a set of time stamps or events associated with an article. For this reason, progress in the recognition of events and temporal expressions in text is a critical area of research.

The automatic recognition of temporal and event expressions in natural language text has recently become an active area of research in computational linguistics and semantics. In this chapter, we report on TimeML, a specification language for events and temporal expressions, which was developed in the context of a six-month workshop, TERQAS (www.time2002.org), funded under the auspices of the AQUAINT program. The ARDA-funded program AQUAINT is a multi-project effort to improve the performance of question answering systems over free text, such as that encountered on the Web. In this chapter, we report on an AQUAINT project to create a specification language for event and temporal expressions in text.

Events in articles are naturally anchored in time within the narrative of a text. For this reason, temporally grounded events are the very foundation from which we reason about how the world changes; that is, event recognition drives basic inferences from text. For example, questions such as the following are not currently supported by question answering systems.

a. Is Gates currently CEO of Microsoft?

b. When did Iraq finally pull out of Kuwait during the war in the 1990s?

c. Did the Enron merger with Dynegy take place?

What characterizes these questions as beyond the scope of current systems is the following: they refer, respectively, to the temporal aspects of the properties of the entities being questioned, the relative ordering of events in the world, and events that are mentioned in news articles but which have never occurred.

There has recently been a renewed interest in temporal and event-based reasoning in language and text, particularly as applied to information extraction and reasoning tasks (cf. Mani and Wilson 2000, ACL Workshop on Spatial and Temporal Reasoning 2001, Annotation Standards for Temporal Information in Natural Language, LREC 2002). Several chapters from the workshop point to promising directions for time representation and identification (cf. Filatova and Hovy, 2001, Schilder and Habel, 2001, Setzer, 2001). Many issues relating to temporal and event identification remain unresolved, however, and it is these issues that TimeML was designed to address. Specifically, four basic problems in event-temporal identification are addressed: (a) time stamping of events (identifying an event and anchoring it in time); (b) ordering events with respect to one another (lexical versus discourse properties of ordering); (c) reasoning with contextually underspecified temporal expressions (temporal functions such as last week and two weeks before); (d) reasoning about the persistence of events (how long does an event or the outcome of an event last).

The specification language, TimeML, is designed to address these issues, in addition to handling basic tense and aspect features.

8.2 Temporal Ontologies and TimeML

Following Hobbs (2002), the development of a time ontology can be seen as the combined specification of six distinct areas:

1. Topological temporal relations
2. Basic temporal entities (e.g. instants, intervals, events)
   a. Properties of temporal entities
   b. Relations between temporal entities
   c. Measuring durations
3. Clock and calendar
   a. Time zones
   b. Clock and calendar units
   c. Deictic time
4. Specification of temporal concepts such as *now, tomorrow, last Monday*
   Sequence of temporal entities
5. Specification of temporal sequence concepts such as:
   quarterly, every other Monday
6. Vague temporal concepts

Unlike most previous attempts at event and temporal specification, TimeML separates the representation of event and temporal expressions from the anchoring or ordering dependencies that may exist in a given text. There are four major data structures that are specified in TimeML (Ingria and Pustejovsky 2002, Pustejovsky et al. 2002): EVENT, TIMEX3, SIGNAL, and LINK. These are described in some detail below. The features distinguishing TimeML from most previous attempts at event and time annotation are summarized below:

1. Extends the TIMEX2 annotation attributes
2. Introduces temporal functions to allow intensionally specified expressions: three years ago, last month;
3. Identifies signals determining interpretation of temporal expressions
   a Temporal prepositions: *for, during, on, at*
   b. Temporal connectives: *before, after, while*
4. Identifies all classes of event expressions
   a. Tensed verbs: *has left, was captured, will resign*
   b. Stative adjectives and other modifiers: *sunken, stalled, on board*
   c. Event nominals: *merger, military operation, Gulf War*
5. Creates dependencies between events and times:
   a. Anchoring: *John left on Monday*
   b. Orderings: *the party happened after midnight*
   c. Embedding: *John said Mary left*

In the design of TimeML, we began with the core of the TIDES TIMEX2 annotation effort (Ferro et al. 2001)[1] and the temporal annotation language presented in Andrea Setzer's thesis (Setzer 2001). Consideration of the details of this representation, however, in conjunction with problems raised in trying to apply it to actual texts, resulted in several changes and extensions to Setzer's original framework. The most significant extension is the logical separation of event descriptions and the relations they enter into, defined relative to temporal expressions or other events. This resulted in a natural reification of these relations as LINK tags.

TimeML considers "events" (and the corresponding tag <EVENT>) a cover term for situations that happen or occur. Events can be punctual or last for a period of time. We also consider as events those predicates describing states or circumstances in which something obtains or holds true. Not all stative predicates are marked up, however, as only those states which participate in an opposition structure in a given text are marked up. Events are generally expressed by means of tensed or untensed verbs, nominalizations, adjectives, predicative clauses, or prepositional phrases. The specification of EVENT is shown in the following.

```
attributes ::= eid class tense aspect
eid ::= EventID
EventID ::= e<integer>
class ::=
'OCCURRENCE'|'PERCEPTION'|'REPORTING'|'ASPECTUAL'
           'STATE'|'I_STATE'|'I_ACTION'|'MODAL'
tense ::= 'PAST' | 'PRESENT' | 'FUTURE' | 'NONE'
```

```
aspect ::= 'PROGRESSIVE' | 'PERFECTIVE' |
           'PERFECTIVE_PROGRESSIVE' | 'NONE'
```

Examples of each of these event types are:

1. Occurrence: *die, crash, build, merge, sell*
2. State: *on board, kidnapped, love*
3. Reporting: *say, report, announce*
4. I-Action: *attempt, try, promise, offer*
5. I-State: *believe, intend, want*
6. Aspectual: *begin, finish, stop, continue*
7. Perception: *see, hear, watch, feel*
8. Modal: *might, should, would*

The TIMEX3 tag is used to mark up explicit temporal expressions, such as times, dates, durations, etc. It is modeled on both Setzer's (2001) TIMEX tag, and the TIDES (Ferro et al. 2002) TIMEX2 tag. There are three major types of TIMEX3 expressions: (1) fully specified temporal expressions, *June 11, 1989, Summer, 2002;* (2) underspecified temporal expressions, *Monday, Next month, last year, two days ago;* (3) durations, *Three months, Two years.*

```
attributes ::= tid type [functionInDocument] [temporalFunction]
               (value|valueFromFunction) [mod]
               [anchorTimeID | anchorEventID]
tid ::= TimeID
TimeID ::= t<integer>
type ::= 'DATE'|'TIME'|'DURATION'
functionInDocument ::= 'CREATION_TIME'|'EXPIRATION_TIME' |
                    'MODIFICATION_TIME'|'PUBLICATION_TIME'|
                            'RELEASE_TIME'|'RECEPTION_TIME'|'NONE'
temporalFunction ::= 'true' | 'false'
{temporalFunction ::= boolean}
value ::= CDATA
{value ::= duration | dateTime | time | date | gYearMonth |
          gYear | gMonthDay | gDay | gMonth}
valueFromFunction ::= IDREF
{valueFromFunction ::= TemporalFunctionID
TemporalFunctionID ::= tf<integer>}
mod ::= 'BEFORE'|'AFTER'|'ON_OR_BEFORE'|'ON_OR_AFTER'|
        'LESS_THAN'|'MORE_THAN'|'EQUAL_OR_LESS'|
        'EQUAL_OR_MORE'|'START'|'MID'|'END'|'APPROX'
anchorTimeID ::= TimeID
anchorEventID ::= EventID
```

The optional attribute, functionInDocument, indicates the function of the TIMEX3 in providing a temporal anchor for other temporal expressions in the document. If this attribute is not explicitly supplied, the default value is "NONE." The nonempty values take their names from the temporal metadata tags in the Prism draft standard (available at www.prismstandard.org/).

The treatment of temporal functions in TimeML allows any timevalue dependent algorithms to delay the computation of the actual (ISO) value of the expression. The following informal paraphrase of some examples illustrates this point, where DCT is the document creation time of the article.

1. *Last week* = (predecessor (week DCT)): That is, we start with a temporal anchor, in this case, the DCT, coerce it to a week, then find the week preceding it.

2. *Last Thursday* = (thursday (predecessor (week DCT)): Similar to the preceding expression, except that we pick out the day named 'thursday' in the predecessor week.
3. *The week before last* = (predecessor (predecessor (week DCT))): Also similar to the first expression, except that we go back two weeks.
4. *Next week* = (successor (week DCT)): The dual of the first expression: we start with the same coercion, but go forward instead of back.

SIGNAL is used to annotate sections of text, typically function words, that indicate how temporal objects are to be related to each other. The material marked by SIGNAL constitutes several types of linguistic elements: indicators of temporal relations such as temporal prepositions (e.g., on, during) and other temporal connectives (e.g., when) and subordinators (e.g., if). The basic functionality of the SIGNAL tag was introduced by Setzer (2001). In TimeML it has been expanded to also mark polarity indicators such as not, no, none, etc., as well as indicators of temporal quantification such as twice, three times, and so forth. The specification for SIGNAL follows:

```
attributes ::= sid
sid ::= ID
{sid ::= SignalID}
SignalID ::= s<integer>
```

To illustrate the application of these three tags, consider the following example annotation:[2]

John left 2 days before the attack.

```
John
<EVENT eid="e1" class="OCCURRENCE" tense="PAST"
aspect="PERFECTIVE">
left
</EVENT>
<MAKEINSTANCE eiid="ei1" eventID="e1"/>
<TIMEX3 tid="t1" type="DURATION" value="P2D"
temporalFunction="false">
2 days
</TIMEX3>
<SIGNAL sid="s1">
before
</SIGNAL>
the
<EVENT eid="e2" class="OCCURRENCE" tense="NONE" aspect="NONE">
attack
</EVENT>
<MAKEINSTANCE eiid="ei2" eventID="e2"/>
```

8.3 LINKS

One of the major innovations introduced in TimeML is the LINK tag. As mentioned above, the set of LINK tags encode the various relations that exist between the temporal elements of a document, as well as establishing ordering between events directly. There are three types of link tags: (1) TLINK: a temporal link representing the temporal relationship holding between events or between an event and a time; (2) SLINK: a subordination link used for contexts introducing relations between two events, or an event and a signal; and (3) ALINK: an aspectual link representing the relationship between an aspectual event and its argument event.

8.3.1 TLINK

TLINK represents the temporal relationship holding between events or between an event and a time, and establishes a link between the involved entities, making explicit if they are:[3]

1. Simultaneous
2. Identical: (referring to the same event)
   John drove to Boston. During his drive he ate a donut.[4]
3. One before the other:
   John left before Mary arrived.
4. One after the other: (cf. 3)
5. One immediately before the other:
   All passengers died when the plane crashed into the mountain.[5]
6. One immediately after the other: (cf. 5)
7. One including the other:
   John arrived in Boston last Thursday.
8. One being included in the other: (cf. 7)
9. One holding during the duration of the other
10. One being the beginning of the other:
    John has lived in Boston since 1998.
11. One being begun by the other: (cf. 10)
12. One being the ending of the other:
    John stayed in Boston till 1999.
13. One being ended by the other: (cf. 12)

The specification for TLINK follows.

```
attributes ::= (eventInstanceID | timeID) [signalID]
                  (relatedtoEvent |relatedtoTime) relType
                  [magnitude]
eventInstanceID ::= ei<integer>
timeID ::= t<integer>
signalID ::= s<integer>
relatedToEvent ::= ei<integer>
relatedToTime ::= t<integer>
relType ::= 'BEFORE'|'AFTER'|'INCLUDES'|'IS_INCLUDED' |
             'HOLDS'|'SIMULTANEOU.S.'|'IAFTER' |'IBEFORE' |
             'IDENTITY'|'BEGINS' |'ENDS' | 'BEGUN_BY' |
             'ENDED_BY'
magnitude ::= t<integer>
```

To illustrate the function of this link, let us return to the sentence above, now adding the annotation of the TLINK, which orders the two events mentioned in the sentence, with a magnitude denoted by value of the temporal expression.

John left 2 days before the attack.

```
<TLINK eventInstanceID="ei1" signalID="s1" relatedToEvent="ei2" rel-
Type="BEFORE" magnitude="t1"/>
```

This link composes two assertions: (1) that John's leaving, e1, is ordered before the attack, e2; and (2) that the interval separating these events has a magnitude equal to the value of the temporal expression, t1.

Quantification within a temporal phrase, however, is a more difficult temporal value to express in terms of a simple and consistent annotation scheme. Consider, for example, the following sentence.

John taught 20 minutes every Monday.

The expression, every Monday, is a temporal function in two respects: first, it is a generalized quantifier and cannot be bound to a conventional MAKEINSTANCE variable; secondly, it contains incomplete information regarding the domain over which the expression is to be interpreted. We introduce the attribute CARDINALITY in the MAKEINSTANCE tag to allow for this interpretation. The resulting TimeML for this example follows.

```
John
<EVENT eid="e1" class="OCCURRENCE" tense="PAST" aspect="NONE">
taught
</EVENT>
<MAKEINSTANCE eiid="ei1" eventID="e1" signalID="s1"
cardinality="EVERY"/>
<TIMEX3 tid="t1" type="DURATION" value="PT20M">
20 minutes
</TIMEX3>
<SIGNAL sid="s1">
every
</SIGNAL>
<TIMEX3 tid="t2" type="DATE" value="XXXX-WXX-1">
Monday
</TIMEX3>
<TLINK eventInstanceID="ei1" relatedToTime="t1"
relType="HOLDS"/>
<TLINK eventInstanceID="ei1" relatedToTime="t2"
relType="IS_INCLUDED"/>
```

8.3.2 SLINK

SLINK or subordination link is used for contexts introducing relations between two events, or an event and a signal, of the following sort:

1. *Modal:* Relation introduced mostly by modal verbs (should, could, would, etc.) and events that introduce a reference to a possible world; these are mainly I STATEs:
   a. John should have bought some wine.
   b. Mary wanted John to buy some wine.
2. *Factive:* Certain verbs introduce an entailment (or presupposition) of the argument's veracity. They include forget in the tensed complement, regret, manage:
   a. John forgot that he was in Boston last year.
   b. Mary regrets that she didn't marry John.
   c. John managed to leave the party.

3. *Counterfactive:* The event introduces a presupposition about the non-veracity of its argument: forget (to), unable to (in past tense), prevent, cancel, avoid, decline, etc.
   a. John forgot to buy some wine.
   b. Mary was unable to marry John.
   c. John prevented the divorce.
4. *Evidential:* Evidential relations are introduced by REPORTING or PERCEPTION:
   a. John said he bought some wine.
   b. Mary saw John carrying only beer.
5. *Negative evidential:* Introduced by REPORTING and some PERCEPTION events conveying negative polarity:
   a. John denied he bought only beer.
6. *Negative:* Introduced only by negative particles (not, nor, neither, etc.), which are marked as SIGNALs, with respect to the events they are modifying:
   a. John didn't forget to buy some wine. b. John did not want to marry Mary.

The specification for the SLINK relation is shown in the following:

```
attributes ::= [eventInstanceID] (subordinatedEvent |
                  subordinatedEventInstance) [signalID]
                  relType [polarity]
eventInstanceID ::= ei<integer>
subordinatedEvent ::= e<integer>
subordinatedEventInstance ::= ei<integer>
signalID ::= s<integer>
relType ::= MODAL'|'NEGATIVE'|'EVIDENTIAL'|'NEG_EVIDENTIAL'
            |'FACTIVE'|'COUNTER_FACTIVE'
```

A modally subordinating predicate such as "want" is typed as introducing a SLINK, as shown in the following.

Bill wants to teach on Monday.

```
Bill
<EVENT eid="e1" class="I_STATE" tense="PRESENT" aspect="NONE">
wants
</EVENT>
<MAKEINSTANCE eiid="ei1" eventID="e1"/>
<SLINK eventInstanceID="ei1" signalID="s1"
subordinatedEvent="e2" relType="MODAL"/>
<SIGNAL sid="s1">
to
</SIGNAL>
<EVENT eid="e2" class="OCCURRENCE" tense="NONE" aspect="NONE">
teach
</EVENT>
<MAKEINSTANCE eiid="ei2" eventID="e2"/>
<SIGNAL sid="s2">
on
</SIGNAL>
<TIMEX3 tid="t1" type="DATE" temporalFunction="true"
value="XXXX-WXX-1">
Monday
</TIMEX3>
<TLINK eventInstanceID="ei2" relatedToTime="t1"
relType="IS_INCLUDED"/>
```

8.3.3 ALINK

The ALINK or sspectual link represents the relationship between an aspectual event and its argument event. Examples of the possible aspectual relations that are encoded are shown below:

1. Initiation:
   John started to read.
2. Culmination:
   John finished assembling the table.
3. Termination:
   John stopped talking.
4. Continuation:
   John kept talking.

```
attributes ::= eventInstanceID [signalID]
relatedToEvent relType
eventInstanceID ::= ei<integer>
signalID ::= s<integer>
eventID ::= e<integer>
relType ::= 'INITIATES'|'CULMINATES'|'TERMINATES'|'CONTINUES'
```

To illustrate the behavior of ALINKs, notice how the aspectual predicate, begin, is treated as a separate event, independent of the logically modified event; the "phase" is introduced as the relation within the ALINK.

The boat began to sink.

```
The boat
<EVENT eid="e1" class="ASPECTUAL" tense="PAST" aspect="NONE">
began
</EVENT>
<MAKEINSTANCE eiid="ei1" eventID="e1"/>
<SIGNAL sid="s1">
to
</SIGNAL>
<EVENT eid="e2" class="OCCURRENCE" tense="NONE" aspect= "NONE">
sink
</EVENT>
<ALINK eventInstanceID="ei1" signalID="s1" relatedToEvent="e2"
relType="INITIATES"/>
```

8.4 TimeML in Question Answering Systems

TimeBank is the gold standard corpus created from the TERQAS workshop effort. To facilitate much of the preprocessing and interoperability of the corpus, we chose articles from document collections that have been adopted by other researchers in the community. These include ACE, DUC, and Propbank. The TimeBank collection of annotated texts consists of 300 texts with careful and detailed annotations of terms denoting events (including states and changes of state as well as actions, occurrences, and processes), temporal expressions, signals (modals, negatives, temporal connectives, etc.) and, most importantly, the links between them.

The original goal of the development of TimeML and the gold standard corpus TimeBank was for eventual use in QA systems. The ability to handle temporally sensitive questions has been, to date, clearly out of the scope of current QA systems. In this section, we discuss the ways in which TimeML has been designed to be embedded within a QA system; specifically, we describe the corpus of questions that was created as part of the TERQAS effort, the classification of these questions, and how they relate to TimeML.

Temporal questions come in many shapes. Only a small number of temporal questions do indeed start with the question word "When." We distinguish between implicit and explicit temporal questions. Explicit temporal questions ask for a temporal expression ("when?" "what time?" "how often" "in which century?" etc.) while implicit temporal questions use temporal expressions to give non-temporal answers (e.g., "who was president of X in 1990?" or "did world steel output increase in the nineties?").

The question corpus includes 100 questions. These questions are distributed across the different categories shown in the question creation tool. The questions were chosen in such a way that all possible values of each individual parameter could be accounted for (although not all possible combinations of parameters were covered). A tool was developed to annotate questions for the purpose of the corpus creation. This tool can be used to specify properties of the questions such as answer type and volatility.[66]

To annotate questions in TimeML, we used the Alembic Workbench (AWB) from MITRE, the same tool used to annotate full documents against the specification. Table 8.2 presents the different parameters used to describe questions.

An example of an annotated question follows.

```
<?xml version='1.0'?>
<!DOCTYPE DOCSENT SYSTEM './tquestion.dtd'>
<TERQAS-QUESTION TQID="31">
   <QUESTION>
      Who was president of Iraq during the invasion of Kuwait?
   </QUESTION>
   <ANS_TYPE> Point </ANS_TYPE>
   <NB_TEMPEX> Zero </NB_TEMPEX>
   <INDEXICAL> Yes </INDEXICAL>
   <NB_EVENTS> Two </NB_EVENTS>
   <POS_ANSWERS> One </POS_ANSWERS>
   <EVENT_CLASSES> State </EVENT_CLASSES>
   <VOLATILITY> Medium term </VOLATILITY>
   <SUBORD_TYPE> None </SUBORD_TYPE>
   <REP_TYPE> PointInTime </REP_TYPE>
   <NE_TYPE> Person </NE_TYPE>
</TERQAS-QUESTION>
```

Finally, here is an example of a question annotated in TimeML:

When did the war between Iran and Iraq end?

```
<TIMEX3 tid="t1" type="DATE" value="QUERY">
When
</TIMEX3>
did the
```

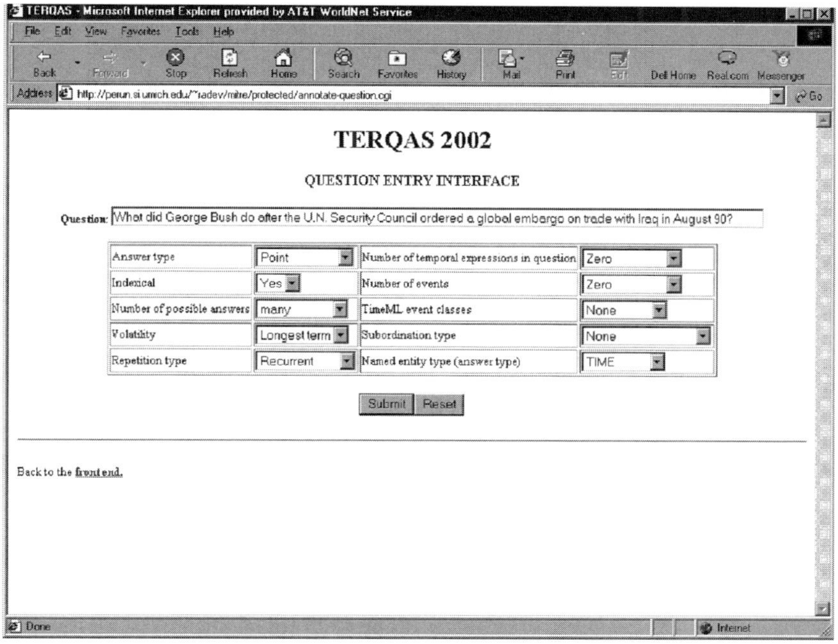

Figure 8.1. Question Annotation Interface

```
<EVENT eid="e1" class="OCCURRENCE" tense="NONE" aspect="NONE">
war
</EVENT>
<MAKEINSTANCE eiid="ei1" eventID="e1"/>
between Iran and Iraq
<EVENT eid="e2" class="ASPECTUAL" tense="PAST" aspect="NONE">
end
</EVENT>
<MAKEINSTANCE eiid="ei2" eventID="e2"/>
?
<ALINK eventInstanceID="ei2" relatedToEvent="ei1" relType="TERMI-
NATES"/>
<TLINK eventInstanceID="ei2" relatedToTime="t1" relType="IS_INCLUD-
ED"/>
```

8.5 Future Developments

Question answering systems need to be sensitive to querying over temporally anchored events, as well as the ordering of events relative to each other. Without such a capability, the expressiveness of the query set for a QA system is greatly limited. In this chapter, we have outlined a specification language that can be used in the automatic markup of events and temporal expressions in natural language texts. The named entities identified by this strategy can then be used in creating semi-structured indexes for reference to events in queries,

Feature	Description	Possible values	Default
ANS_TYPE	the type of the answer	Duration, Frequency, Point, Non-temporal, Point	Point
NB_TEMPEX	number of TEMPEX expressions in question	Zero, One, Two, Three or more	Zero
INDEXICAL	is the question indexical	Yes, No	Yes
NB_EVENTS	how many events are mentioned in the question	Zero, One, Two, Three or more	Zero
POS_ANSWERS	how many possible answers can the question have	many, a few, less than two, many	Many
EVENT_CLASSES	types of events	None, occurrence, perception, aspectual, intending, state, reporting	None
VOLATILITY	how often does the answer change	Longest term, Medium term, Short term, Ephemeral	Ephemeral
SUBORD_TYPE	subordination type	None, Modal, Evidential, Negative-evidential, Factive	None
REP_TYPE	does the question refer to a repetitive event	Recurrent, PointInTime, Period, MultipleTimes	PointInTime
NE_TYPE	what named entity type (if any) is the expected answer to the question	Time, Location, Person, Number, Other	Time

Table 8.2. Question Parameters

or they might be accessed directly from database tables constructed from the entities. TimeML is a good starting point for reference to events and times in QA systems because it systematically anchors event predicates to a broad range of temporally denotating expressions; it provides a language for ordering event expressions in text relative to one another, both intrasententially and in discourse; and it provides a semantics for underspecified temporal expressions, thereby allowing for a delayed interpretation. It is hoped that this effort will provide a platform on which to build a multi-lingual, multi-domain standard for the representation of events and temporal expressions.[7]

Notes

1. TIMEX2 introduces a value attribute whose value is an ISO time representation in the ISO 8601 standard.

2. MAKEINSTANCE is a realization link; it indicates different instances of a given event. One can create as many instances as are motivated by the text. All relations indicated by the other links are stated over these instances. Because of this, every EVENT introduces at least one corresponding MAKEINSTANCE.

3. See Allen (1984) , Allen and Kautz, (1985) for motivation.

4. One reviewer has pointed out that the function of the during-expression signals containment rather than identity. Although this is correct, the event denoted by the referring expression, his drive, is legitimately identical to the event reified by the deictic tense in the previous sentence. Only in composition with the preposition does the containment function emerge.

5. In terms of causal reasoning, these two events must be ordered rather than simultaneous.

6. Available at http://perun.si.umich.edu/~radev/mitre/protected/annotate-question.cgi.

7. Further information may be found at www.timeml.org.

James Pustejovsky is a professor of computer science at Brandeis University.

Roser Saurí is a graduate student in the Laboratory for Linguistics and Computation at Brandeis University.

José M. Castaño is a graduate student in the Laboratory for Lingustics and Computation at Brandeis University.

Dragomir Radev is an assistant professor at the University of Michigan and leads the Computational Linguistics and Information Retrieval group. He holds a Ph.D. in computer science from Columbia University. Dragomir can be reached at radev@umich.edu.

Rob Gaizauskas is a professor of computer science at the University of Sheffield, Sheffield, U.K.

Andrea Setzer is a research assistant on the COMIC project at the University of Sheffield.

Beth Sunheim is affiliated with the Space and Naval Warfare Systems Command at the U.S. Navy.

Graham Katz is a professor at the Instite for Cognitive Science, University of Osnabrück.

Chapter 9

Answering Questions About Moving Objects in Videos

Boris Katz, Jimmy Lin, Chris Stauffer, and Eric Grimson

9.1 Introduction

Although many advances have been made in question answering over the last few years, most existing systems are exclusively text-based (Voorhees 2002). While such systems are undoubtedly useful, information exists in many other types of media as well; a truly effective information access system should not only be able to answer questions about text, but also about pictures, movies, sounds, etc.

Our research centers on extending question answering capabilities to new domains: specifically, video footage captured in a surveillance setting. We have developed Spot, a system that answers questions about moving objects found in video footage. In response to user questions, our system returns dynamically generated video clips that directly satisfy the user query. For example, when the user asks "Show me all southbound cars," Spot displays a video that consists solely of cars heading south; all other traffic is omitted. This research effort is made possible by integrating vision and language technologies developed at the MIT Computer Science and Artificial Intelligence Laboratory.

Our prototype video-surveillance question answering system is situated in a general framework for integrating vision and language systems, called CLiViR (common linguistic-visual representation). In order to exploit the synergies that arise from fusing multimodal information streams, we are developing common representations capable of capturing salient aspects of both language and vision. This general framework supports four major capabilities: event recognition, question answering, event description, and event filtering.

Although there exist information retrieval systems that operate on video clips and still images (Aslandogan and Yu 1999, Smeaton et al. 2001), the vast majority of them treat multimedia segments as opaque objects. For the most part, current multimedia information retrieval systems utilize textual data,

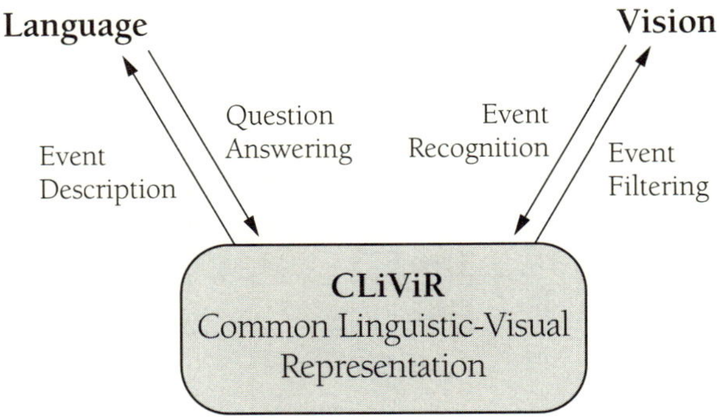

Figure 9.1. Capabilities Provided by CLiViR Framework

such as captions and transcribed speech, as descriptors of content for indexing purposes. For many types of media, the required textual metadata is hard to obtain. Furthermore, the content of multimedia segments cannot be adequately captured by representations purely derived from text; these representations will necessarily be impoverished. Although there has been research on automatically extracting features from video and images, it has been limited to such information as color, shape, and texture; these low-level features alone are insufficient to capture the semantic content of non-textual segments. In addition, automatically translating user queries into sets of appropriate low-level features remains a challenge.

In certain domains it is possible to integrate computer vision and natural language technology in order to extract high-level events from video input and generate symbolic representations that capture the semantics of those events. We attempt to break the inter-media barrier by developing shared representations that are capable of bridging different modalities.

9.1.1 Common Framework

CLiViR lies at the heart of our effort to integrate vision and language. The central goal is to develop a framework that supports practically-grounded shared representations capable of bridging the visual and linguistic domains. Our desire is to capture the salient aspects of both visual and linguistic data relevant for answering user questions, while discarding irrelevant details. Our framework supports four major capabilities that cross the boundaries of language and vision (see figure 9.1):

Event Recognition. CLiViR serves as an "event language" for describing visual scenes. Our representation abstracts away raw video into symbolic structures that can be easily analyzed and manipulated.

Question Answering. Natural language questions can be translated into

Figure 9.2. Still Frames Taken From Video Dynamically Generated by Spot

queries in CLiViR, and then matched against recognized events. With such capabilities, users can ask questions in English and get back appropriate answers, either video clips or textual descriptions. Because the matching is done on symbolic representations, the system can provide concise responses that capture large variations in the video data.

Event Description. Our common representation supports natural language generation, so that users can request "digested summaries" of a particular scene, e.g., "In the last five minutes, five cars passed in front of the building. A blue van stopped across the street for approximately a minute and then drove off."

Event Filtering. CLiViR allows users to issue standing queries that filter the incoming video in real-time, e.g., "Notify me whenever a black sedan pulls up into the driveway."

Our development of CLiViR is driven by both theoretical and practical considerations. On one hand, we believe that by leveraging existing work in knowledge representation and cognitive psychology, it is possible to synthesize theories of meaning expressive enough to capture linguistic and visual knowledge. On the other hand, our commitment to working with unaltered, real-world video will ground our system in realistic scenarios, ensuring robustness and scalability. In essence, we are developing a platform capable of validating theories of representation against real-world data.

9.1.2 Spot: A Prototype

We have built a prototype information access system, called Spot, that can answer interesting questions about video surveillance footage taken around the Technology Square area in Cambridge, Massachusetts. The scene consists of a large parking garage to the west, a white office building to the east, and a north-south roadway that runs between the two structures. The area experiences moderate to heavy amounts of both pedestrian and vehicular traffic, depending on the time of day. A typical video segment shows cars leaving and entering the parking garage, vehicles (e.g., cars and delivery trucks) driving both northbound and southbound, and pedestrians walking around.

Our Spot system analyzes raw footage and attempts to recognize salient events in the video; these events, captured in a symbolic representation, are stored in a knowledge base and indexed for convenient retrieval. When asked a natural language question, Spot first transforms it into a symbolic query, which is then matched against the knowledge base of indexed events. Based on the match, Spot dynamically assembles an abridged video clip satisfying the user request. Currently, we focus on various types of motion within the scene. For example, when a user asks "Show me cars pulling up to the white office building", the system responds with a video clip showing cars entering the driveway of that particular building; all other vehicular and pedestrian traffic is omitted. Figure 9.2 shows several still frames from the answer.

Our prototype can presently answer a variety of interesting questions, e.g.,

Show me cars dropping off people in front of the white building.
Did any cars leave the garage towards the north?
How many cars pulled up in front of the office building?
Show me cars entering Technology Square.
Give me all northbound traffic.

Spot is a proof of concept demonstrating the viability of question answering for video surveillance applications. Much in the same way that traditional question answering systems can respond to queries about textual documents, Spot allows users to ask interesting questions about objects moving in a particular scene.

9.1.3 Underlying Technology

Our Spot system is the result of integrating computer vision and natural language understanding technology. Our prototype is supported by two systems developed at the MIT Computer Science and Artificial Intelligence Laboratory: a real-time motion tracking system and the START Natural Language System.

9.1.4 Robust Object Tracking

By combining the latest in both computer vision and machine learning techniques, we have developed systems that can robustly track multiple moving objects in both indoor and outdoor settings. Under a bottom-up, data-driven framework called Perceptual Data Mining (PDM) (Stauffer 2002), we have created autonomous perceptual systems that can be introduced into almost any environment and, through experience, learn to model the active objects of that environment (Stauffer and Grimson 2000). Over the last five years, we have processed billions of images. Using novel attention mechanisms and adaptive background estimation techniques, our system can isolate moving objects from stationary background scenery.

Our motion-tracking algorithm is based on an adaptive background subtraction method that models each pixel as a mixture of Gaussians and uses an on-line approximation to update the model. The Gaussians are then eval-

Figure 9.3. A Composite of Motion Tracks Detected by Our System in Two Different Settings: an Airport Tarmac (left), and an Entrance Gate to an Office Park (right)

uated using a simple heuristic to decide whether or not a pixel is part of the background process. Foreground pixels are segmented into regions by a two-pass, connected components algorithm. Objects are tracked across frames by using a linearly predictive multiple hypotheses tracking algorithm, which incorporates both position and size. Our approach is able to robustly ignore environmental effects, e.g., flags fluttering or trees swaying in the wind, etc., and handle different weather conditions, e.g., rain or snow. Furthermore, our system is capable of maintaining tracks through cluttered areas, dealing with overlapping objects, and adjusting to gradual lighting changes.

With our technology, it is possible to observe and characterize motions in a particular scene over long periods of time. By applying unsupervised classification techniques to the observed trajectories of moving objects, we can categorize patterns of usage in a site; these include common paths of movement through the site based on type of object as well as common patterns of usage as a function of time of day. As an example, figure 9.3 shows two scenes, a tarmac at an airport and a gate of an office complex, with motion tracks superimposed. In the airport environment, our system is able to detect airplanes taking off and landing in the distance, typical taxi paths, and motion of cars along the roads. In the office gate setting, our system is able to observe cars entering and leaving, as well as pedestrians walking along the road. This classification provides us with a basis for flagging unusual behaviors, for retrieving similar instances of behaviors, and for gathering statistics on site usage.

9.1.5 Natural Language Understanding

The other component that supports the Spot system is natural language understanding technology, in the form of the START information access system (Katz 1997, Katz et al. 2002). In December 1993, START became the first QA system available for question answering on the world wide web. Since then, it

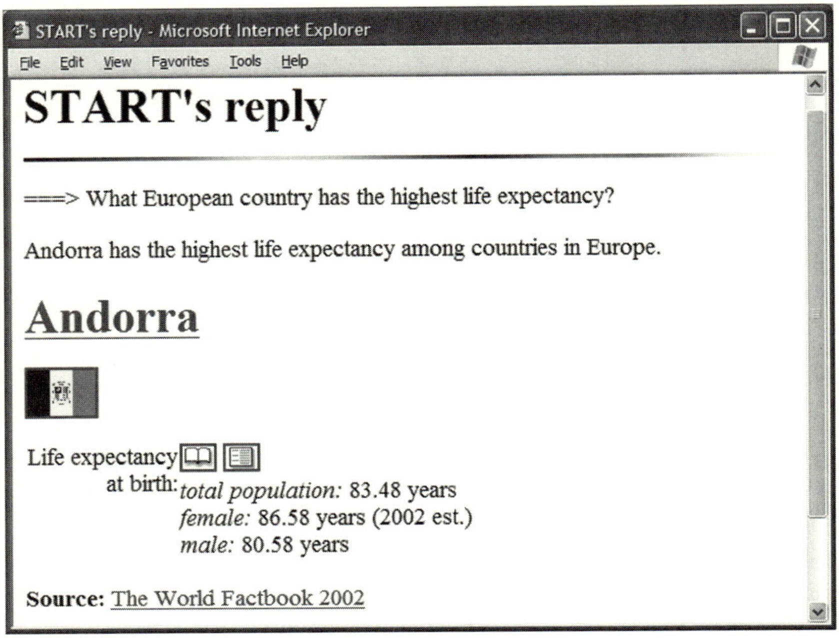

Figure 9.4. START Answering the Question "What European Country Has the Highest Life Expectancy?"

has engaged in exchanges with hundreds of thousands of users all over the world, supplying them with useful knowledge. See chapter 16 in this volume for a more detailed description of our system.

The START system is grounded in a technique called natural language annotation, in which English phrases and sentences are used to describe information segments and the types of questions that they are capable of answering. The system parses these annotations, converts the parsed structures into a set of ternary expressions (Katz 1988), and stores them in a knowledge base with pointers back to the original information segments they describe. To answer a question, the user query is also converted into a set of ternary expressions, which are then compared to the annotations stored in the knowledge base. Because this match occurs at the level of syntactic structures, linguistically sophisticated machinery such as synonymy/hyponymy, ontologies, and structural transformational rules are all brought to bear on the matching process. Linguistic techniques allow the system to achieve capabilities beyond simple keyword matching, for example, handling complex syntactic alternations (Katz and Levin 1988). If a match is found between ternary expressions derived from annotations and those derived from the query, the segment corresponding to the annotations is returned to the user as the answer. An important feature of the annotation concept is that any information segment can be annotated: not only text, but also images, multimedia, and even procedures. Figure 9.4 shows a screenshot of START answering a user question with both text and images.

9.2 Integrating Vision and Language

In response to a user's English question, Spot queries its knowledge base of recognized events to dynamically generate a video clip that satisfies the user's information need. This section describes the question answering process in greater detail.

The basic unit of output from the motion tracking system is a track, which traces the motion of a single object over time. A track is comprised of a sequence of track instances. A track instance depicts a tracked object at a particular moment in time. Each track instance is tagged with a unique identifier and timestamp, and also contains information about the object's screen coordinates, size, and velocity vector, and other meta information. In addition, each track instance contains the actual image of the object and its silhouette, making it possible to reconstruct a movie of the object in motion.

We have developed a symbolic representation that abstracts away from the raw tracking stream. Our representation captures only the salient aspects of the motion observed, and allows for a compact description of the visual data. A compact, yet expressive representation is crucial because the tracking information provided by the vision system is continuous and extremely large—a single camera is capable of generating over one hundred thousand images an hour, most of which may not be relevant to the user.

The basis of our representation is adapted from Jackendoff's linguistic representation of motion and paths (Jackendoff 1983, 1990). This representation is a component of lexical conceptual structures (LCS), a syntactically-grounded semantic representation that captures many cross-linguistic generalizations. It has been successfully used in applications such as interlingual machine translation (Dorr 1992).

As an example, a car leaving the garage would be represented by the following (simplified) expression:

MOVE(Object213, [PATH Source(Garage57)])

In this representation, objects moving along paths are specified by a series of path primitives. These primitives capture the relationship between the object in motion and other (mostly stationary) objects. Path primitives are ideal for serving as the intermediary between vision and language. They correspond to features that can be easily extracted from raw video (using only screen coordinates and other tracking information). In addition, natural language queries about motion are most naturally specified in terms of prepositional phrases, which correspond to path primitives. Thus, our framework for capturing motion and paths serves not only as an expressive representation, but also as a powerful query language. Our structures can contain any number of path primitives; under-specification can be used to indicate missing or unknown knowledge.

An essential component of our representational framework is the mapping from symbolic locations to on-screen coordinates. Currently, this is accomplished manually: a human must identify the interesting landmarks in a particular scene and map the screen location of those landmarks to their symbolic representations. In the future, such mappings could be constructed automatically or semi-automatically by clustering visible behavior into interesting regions and positing the existence of relevant landmarks in the scene.

To efficiently answer natural language questions, we have constructed a knowledge base for storing representations derived from raw video. Spot queries this store using partially instantiated CLiViR structures with unbound variables.

9.2.1 Answering Questions

Consider the query "Show me all cars leaving the garage." START translates the English question into the following query:

Query(MOVE(car?, [PATH Source(Garage57)]))

Since we have not yet integrated object recognition technology into Spot, size is used as a surrogate for object detection, i.e., blobs above a certain size are classified as "cars."

The translation of natural language questions into CLiViR queries is accomplished by augmenting the lexical entries of verbs such as *leave* and *enter* with fragments of CLiViR queries that are dynamically assembled and instantiated during parse-time. Such lexical knowledge is stored alongside the subcategorization frames associated with each verb. In this particular example, the direct object of *leave,* "the garage," is extracted from the parse tree, translated into its corresponding CLiViR location, Garage57, and instantiated as the argument of the "Source" primitive of the path. The mapping from natural language locations to CLiViR locations is specified in terms of nouns and various syntactic constraints on those nouns (e.g., adjectives). Because our lexicon contains information about synonymy, different terms such as *parking structure* and *parking garage* all map to the same CLiViR symbol. Cardinal directions like *north* and *south* are treated as special instances of locations.

The resulting query is then executed against the database of stored event structures. In response, Spot dynamically generates video that contains only motion tracks satisfying the user request. START's syntactic machinery automatically allows Spot to handle variations in language, e.g.:

Did any cars leave the garage?
Give me all cars that exited the garage.

Display cars leaving the garage.

As another example, START's knowledge about natural language allows Spot to translate the question "Show me all southbound traffic." into the query

Query(MOVE(car?, [PATH Source(Road17) Direction(South)]))

Accordingly, Spot displays a video showing only vehicles driving south.

9.3 Related Work

Object and event recognition in the general domain is far beyond the capabilities of current technology. Instead, current video and image retrieval systems rely on low-level features such as color, texture, and shape that can be automatically extracted; see Aslandogan and Yu (1999) and Yoshitaka and Ichikawa (1999) for a survey. However, such systems are fundamentally incapable of capturing high-level semantics.

A method for overcoming the limitations of low-level feature indexing is to utilize textual annotations that may accompany multimedia content. For example, image retrieval systems have been built around the use of image captions (Smeaton and Qigley 1996, Wactlar et al. 2000); similarly, video retrieval systems have incorporated textual transcripts (either taken from closed-captions or generated by speech recognition systems) and other manually entered annotations (Smeaton et al. 2001). There are several drawbacks to this approach. Often unstructured text is simply not the best representation for multimedia content. Furthermore, descriptive annotations often cannot be obtained automatically and require human labor to gather. In contrast, one major advantage offered by our approach stems from the compositional nature of our semantic representation. Instead of using fixed annotations to described predefined multimedia segments, our CLiViR framework allows complex events to be built up from simple primitives. Although we must still specify the semantics for individual primitives, a compositional semantics allows unparalleled flexibility and the ability to describe novel unseen events.

Other attempts to automatically extract higher-level semantics from multimedia segments include pseudo-semantic classification, where items are broken down into broad, generic categories like nature vs. man-made or indoor vs. outdoor (Smith et al. 2001, Chen et al. 1999). Object recognition technology has also been applied to image and video retrieval, although most efforts have been focused on specific objects, e.g., faces, numbers, etc. Video Semantic Directed Graph (Day et al. 1995), an object oriented framework for representing video sequences, focuses on modeling physical objects and their appearance or disappearance rather than events and activities. In contrast to these approaches, we are attempting to develop automatic methods for extracting and modeling high-level semantic events.

9.4 Next Steps

Although our current path representation is limited in scope and in the types of questions that it can answer, we believe that Jackendoff's LCS representation serves as a solid basic foundation upon which to build more expressive structures. Our immediate goal is to augment existing representations with attributes such as time, speed, color, size, etc., to allow richer questions:

Show me the last delivery truck that stopped in front of the office.
How many people walked out of the building in the last 15 minutes?
Display all blue cars entering the garage from the south this morning.

We are presently in the process of developing a language that can manipulate primitive building blocks such as paths and path primitives to craft more complex events. A significant portion of this effort focuses on exploring possible ways in which primitives can be combined to form more complex events such as sequences or causal chains. From this, we hope to develop a meaningful set of "connectors" to explicitly relate primitive events. This event language would allow users to ask very interesting questions:

In the last hour, did any car pull up to the curb and let out passengers?
Have any trucks circled the building more than twice within the last day?

With traditional video-retrieval systems, it is often very difficult to construct meaningful queries in terms of low-level features like textures and colors, e.g., for events such as a car dropping a passenger off at the curb or a van making a U-turn. Yet, many of these complex events can be easily specified in natural language. By building a suitable abstraction between language and vision for capturing high-level semantic events, we can build systems that provide users with effective access to video information.

Furthermore, traditional information-retrieval-based question answering technology can be integrated with a system like Spot to form a generalized multimodal information access system. Such an integration would provide users with powerful tools for analyzing situations from different perspectives. For example, consider a busy freeway intersection: integration of video and textual data would allow a user to understand anomalous traffic patterns (detected by video) by consulting traffic and weather reports (textual data).

Input using multiple modalities is another direction that we would like to explore. In our domain of visual surveillance, gestures could play an important role as a possible mode of querying. For example, a user could ask "Show me all cars that went like this [gesturing a path]." Or "Did anyone leave this building [pointing to a specific office building] in the last hour?"

An important aspect of video sequences that cannot be easily captured by Jackendoff's LCS representation is the notion of time and temporal intervals. For modeling temporal aspects of activity, Allen's work (1983) on qualitative relations between temporal intervals is highly relevant. Correspondingly, there has been some work on relations in the spatial domain that we could capitalize on (Chang et al. 1987, Egenhofer and Franzosa 1991). In addition, representations focusing on change and transitions between states (Borchardt 1992), could also be helpful in the development of CLiViR.

9.5 Challenges

Our endeavor seeks to bring together maturing technologies from different fields to tackle fundamental problems in artificial intelligence. Although increasing trends towards specialization have resulted in many spectacular breakthroughs in narrow domains, the fragmentation of artificial intelligence research into a multitude of sub-disciplines has lead to stagnation of progress in "grand challenges." We believe that technologies from various disparate areas are mature enough to support integration into a common framework, and that the potential synergies resulting from such integration will allow us to develop applications with far-reaching consequences.

Nevertheless, in pursuing our objectives, we may encounter both theoretical and practical challenges. The inherent assumption of our shared representation is the decompositional nature of knowledge across different modalities. Although preliminary successes are encouraging, it remains an open research question whether complex events can indeed be broken down into simple primitives. Furthermore, can primitives then be assembled to productively describe novel and unanticipated events? If the expansion of a system like Spot into new domains leads to an endless proliferation of new primitives, then perhaps our common-representation approach to integrating vision and language is untenable. Perhaps, even if this were the case, the failure of our approach would teach us something about the nature of knowledge itself.

Aside from theoretical considerations, there are practical concerns with the scaling of video knowledge bases. Currently, Spot can successfully handle days worth of video (on the order of hundreds of megabytes). However, real-world applications might require storage of months, and maybe even years, of footage. The vast amounts of data involved, coupled with the rich symbolic structures derived from them, create a potential problem in the storage, indexing, and retrieval of video knowledge. Nevertheless, we are confident that such issues can be addressed through increased computing power and better algorithms.

9.6 Conclusion

The integration of vision and language technologies presents both difficult challenges and exciting opportunities for information access systems. We have taken several steps towards crossing the chasm between different modalities—not only have we implemented a prototype QA system for video surveillance footage, but also sketched a general framework for integrating the visual and linguistic domains under a shared representation.

Psychologists have long believed that language and vision are two very important aspects of cognition that contribute to intelligence. People are able to effortlessly integrate visual and linguistic data to reason and learn, an ability far beyond that of present-day computers. By creating a framework for bridging vision and language, not only can we build more effective information access systems, but perhaps we can also shed some light on the wonders of human cognition.

Acknowledgments

We would like to thank Gary Borchardt, Sue Felshin, Greg Marton, and Stefanie Tellex for their comments on earlier drafts of this chapter. This research was funded in part by MIT's Lincoln Laboratory and the Oxygen Project.

Boris Katz is a principal research scientist and head of the InfoLab group at the Computer Science and Artificial Intelligence Laboratory at the Massachusetts Institute of Technology.

Jimmy Lin is a Ph.D. student in the Electrical Engineering and Computer Science Department at the Massachusetts Institute of Technology.

Chris Stauffer is a post doctoral associate in the Electrical Engineering and Computer Science Department at the Massachusetts Institute of Technology.

Eric Grimson is the Bernard Gordon Professor of Medical Engineering and a professor of computer science and engineering at the Massachusetts Institute of Technology.

Section Four

Interactive and Scenario-Based QA

An important new direction in QA is the ability to exploit context in interactive sessions. This section considers several new directions such as the use of interactive dialogue to clarify and refine questions and the use of context to interpret complex questions.

The first chapter, by Sharon Small, Tomek Strzalkowski, Ting Liu, Nobuyuki Shimizu, and Boris Yamron (State University of New York), considers interactive question answering for analysts to address exploratory, analytical questions such as "What has been Russia's reaction to the U.S. bombing of Kosovo?" Interactivity is required because the underspecification of query requires clarification dialogue and it may not be possible to answer with a single shot, as in factoid QA (e.g., providing a named entity). Recent factoid questions answering systems deduce this expected answer type from the form of the question and a finite list of possible answer types. For example, "Who was the first man in space" expects a "person" as the answer, while "How long was the Titanic?" expects some length measure as an answer, probably in yards and feet, or meters.

In their HITIQA system, the authors report the use of N-gram-based clustering of text passages and concept extraction to uncover the main topics, themes and entities in the retrieved set. Typically three to six clusters are generated out of the top 50 documents. Event frames are used to bridge the query to the document. These include generic templates, consisting of a small number of attributes, such as location, person, country, organization, etc., as well domain specific ones for the non-proliferation domain, e.g., transfer missile-parts from North Korea to Egypt. The authors built extractors using Sheffield's GATE[1] system and more recently using BBN's Identifinder software, which extracts 24 types of entities. There are both goal frames from the user's query and data frames from clusters of documents. For example, given the query "How has pollution in the Black Sea affected the fishing industry, and what are the sources of this pollution?" the HITIQA system will produce the goal frame with Topic: [pollution, industry, sources], Location: [Black Sea], and Industry: [fishing]. At this point, the attributes of goal and data frames are compared. Three types of clarification dialogue with the user at the information semantic level then occur (the first two are implemented): (1) narrowing dialogue, which reduces the size of the answer set, i.e., number of frames with zero conflicts; (2) broadening dialogue, to move some of the 1-conflict and maybe 2-conflict, etc., frames into the zero-conflict zone by asking questions to the user; and (3) fact seeking dialogue, which asks the user to supply missing values for certain attributes such as date or location.

Frame information can be utilized to automatically generate a "headline" by exploiting the semantics of thematic frames where attributes are assigned specific roles. For example, if the user asks "Do we have any data about Syria having nerve gas manufacturing capability?" HITIQA responds including the headline "SYRIA REPORTED TO DEVELOP SARIN NERVE GAS, WARHEADS AND MISSILES". A visual display allows the user to see all the frames in a compact visual form and also to directly manipulate frame relevance. In short, interactivity enables the system to engage in dialogues to narrow or broaden interpretation of user queries.

Whereas interactivity plays an essential role in query refinement and clarification, finding answers to complex questions is the focus of the next chapter by Anne Diekema, Ozgur Yilmazel, Jiangping Chen, Sarah Harwell, Lan He, and Elizabeth Liddy from Syracuse University. In contrast to the short, factoid-focused TREC (trec.nist.gov, Voorhees 2000; Voorhees and Tice 2000), this NASA and AT&T funded effort focuses on real-time, complex questions from Cornell and Syracuse University aeronautical engineering undergraduates regarding Reusable Launch Vehicles. Question answering is used from within the collaborative learning environment, AIDE (Advanced Interactive Discovery Environment for Engineering Education). A novel question negotiation module based on the traditional reference library interview serves as a bridge to flag and correct miscommunications between user and system.

CNLP AIDE QA system has four primary modules: (1) document processing (NLP); (2) language-to-logic (L2L); (3) search engine; and (4) answer providing passages (returning the top 20 passages). Questions are classified as being best answered using an entity-based approach, a pattern-based approach, or a context-based approach. Answers come from technical content, such as textbooks, technical papers, and websites.

The authors' analysis of 342 student questions indicated they included a large number of domain-specific phrases, including proper noun, common-noun and verb phrases. They found questions to be long, with complex syntax containing several prepositional phrases as modifiers (e.g., "how difficult is it to mold and shape graphite-epoxies compared with alloys or ceramics that may be used for thermal protective applications?"). They identify linguistic patterns that can be used to categorize questions into classes. The 342 questions were distributed among the types as follows: Wh- (23%), Yes / No (15%), How (14%), Quantification (12%), Definition (10%), Why (4.7%), Conditional (3.5%), and Alternative (3.2%). Each question type could have a "focus", the type of information needed in an answer (e.g., "how" answers involve level or manner; "quantification" answers involve number, money, time, weight, temperature, or volume).

The authors point out many forms of ill formed queries including too broad a query, queries whose answers, even though correct, do not meet the unstated needs of the user, or a question that is based on a misunderstanding, either of the system or of the subject. Queries also can have ambiguous keywords, erroneous details or faulty assumptions about the world or subject.

Motivated by library science, the authors aim to model a reference interview in which an information need is broken down into multiple questions, paraphrases of the question, follow up questions, and answer feedback. They point out that each type of question requires a separate query negotiation process based on its classification. For example the factoid question "What is the weight of the space shuttle?" can be paraphrased to "Do you want to know how much the <OBJECT> weighs?". If the user responds yes, the amount can be provided; if not, a more complex explanation can be provided. The authors conclude by proposing a new interactive QA model which includes modules for document processing, question interpretation and negotiation, a search engine, answer passages, and answer satisfaction.

The final chapter in this section reports on the combination of a dialogue system with information extraction techniques. Arne Jönsson, Frida Andén, Lars Degerstedt, Annika Flycht-Eriksson, Magnus Merkel, and Sara Norberg from Linköping University explore these ideas in BIRDQUEST, a QA dialogue system based on a Nordic bird encyclopedia provided on the web to viewers of a nature TV program. The authors define dialogue as including context (e.g., anaphora, ellipsis), query clarification/refinement (e.g., does size mean length or wingspan?; what type of loon is meant by loons?), and follow up questions.

The authors note that users often have different perspectives of the domain in question compared to the concepts expressed and used in reference material written by domain experts, such as a bird encyclopedia. For instance, in the case of bird anatomy, an expert would use specialized terms to refer to different kinds of feathers whereas a novice would use more every-day descriptions. It is therefore important to identify these different views on the ontology.
An analysis of the bird encyclopedia yielded 8 objects (various groupings of birds, and geographical locations), 30 attributes, and 3 relations. Four new objects and six new attributes were introduced by the analysis of the question corpus. The resulting ontology contained 12 objects, 36 attributes and 3 relations. The system only reasons about color or shape to a limited extent, as the domain ontology does not include a representation of all body parts. While

there are over 100 different body parts, typically only 3 are represented in books or described in relation to one another (e.g., "The Blyth's Reed Warbler looks like the European Reed Warbler and the Marsh Warbler, but the upper parts' brown colour is slightly grayer.")

A corpus of 264 questions about birds was collected by the Swedish Public Service Television Company on a web site for one of their nature programs. An interaction component processes utterances in five phases: linguistic analysis, pragmatic interpretation, task handling, generation, and memorization. Questions can be vague with respect to the (1) object class (e.g., a loon can be one of many), (2) properties (e.g., appearance maps onto size, color, shape), or (3) mappings of vague properties to ones suitable for database access (e.g., size maps onto many DB sub-properties).

The authors evaluated their system with 27 dialogues containing a total number of 518 user utterances. About half were successful, a quarter of user queries contained errors, and BIRDQUEST failed on slightly over a quarter of the utterances. Of 180 successful system responses, 128 required dialogue. This was split among dialogue refinements (31), vague properties (28), and vague property mappings to DB (64). For 55 responses there was no relevant information in the database. As the BIRDQUEST domain illustrates, domain ontology and dialogue management are essential for successful question answering.

Note

1. Generalized architecture for text engineering (GATE) is an information extraction system developed at the University of Sheffield (Cunningham, 2000).

Chapter 10

A Data Driven Approach to Interactive QA

Sharon Small, Tomek Strzalkowski, Ting Liu, Nobuyuki Shimizu, & Boris Yamrom

10.1 Introduction

The HITIQA project is part of the Advanced Research and Development Activity (ARDA) Advanced Question and Answering for Intelligence (AQUAINT) program that aims to make significant advances in the state of the art of automated question answering. In this chapter we focus on two aspects of our work: (1) question semantics: how the system "understands" user requests; and (2) human-computer dialogue: how the user and the system negotiate this understanding.

We will also discuss very preliminary evaluation results from a series of pilot tests of the system conducted by intelligence analysts via a remote internet link.

10.2 Factoid Versus Analytical

The objective in HITIQA is to allow the user to submit and obtain answers to exploratory, analytical questions. There are very significant differences between factoid or fact-finding, and analytical question answering. A factoid question seeks pieces of information that would make a corresponding statement true (i.e., they become facts): "How many states are in the U.S.?" / "There are X states in the U.S." In this sense, a factoid question usually has just one correct answer that can generally be judged for its truthfulness. By contrast, an analytical question is when the "truth" of the answer is more a matter of opinion and may depend upon the context in which the question is asked. Answers to analytical questions are rarely unilateral; indeed, a mere "correct" answer may have limited value, and in some cases may not even be determinate ("Which college is the best?" "How do I stop my baby's crying?"). Instead, answers to analytical questions are often judged as helpful, or useful, or satisfactory, etc. "Technically correct" answers (e.g., "feed the baby milk") may be considered as irrelevant or at best unresponsive.

Factoid questions display a fairly distinctive "answer type," which is the type of the information piece needed to fulfill the statement. Recent automated systems for answering factoid questions deduct this expected answer type from the form of the question and a finite list of possible answer types. For example, "Who was the first man in space?" expects a "person" as the answer, while "How long was the *Titanic?*" expects some length measure as an answer-probably in yards and feet, or meters. This is generally a very good strategy, which has been exploited successfully in a number of automated QA systems that appeared in recent years, especially in the context of TREC QA[1] evaluations (Harabagiu et al. 2000, Hovy et al. 2000, Prager at al. 2001).

The above process is not easily applied to analytical questions. This is because the type of an answer for analytical questions cannot always be anticipated due to their inherently exploratory character. In contrast to a factoid question, an analytical question has an unlimited variety of syntactic forms with only a loose connection between their syntax and the expected answer. Given the unlimited potential for the formation of analytical questions, it would be counter-productive to restrict them to a fixed number of question/answer types. Even finding a non-strictly factual answer to an otherwise simple question about *Titanic* length (e.g., "two football fields") would push the limits of the answer-typing approach. Therefore, the formation of an answer should instead be guided by the topics the user is interested in, as recognized in the question and/or through the interactive dialogue, rather than by a single type as inferred from the question in a factoid system.

10.3 Document Retrieval

When the user poses a question to a system sitting atop a huge database of unstructured data (text files), the first order of business is to reduce that pile to perhaps a handful of documents where the answer is likely to be found. This means, most often, some form of document retrieval, using fast but nonexact selection methods. In order to accomplish this, users' natural language questions need to be tokenized, converted into search queries, and sent to a document retrieval engine, such as Google (www.google.com), SMART (Buckley 1985), InQuery (Callan et al. 1992), OKAPI (Robertson et al. 2000), etc. In the experiments with the HITIQA prototype, document retrieval is used to return the top 50 documents from a large text archive comprised of the AQUAINT corpus[2] and a smaller collection of web-harvested documents. Currently, this archive can be searched using one of the two available IR systems (SMART, InQuery); in the future, multiple search engines will return documents and other information objects from different parts of distributed, multimodal data sources.

10.4 Data Driven Semantics of Questions

The set of documents and text passages returned from the initial search is not just a random subset of the database. Depending upon the quality of the text retrieval system available, this set can be considered as a first stab at understanding the user's question by the machine. Again, given the available resources, this is the best the system can do under the circumstances. Therefore, we may as well consider this collection of retrieved texts (the retrieved set) as the meaning of the question as understood by the system. This is a fair assessment: the better our search capabilities, the closer this set would be to what the user may accept as an answer to the question.

It should be clear that better search does not mean just better precision or better recall; it means both, and it also means utility, novelty, and context. In other words, while new information has the highest value to the user, an independent confirmation makes it more reliable. On the other hand, the importance of relevant information is often relative to other, perhaps only marginally related, information; such additional information provides a context or backdrop for the current topic and gives analysts a fuller picture of the relative importance of key facts. Therefore, the search needs to cast a net wide enough to capture more than just the most directly relevant pieces.

10.5 Clustering and Framing

Clustering. Information contained in the documents in the retrieved set is first clustered to uncover any salient themes running through it. This classification is partially orthogonal to the relevance ranking used in document search because it is reinforced by mutual similarities of text fragments within the set (i.e., by repetition of the same theme or pattern) rather than by similarity to the question. While occasionally these two classifications do converge, more often they form a two-dimensional space of things that are important because they are highly similar to the question and things that are important because they show up in numbers. Other dimensions can be added as well, for example time, geographical location, etc., as well as information quality including source, reliability and so forth. Other thrusts in the HITIQA project address these issues (Tang et al. 2003).

We use *n*-gram-based clustering of text passages and concept extraction to uncover the main topics, themes, and entities in the retrieved set. Retrieved documents are first broken into naturally occurring paragraphs. Duplicate paragraphs are filtered out and the remaining passages are clustered using a two-step process, which is a combination of hierarchical clustering and n-bin classification (details of the clustering algorithm can be found in Hardy et al. 2002). The hierarchical clustering phase forms a small number of highly connected clusters based on strong similarity criteria derived from variable length word n-gram overlap. Typically three to six clusters are generated out of the top 50 documents, which may yield as many as 1,000 passages, although only a small subset of these will enter the initial clusters (cluster seeds). The goal here is to have each cluster represent a salient theme within the retrieved set: usually an alternative or complimentary interpretation of the user's question. This is of course not always possible, and some clusters may end up merely accidental aggregations of text snippets.

Framing. In HITIQA we use a text framing technique to delineate the gap between the meaning of the user's question and the system "understanding" of this question. The framing is an attempt to impose a partial structure on the text that would allow for systematic comparison among different text pieces and also against the question. In particular, the framing process may reveal that some topics and themes within the retrieved set are not what the user had explicitly asked for, and thus may be unaware of their existence. Nonetheless these may be highly correlated with the desired answer, and may indeed carry important information.

In the current version of the system, most frames are fairly generic templates, consisting of a small number of attributes, such as location, person, country, organization, etc. The intent is of course to capture an event or a relation (for which we reserve a special attribute topic), but the generic frame makes no specific assumptions about the roles of its attributes with respect to topic event or relation. We have also developed a small number of relation templates, specifically for the weapons nonproliferation domain, which is one of the sources of our data. Within this domain, topically specialized frames can be defined, such as transfer, treaty, development, etc. For example, the transfer frame (capturing all transfer events of weapons, technologies, components, etc.) assigns semantic roles to its attributes (e.g., source, destination, weapon type). While this may not capture the entire meaning of the text fragment, it nonetheless allows the system to make a crude comparison: this document says Egypt obtained missile components from North Korea (transfer missile-parts from N. Korea to Egypt), while another document says Egypt transferred weapon technology to Korea.

Most of the frame attributes are defined in advance, however dynamic frame expansion is also possible. Each of the attributes in a frame is equipped with an extractor function which specializes in locating and extracting instances of this attribute in the running text. The extractors are implemented using information extraction utilities which form the kernel of Sheffield's Generalized Architecture for Text Engineering (GATE)[3] system. We have modified GATE to separate organizations into companies and other organizations, and we have also expanded by adding new concepts such as industries. More recently we have been using BBN's Identifinder software, which extracts 24 types of entities.

The framing process resembles strongly the template filling task in information extraction (cf. Message Understanding Conference (MUC)[4] evaluations), with one significant exception. The MUC template task was to fill in a single template using information from an entire document (Humphreys et al. 1998). In the framing process, on the other hand, templates are filled by entities extracted from clusters of small size, very similar passages. The added redundancy of information makes this a less error-prone task-our experience has thus far been more positive than the MUC evaluation results might indicate. Furthermore, clusters containing adjacent text passages would be framed independently and then merged by combining values of frame attributes.[5]

A very similar process is applied to the user's question, resulting in a goal frame which can be subsequently compared to the data frames obtained from the retrieved set. For example, the goal frame generated from the question, "How has pollution in the Black Sea affected the fishing industry, and what are the sources of this pollution?" is shown in figure 10.1. We should note that this is a generic frame and the attributes have no special roles beyond their usual interpretation.

The frames obtained from the clusters in the retrieved set (or data frames) are then compared to the goal frame. We pay particular attention to matching the topic attribute, before any other attributes are considered. As explained before, the topic attribute is expected to contain the main event or relation expressed in text. If any of the goal frame topics are present anywhere in the data cluster, then it becomes the data frame's topic as well. If more than one match is found, the subsequent matches become sub-topics of the data frame. On the other hand, if no explicit match is found against the goal frame topic, we attempt to select the topic from the list of WordNet generated hypernyms.

A sample data frame generated from a passage retrieved in response to the query about the Black Sea is shown in figure 10.2.

After the initial framing is done, an additional frame merging step is attempted for the frames assigned to the same topic. Frames judged to be related to the same event (same topic, overlap on key attribute values), are merged and values of their attributes are combined.

10.5.1 Judging Frame Relevance

We judge a particular data frame as relevant, and subsequently the corresponding segment of text as relevant, by comparison to the goal frame. A data frame is given a negative point for each value mismatch (called conflict) between its attributes and the goal frame. If a data frame has no conflicts, it is given the highest relevance rank, and a conflict score of zero. All other data

Topic: [pollution, industry, sources]
Location: [Black Sea]
Industry: [fishing]
Text: How has pollution in the Black Sea affected the fishing industry, and what are the sources of this pollution?

Figure 10.1. HITIQA-Generated Goal Frame

frames are scored with an incrementing conflict value, one for frames with one conflict with the goal frame, two for two conflicts etc. Frames that conflict with all information found in the query are given a score of 99 indicating the lowest relevancy rank. We should note here that such frames may sit over passages with some keyword overlap with the query, but presumably such overlap is semantically meaningless. Currently, frames with a conflict score of 99 are excluded from further processing.

10.5.2 Enabling Dialogue with the User

Framed information represents the system's partial understanding of the user question; specifically, zero-conflict frames constitute elements of the answer. An answer can now be composed from the underlying text passages, or by generation, using attribute values from the frame. However, a large and diverse population of near-miss frames may indicate that only part of the answer has been captured; conversely a large number of zero frames may suggest that a narrower interpretation of the question is warranted. Whether any of these conditions require revisions to the answer space can be determined through a dialogue with the user.

HITIQA automatically evaluates the semantic correlation between frames and initiates a clarification dialogue with the user. The purpose of the dialogue is to help bridge the gap between the user's expectations and the system's heretofore "understanding" of the question. In clarification dialogue the system solicits more details from the user about what information he or she is seeking, based on the composition of the entire answer space, including the near-miss frames. The main principle here is that the dialogue is at the information semantic level, not at the information organization level. Moreover, the dialogue relates directly to the subject matter addressed by the question: it is of course a challenge to make sure that what happens next is indeed a logical follow up to the question. Consider the following exchange:

USER: What is being done to combat AIDS epidemic in Africa?

HITIQA: Are you interested in information about International AIDS Conference?

USER: yes, but only as related to access to AIDS medication and prevention.

Thus, the dialogue relates directly to the topic of the user inquiry, and of course it may subsequently proceed in any direction. Here is another example recorded in a recent session with HITIQA:

Topic: pollution
Subtopic: [sources]
Location: [Black Sea]
Industry: [fisheries, tourism]
Text: [In a period of only three decades (1960's-1980's), the **Black Sea** has suffered the catastrophic degradation of a major part of its natural resources. Particularly acute problems have arisen as a result of **pollution** (notably from nutrients, fecal material, solid waste and oil), a catastrophic decline in commercial fish stocks, a severe decrease in **tourism** and an uncoordinated approach towards coastal zone management. Increased loads of nutrients from rivers and coastal **sources** caused an overproduction of phytoplankton leading to extensive eutrophication and often extremely low dissolved oxygen concentrations. The entire ecosystem began to collapse. This problem, coupled with **pollution** and irrational exploitation of fish stocks, started a sharp decline in **fisheries** resources.]
Relevance: Matches on all elements found in goalframe

Figure 10.2. A HITIQA-Generated Data Frame
(Words in Bold Were Used to Fill the Frame)

USER: How did al-Qaida conduct its efforts to acquire weapons of mass destruction?
HITIQA: We have this information about bin Laden, not about al-Qaida; would you like to see this?
USER: Yes, sure.

On the other hand, the user should never be asked if a particular keyword is useful or not, or if a document is relevant or not. The only exception to this rule is when a misspelling or omission of a key concept is detected in the user input - we could occasionally try "Did you mean ..."[6] However, our experience shows that these can be quite irritating to most users.

In HITIQA we adopted a three-pronged dialogue strategy, based on the organization of the answer space: (1) Narrowing dialogue: ask questions that would allow the system to reduce the size of the answer set. This is to narrow the interpretation of the question and to reduce the number of zero frames. (2) Broadening dialogue: ask questions that would allow the system to decide if the answer set needs to be expanded by information just outside of it (near-misses). This is to move some of the 1-conflict and maybe 2-conflict, etc., frames into the zero-conflict zone. (3) Fact seeking dialogue: ask the user to supply missing values for certain attributes such as date or location, etc. Furthermore, allow the user to ask questions seeking additional facts and specific examples, or similar situations.

Of the above, we have thus far implemented the first two options as part of the preliminary clarification dialogue. The clarification dialogue is when the user and the system negotiate the task that needs to be performed. We call this a "triaging stage" of the interaction, as opposed to the actual problem solving stage (item 3 above). In practice, these two stages are not necessarily separated and may be overlapping throughout the entire interaction.

10.5.3 Clarification Dialogue

Data frames with a conflict score of zero form the initial kernel answer space. Depending upon the size of this set and the presence of other frames outside of it, the system either proceeds to generate the answer or initiates a dialogue with the user. For example, if the answer space appears too large or varied, e.g., consists of many different topics, the system may ask the user how to narrow it. Alternatively, the presence of large groups of text frames with near-miss frames assigned to them (i.e., frames with 1 or 2 conflicts with the goal frame) may indicate that the answer space is actually larger, and the user will be consulted about a possible broadening of the question. Currently, we only initiate a clarification dialogue for 1-conflict frames.

A 1-conflict frame has only a single attribute mismatch with the goal frame. This could be a mismatch on any attribute, for example, location, or organization, or time, etc. A special case arises when the conflict occurs on the topic attribute. Since all other attributes match, we may be looking at potentially different events or situations involving the same entities, or occurring at the same location or time. The purpose of the clarification dialogue in this case is to probe which of these topics may be of interest to the user. This is illustrated in the exchange recorded during an evaluation session with an intelligence analyst (see figure 10.3).

To understand what happened here, we need to note first that the goal frame for the user question does not have any specific value assigned to its topic attribute. This of course is as we would expect it: the question does not give us a hint as to what information we need to look for or may be hoping to find about Sanchez. This also means that all the data frames obtained from the retrieved set for this question will have at least one conflict with the goal frame, and thus will be classified as either near-misses or outliers. One such 1-conflict near-miss frame is shown in figure 10.3: its topic is "civil rights," from the list of WordNet generated hypernyms, and it is about Sanchez. HITIQA thus asks if "civil rights" is a topic of interest to the user. If the user responds positively, this topic will be added to the goal frame, and thus to the answer space. Subsequently, all 1-conflict frames with a civil-rights topic will be re-scored to zero conflicts. Similarly, 2-conflict frames with civil-rights topics will be rescored to 1-conflict, etc. The above dialogue strategy is applicable to other attribute mismatch cases, and produces intelligent-sounding responses from the system.

The clarification dialogue will continue on the topic level until all the significant sets of NEAR-MISS frames are either included in the answer space (through user broadening the scope of the question that removes the initial

User: Who is Elizardo Sanchez?

HITIQA: Are you interested in seeing information about civil rights as it is related to Elizardo Sanchez?

Topic: civil-rights
Subtopic: []
Location: [Cuba, Cuba, Cuba]
Companies: []
People: [Sanchez, Sanchez]
Document date: [2000, 1, 11]
Source: HAVANA (AP) –
Text: [``I consider that the situation for civil and political rights in **Cuba** has worsened over the **past year**... owing to that **Cuba** continues to be the only closed society in this hemisphere," **Sanchez** said. ``There have been no significant release of prisoners, the number of people sanctioned or processed for political motives increased. **Sanchez**, who himself spent many years in **Cuban** prisons, is among the communist island's best known opposition activists. The commission he heads issues a report on civil rights every six months, along with a list of people it considers to be imprisoned for political motives.]

Figure 10.3. A 1-Conflict Frame Utilized in Generating the Sanchez Dialogue

conflicts) or dismissed as not relevant. When HITIQA reaches this point it will re-evaluate the data frames in its answer space. If there are too many answer frames now (more than a pre-determined upper threshold), the dialogue manager will ask the user to narrow the question using another frame attribute. On the other hand, if the size of the new answer space is still small and there are many unresolved near-miss frames, the dialogue manager will suggest to the user ways of further broadening the answer space, thus making more data frames relevant, or possibly retrieving new documents by adding terms acquired through the clarification dialogue. When the number of frames is within the acceptable range, HITIQA will generate the answer using the text from the frames in the current answer space. The user may end the dialogue at any point and have an answer generated given the current state of the frames.

10.5.4 Answer Generation

In the first version of HITIQA, the answer is simply composed of text passages underlying the zero conflict frames. The text of these frames is ordered by date and output to the user. Typically, an answer to analytical type questions will require a few pages of information. The example below shows the first portion of the answer generated by HITIQA for the Black Sea query.

USER: How has pollution in the Black Sea affected the fishing industry, and what are the sources of this pollution?

HITIQA: The Black Sea is widely recognized as one of the regional seas most damaged by human activity. Almost one third of the entire land area of continental Europe drains into this sea (...) The management of the Black Sea itself is the shared responsibility of the six coastal countries: Bulgaria, Georgia, Romania, Russia, Turkey, and Ukraine...

Our current work on answer generation is focused on fusion of more succinct and informative answer summaries. The first step in this process is to define a process by which the frame information can be utilized to automatically generate a "headline" for the underlying text passage. For example:

USER: Do we have any data about Syria having nerve gas manufacturing capability?

HITIQA: **SYRIA REPORTED TO DEVELOP SARIN NERVE GAS, WARHEADS AND MISSILES:**

Syria is said to possess a large number of warheads filled with VX and sarin nerve gas, which can be mounted on Scud-B and Scud-C missiles. It is reported to have factories near Damascus and Homs that are producing hundreds of tons of mustard gas and sarin nerve agent.

This "headline" is generated by exploiting the semantics of thematic frames where attributes are assigned specific roles. In general, the more precise the semantics of a frame, the more satisfactory headline is generated. For generic frames (like those used in the Sanchez examples in section 10.5.3) it would be much harder to automatically come up with the right wording for a headline.

The work on answer fusion is in the initial stages. Eventually, we envision that headlines of multiple text passages will form a fused summary of the answer, something that the user can view first.

10.6 Visual Navigation through Answer Space

We use visualization techniques to supplement the dialogue and give the user more control over the data if they so choose. Visual display allows the user to see all the frames in a compact visual form and also to directly manipulate frame relevance. Figure 10.4 shows typical top level visualization panels. Each panel is split into two halves. The top half displays frames or group of frames, the lower half displays the legend. Frames are represented by colored circles, and are arranged by their scores and by their topic attribute values. Scores are represented using a color palette (bottom, left), from the most relevant (blue) to least relevant (red), using the accepted convention for denoting elevations on geographical maps. Annotated spokes on the circles represent key attributes of the frame. Each attribute has a fixed location on circle perimeter, so they can be visually located even when annotation is removed. This multiparametric visualization technique has been shown to be effective (Grinstein et al. 1993). The text window in the lower right corner is used to display frame text.

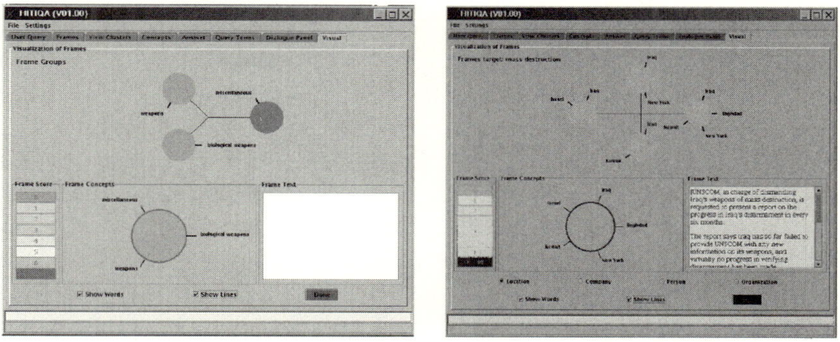

Figure 10.4. Group Level Display and Frame Level Display

The user can change relevancy of selected frame groups or individual frames. By positioning the cursor over a frame group or a frame and clicking the right mouse button, the user changes the conflict-score of the selection according to the following logic: If the score is not equal to zero, it will become zero, and if the score is zero it becomes 99. Users also can reset the scores of all frames to their original (at the visual initiation time) values. With the left mouse button click, when the cursor is positioned over the group of frames, the user can switch to the display of the individual frames of this group. In figure 10.4, the left screen shows three groups of frames (two 0-conflict and one 99-conflict), while the right panel displays four individual frames in one of the groups (represented by the lower blue circle on the left panel). By clicking the left mouse button again the user returns to the group level display; thus the left mouse button is used as a toggle between the individual frames and the groups of frames display.

When individual frames are displayed, the user may choose which attributes should be visualized by selecting from the menu in the legend window. This is controlled by a set of radio buttons with the names of attributes. When the user rolls the mouse over a frame circle, the actual document text is displayed in the small window on the right. The combination of attribute, frame, group and score manipulations allows for fast traversal of the answer space. Moving from the visual dialog to the textual dialog and back is seamless in a sense that any changes to the frame scores in one modality are immediately accessible to the user in another modality. When the "Done" button is clicked, HITIQA will either generate a new dialogue query if needed or generate the answer. We noted that users frequently return to visualization panel after the final answer has been generated, in order to verify that no important item has been overlooked. They can add and remove frames from the answer space and HITIQA will always seamlessly pickup a new dialogue or generate a new answer.

10.7 Future Work

This chapter describes a work in progress. We expect that the initial specification of content frame will evolve as we subject the initial system to more demanding evaluations. Currently, the frames are not topically specialized, and this appears the most logical next refinement, i.e., develop several (10–30) types of frames covering different classes of events, from politics to medicine to science to international economics, etc. This is expected to increase the accuracy of the dialogue as is the interactive visualization which is also under development. Answer generation will involve fusion of information on the frame level, and is currently in an initial phase of implementation.

Acknowledgments

This chapter is based on work supported by ARDA's AQUAINT Program under contract number 2002-H790400-000. We would like to thank Ralph Weischedel of Verizon/BBN for making Identifinder available for this project.

Notes

1. TREC QA is the annual Question Answering evaluation sponsored by the U.S. National Institute of Standards and Technology www.trec.nist.gov.

2. The AQUAINT corpus of news articles from a variety of sources covering 1998-2000 is available to the research community through the Linguistic Data Consortium.

3. GATE is an information extraction system developed at the University of Sheffield (Cunningham 2000).

4. MUC, funded by DARPA, involved the evaluation of information extraction systems applied to a common task.

5. We should note that selecting the right frame type for a passage is an important precondition to "understanding."

6. This option is not currently implemented in HITIQA.

Sharon G. Small is a research scientist at the ILS Institute at SUNY Albany. She is currently working on the HITIQA project, under the ARDA AQUAINT program. She can be reached at small@albany.edu.

Tomek Strzalkowski is an associate professor of computer science at the State University of New York at Albany.

Ting Liu, is a Ph.D. student in computer science at the State University of New York at Albany.

Nobuyuki Shimizu is currently finishing his doctorate degree in computer science at SUNY/Albany. His interests include machine learning and natural language understanding. He can be reached at www.nobuyuki.shimizu.name .

Boris Yamrom is a professor of mathematics and computer science at Lehman College of the City University of New York.

Chapter 11

Finding Answers to Complex Questions

Anne R. Diekema, Ozgur Yilmazel, Jiangping Chen, Sarah Harwell, Lan He,& Elizabeth D. Liddy

11.1 Introduction

While there was significant early research in question-answering (QA) in the fields of logic and linguistics (Belnap 1963, Belnap and Steel 1976), automatic QA research has been largely driven by the Text Retrieval Conference (TREC), cosponsored by the National Institute of Standards and Technology (NIST) and the Defense Advanced Research Projects Agency (DARPA). The purpose of TREC is to support research in the area of information retrieval by organizing yearly large-scale system evaluations of a variety of retrieval related tasks (tracks). Although progress has been made since QA was first added as a track at TREC in 1999 (Voorhees 2000), the research has largely converged on shorter, fact-based, general domain questions, many of whose answers can be found using a redundancy of potential answers on the Web. While these simpler approaches may work well for factoid questions, having a relatively successful QA system tailored to the TREC question-answering task (Diekema et al. 2001) does not necessarily ensure success in question-answering applications outside TREC.

As QA fully emerges as a field in its own right, a broader definition of QA is developing which encompasses a wider range of question types and answer types than those represented in the TREC QA paradigm. Important in this definition is the notion of context, i.e., who is the user?...what is the task they are attempting to accomplish when they ask a question?...what constitutes a useful answer to them?...what format should the answer be presented in?...might the most useful answer be an unsupported factoid?...or an answer-providing passage?...or the full document?...or a cell value highlighted in a table? As the field advances from the somewhat homogenous approaches initially adopted across QA systems (Hirschman and Gaizauskas 2001), the lessons learned from deployment of QA systems into real user environments are providing insights into requirements for next generation QA systems.

In this chapter, we motivate one potential type of future QA system that deals with questions more complex than simple factoid questions and which provides answers with their supporting context. Our approach is based on the issues we faced when developing and delivering a QA system to deal with real time questions in the domain of reusable launch vehicles (RLVs) within the larger field of aerospace engineering. This particular domain, the actual users of the system, and the questions asked, all demanded a change in our question-answering strategy. First, the chapter will present background on the project that provided the context and a description of the system that was deployed. Next, the chapter analyzes the questions put to the system by the users and discusses the implications that this analysis and the user evaluation study had on our design of a QA system of the future.

11.2 Background

We have developed a QA system (Liddy 2002) with funding from NASA and AT&T for use within a collaborative learning environment for undergraduate students majoring in aeronautical engineering at Cornell University and Syracuse University. The students are taking courses that are taught within the advanced interactive discovery environment for engineering education (AIDE) environment. The students are able to ask questions and quickly get answers in the midst of their hands-on collaborations within the AIDE or while working independently. The collection against which the questions are asked is comprised of textbooks, technical papers, and websites that have been pre-selected by the engineering faculty of both universities for their relevance and pedagogical value.

The students' questions are not typically simple factoid questions, but tend to be more complex and require more than bare answers, such as: "What are the changes made to the design of the Shuttle SRM since the *Challenger* accident?"

The system provides up to 20 short answers on the answer page. The student can then click on a link that provides access to the full document. In case the link is dead, or the student is otherwise having trouble accessing the page, a cached version is also provided. The system has undergone a first round of user testing, the results of which are reported later in this chapter.

11.3 System Overview

The architecture of the current Center for Natural Language Processing (CNLP) AIDE QA system (see unshaded portions in figure 11.1) consists of

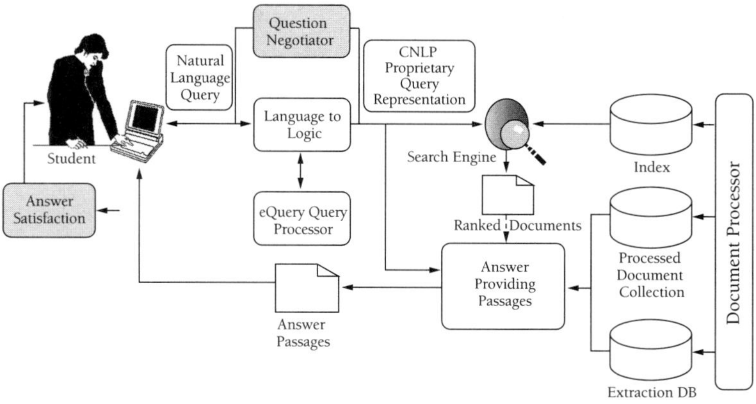

Figure 11.1. System Architecture

four modules: (1) document processing; (2) language-to-logic (L2L); (3) search engine, and (4) answer-providing passages. Given that the instructors want to vet the documents that will be used to answer the students' questions, it is possible to do document processing offline. When a user submits a question to the system, the question is first sent to the L2L module, which generates the L2L query representation and identifies the question focus. The search engine module then searches the index and returns the top 50 relevant passages. At last, the L2L query representation, question focus, and the retrieved passages are passed to the answer-providing passages module, which returns the top 20 most relevant answer passages.

Three months into the project, we conducted an informal evaluation of the system. Twenty-seven students responded. While many students expressed satisfaction with the system and the answers to their questions, half of the negative comments mentioned the need to improve the accuracy of our answers. Although our system contained vetted documents that were highly relevant to their questions, the students perceived Google as their preferred system. While preference for the system that has been in use longer than the system being introduced is a typical finding, we still wanted to better understand the causes of this evaluation result. We began to analyze: (1) the nature of the students' questions, (2) the kinds of answers the students expected and wanted, and (3) how their questions and expected answers differed from the TREC questions of our past experience.

11.4 Analysis of NASA Questions

Characteristics of NASA Questions. For our analysis, we closely examined 342 questions that were asked of the system by students in the aeronautical engineering program. This analysis found these questions to be similar in language usage to scientific writing generally. They are: Objective-personal pronouns seldom appear in the questions, and even if they do, they are not very useful in representing the semantics of the questions; Plain-the adjectives and adverbs used are necessary modifiers and are used either to convey a certain feature or to specify a level; Precise-the questions require certain prepositional phrases to convey the temporal, spatial, or conceptual domain of an occurrence.

These questions were observed to present the following linguistic features:

1. A large number of domain-specific phrases, including Proper Noun phrases, common-noun phrases, and verb phrases.

The domain-specific noun phrases and verb phrases are essential for complete understanding of the meaning of the questions. A preliminary analysis shows that these noun phrases can be classified into 49 categories and the verb phrases can be classified into 41 categories. Examples of the classes for noun phrases are system, application, reason, alternative, weight, part, structure, and risk. The classes for verb phrases include compositional, dependency, reference, tendency, examination, and alteration. These classifications of the noun and verb phrases are important for proper representation and identification of the key components of a question together with the relations among components of a question. They are also used for question focus identification, which will be discussed later.

2. There are clear linguistic patterns that can be used to categorize questions into classes. A question type classification is presented in table 11.1.
3. These questions are comparatively longer, with complex syntax containing several prepositional phrases as modifiers (see sample questions in table 11.1).

Question Type and Question Focus. To identify the focus of a question, the L2L Module first determines the question type (Chen et al. 2002). As shown in table 11.1, eight different question types emerged from the analysis of questions in this application. Some of the question types are the same as the TREC questions, but some are new types, such as yes/no questions and alternative questions. While there are a large number of Wh-questions, only a portion of them are simple factoid questions. To capture this, we divided the Wh- questions into simple and complex types. Table 11.1 also shows the distribution of the 342 questions. Each question type was identified based on lexical and/or syntactic information. As discussed above, noun phrases, verb phrases, and prepositional phrases in the questions were categorized into classes with attached semantic relations. For this classification, a domain expert was consulted for the definition of those phrases in students' questions with which our team was unfamiliar. A list of sample question focuses is shown in the third column of table 11.1. "Unknown" is assigned to questions for which the system cannot identify a proper question focus. These questions may need special processing or interaction with the user. The system approach to focus identification and phrase analysis is detailed in Diekema et al. (2001).

Type/Cat.	Definition / Frequency	Example / Sample Focus
Wh-	Questions starting with What, When, and Where. Some are simple factoid questions, others are quite complex.	*What are the downselect criteria for design of the thermal protection system for the second generation RLV?*
Wh-simple	80 (23.4%)	time, material, cost, part, position
Wh-complex	49 (14.3%)	process, comparison, feature, goal, application, method, mission, danger, design, unknown
Yes / No	Require a yes or no response, but may mask a complex inquiry.	*Doesn't the simplification of the complex honeycomb design for the thermal protection system of a Reusable Launch Vehicle jeopardize the accuracy of results?*
Yes/No	51 (14.9%)	unknown
How	Require an explanation.	*How difficult is it to mold and shape graphite-epoxies compared with alloys or ceramics that may be used for thermal protective applications?*
How	48 (14.0%)	level, manner
Quantification	Looking for a specific amount, such as cost, weight, number, maximum, volume, etc.	*What is the highest temperature the space shuttle undersurface experiences during its mission?*
Quantification	41 (12.0%)	number, money, time, weight, temperature, volume
Conditional	Inquiry indicates a condition that the answer needs to take into account. Indicated by phrases such as: *in addition to, aside from, other than, etc.*	*Aside from contact of two tiles that can be damaging, are there any other reasons why insulating tiles on Reusable Launch Vehicles must be isolated from one another?*
Conditional	12 (3.5%)	Manner, unknown
Alternative	User provides several alternatives, one of which needs to be proven true, e.g. *A or B or C.*	*Are Thermal Protection systems of spacecrafts commonly composed of one panel or a collection of smaller tiles?*
Alternative	11 (3.2%)	unknown
Why	Require an explanation.	*Why are all shear loads and twisting moments set to zero for the preliminary design phase of TPS?*
Why	16 (4.7%)	reason
Definition	Looking for a formal or semi-formal definition of an element, process, material, etc.	What is a liquid metal?
Definition	34 (10.0%)	definition

Table 11.1. NASA AIDE Question Types, Distributions, and Focuses

11.4.1 Complexity of NASA questions

NASA questions differ from TREC questions in several respects. First, a NASA question is written in real time by a student whose question can be ambiguous, or dependent upon implicit knowledge that isn't explicitly stated in the question. Real-time questions are often hurried and rife with malformed syntax and spelling errors. Due to the nature of the subject area and the fact that the QA system supports an educational endeavor, the NASA questions are complex, needing complex answers or sometimes returning information from which the answer needs to be inferred by the student once the answer-providing passages are read.

For example the simple question: "How dsose the shuttle fly?" (leaving aside its obvious typo) is so broad as to thoroughly confound even a reference librarian, let alone an automatic QA system. Does the student wish to know that the shuttle flies upside down, i.e., the physical orientation of the space shuttle as it flies? Or is the student looking for specifications related to the way the space shuttle flies during its launch, the way it orbits when it arrives in space, or its re-entry into our atmosphere? Or does the student need information about the way the shuttle navigates?

The question: "Do welding sites yield any structural weaknesses that could be a threat for failure?" is not specific, i.e., it doesn't specify where or on what the welding sites are located. We can assume (as humans who know what course the students are taking) that the welding sites are probably located on the space shuttle, but QA systems of today do not typically make this type of assumption.

For another type of question that appears simple, e.g., "At what temperatures do liquid metals typically exist?" the QA system would typically look for "liquid metals," plus a particular semantic class of verb, and a temperature (determined by the L2L focus analyzer). However, the actual answer is much more complex. Melting points depend on the type of liquid metal, with binary liquids having a narrow melting point (e.g., mercury -39 C), liquid metals made of heavier elements having a lower melting point (unspecified), and alkali metals having melting points below 200 C. This answer can be found in one document, but over several paragraphs, and it is still not the complete answer because it fails to specify the exact temperatures of liquid metals made of heavier melting points.

A fourth type of complex question requires comparison of two different elements from two different documents where the answer has to be synthesized by the actual questioner. For example: "What advantages/disadvantages does an aluminum alloy have over Ti alloy as the core for a honeycomb design?" It is unlikely that the system will find a particular sentence or paragraph that will answer this question thoroughly. This type of question requires higher order thought processes that utilize synthesis and analysis of existing information within the document collection. To assist the questioner, the system must be able to parse the question into different parts, e.g., return a passage on the strengths and weaknesses of "aluminum alloy" for honeycomb design, as well as return a passage that talks about the advantages and disadvantages of "Ti alloy" for honeycomb design. It will then be necessary for the system or the questioner to deduce an answer from the pieces of returned information.

Research has shown that "ill-formed queries" can be expected when dealing with users of any system. Reference librarians are familiar with the general patterns that can be expected when dealing with real-time questions. These problems fall into the following categories (Ross et al 2002): (1) Too broad a query; (2) Queries whose answer, even though correct, does not meet the unstated needs of the user; (3) A question that is based on a misunderstanding, either of the system or of the subject; (4) Ambiguous keywords; (5) A question based on erroneous details or memory that is wrong; and (6) A question containing a faulty assumption about the world or subject.

Any QA system that deals with real-time questions from users will need to develop strategies to deal with these types of questions successfully.

11.5 Human Query Negotiation

Reference librarians have successfully fielded ambiguous and open-ended questions for years using the reference interview to narrow a broad question and clarify an apparently unfocused question. The reference interview tries to "elicit from the user sufficient information about the real need to enable the librarian to understand it enough to begin searching" (Ross et al. 2002). The question is "clarified, narrowed down, made more detailed and contextualized" (Ross et al. 2002). Real questions from real users are often "'ill-formed' with respect to the information system; i.e., they do not match the structure of 'expectations' of the system" (Ross et al. 2002). A reference interview translates the user's query into a representation the library system can interpret correctly. Straightforward questions might be well served by the "focus" approach, but we believe the more complex questions need an alternative process to help the system interpret the question correctly. One possible solution for a QA system faced with broad or ambiguous questions is query clarification, where the system asks the questioner for more information in order to return better results. We posit that utilizing reference interview theory to provide a framework for automatic query negotiation between the system and the questioner will make system QA more accurate and satisfying.

A reference interview has three parts: questioning the questioner, locating the answer, and returning the answer to the user (Bopp and Smith 2001). The reference interview typically begins by restating the question to the user in order to allow the patron to refine his or her thoughts and to ensure that the librarian has understood the query accurately. Based on the initial question, the librarian might respond with an open-ended question. For example, when the system is faced with a question as ambiguous as "How does a shuttle fly?" it might best respond, "What part of flying a shuttle would you like to explore?" thus allowing the patron to rephrase his or her question and make it more specific.

Since we are basing the automatic query negotiation on the model of the reference interview, which is an actual conversation between librarian and user, certain modifications of the question negotiation process are in order. It is important to verify first that the question has been understood correctly. After the information need has been established, follow-up interview questions by the system might be in order to further clarify what the user is looking for. Finally, once the answer has been provided, the user should be asked whether the answer is what he or she was looking for. If not, the process begins again. The implementation of each of these stages in the interactive QA process is further detailed in section 11.6 (see figure 11.3 for a sample interaction).

11.6 Architecture of an Interactive Question Answering System

From a technical perspective, the system can be described as follows: domain specific documents are collected, preprocessed, split into sections, indexed,

User:	How are layers in TABI bonded together?
Computer:	Do you mean How are layers in TABI bonded together?
User:	Yes
Computer:	Our databases expand *TABI to tailorable advanced blanket insulation*. Please press enter if this is correct.
User:	Enter
Computer:	Are you looking for an explanation? (Computer is alerted to this possibility using the classification schema shown in table 1).
User:	Yes
Computer:	The subject of your question is *layers* in *tailorable advanced blanket insulation*. The action is *bonded*. Is this correct?
User:	Yes
Computer:	We show the following synonyms for bonded: 1 SHACKLE, chains, fetter(s), gyve(s), iron(s) 2 CONTRACT, agreement, bargain, compact, convention, covenant, pact, transaction 3 ADHERENCE 1, adhesion, cling, clinging, coherence, cohesion, stickage, sticking 4 GUARANTEE 1, bail, guaranty, security, surety, warranty Please choose the appropriate sense.
User:	4
	Computer then returns appropriate passages.
Computer:	Does this answer your question?
User:	No.
Computer:	Would you like to try again? Use the following hints in rephrasing your question (e.g., be as specific as possible, make sure the spelling is correct, think about what kind of answer you want).

Figure 11.2. Sample Interaction

and tagged offline at multiple levels of linguistic analysis the same as before. A user who comes to the system can ask a natural language question immediately, or go to the pages containing help information explaining the system's processing and then submit a question. The system will conduct spell checking, acronym expansion, and focus identification after receiving the question. Next, the query negotiation process will be activated to refine the question. The user will have total control of the negotiation process and can stop at any point. The finalized question will then go through passage retrieval and answer finding. The system will return 20 possible answer-providing passages and display them to the user. The user will be given the opportunity to evaluate these answers. The system will provide several options if the user is not satisfied, including rephrasing the question for another search attempt, asking an expert for the answer, or returning answers from other resources.

The QA system will have the following modules: (1) document processing; (2) question interpretation and negotiation which has three components: question entry/revision page, question interpreter, and question negotiator; (3) search engine; (4) answer providing passage provision; and (5) answer satisfaction. The document processing, search engine, and answer providing passage provision modules stay the same as in the current system model. Question interpretation and negotiation and answer satisfaction modules are new and are described in detail below and can be seen in figure 11.1 as the shaded modules.

11.6.1 Question Interpretation and Negotiation Module

Question Entry/Revision Page. On this page, the user may type in the question, review the rephrased question returned by the system, or go to the help page for more information. This page will be brought up at each interaction between the system and the user. The user can ask a natural-language question immediately, or go to the help pages containing a description of question techniques, an explanation of what kinds of questions can be best answered by the system, sample questions, and a collection of domain specific terms and their definitions or de-abbreviations.

Question Interpreter. This module includes spell-checking and acronym expansion. If unusual spellings are detected, the system will ask the user whether they are intended and suggest alternative spellings. At this stage the system will ask the user to pick the full form of any acronym used in the question. The original L2L module will be extended to facilitate interactive QA. In addition to identifying the question's focus, the L2L module combines linguistic features such as phrases, categorizations, and extractions to construct what we call "semantic expected-answer frames" based on an understanding of users' queries.

For those questions where the system automatically creates a semantic expected-answer frame, the goal is to establish one or more of the following extraction segments: type, frame type, and content.

The frame type indicates whether the extraction is about a named entity, an entity, or an event. This information is not only important for finding the answer, but also in the dialog between the system and the user. By showing the user what the system understands as an expected answer and soliciting feedback, a much more exact picture of the expected answer is likely to emerge. Extraction content is textual information from the document that can be found in the answer frame that identifies logical relations between the question's terms and term importance.

For example, the question: "Are thermal protection systems of spacecrafts

Answer Frame
event (frame type): composed of
agent: Thermal Protection systems
(two possible answers expected)
object: panel
object: tile
entity (frame type) : panel
    type=part
entity (frame type): tile
    type=part

Figure 11.3. Answer Frame

commonly composed of one panel or a collection of smaller tiles?" would produce an answer frame as in figure 11.3.

The semantic expected answer frames will be fed into the question negotiator component to be shown to the user and to receive feedback on the system's understanding of the question.

Question Negotiator. The question negotiator begins the conversation between the system and the user. Complex questions such as How, Why, Alternative, and Conditional questions (and to some extent Yes/No questions) require complex answers and may not be satisfied by the traditional "focus" approach. Each time the system does not understand the focus for a question, it turns to the question negotiator for help in refining the question. In each interaction, the system will carry out one of the following actions: rephrase the question, ask for more information from the user, or end the interaction to start the answer-finding process.

For some questions, the information need is easily determined by the system. The question: "What is the weight of the space shuttle?" clearly asks for a weight of a certain item. This type of question is currently recognized by our system as it is familiar with weight measures (i.e., tons, kilos, pounds) and can provide a short factual answer. It is therefore fairly straightforward to add an extra step where the system paraphrases a weight question: "Do you want to know how much the <OBJECT> weighs?"

Paraphrasing the question becomes more complicated when questions are open-ended ("Why must there be a buffer between tiles on the thermal protection system surface?"), or ambiguous ("How does an X-Ray spectrometer locate stress fields?"). For those questions that cannot be paraphrased as easily, the question needs to be processed in more detail. During this process, information about the entities, events, and relations is extracted and presented in human-readable form. The user can quickly see whether the system has understood the question. If so, the system proceeds to the next step in the reference interview.

Each type of question would require a separate query negotiation process based on its classification. For example, an alternative question would be split into two or more questions. The question: "Are Thermal Protection systems of spacecrafts commonly composed of one panel or a collection of smaller tiles?" would necessitate splitting the later part of the question into the two different parts, so that the answer documents could be retrieved using the questions, "Are TPS of spacecrafts commonly composed of one panel" and "Are TPS or spacecrafts commonly composed of a collection of smaller tiles?" The returned answer passages would be ranked for each separate question allowing the user to compare and synthesize the question alternatives.

If the L2L conversion process returns a question missing key information (e.g., no focus), the system will then ask the user to supply additional information pertaining to the question. The user will be able to alter the question as understood by the system. For example, if the system returned the wrong subject, the user can type over the incorrect subject and resubmit the question with corrections.

11.6.2 Answer Satisfaction

The user is then shown a page that allows feedback about the answers provided. If the answer is unsatisfactory, the user will be provided with three options: (1) the user can choose to return to the question entry/revision page to begin the process with an alternative question; (2) the user will be able to ask the question using the resources from the web, or; (3) the user can choose to get help from a subject specialist.

11.7 Conclusion

This chapter is based on our findings in a real-world environment where we are providing a QA system to a real set of users with particular tasks required of them. We have found that the nature of queries (examples of which are included throughout this chapter) generated by real users, as well as the breadth vs. narrowness of what constitutes a useful answer, diverges substantially from the TREC experimental setup. While the TREC approach may be required for comparative testing of multiple systems, we have found that answering complex questions in a real-time environment requires a quite different approach. We propose to provide this type of QA system capability by incorporating the well-known reference interview process from library science into the automatic question-answering process. By helping the user to formulate questions that the system can understand and to reformulate complex questions based on the system's feedback, we believe we can improve the question-answering process for such real world environments.

Acknowledgments

This research was supported by funding from National Aeronautics and Space Administration under NCC1-01-004, the State of New York, and AT&T.

Anne Diekema is a research asssistant professor at the Center for Natural Language Processing in the School of Information Studies at Syracuse University. Her research interests include cross-language information retrieval, natural language processing, and information retrieval. For further information and contact, see www.cnlp.org.

Ozgur Yilmazel is a senior software engineer at the Center for Natural Language Processing in the School of Information Studies at Syracuse University. His research interests include QA, information retrieval, and text categorization. For further information and contact, see www.cnlp.org.

Jiangping Chen is an assistant professor in the School of Library and Information Sciences at University of North Texas. Her research interests include cross language information retrieval and Chinese information processing. She can be reached at jpchen@unt.edu.

Sarah Harwell is a research analyst at the Center for Natural Language Processing in the School of Information Studies at Syracuse University. Her research interests include question-answering, text classification, and natural language processing. For further information and contact, see www.cnlp.org.

Lan He is a research analyst at the Center for Natural Language Processing in the School of Information Studies at Syracuse University. Her research interests include coreference resolution and question-answering. For further information and contact, see www. cnlp.org.

Elizabeth D. Liddy is a professor in the School of Information Studies at Syracuse University and director of its Center for Natural Language Processing. Her research interests include natural language processing, question-answering, and text mining. For further information and contact, see www.cnlp.org.

Chapter 12

Experiences From Combining Dialogue System Development With Information Extraction Techniques

Arne Jönsson, Frida Andén, Lars Degerstedt, Annika Flycht-Eriksson, Magnus Merkel, and Sara Norberg

12.1 Introduction

In the field of question answering, information extraction (IE) techniques have been used successfully for retrieving answers to fact-based questions from unstructured information (Moldovan et al. 2002, Voorhees 2002), but the QA approach has not yet reached the level of sophistication for handling connected dialogue as is present in dialogue systems tailored to background systems with structured data. Dialogue capabilities allow, for example, for more precise formulation of information requests and follow-up questions. A desired improvement to future QA systems would therefore be to incorporate advanced dialogue management in order to facilitate more natural interaction between the system and its users (Burger et al. 2001). This means that dialogue systems either have to be adapted to handling unstructured information dynamically, on the fly, as in QA systems, or be provided by structured information in database formats, derived from a text collection. The latter could be performed with information extraction techniques that pull out relevant information from textual documents and compile it to a usable database.

In this chapter we investigate how the precompiled approach works, by developing a dialogue system where information is automatically extracted from a text book which then can be accessed through natural language dialogue. This allows us to (a) use and evaluate existing methods for information extraction and dialogue, and (b) to investigate how much of the development must become shared for both enterprises as a "minimal assessment." We present one

U1:	Which birds nest in Africa
S2:	Montagu's harrier, common kestrel, Eurasian hobby, Kentish plover, Gull-billed tern, Stock dove and European Bee-eater
U3:	How large is the common kestrel
S4:	- A common kestrel is about 35 cm long from beak to tip of the tail.
	- A common kestrel's wingspan is about 80 cm.
U5:	How many eggs does it lay
S6:	A common kestrel lays approx. 3-6 eggs
U7:	Loon
S8:	Select one of the following loons: Yellow-billed loon, black-throated loon, red-throated loon and great northern loon
U9:	red-throated loon
S10:	A red-throated loon lays approx. 1-2 eggs
U11:	Where does it nest
S12:	Red-throated loons geographic nesting area: Is the one of the four loons that nest northernmost

Figure 12.1. English Translation of a BIRDQUEST Dialogue

such system, BIRDQUEST, where sharing of knowledge resources is utilized. It was implemented by an incremental approach for ontology creation, information extraction, and interactive dialogue following an iterative scheme. This can also be seen as a first step towards the more advanced goal of dialogue with dynamically extracted text information.

12.2 BirdQuest

BIRDQUEST was developed for a web site where people, watching nature programs on TV, can ask questions related to the TV program, in this case questions on Nordic birds. Figure 12.1 shows a dialogue with BIRDQUEST translated to English. U1-S2 shows a complex search in the database. In utterance U3 the user asks for the property "size" which, as seen in S4, has two different aspects, "wingspan" and "length." In U5 the user uses a pronoun to refer to the object in focus, i.e., "common kestrel," and in U7 the user implicitly refers to the same property, i.e., "eggs," but for a different bird, "loon." However, there are many loons, so BIRDQUEST asks the user to select one in S8. The user does that in U9 and the user gets a response based on the property provided in utterance U5 and the bird species in U7-U9

The BIRDQUEST application was built using the dialogue system framework MALIN, a code and application development framework that has evolved for a long time over several earlier dialogue system projects. The code base of MALIN was adapted partly by additions of new content for its information resources, such as a grammar, and partly by adjustments and pattern reuse of source code (currently Java). Application development follows a similar iterative basic scheme for any application but may vary depending on certain details depending on the domain.

For BIRDQUEST the MALIN framework is set up to function as the basis of an information processing component together with an interaction component. The information processing component takes collections of unstructured or semi-structured documents and transforms them into structured information that can be used by the interaction component during interaction with the user. The unstructured information on birds in a bird encyclopedia (Staav and Fransson 1991) was marked up as XML entities using simple patterns for tagging named entities, such as bird names, colors, measurements, etc. This information was then used as a basis for information extraction to create and fill a database with structured information. The transformation is based on information extraction techniques, and the documents are analyzed in several stages going through lexical and morphological, syntactical, and domain analysis, in each step adding more structure to the documents. The interaction component is responsible for the dialogue interaction with the user. It collaborates with the user to produce a question and accesses the structured information sources to retrieve an answer to that question.

As a basis for the processing of documents and user questions a number of knowledge sources are utilized. Some are highly specialized and only used by one or a few sub modules of a component, for example the dialogue model in the interaction component, while others are more general and used for several tasks in both components, e.g., the domain ontology.

Shared data sources are used for communication between the two components. A common agreement on lexical, grammatical, and ontological knowledge is therefore required. The important starting point for the combined information extraction/dialogue system development of BIRDQUEST was a dialogue corpus collected for this domain.

12.3 Domain Ontology

The ontology is the most complex knowledge source, and it must also be shared by both components. The term ontology is used very differently in various areas of computer science, ranging from simple taxonomies, meta data schemes, to logical theories. A general and commonly used definition, adopted here, is that "An ontology is a formal, explicit specification of a shared conceptualization" (Gruber 1993). A more practical view is to consider an ontology as "a world model used as a computational resource for solving a particular set of problems" (Mahesh and Nirenburg 1995).

The ontology in BIRDQUEST supports the interaction component's tasks of cooperatively formulating information requests together with the user and of accessing and retrieving the requested information. It should also model the type of information to be extracted from the source document and stored in the database. Since the bird encyclopedia almost exclusively contained information of a factual character with focus on objects, the BIRDQUEST ontology was restricted to modeling this type of information in terms of the objects and their properties, which were further divided in attributes and relations.

Users often have different perspectives of the domain in question compared to the concepts expressed and used in reference material written by domain experts, such as a bird encyclopedia. For instance, in the case of bird anatomy, an expert would use specialized terms to refer to different kinds of feathers, whereas a novice would use more every-day descriptions. Thus, we need to identify the different views on the ontology. For BIRDQUEST a user conceptualization was developed from a question corpus and a system conceptualization was based on the textual documents. The former captures the concepts utilized for dialogue interaction, and the latter the concepts needed to translate user requests to SQL requests.

The organization and structure of the bird encyclopedia were taken as a starting point for identification of system-oriented ontology concepts. It used the K H Voous system for dividing birds into orders, families, and species. For each of the categories information about certain properties was presented, most of which were species specific. The book was manually analyzed to identify the objects, attributes, and relations relevant for the purpose of information extraction. The analysis gave a total of 8 objects (various groupings of birds, and geographical locations), 30 attributes, and 3 relations.

The corpus used to detect user-oriented concepts consists of 264 questions about birds. It was collected by The Swedish Public Service Television Company on a web site for one of their nature programs, where the public could send in questions. The analysis of the corpus focused on questions that were deemed as within the boundaries of the application leaving out, for example, questions concerning veterinarian treatment of birds or explanations of behaviors. The analysis of the remaining questions in the corpus revealed that the users' view of the domain in most cases corresponds to the one found in the encyclopedia, but a small number of new categories and several new attributes were identified.

Taking the system-oriented conceptualization as a starting point the new categories of birds found in the question corpora were added. Allowing multiple inheritance, new links between existing categories and new categories were included. Conflicting concepts were resolved in various ways. One example is the use of the word "large" in the utterance Which is the largest bird? There is not a single corresponding concept for the word "large" in the domain ontology; instead a user ontology concept, "size," is introduced which in turn is mapped to the two domain ontology concepts: "wingspan" and "length." This mapping is domain dependent and consequently not done in the lexicon but in the ontology, as being large does not imply, for instance, having large wingspan in all domains.

The ontological knowledge was represented in two separate parts, one containing the concepts and their taxonomical relations, and one holding the facts, i.e., object instances and their taxonomical relations. With 4 new objects and 6 new attributes introduced by the analysis of the question corpus, the resulting ontology contained 12 objects, 36 attributes, and 3 relations. The factual part was then automatically generated by extraction of instances from the bird encyclopedia.

12.4 Information Extraction

The goal of the information processing component was to identify and extract the objects and properties in the text that were relevant to the user questions. This included identifying species and families, and finding different types of properties on the family level as well as on the species level. It also included finding relations in the text, like which family a species belongs to. The selection of what information to extract was guided by the ontology. The objective was to only fill the database with relevant information and ignore text segments that did not meet the needs of the users. The information processing component extracts atomic values as well as segments of text, with the purpose of providing text segments that could be provided as answers to the user. Atomic values were extracted only when the question corpus indicated that comparisons between birds would be needed. The possibility of extracting atomic values exists for all the records in the database.

Information extraction is fairly standard and broken down into several distinct stages. The first stage is tokenization and preprocessing followed by syntactic parsing of the text where functional dependencies and part-of-speech tags are obtained. Named entity recognition is the next step where the focus lies on finding the names of the species, families etc. The named entity recognizer utilizes a lexicon to identify and tag geographic sites, colors, body parts, names of species, and families, Latin names, food, etc. After NE recognition the text segments relevant to each species are identified and tagged. Patterns are then used to find and extract the relevant facts in the text. The patterns are compiled into one set of pattern instructions that is run in batch. The properties that can be extracted from the text are the properties that are leaf nodes in the ontology. After the pattern matching has taken place the results are transformed to relational database format to serve as background information in the dialogue system. The database contains two main tables, one for bird species and one for bird families.

Several difficulties were encountered when extracting information from the bird encyclopedia. The book contained varying amounts of facts about the birds; some of the species were described in detail while descriptions of other species had very little information. Also, birds were described by their most characteristic features, which led to omission of many traits. A related problem was that pictures of the birds and maps of their distribution complemented the text. Because of this, text often referred to maps and images, and left out the information that could be seen there, e.g., outside the map the Black-throated diver nests in Russia and China.

Some of the extracted features are not present in the final database. This is due to the high degree of variation in the text describing certain facts that makes them difficult to be of any use to the dialogue system. Such features are therefore ignored. To reason about the colors and shapes of body parts, for example, the ontology would have to be extended to include a representation of what body parts are meronyms to others. There are over 100 different body parts to choose from. Furthermore, for each species only the most characteristic body parts are described, seldom more than three parts, and the variation is huge among these. Colors are also often described in relation to other birds, e.g., The Blyth's Reed Warbler looks like the European Reed Warbler and the Marsh Warbler but the upper parts' brown colour is slightly grayer, and an inference tool would then need to assemble information from these different species in order to provide a complete colour description.

12.5 Dialogue and Domain Knowledge Management

The Interaction component processes utterances in five phases: linguistic analysis, pragmatic interpretation, task handling, generation and memorization. During the pragmatic interpretation phase, dialogue history and local focus are used to create a complete dialogue move from the incoming linguistically analyzed user utterance. This move is subsequently handled, during the task handling phase, either by generating a clarification initiative or by accessing and retrieving information from the BIRDQUEST information sources (the database or the domain ontology), depending on how the dialogue move is classified. Task handling results in a system utterance structure, which is on a format compatible with that of the user dialogue move, in order to facilitate later focus inheritance. During the generation phase, the system utterance is transformed into the multimedia surface format, which yields appropriate formatted textual results, images and sounds for the user interface. In the memorization phase, current user, and system moves are recorded in dialogue memory.

By analyzing the question corpus and the information text, the names and value domains of the objects and properties parameters were selected, based on the domain ontology. In reality there are many more potential types of objects and properties both in the information text and in the question corpus. The selection of objects was in some ways straightforward, since the obvious objects are birds. Other objects, like the kinds of food that are eaten by the birds, (e.g., fish), or places the birds stay, (e.g., countries they migrate to during wintertime), were not chosen mainly because there was very little or no information about these potential objects in the information text, so there would be no information about them for the system to present.

There is, however, still a point to handling the above conceptual entities of the system. Since the information is put into a relational database it is possible to make inferences about the data. Fields and records in the database can be searched and matched against a text string by using regular expressions (and/or by simple annotations of text). Texts about the birds' migration places and foods contain many objects. By including some of these and interpreting them as values they can be matched against the text fields in the database. This makes it possible to "stretch" the scope of the extracted text segments, for instance, to derive the names of the birds that migrate to a specific place or eat a specific type of food from the food text field in the database.

Using information extraction techniques means that knowledge sources can incorporate more elaborate linguistic content, such as ontological data. Consequently all dialogue capabilities of BIRDQUEST must be adjusted to handle and exploit such resources in its various phases and steps of execution. For pragmatic interpretation, this amounts to handling properties of various levels of ontological abstraction. For domain knowledge source management it amounts to handling both information made explicit in the data model, and derived results. For user dialogue acts that are still under-specified after contextual data has been added, ontological information and data models help to give valuable requests for more information and point out what the system can handle.

Since the ontology incorporates both user- and system-derived concepts, it plays a crucial role in bridging the terminology of user requests and the extracted information in the database. Users are often too vague in their requests and the ontology can then be used to support clarifications and mappings to system concepts. In BIRDQUEST three types of under-specified requests occur. As illustrated by U7-S8 in figure 12.1 objects can be under-specified, for example, the bird family "Loon," refers to a number of different species of bird. In this case information about which species belong to the given family is gathered from the part of the ontology that contains facts, and the user is asked to choose one of them. Properties can also be too vague, i.e., the question "What does it look like?" in which the user must specify if the property "Appearance" should be "Plumage" or "Size." The third type concerns mappings of vague properties to ones suitable for database access, as illustrated by U3-S4 in figure 12.1 where the sub-properties to "Size" are collected from the ontology in order to access and collect the values from the database.

	No of utterances	Percentage of user utterances
Interpretable Requests	189	37%
Co-operative CR Responses	55	11%
Uncooperative CR Responses	11	2%
Out of scope	121	23%
Misinterpreted	141	27%

Table 12.1. User Utterances

12.6 User Evaluation of BIRDQUEST

BIRDQUEST is intended to be used by casual users without previous experience of dialogue systems or extensive knowledge of birds. The system was therefore evaluated in a walk-up and use situation similar to a real use situation during a day when the public was invited to the university. We had six machines running BIRDQUEST during 2 hours and 30 minutes and collected dialogues from 27 users. They received minimal instructions in advance; they were only told that the system can answer questions on Nordic birds, that it understands Swedish, and that the dialogue would be recorded. The resulting corpus consisting of 27 dialogues have a total number of 518 user utterances, with a mean of 19 for each user. However, with individual differences, e.g., three users were posing more than 40 utterances to the system and three users were posing less than 5.

The dialogues were tagged in order to provide statistics over successful and problematic information exchanges (Flycht-Eriksson and Jönsson 2003).

The user utterances are categorized in table 12.1 and the categorization of responses from BIRDQUEST is presented in table 12.2. Table 12.1 shows that approximately half of the users' utterances (48%) were involved in successful information exchanges where the user initiated an information request or answered a clarification request from the system. We also see that 25% of the users' utterances are erroneous in some way and that BIRDQUEST failed on 27% of the utterances.

From table 12.2 we see that BIRDQUEST presented 180 successful responses. A successful response is a response where BIRDQUEST presents information found in the database. A response where the bird encyclopedia does not include the information and BIRDQUEST responds, e.g., information on wingspan is missing for magpie, is also considered successful. The reason being that BIRDQUEST successfully accessed the database and presented whatever information was there, including cases where there was no information in the database. Among the 180 there are 55 such responses, so they are not rare, and it shows one of the many interesting problems we encountered in the de-

	No of utterances	Percentage of system utterances
Successful response	180	35%
Clarification request	70	13%
Incorrect response	15	3%
Incorrect focus	16	3%
Error message	240	46%

Table 12.2. System Utterances

velopment of a dialogue system based on information extraction from a textbook.

As discussed in the previous section the ontology was used for clarifications. The first type of clarification, where the object needs to be specialized, was initiated in 31 of 180 user requests for information. The second type regarding vague user properties occurred in 28 instances. Finally, mapping of vague properties to ones suitable for database access was carried out in 64 cases. There were also five cases in which the user requested information about birds of the categories "small birds," "migratory birds," and "sedentary birds," which had not been implemented and could therefore not be handled. The high number of clarifications and mapping of properties for database access shows the usefulness of the domain ontology. For further details on the evaluation see (Flycht-Eriksson and Jönsson 2003).

12.7 Evaluation of the Development Process

The BIRDQUEST ontology and interaction component have been developed iteratively, where running prototype systems have been incrementally extended with more dialogue capabilities following well established steps (Degerstedt and Jönsson 2001). The collected dialogue corpus has been the driving force for the iterative work flow. Increments of dialogue functionality have been made simultaneously to both knowledge and data resources, such as the grammars and ontology, and source code functionality of the dialogue system. The information extraction component has been used in parallel to extend, and at some points alter, the database content of the final system.

We have interviewed five developers of BIRDQUEST about the feasibility of the suggested pre-compiled approach. Three of the developers have been interviewed about source code development and information source engineering, one developer about ontological resource development, and one developer concerning information processing. The interviews showed that both work with the information processing component and the interaction component became closely time-dependent on the design of the ontology. Several interviews indicated that one would like to have the ontology done before the remaining parts, but that in practice the dependencies became iterative in nature. Thus, for a domain where a suitable ontology already exists, the rest of the development could be substantially more efficient.

The development of the ontology was in itself relatively straightforward. However, the overlap between the ontology and the lexicon was a source of inconsistency. Several developers expressed that modeling the domain in terms of objects and properties was not straight-forward in practice. Deciding whether an entity is an object or a property must facilitate both management of focal inheritance and the SQL data lookup. As a consequence, a large part of the practical development work was concerned with making the SQL templates robust and complete with respect to possible user dialogue moves. A suggested improvement concerned details of the internal representation of the dialogue moves, in order to facilitate this. Relational expressions, e.g., requests concerning comparisons between different bird species, were also perceived as hard to represent within the current framework. It was difficult to change the knowledge representation due to its dependencies between information extraction, the interaction component, and the ontology.

For the interaction component, most of the development effort was on task handling. This was the phase most closely related to the ontology and the domain. Consequently less work was on pragmatic interpretation. However, these two phases were perceived by the developers to be closely related in practice, and the pragmatic interpretation tended to depend on prior work of the task handling: "decide how to handle complete user requests before handling ones that arise through dialogue." This made the interaction component unstable at times, and decreased the system's performance to some extent.

The iterative dependencies between the two interdependent architectural components also made testing crucial. In the current implementation, testing was done manually, using simple handwritten test code at best. Testing for backwards compatibility had to be done both with respect to context of dialogue and conceptual taxonomy. Newly added functionality easily re-introduced faults in previously working code, in one of these dimensions. This was also perceived as originating from the iterative strategy of how to extend the system incrementally by adding dialogue abilities based on a dialogue corpus.

To sum up, the design of the database access, model, and contents becomes an elaborate endeavor when information extraction is introduced for interaction with dialogue. Thus, development related to the database became more iterative in nature, which is an overhead that one often tries to avoid due to its inherent complexity. This also suggests one of the limitations for a pre-compiled approach—at some point manual incremental changes of the database simply make adjustments of the interaction component a much too expensive enterprise, in terms of both man hours and maintenance of system correctness. At that point one should probably search for an alternative or complementary method. But in cases where the domain, or parts of it, is fixed and ontological structures exist in advance of the project, the pre-compiled approach will work effectively.

12.8 Summary

We have presented BIRDQUEST, a system that utilizes dialogue interaction to help users formulate requests for information that has been automatically extracted from a text book. Results from an evaluation of BIRDQUEST showed that it is possible to develop such a system, and that users get a fair amount of information that they would not have been able to get if the system had not allowed for connected dialogue and used a domain ontology. The evaluation also revealed a number of issues for further development of this type of systems. A more fine-grained ontology with a more complex representation would allow for more inferences and detect information with more details. This is crucial both for the information extraction component and dialogue management. Combining general and core ontologies efficiently with domain ontologies is also important for rapid application development.

More knowledge on the relationship between question types and answer types can guide the information extraction and aid the dialogue management (cf. Zukerman and Horvitz 2001). The problem of collecting user questions that will guide the design of dialogue systems must, however, be dealt with. Factoid questions are relatively easy to collect from real usage and reapply in QA systems. Information systems with dialogue capabilities require empirical data containing connected dialogue.

Moving between domains and tasks require customization, in most cases more than you want. Better tools to make the process of building extraction patterns more efficient must be developed. Several researchers have pointed this out within the IE framework (cf. Yangarber and Grishman 1997), but in advanced QA and dialogue systems, the problem is to identify the user tasks in relation to the document base. Distilling important user tasks from a question corpus is complicated. And yet the users and the texts are the ones that set the limits and possibilities of the system.

BIRDQUEST was developed for a closed domain; future research includes the move to multi domain and then to open domain applications. It is still very much an open question as to what extent the techniques for IE, shared knowledge sources, and dialogue management presented in this article can be applied to such applications. An interesting mixed approach is to use a simpler information extraction technique as fallback strategy when the precompiled approach fails.

Acknowledgement

This research is financed by Vinnova, Swedish Agency for Innovation Systems and SITI, The Swedish Research Institute for Information Technology. We are indebted to anonymous reviewers for valuable suggestions for improvement of the article.

Arne Jönsson is an associate professor of computer science at Linköping University, Sweden, specializing in design and development of multimodal dialogue systems. He can be reached at www.ida.liu.se/~arnjo.

Frida Andén is a research assistant at the Santa Anna IT Research Institute in Linköping, Sweden.

Lars Degerstedt is a research engineer in the Department of Computer and Information Science, Linköping University.

Annika Flycht-Eriksson is a graduate student in the Department of Computer and Information Science, Linköping University.

Magnus Merkel is an assistant professor of computational linguistics at Linköping University, Sweden. His research interests include translation tools, corpus linguistics and information extraction. He can be reached at www.ida.liu.se/~magme.

Sara Norberg is a research assistant at the Santa Anna IT Research Institute in Linköping, Sweden.

Section Five

Reuse

The best of TREC systems are able to answer factual questions, analogous to trivia questions, 70% of the time, while searching a million newswire documents. In TREC, two types of reuse have been addressed: redundant questions and context processing. The former case is exemplified by the TREC-9 "same question, different wording" (e.g., recognizing that "What dates are the Sydney Olympics on?" and "What are the dates of the Summer Olympics in Sydney?" are equivalent). The context processing case (TREC-10 Context) consists of resolving co-reference or ellipsis in sequences of questions such as: "What type of vessel was the Varyag?" "In what facility was it constructed?", "In what country is this facility located?" Since exact or similar questions will likely reoccur, reuse of previous solutions promises to be both economical and help ensure answer consistency. Moreover, as these chapters illustrate, reuse can occur both in question and answer. The two chapters in this section present, in a complementary fashion, both a broad study of question answering together with a focused system that reuses popular frequently ask question sites.

In the first chapter, the team of Marc Light (University of Iowa/MITRE), Abraham Ittycheriah (IBM T. J. Watson), Andrew Latto (Gensym), and Nancy McCraken (Syracuse University) report eleven categories of reuse that were found in user-generated question sets. Building a corpus of reuse examples, the authors consider what types of "reuse" exist and how a system might capitalize on various reuse opportunities.

Reuse can occur both in the case where a single user asks a series of questions or multiple users ask questions about same topic. The authors generated at several sites question sets to exercise these situations. For example, at IBM, twenty-one topics were created on current newsworthy events and 147 questions were generated to answer a notional research report. Syracuse University graduate students and research staff generated 10 question/answer sequences on any research topic they desired. Question sequences were developed incrementally, not a priori, resulting in 74 total questions on 8 single user topics. Finally, researchers at MITRE created multiple user question/answer sets. A corpus of question answers was then created including the Syracuse topics plus more from a million entry log of questions from a popular web keyword search

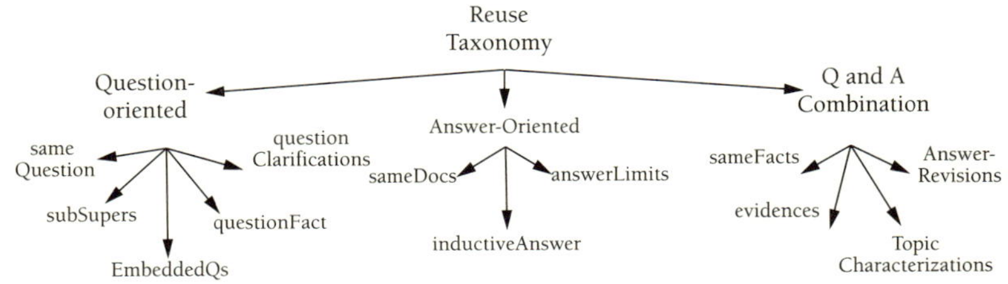

engine. This resulted in over 2000 questions for 15 topics, averaging 154 questions per topic with a range from 8-631 questions per topic.

The graph on this page illustrates the three broad categories of identified question-answering reuse. Question-oriented reuse includes variations of the same question (e.g., "Which team won the Stanley Cup in 1994?" and "Who won the Stanley Cup playoffs in 1994?"). A second type are questions that are part of another as in "When does the summer 2000 Olympics start?" and "When are the Summer 2000 Olympics?", the later which encompasses the former. A third type has questions embedded. For example the answer to "How much calcium should an adult woman get in her diet?" is required or embedded in the question "How much Vitamin D do you need to absorb the recommended amount of calcium?" Similarly, it is useful to know what the dietary sources of calcium are before finding out how they fit into an overall diet. A fourth type of question reuse is question facts as in "How many awards did "Gone with the Wind" win?" or "Who starred in gone with the wind?" from which we can learn that the object "Gone with the Wind" has awards and stars in it. Finally, question clarification reuse occurs when a second question clarifies terminology or meaning of the first as in the sequence "Who poses the biggest threat to the United States?" followed by "What countries are developing weapons of mass destruction?" in which the second question defines the threat mentioned in the first.

A second general class of reuse occurs with answers, which might come from the same document, be induced from the knowledge of previous questions and answers, or be limited by the answer to a previous question. A third general class of reuse occurs with combinations of questions and answers, such as when the same fact is needed to answer two different questions, when answers to one question might provide evidence for or against answers to another question, when topics identified in preceeding questions can assist in the interpretation of subsequent questions, and when an earlier answer to a question needs to be revised based on an answer to a subsequent question.

The authors conclude by discussing strategies for implementing reuse. These include keep a cache of previous questions and answers (analogous to an FAQ, but perhaps more richly indexed), building topic detection and tracking for question sets, and building classifiers that take the current question and a previous question on the same topic and assigns a reuse category to the pair (most likely the NULL category, but, for example, a classifier could be built to identitify sameQuestions). They also suggest engaging the user in assisting the reuse process and indicate the need to assess reuse capabilities by evaluating QA systems with and without them turned on.

Whereas the first chapter in this section addresses the taxonomy of question answer reuse, the second chapter by Noriko Tomuro and Steven L. Lytinen (DePaul University) focuses exclusively on learning with frequently asked question (FAQ) files. They argue that FAQ data is found data, with 2,490 internet FAQs. With effective question paraphrase matching, it is possible to directly retrieve answers. Somewhat unexpectedly, their analysis showed that over 60% of questions in FAQs and in AskJeeves are open ended Q's (e.g., how, why, y/n questions) rather than closed or factoid questions.

The authors propose the FAQFinder system. It performs Q-to-Q matching and Q-to-A-matching. Matching is done with vector term similarity, term coverage, semantic similarity counting WordNet hypernym/hyponym links, and question type similarity (using C5.0). The combination of these metrics outperforms any individual metric, yielding a matching accuracy of 85%. The author's error analysis illustrates Q-to-Q matching errors fall into difficult paraphrases (e.g., semantically related lexemes with differing parts of speech such as "die" and "fatal") and unexpected matches. In the later, for example, the questions are dissimilar but the answer is nevertheless in the response to the question.

For Q-to-A matching, the good and bad news is that answers are longer than questions. Therefore, there is more content to match and more to search for an answer. Conventional factoid QA techniques that search for items such as named entities (e.g., people, organizations, locations, time, money), attributes (e.g., age, time) or relations, do not always work with the more frequent open ended answers. New techniques are required to include "meta-linguistic features" such as the number and style of paragraphs and domain independent words (e.g., "step," "first," "because"). The authors analyzed 253 randomly selected Q and A pairs from various FAQ files which included 123 procedure or "how-to" Q and As. They constructed a decision tree using C5.0 from the 253 PRC answers including six key features: the number of paragraphs, sentences, imperative sentence, procedural key words such as "step", "way", or "first", non-procedural words such as "because," "yes," "no," and occurrences of "if." The resulting classification accuracy was 90.1%.

The authors conclude by outlining some key areas from research including anaphora and ellipsis, which are heavily used in 20% of the FAQ files. Passage retrieval research is also needed to extract the relevant parts of FAQs. Finally, techniques for answer formulation might also be induced from expert answers.

Chapter 13

Reuse in Question Answering: A Preliminary Study

Marc Light, Abraham Ittycheriah, Andrew Latto, and Nancy McCracken

13.1 Introduction

Current information retrieval systems and search engines help users find documents that are relevant to their needs, but leave it to the user to extract the useful information in those documents. In particular, users often have questions for which they would like answers, not documents. QA systems aim to allow users to ask questions such as "Which terrorist organizations have issued threats on U.S. embassies this year?" and to receive succinct answers. Many initial end-to-end systems have been built and evaluated as part of the TREC question answering track (Voorhees and Tice 1999; Voorhees and Harmon 2000). The best systems are able to answer factual questions, similar in style to trivia questions, 70% of the time, while searching a million newswire documents.

Although answering isolated factual questions against newswire text is useful in many user scenarios, there are numerous improvements that could increase the impact of the technology. This book presents many such variations of the generic question answering theme. Here we focus on the idea that if a QA system accumulates questions, answers, and other auxiliary information, this information could then be "reused" to enable the system to better answer future questions. In this way, a system could duplicate a human's ability to gain knowledge in an area as she or he answers questions. However, it was not immediately clear how to implement this ability in a general way. This chapter presents the results of an initial investigation of "reuse" in question answering. Specifically, it addresses two issues: what types of "reuse" exist and how might a system capitalize on the different reuse opportunities? Thus, the contribution of this chapter is that it provides a classification of the possible relationships between questions that provide reuse opportunities, and it provides a corpus of examples.

Our method of study includes collecting and analyzing examples of reuse possibilities in real-world question-answering scenarios. In particular this chapter describes a corpus of questions, the *reuse corpus*, that the authors collected. (The reuse corpus is freely available from the authors.) Using this corpus, we found eleven categories of reuse. In addition, we explored (without actual implementations) different ways systems could operationalize reuse.

Certainly, many of the reuse categories seem very difficult to implement. We did not focus exclusively on "easy" reuse examples but instead we looked into all examples of reuse a human might be able to handle. Many tasks in question answering require AI-complete technology for perfect performance. However, many of these same tasks can be performed with usable performance using simple techniques. Finally, we did not address the difficult problem of what happens when previous information was or has become incorrect. The topic of reliability of answers is a separate though crucial research topic with respect to reuse.

Before going any further, let us look at an example. Consider a scenario where a number of users are asking questions about anthrax, a topic that was previously unexplored by the user base and the QA system's developers. A sequence of questions and document excerpts might be as follows:

Q1: What are some medicines that treat anthrax?
D1: The FDA has approved Cipro (ciprofloxacin), tetracyclines including doxycycline, and penicillins to treat anthrax. (from www.medlineplus.com)

Q2: What are some of the side effects of anthrax medicines?
D2: *Physician's Desk Reference* reports that of 2,799 patients who took Cipro during clinical investigations, 16.5 percent had adverse reactions that were possibly or probably related to the drug. The most frequently reported reactions; nausea, diarrhea, vomiting, abdominal discomfort, headache, restlessness, rashes. (from www.medlineplus.com)

Q3: Who manufactures anthrax medicine?
D3: Cipro is produced in the U.S. by the German pharmaceutical company Bayer AG. (constructed)[1]

This sequence might be from a single user or from different users. The important feature of these question-passage pairs is that Q2 and Q3 should be easier to answer if the system can make use of the answer to Q1. For example, knowing that Cipro is a medicine and that it is used to treat anthrax should help the system find information about the side effects of anthrax medicines. Note that D2 and D3 do not mention anthrax.[2]

It is useful at this point to contrast reuse with two topics that have recently received attention in the question answering community: simple context processing and redundant questions.

Redundant questions were explored in TREC-9 where a number of questions were reformulated and included in the test set. When detection of a reformulated question is possible, the information obtained in answering the previous question can be applied, as we discuss in this chapter. The Falcon system

(Harabagiu et al. 2000) performed well on these reformulated questions. This idea has been the basis of many help-desk applications such as askJeeves (ask.com), which use a base of frequently asked questions (FAQs) to find answers to the same question. However, our investigation explores a much wider variety of ways in which there is information reuse in the question answering process.

Context processing was explored, in a preliminary fashion, by the TREC-10 QA context subtrack. This track contained sequences of questions in which the QA system needed to resolve anaphora and coreference in general, and ellipses. See Harabagiu et al. (2001) for a description of a system designed for this task. Such information is useful for reuse but does not subsume it. For example, *cipro* and *penicillin* are not coreferential with anthrax medicines in the examples above.

A difference with the TREC evaluations and the research presented here is that this research characterizes different kinds of "reuse" and explores the issue by collecting a database of different reuse aspects, as well as exploring a large corpus of questions to discover opportunities for "reuse." However, methods discovered in the TREC systems, such as caching questions and measuring question similarity, will play a role in the implementation of some types of reuse discussed here.

While our investigation of reuse is broader than the TREC subtracks mentioned above, the general topic of reusing information is broader still. Case-based reasoning (CBR) addresses the issue of reusing information by storing knowledge in cases which are added to and updated during the operation of the system. In general CBR solves problems by storing a number of cases, which gives problem solving knowledge at an operational level (Kolodner 1993). For each problem instance, an index of problem types is used to retrieve appropriate cases, and adaptation strategies are used to apply the case to find a solution. Evaluation and repair are then used to update the store of cases so that the CBR system becomes more competent over time. CBR can be applied to question answering where the cases are strategies to answer types of questions, as in the FAQFinder system (Burke et al. 1997). CBR has been adapted to other textual applications such as the document retrieval system (Lenz et al. 1998).

Knowledge-based QA systems address one aspect of the reusing of information by allowing the QA system to store and retrieve information other than just the text documents. In the question answering system of Clark et al. (1999), a knowledge base is used to augment the information in the text documents and to fill in an answer schema. In the Webnotator system of Katz et al. (2001), the START QA system is augmented by allowing users to add information to a knowledge base that can later be used for finding answers.

Although the ultimate goal is to implement a module that could handle different types of reuse, the goal of our research was to take the first step in this direction. We attempted to introduce and demarcate the topic of reuse in question answering, develop a set of categories of reuse, find examples of these categories of reuse, sketch possible implementation and evaluation methods for reuse, and make recommendations with respect to future work on reuse.

13.2 Constructing the Reuse Corpus

We imagined two situations where reuse would be possible: a single user asked a series of questions all about a particular topic; or many users, possibly at different times and places, ask questions about a particular topic. Common to both situations is the fact that there are sets of single topic questions where questions belong to a set by virtue of their topic. The first questions are from single user sets where a single user asked and ultimately answered a sequence of questions while performing a particular information gathering task. One example is finding information on calcium needed in a woman's diet. Note that such question sets are really question answer sequences. The second type of question set contains questions from multiple users where the users may be unaware that the other users interested in the topic exist or that they are also asking the system questions. Continuing the example above, a search for *calcium* was performed on questions collected from a web search engine log.

At the outset, we were unsure how to get realistic question sets that might contain reuse opportunities. There are many ways that one could collect both single user and multiple user sets. For the single user question sets IBM and Syracuse devised two different methods of collections and performed their methods independently. Because of the availability of a web search engine log, MITRE chose to collect the sets by doing keyword searches on this log.

At IBM, 21 topics were chosen to represent current newsworthy events. The question sequences were generated by an independent person and one of the co-authors. The directions for generating these questions were to write questions whose answers might enable writing a research report on the topic. One hundred forty-seven questions were generated in this manner and then answers were searched for on the internet using a common search engine. The following are the topics used: challenger space craft, choosing between Mac and PC, Columbine, Dave Koresh, Death Penalty, Ebay, End of Apartheid, global warming, human cloning, Martha Stewart corporation, NAFTA, pathfinder on Mars, modern terrorism, the Brady Bill, the collapse of the Soviet Union, Enron, Israeli-Palestinian conflict, Timothy McVeigh, the Taliban, World Trade Center, the World Wide Web.

At Syracuse, graduate students and research staff assisted in generating question sequences. The goal was for each of 10 people to generate a sequence of 10 questions and answers on an information gathering task of interest to them. The problem was stated to them in terms of researching a topic of interest or in accomplishing some task. In the absence of a QA system, each person emulated such a system by using a search engine, or other web searching techniques, to first find documents that contained the answer to the question and then to find the answer in a document. The URL was recorded for each answer document, where feasible. The subjects were also instructed not to generate the question sequence in advance, but to generate questions as they went, either from their own knowledge or from reading answer documents from earlier questions. The resulting questions were usually just one sentence without complex structure. Many questions had simple factual answers, but others asked about more complex issues. And some question sequences consisted almost entirely of questions that were too general for the short answer format, e.g., "How do I build a manipulable arm for a robot?" The more general sequences were eliminated[3] to obtain 74 total questions on 8 single user topics. The Syracuse single user topics were: heel pain, calcium, ice cream, poetry, Saskatoon (Saskatchewan, Canada), special education, and Washington, D.C.

The multiple users sets were collected at MITRE. The topics included Syracuse's single user topics and a number of additional topics: Tiger Woods, digital cameras, Tupac Shakur, the Oscars, the Stanley Cup, and the 2000 Summer Olympics. The questions came from a popular web keyword search engine during the summer of 2000. Over many weeks, queries to the search engine were logged.[4] A regular expression was used to find questions in the log that looked for *who, whom, what, when, where, why, how,* and *which* anywhere in the line or queries starting with *is, name, show,* or *find me.* Over a million questions were extracted. This question corpus was then searched using relevant keywords for the topics, primarily the topic names themselves. There were over 2,000 questions for the 15 topics. Falcons had the least with 8 questions, and poetry had the most with 631. The average was 154.

The questions from these three sources were then placed in a standard format and combined to form the Reuse Corpus. Each question was given a unique identifier and this identifier is given in the examples below prefixed by I. Instances of reuse categories were then annotated. We both analyzed a portion of the corpus one question at a time, looking for instances of any sort of reuse opportunity and we scanned the questions with a particular category of reuse in mind. Although we found a number of instances of the different categories, we are far from finishing a complete analysis of the corpus.

13.3 Reuse Categories

To review: a reuse opportunity occurs when the fact that a QA system has processed one question can allow the system to provide improved subsequent performance. This possibility is dependent on the relationship between the original and the subsequent questions asked of the system. We have attempted to provide a classification of the possible relationships between questions that provide reuse opportunities. We first break these relationships down into three broad clusters. The first cluster consists of those reuse opportunities that only require the system to track the questions it is asked. The second cluster involves those questions in which the reuse opportunity is apparent merely from looking at the answers to the questions. A third cluster consists of those reuse categories where both the questions and answers must be examined in order to see the reuse possibilities. Each of these three clusters is then further broken down into categories.

13.4 Question-Oriented Cluster

The most straightforward reuse category, *sameQuestions,* occurs when multiple users of a QA system ask the same question. The question may be asked in an identical form, or in a reformulation which can potentially be recognized by the system as having the same semantic content. What we refer to as the sameQuestions reuse category is essentially the same as question reformulation in TREC-9. Two examples from our annotated corpus are given below:

Q(I:235): What countries have qualified in soccer for the 2000 Olympics
Q(I:237): What countries will compete in soccer at the Olympics in 2000?
Q(I: 84): What is the moral status of human cloning?
Q(I: 87): What are the ethical issues for human cloning?

Another relatively simple opportunity for reuse, *subSuperQuestions,* occurs when the information requested by one question is a subset of the information asked for in another. If the question asking for the smaller quantity of information is encountered first, the system already has a partial answer for the question asking for more information. If the question asking for the larger quantity of information is asked first, and this reuse opportunity is recognized by the system, the performance benefit is even greater.

Q(I: 328: How to wrap an achilles tendon to relieve pain?
Q(I: 327): How do I treat a sore achilles tendon?
Q(I: 98: Who are the Taliban
Q(I: 100: What is the Taliban's religious background ?

In the first pair above, a correct answer to the first question is a component of an answer to the second question, but does not provide a complete answer, since there may be other ways to treat a sore achilles tendon other than wrapping. In the second pair, a description of the Taliban's religious background provides a partial, but not a complete, description of who the Taliban is.

Another type of reuse, *embeddedQuestions,* was discussed in the introduction: knowing that cipro and penicillin are anthrax medicines allows a system to more effectively find answers to questions about the side effects and manufacturers of these medicines. If question Q2 were to be asked in isolation, a human question answerer is likely to first try to figure out what medicines treat anthrax, i.e., question Q1. Let us consider two more examples. In question I:12, knowing how much calcium is recommended could play a role in finding out how much Vitamin D is needed. Similarly, in question I:18, it is useful to know what the dietary sources of calcium are before one tries to find out how they fit into an overall diet.

Q(I: 11): How much calcium should an adult woman get in her diet
Q(I: 12): How much Vitamin D do you need in order to absorb the recommended calcium
Q(I: 15: What are good dietary sources of calcium
Q(I: 18: How do the calcium sources fit into the overall diet?

The relation between questions often involves a pair of noun phrases. For example, *anthrax medicines, recommended calcium amount,* and *calcium sources* are normalized forms of a noun phrase in their respective question pairs. The relation involves coreference but recognizing the coreference is just the beginning. A system could use the answer to the "embedded" question, e.g., question I:11 and I:15, in order to produce better answers to I:12 and I:18 respectively. For example it may be written in some document that you need a milligram of Vitamin D for every gram of calcium. If you know that you need 10 grams of calcium each day, then you could deduce that you need 10 milligrams of vitamin D. The point is that *recommended calcium* in I:12 refers, in some sense, to the answer to I:11. Similarly, *calcium sources* refers to the answer of I:15.[5] In contrast, noticing the coreference relation is enough for processing TREC-10 context questions:

Q(I: CTX7a):What type of vessel was the modern *Varyag?*
Q(I: CTX7b): In what facility was *it* constructed?
Q(I: CTX7c):In what country is *this facility* located?
Q(I: CTX7e):How many aircraft was *it* designed to carry?

In the *questionFacts* category, the questions themselves contain information that can be useful for answering later questions. For example, the manufacturer of Tiger Woods' ball can be extracted from I:2014 and this might be useful for answering I:2019.

Q(I: 2014): What's the name of the Nike golf ball Tiger Woods uses
Q(I: 2019): What golf ball did tiger woods use in the us open

Such information may also be less direct. For example, the quotes in the first question below indicate that *Gone with the Wind* is a title. This information might be useful when trying to find answers to the second question.

Q: How many awards did "*Gone with the Wind*" win?
Q: Who starred in gone with the wind?

Question answering systems often have trouble answering vague and unclear questions. This difficulty is exacerbated by always attempting to answer questions in isolation, rather than making use of reuse opportunities by examining related questions. The content of these related questions, even if they are asked by different users of the QA system, can provide useful data that clarifies for the system the intended meaning of the vague or unclear question. We refer to this category of reuse as *questionClarifications*. Consider the pair of questions below. In the first, there are many categories of possible threats, and the question answering system may not understand what sort of threat is being discussed. In addition, the use of the word *who* may mislead a naïve system into restricting its search to individual people, rather than countries and organizations, that pose a threat to the United States. However from the second question, the system could infer that weapons of mass destruction were an important category of threat to consider, and that countries as well as individuals should be considered as possible answers.

Q(I: 80): Who poses the biggest threat to the United States ?
Q(I: 81): What countries are developing weapons of mass destruction ?

13.4.1 Answer-Oriented Clusters

The questions in the type of reuse, *sameDocuments*, are related because they could be answered by one document. These questions occur in both the question sequences and in the multi-user questions where questions in one topic area could be answered by a document discussing various aspects of this topic. This type of reuse has an obvious operational realization: save a core pool of documents (or knowledge base of information obtained by processing those documents) on particular topics.

In the Reuse Corpus, the occurrence of using the same documents to answer two or more questions was so ubiquitous that we only annotated a few of these instances of reuse. One specific example is the question sequence topic of heel pain; there are three questions specifically about Achilles tendonitis. It is common for a web document on medical conditions to define the condition, give the causes and symptoms, and give recommended treatments.

Q(I: 3): What is achilles tendonitis
A: Inflammation of the Achilles tendon

Q(I: 4): What are the causes of achilles tendonitis
A: Excessive running or jumping especially without proper stretching and strengthening are the most common causes of Achilles tendonitis. Uphill running in particular can cause this condition

Q(I: 5): How can achilles tendonitis be treated
A: (Answer is too long to be given here.)

A series of questions about a particular event often provide *sameDocuments* examples. For example, often a news article will summarize many facts about the event. The questions below are all answered by the following excerpt from a news story from www.thedailycamera.com.

Q(I: 136): Where is Columbine High School?
A: Littleton, CO

Q(I: 137): When and what happened at Columbine ?

A: Two students walked into the school at 11:15 a.m. and fired shots from a multi-gun arsenal and lobbed homemade bombs throughout the school

Q(I: 139): How many people died ?
A: Twelve students and a teacher

"On April 20, 1999, two students walked non-chalantly into Columbine High School at 11:15 a.m. and fired shots from a multi-gun arsenal and lobbed homemade bombs throughout the school. At the end of the rampage, 12 students, one teacher and the gunmen were dead. The following articles, photos, audio clips and polls recount the events of that day as well as the recovery of the wounded and the remembrance of the victims. Below, are articles from the first five days after the shooting. At right, key stories are divided into certain issues surrounding the tragedy."

In the *inductiveAnswers* type of reuse, the knowledge of previous questions and answers allows the answer to a new question to be induced. In some cases, parts of the answer can be induced and in others it may just be noted that the answer is similar to previous ones. In either case, the answer is to be considered a hypothesis that must be checked. Operationally, this may enable the system to find answers faster or to find better answers than a more direct answer. In the questions below, if a system has found the answer to any one of the questions to be the manufacturer Titleist, then it could guess that the manufacturer of the other types of golf clubs is the same.

Q(I: 2011): What irons does tiger woods use?
A: Titleist

Q(I: 2012): what loft one wood does tiger woods use?
A: Titleist

Q(I: 2013): what putter does Tiger Woods use?
A: Titleist

Another category of reuse, *answerLimits,* occurs when the answer to a question provides information that limits the possible answers to a second question. This can aid the system in searching for an answer to the second question.

Q(I:53): What is the weather like in Saskatoon, especially in the winter?
A: Generally not too much precipitation, and it can get very cold in the winter.

Q(I: 54): What is there to do outdoors in Saskatoon?

The answer to the first question would provide the useful information that possible answers to the second question might well include snow skiing, but would be very unlikely to include water skiing. This example is also notable in that it shows that the more common-sense real-world knowledge is possessed by a QA system, the more opportunities for reuse it will be able to recognize and make use of. Only a system that had some understanding of the appropriate temperatures for various real-world activities would be capable of recognizing this particular example of reuse opportunity.

13.4.2 Question and Answer Combination Clusters

The following types of reuse require caching both questions and answers to previous questions.

The *sameFacts* type occurs when the same fact is needed to answer two different questions, even though it is not apparent that the questions are not asking for the same information until at least one of them has been answered. Consider the questions below. The single fact "Cipro cures anthrax" provides an answer to both questions, so a system that has answered one of these two questions, and recorded this fact, can answer the second question with no further processing.

Q: What medicines cure anthrax?
A: Cipro, and other antibiotics

Q: What does Cipro cure?
A: anthrax

The *topicCharacterizations* reuse category concerns groups of questions that together identify a topic. For example, words from some of the questions may help to disambiguate other question words. In the following example, the word *tennis,* which characterizes the first question, can assist in disambiguating which King is being mentioned in the subsequent question.

Q: Who did Billy Jean King beat in battle of the sexes?
A: When tennis champion Billie Jean King accepted the half-humorous challenge Bobby Riggs threw down in 1973, most women (and a lot of men) watched the televised "Battle of the Sexes" with rapt attention.

Q: How many titles did King win?

The idea of the *evidences* category is that some complex questions benefit from related questions that provide evidence for or against particular answers to the question. In the examples below, in order to answer the first question, it would be useful to have the answers for the remaining questions.

Q(I: 2058): Is tupac still alive?
Q(I: 2081): where can i find a picture of tupacs death
Q(I: 2063): what happened between tupac and suge knight
Q(I: 2143): who killed tupac shackur

If the system could provide pictures of Tupac's death or name the killer or know a time, this would help answer negatively to question I:2058. The relation between these questions is heavily dependent on world knowledge and thus operationalizing this form of reuse would initially require a restricted domain such as events of unnatural death. It is this event-specific knowledge that sets apart examples of the evidences reuse category from subSuperQuestions and embeddedQuestions categories.

When a particular type of reuse is detected and applied to a pair of questions, the possibility arises that earlier answers may need modification. We have called this category *answerRevisions*. It is not strictly a form of reuse but rather an action that might be taken when a reuse condition is detected. In the reuse corpus, an instance of this can be found in the following Q and A pairs.

Q(I: 11): How much calcium should an adult woman get in her diet?
A: Adult women need 1000-1500mg per day (pre- and post-menopausal) and also need Vitamin D to absorb the calcium. But they should not take over 500mg at one meal.

Q(I: 19): What are the factors that increase calcium excretion?
A: high protein diet, caffeine, alcohol, sodium, low exercise. Note that the minimum daily requirements seem to assume some of these, so a lifestyle without these factors may require fewer mgs of calcium per day.

Once the answer to the second question is found, the first answer should be modified to indicate further clarifications.

13.4.3 Strategies for Implementing Reuse

There are a variety of techniques that might enable a question answering system to improve performance via the reuse categories we have identified. The simplest reuse technique is to keep a cache of all questions previously asked of the system, and the answers provided by the system. This gives a potential performance benefit for questions that exemplify the reuse categories in the question-oriented cluster, namely sameQuestion, subSuperQuestions, embeddedQuestions, questionFacts, and questionClarifications. In order to achieve this enhanced performance, the question answering system must be sufficiently sophisticated to identify the relationship between the questions asked, and recognize that the relationship is from a given reuse category.

A question answering system has additional reuse potential when, it keeps a record of the answers it uses and the documents used by the system to obtain these answers. This should make reuse that falls in the sameDocuments category fairly straightforward, and can potentially enable reuse in the more complex categories, such as inductiveAnswers, answerLimits, sameFacts, and topicCharacterizations.

In all cases, two requisite tasks are the recognition by the system of the relationship between the various Q and A pairs, and the categorization of these relationships into the various reuse categories we have identified. One way to view these tasks is as a question clustering module that recognizes that two questions are about the same topic and a question set classifier that assigns reuse labels to question sets where the set might contain two questions. Common clustering and classification techniques could then be applied.

The system may be able to involve the user in an attempt to identify such relationships. This would involve a non-trivial interaction with the user. A system might employ a model where the user provides direct feedback about the answers and documents and perhaps even about the inner workings of the system. For example, the user may indicate whether she finds the answer provided by the system satisfactory. Maintaining a record of this information has utility when the system identifies reuse in the sameQuestion or subSuperQuestions categories. If the system provides access to several corpus documents in response to a question, there is additional information available in the form of which documents the user actually accesses, and in what order. The user could also provide the system with information concerning the perceived usefulness of these documents.

An important area for future research is the possible modes of user feedback in a QA system, and the ways in which this feedback can assist the system both in identifying and categorizing reuse opportunities, and obtaining maximum performance enhancement as a result of the reuse. Several other chapters in this book discuss lines of research in interactive QA systems that could be used for the type of dialog and user feedback needed for question reuse.

Regardless of the method used to implement reuse, one will have to evaluate its effectiveness. A simple method would be to compare its performance with that of the system with the reuse mechanisms turned off. One could perform user-centric evaluations such as in the TREC interactive track or the more traditional information retrieval evaluations like the TREC QA track evaluations. In either case, one would hope for an improvement in performance employing the reuse mechanisms when compared to the performance of the baseline system.

13.5 Future Work

This chapter represents a start on collecting and analyzing data on reuse possibilities in question sets. However, more work of this kind is needed. For example, our goal was to find examples of reuse and to investigate the different categories. A more complete annotation of the corpus should be performed. In addition, when we developed the corpus of questions, we did not have firm goals about the types of topics that QA systems would be particularly interested in. Our topics were often of general scope and also topics about issues. We believe that topics that contained more people and events are also of great interest to QA systems, and it would be good to collect examples of them. It would also be valuable to query against a different document set. One example would be the TREC QA document collection. One method would be to start with a TREC QA question and to develop a topic and sequence around that question. Finally, we have not collected enough annotations of reuse to estimate the distribution of the categories of reuse. Such a distribution would be a measure of the importance of the various categories.

13.6 Conclusion

In this chapter we have introduced and demarcated the topic of reuse in question answering, developed a set of categories of reuse, found examples of these categories, discussed strategies for implementing reuse, and outlined future work. It is our hope that this chapter, combined with its corresponding question corpus and annotations, will provide a starting point for further research in reuse.

Acknowledgements

This work was performed in support of the Northeast Regional Research Center (NRRC) which is sponsored by the Advanced Research and Development Activity (ARDA), a U.S. Government entity which sponsors and promotes research of import to the Intelligence Community which includes but is not limited to the CIA, DIA, NSA, NIMA, and NRO.

Notes

1. Constructed answers or questions were not "found" in the Reuse Corpus. Instead they were made up by the authors to illustrate a point.
2. We are indebted to Alexander Morgan for examples Q1, Q2, and Q3.
3. Since we do not claim that our reuse categories are exhaustive, eliminating some sequences is not theoretically problematic. We felt that we had a better chance of finding examples of reuse if we focused on the short answer questions.
4. We are indebted to John Henderson for this collection.
5. We would like to thank Bonnie Webber for her useful comments on this section.

Marc Light is an assistant professor in the Department of Linguistics, School of Library and Information Science at the University of Iowa.

Abraham Ittycheriah is a research staff member at the IBM T. J. Watson Research Center, Yorktown Heights, New York. His interests are in applying statistical approaches for natural language processing problems. He can be reached at abei@us.ibm.com.

Andrew Latto is a software engineer at Gensym, Inc., Burlington, Massachusetts. He can be reached at andy.latto@pobox.com.

Nancy McCracken is a research professor of information studies at Syracuse University, specializing in natural language processing. She can be reached at njm@ecs.syr.edu.

Chapter 14

Retrieval Models and Q and A Learning With FAQ Files

Noriko Tomuro and Steven L. Lytinen

14.1 Introduction

The idea of compiling knowledge into frequently-asked question (FAQ) files has existed for some time. The Usenet became an early repository of on-line FAQ files, and currently the Internet FAQ Archives web site (http://www.faqs.org) has 2490 "popular" FAQs archived. There are many other sources of FAQ files. Call-center manuals are also often structured as FAQ files. As the world wide web has become widely accessible, FAQ files have also become a popular way for web sites to store knowledge and convey answers to customers/site users about questions that these users would commonly ask. Thus, answers to a very wide variety of questions can be found in FAQ files, and developing applications and techniques for question answering tailored to FAQ files is an important thrust in question answering.

An FAQ file typically contains several question-and-answer (Q and A) pairs where questions are preanswered and compiled by domain experts. Thus, finding answers from FAQ files essentially is to reuse previously answered questions instead of finding answers from scratch every time—an economical solution. Due to this semistructured format, retrieval models for FAQ files place emphasis on different techniques than retrieval models for unstructured documents. First, the primary focus is on finding an FAQ question (not answer) which is similar to the user query/question, that is, a *Q-to-Q match*. In essence, this is the task of recognizing *question paraphrases*—two or more questions which ask the same thing(s) but are formulated in different ways. Recently, the issue of paraphrase recognition has been receiving attention in question-answering research as a way to fill the gap between words in a question and those in an answer. Most approaches try to enumerate paraphrase patterns, for instance "How much does X cost?" $\Rightarrow$ "X costs Y" $\equiv$ "the price of X is Y" (Lin and Pantel, 2001; Hermjakob, Abdessamad, and Marcu, 2002).

Type	FAQ files	FAQFinder	AskJeeves
Open ended	8079 (62%)	435 (70%)	2131 (62%)
Specific	4859 (38%)	185 (30%)	1322 (38%)
Total	12938 (100%)	620 (100%)	3453 (100%)

Table 14.1. Proportions of Open-Ended Questions

However, these patterns express variations of potential answer sentences (to be matched with a given question), not of questions. To do Q-to-Q match, systems must be able to account for variations of interrogative words/phrases, such as "How do I make *X*?" ⇒ "What is involved in making *X*?"

Second, many questions answered in FAQ files are general and open-ended, such as "how," "why," and "yes/no" questions,[1] in contrast to narrow, specific questions which ask for simple facts, such as those asked in TREC QA tasks (Voorhees 2000). Although FAQ answers are prepackaged "canned answers," it is not necessary for the retrieval models to pinpoint (or generate) exact answers, those types of general questions must be properly analyzed and comprehensively covered in FAQ-based systems. An interesting observation is that many questions asked by users of real-world QA systems, including FAQFinder (Burke et al. 1997) and AskJeeves (http://www.askjeeves.com), are indeed such questions as well. This implies that in practice, people often seek substantial information from real QA systems. Table 14.1 shows the proportions of open-ended questions ("how'" "why," "yes/no") observed in sample data randomly selected from FAQ files, FAQFinder user logs and AskJeeves user logs.

In addition to Q-to-Q matching, retrieval models for FAQ files may also include an effort to match questions directly with answers, that is, a *Q-to-A match.* Since both question and answer are available in an FAQ file, it may be useful at times to find answers from the answer part of the Q and A pairs, either when no similar FAQ questions are found, or in addition to the Q-to-Q match.

This chapter describes ongoing research on a real-world FAQ-based QA system called FAQFinder (Burke et al. 1997, Lytinen and Tomuro 2002). The focus of our research has been primarily on Q-to-Q matching. In this chapter, we first describe the system's current Q-to-Q matching strategy and report its retrieval performance to date. Then we present our latest work on Q-to-A matching. Finally we discuss future research directions, including Q and A learning, that apply to FAQ-based question-answering systems in general.

14.2 Overview of FAQFinder: Q-to-Q Match

FAQFinder is a web-based natural language QA system. Currently the system uses a library of approximately 600 Usenet FAQ files as the knowledge base, and tries to find an answer to a user's question by matching it against the ques-

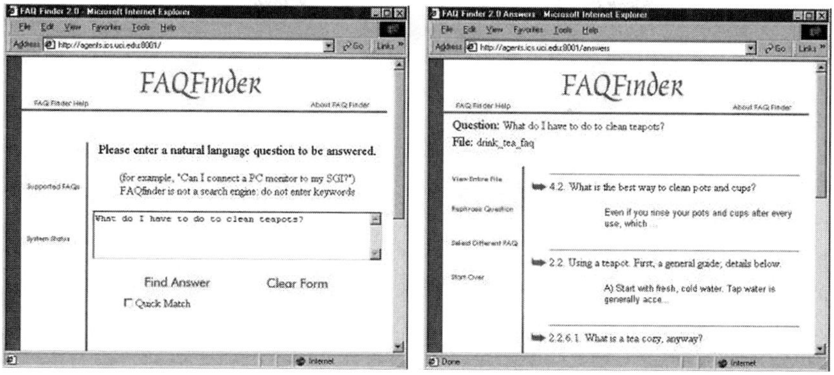

Figure 14.1. FAQFinder Initial Screen (Left Panel) and Five Best-Matching FAQ Questions (Right Panel)

tion part of the Q and A pairs in the FAQ files (i.e., FAQ questions). Figure 14.1 shows an example session with FAQFinder. After the user has typed a question (left panel), FAQFinder matches it with an FAQ question in two stages. In the first stage, the system displays FAQ files that are judged most likely to be relevant to the user's question. The SMART information retrieval system (Salton 1971) is used to select these files. Then in the second stage, after the user chooses one of the FAQ files from this list, (up to) 5 best-matching FAQ questions from that file are displayed, with their answers (right panel).

The second stage of processing uses a combination of four metrics to judge the similarity between a user question and an FAQ question. These metrics measure different aspects/dimensions of the similarity of the two questions; thus, they are complementary to each other. The metrics are (1) term vector similarity, (2) coverage, (3) semantic similarity, and (4) question type similarity. Each metric is normalized to produce a value of between 0 and 1, where 1 indicates the strongest similarity. In the current version of FAQFinder, overall similarity is computed by averaging the four metrics together. Below we describe the four metrics in detail.

14.2.1 Vector, Coverage, and Semantic Similarity

The first metric, *term vector similarity,* is computed using tf·idf (Salton and McGill 1983), a standard IR measure. In the context of Q-to-Q match, each (user or FAQ) question is considered a "document," and represented by a vector of word/term frequencies (after some closed-class terms are discarded using a stop list, as is standard in IR). The similarity score is computed as the cosine of two term vectors.

The second metric, *coverage,* is computed as the percentage of words in the user question that also appear in the FAQ question. This metric is intended to ensure that a matched FAQ question is covering the important concepts/keywords mentioned in the user question.

The third metric, *semantic similarity*, is computed by using the semantic distances between all terms in the user question and all terms in the FAQ question. To obtain a semantic distance between two terms, FAQFinder utilizes the WordNet (Miller 1990) hierarchy, and finds the shortest path between WordNet concepts (called *synsets*) referred to by the terms through hypernym/hyponym links. Detailed description of the computation of this metric is found in Lytinen, Tomuro, and Repede (2000).

14.2.2 Question Type Similarity

The fourth metric used in FAQFinder is *question type similarity*. This metric is based on a set of 12 question types (shown below) which we had developed in our previous work (Tomuro and Lytinen 2001). Notice our question types are quite general — since FAQFinder is a general Q and A system, we need a comprehensive set of question types that cover a more general class of questions.

1. DEF (definition)	2. REF (refernce)
3. TME (time)	4. LOC (location)
5. ENT (entity)	6. RSN (reason)
7. PRC (rpcedure)	8. MNR (manner
9. DEG (degree)	10. ART (atrans)
11. INT (interval)	12. YNQ (yes-no)

Our question types were defined based on the paraphrasing patterns of interrogatives. For instance, types PRC and MNR both include "how" questions, such as "How should I store beer?" (PRC) and "How did the solar system form?" (MNR). Even the meanings of "how" in these sentences are the same: "In what manner or way" (*Webster's Collegiate Dictionary*, sense 1 of "how"). However, some of the paraphrasing patterns for PRC questions do not apply to MNR questions. For example:

"What do I have to do to store beer?"
* "What did the solar system have to do to form?"

Also, we defined a type ATR (ATRANS in conceptual dependency (Schank 1973) as a special case of PRC. An example question of this type would be "How can I get tickets for the Indy 500?" Not only do ATR questions undergo the paraphrasing patterns of PRC questions, they also allow rephrasings which ask for the location or entity of the thing(s) being sought, for instance, "Where can I get tickets for the Indy 500?" and "Who sells tickets for the Indy 500?"

The question type similarity is computed by comparing the question types of user and FAQ questions. Note this metric looks at original questions, before the stop-list is applied. The question type for a question is determined by automatically classifying it using C5.0: the commercial version of the C4.5 decision tree induction system (Quinlan 1994).[2] In our previous work, we had trained C5.0 with 7637 questions selected randomly from 150 FAQ files and produced a decision tree that classifies a question according to the 12 question types. The classification accuracy for the training data was 85.3%. We will use this tree in the evaluation of FAQFinder, which we describe in the next section.

14.3 Evaluation of FAQFinder

To test the performance of FAQFinder, and to measure the effect of the four similarity metrics on the system's overall performance, we developed two test sets of user questions. The first test set consisted of a set of paraphrases of some FAQ questions. To gather paraphrases, we randomly chose 35 questions of various question types from the FAQ files and posted them on a Web site. Visitors to the site were shown an arbitrary sampling of those questions and were asked to rephrase them. After leaving the site on the Web for a period of 2 weeks, we had gathered a set of 679 example questions. The second test set consisted of a set of 153 questions typed by FAQFinder users, arbitrarily chosen from the system server logs.

We ran FAQFinder on both test sets. For the paraphrase test set, since the 679 questions in the test set were all generated from the original 35 FAQ questions, the correct match for each paraphrase was the original FAQ question from which it was generated. For the FAQFinder log test set, we manually inspected the FAQ files and determined which (if any) was the best matching question.

We evaluated the system performance by examining the trade-off between recall and *rejection* for varying threshold values. Recall is defined as the percentage of *answerable* user questions (i.e., questions in the test sets whose answers exist in some FAQ file) for which the system returned their matching/correct FAQ questions in the top 5 matches (after the threshold cut-off). Rejection is defined as the percentage of *unanswerable* user questions (i.e., questions in the test sets for which no answer exists in any FAQ file) for which the system displays no matches to the user (again after the threshold cut-off). We used rejection rather than the standard precision metric because it is a more pure measure of system performance on unanswerable questions (precision also measures the number of irrelevant answers (up to 5) returned for answerable questions). The FAQFinder log test set contained 91 answerable and 62 unanswerable questions. As for the paraphrase test set, since there were no unanswerable questions, we measured rejection by running the system on the same set of 679 test questions with the correct FAQ question removed.

Figure 14.2 shows FAQFinder's performance, as well as the performance of each individual similarity metric, on the two test sets. As the figure illustrates, the combination of the four similarity metrics produces better performance than do the individual metrics. In the case of the paraphrase test set, the dif-

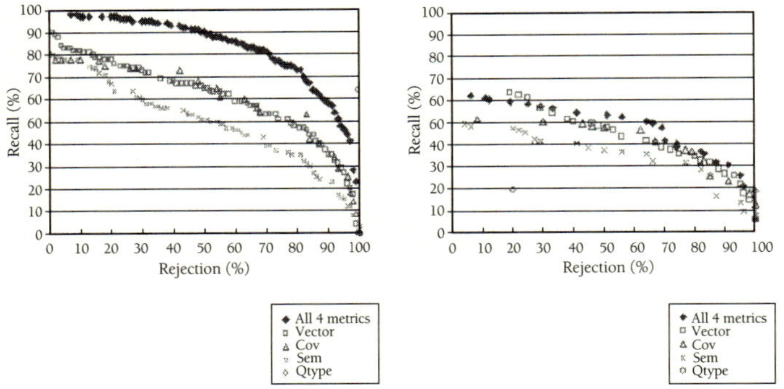

Figure 14.2. Ablation Study for Paraphrase Test Set (Left Panel); Ablation Study for FAQ Finder Log Test Set (Right Panel)

ference is dramatic, showing a synergistic effect of combining complimentary metrics. Also, overall recall is quite high, remaining above 90% for rejection rates as high as 50%. However in the case of the FAQFinder log test set, the effect of combining measures is rather marginal. An immediate reason for this would be the way in which the paraphrase test set was originally generated; when asked to write paraphrases of FAQ questions, our web site users often used many of the same or similar words as the original questions, thus the paraphrases were naturally more similar than questions typed in by actual FAQFinder users.[3] This fact is also reflected on the difference of the general system performance: for instance, at 0% rejection recall is almost perfect (99%) for the paraphrase test set, whereas it is only 62% for the FAQFinder log test set.

To gain insights on how we could improve the retrieval performance, we inspected the failed matches (i.e., test questions to which the correct FAQ questions were not ranked within the top 5 matches). There were 10 and 35 such instances in the two test sets respectively. Upon inspection, we discovered that there were roughly three types of errors: (1) *difficult paraphrasing*, (2) *unexpected match*, and (3) other errors. Table 14.2 shows the breakdown.

Difficult paraphrasing includes cases where the paraphrasing pattern/relation between a user question and its correct FAQ question is difficult to identify. For example, the correct FAQ question to a user question "Is CF fatal?" is "Do people die from CF?" (where CF stands for "chronic fatigue"). Those two questions are obviously paraphrases of each other, but the system failed to recognize them because it currently does not encode phrasal paraphrases (e.g., "*X* is fatal" ≡ "people die from *X*"). Even if we try to match single words "fatal" and "die," our current WordNet-based semantic similarity does not facilitate

Error type	Paraphrase	FAQFinder log
A. Difficult paraphrasing	10 (100%)	6 (17%)
B. Unexpected match	0 (0%)	21 (60%)
C. Other errors	0 (0%)	8 (23%)
Total	10 (100%)	35 (100%)

Table 14.2. Types of Errors in Failed Matches

inferences between words of different part-of-speech categories. Other paraphrase patterns are more difficult and subtle, and require inferences based on deep semantic or common-sense knowledge, such as "How can I separate my credit history from my exhusband's?" vs. "How do I take my exhusband's debts off of my credit report?" Although the meanings of those questions may not be exactly identical, they are close enough (i.e., near-paraphrases) such that we wish to be able to recognize them by Q-to-Q matching (without resorting to a search through the entire FAQ file for the actual answer). To do so, we must enhance our current Q-to-Q matching scheme, in particular the semantic inference capability. In future work, we are planning to incorporate a large database of paraphrase patterns described in Lin and Pantel (2001) and examine its applicability to our data.

Unexpected matches, on the other hand, include cases where the user question and FAQ question are dissimilar or even unrelated (thus they are not paraphrases of each other) but the answer happens to be contained in the FAQ answer part. A good example would be a user question "Is the picture quality of satellite TV identical to cable or broadcast TV?" In the Satellite-TV-FAQ, the answer to this question is found in the answer part of the question "Who should own a satellite system?" But the system retrieved other FAQ questions which were more (lexically) similar. Another example is "Is caffeine linked to high blood pressure or asthma?"—answered in the caffeine-faq, under the question "What happens when you overdose?" In those cases, it is not possible to tell if the user's questions are really answered by those FAQ questions by looking at the questions alone (even with some semantic inferences). In other words, the problem of unexpected match is a limitation of Q-to-Q matching.

Lastly, other errors included preprocessing errors, such as those by tokenizer and part-of-speech tagger, and incorrect answer keys assigned by the human coder.

14.4 Q-to-A Match

In addition to Q-to-Q match, we are currently investigating the possibility of matching a user question directly with the answer part of the Q and A pairs.

Since the answer part of a Q and A pair most often contains more information/words than the question part, it is more indicative of what the Q and A is about and may allow us to do more precise matching. Q-to-A matching would be also useful when Q-to-Q match fails—in the case of unexpected matches discussed in the previous section.

The Q-to-A match in FAQFinder is fundamentally the same as finding answers from unstructured documents—by looking at each FAQ answer block as a document, except that, since FAQ answers are "canned answers," the system does not in principle attempt to pinpoint exact answers. So for narrow specific questions, most of the answer-finding techniques developed so far in question-answering research such as that done by some TREC QA track systems (Harabagiu, Pasca, and Maiorano, 2000, Hovy et al. 2001) would apply directly. However, large proportions of questions entered by the FAQFinder users are complex and open-ended (as shown earlier in table 14.1), therefore we must develop different novel techniques to deal with long answers. While finding answers to specific questions often relies heavily on the semantic categories of the words in user questions and potential answers (e.g., MONEY, TIME), it seems indicative that features for complex questions include meta-linguistic features (e.g., the number and style of the answer paragraph(s)) and domain-independent words (e.g., "step", "because"). To test our hypothesis, we conducted a preliminary experiment where we selected several such features (which hereafter we call "meta-linguistic features") and observed the retrieval performance for "how-to" questions. The result we obtained, as described in section 14.4.1, showed significant improvements by the use of meta-linguistic features.

14.4.1 Meta-Linguistic Features

To develop our intuitions about "how-to" answers, we first randomly selected a set of 253 Q and A pairs from various FAQ files, consisting of 123 Q and A's of type PRC (procedure) and 130 non-PRC Q and A's. Note that, in the current experiment, we tested only PRC questions to examine the potential of our approach; we plan to examine questions of other types in future work.

After inspecting the data, we (manually) decided on the following six features as good indicators of a PRC answer block: (1) Number of paragraphs, (2) Number of sentences, (3) Number of imperative sentences, (4) Number of occurrences of PRC keywords (e.g., "step," "way," "first"), (5) Number of occurrences of non-PRC keywords (e.g., "because," "yes," "no"), (6) Number of occurrences of "if."

Then we constructed a decision tree using C5.0 from those 253 PRC answers. All six features appeared in the tree, and the classification accuracy was 90.1%.

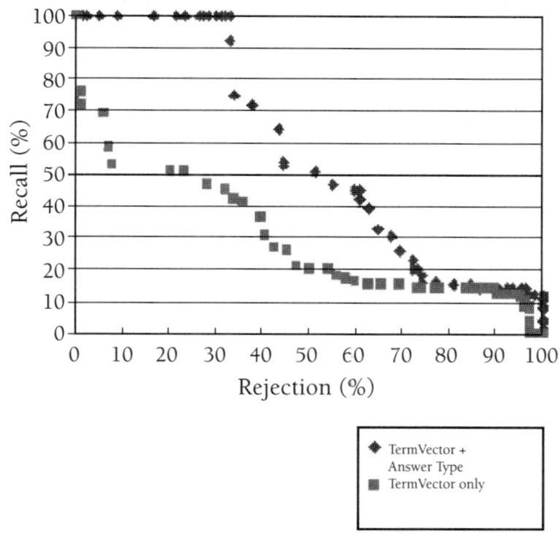

Figure 14.3. Recall Versus. Rejection for Paraphrase Dataset

14.4.2 The Experiment

Using the six meta-linguistic features, we conducted an experiment to see how much those features could help improve the retrieval of "how-to" questions. We chose term vector similarity (tf·idf) as the baseline measure for matching a user question with an FAQ answer, and compared the system's performance with and without using the additional measure of automatic answer type classification (how-to versus nonhow-to). Note that, here in the context of Q-to-A match, the two term vectors compared are a paraphrased test question and an FAQ answer instead of an FAQ question.

For the test set, we used a subset of the paraphrase dataset we used in the Q-to-Q match experiment, consisting of 117 questions of type PRC. This set is essentially the held-out test set (thus, the system was trained on one set of Q and A's and tested with another set of totally unseen Q and A's). The answer type classification is determined by running the C5.0 decision tree classifier obtained in the last section. The classifier returns a value of either 1 (for a how-to answer) or 0 (for a nonhow-to answer). Then, the overall similarity between a test question and an FAQ answer is computed as a weighted sum of the two measures, where in the current experiment, we used the distribution of 90% on term vector similarity and 10% on answer type classification. The combined score would be between 0 and 1, where 1 indicates the strongest similarity.

Figure 14.3 shows the recall vs. rejection curves. Rejection was computed in the same way as Q-to-Q match, by removing the correct answers. As the figure shows, the additional use of answer type classification showed a dramatic improvement. Although the current experiment is still preliminary and only tests for how-to questions/answers, we consider this result to be an excellent indicator for the potential usefulness of meta-linguistic features in retrieving long answers. In future work, we are planning to identify features for other question types that require long answers, and conduct a comprehensive end-to-end retrieval experiment using both Q-to-Q and Q-to-A matches.

14.5 Future Directions

There are several interesting future research directions for question answering with FAQ files. We list some of them below.

14.5.1 Integrated Measure for Question Paraphrase Recognition

The current Q-to-Q similarity measure used in FAQFinder is a combination of four independent metrics. Although the metrics are additive and complementary to each other, they cannot capture the relations and interactions between them. For instance, when a question "What is the best way to clean teapots?" is pre-processed, the word "way" is used in the computation of vector, semantic, and coverage similarities, and thus is considered a content-word. But with respect to question type, this word serves as a predictor for type PRC (and ATR), and is considered a noncontent word.

In an effort to develop an alternative, integrated similarity measure, we have recently defined a set of question paraphrase patterns (Tomuro 2003) as the first attempt. Those patterns are intended to specify and remove syntactic superstructures imposed by interrogative words/phrases (such as "How do I .." and "What is the best way to .."), and represent questions canonically using semantic case frames. A preliminary investigation, although with a small sample data, showed a quite promising result. We are currently investigating ways to combine them with paraphrase patterns of content words (along the lines of (Lin and Pantel 2001) which we mentioned in the evaluation of Q-to-Q match). An interesting alternative would be to take a less knowledge-intensive approach, for instance by keyword expansion and prioritized matching (Sneider 1999).

14.5.2 Passage-Based Answer Retrieval

Another important direction is to investigate how to retrieve a part of an FAQ answer for long answers. In our Q-to-A experiment, a whole FAQ answer was taken as one answer unit. But typically FAQ answers give long explanations and discuss surrounding issues. Each of those parts can be an answer to a different question by itself. This issue is also addressed in Chapter 13 in this book, as well as Light et al. (2003).

To retrieve long segments in FAQ answers, the system must incorporate a passage-based retrieval scheme. To that end, we anticipate cue/focus phrases as well as meta-linguistic features will be effective. For baseline measures, statistical approaches used in Berger and Mittal (2000) (in which a passage in an FAQ file is viewed as a summary of the file relative to a given query) seem a good starting point.

14.5.3 Learning of Answer Formulation

Aside from FAQFinder, FAQ files are also an excellent resource for learning models for query-relevant answer formulation. Since FAQ files are written by domain experts, FAQ answers can be used as model answers from which we can develop criteria for the level and extent of expertise to be found in automatically extracted or generated answers/summaries. The structures of answer content/argument can also be learned from FAQ answers. For instance, an answer to a why question generally starts out with explanations of the reason(s), then discusses ways to fix the problem(s), and finally concludes with tips and advice. We anticipate the techniques developed for the passage-based answer retrieval can be utilized to automatically identify such structures.

14.6 Conclusions

FAQ files can be a rich source of information for question answering. The number and range of FAQ files is large and growing. While an FAQ-based QA system such as FAQFinder is limited to providing answers which have already been written by human experts, we can capitalize on the semistructured nature of FAQ files to retrieve answers efficiently by answer reuse, and to find potential answers that may not be otherwise found by narrowly-scoped question-answering techniques. For example, the "how-to" and "why" types of questions that FAQFinder is able to answer are beyond the scope of the sorts of questions which are included in the TREC QA track.

The majority of our work on FAQFinder has been on refining the Q-to-Q matching techniques. Our preliminary work on Q-to-A matching shows good promise, especially for the types of questions which tend to have long, complex answers. We are hopeful that the full addition of Q-to-A matching will effectively complement Q-to-Q matching and help improve the system's performance.

Notes

1. Yes/no questions are often indirect requests for other types of information, and a good answer is rarely a simple yes/no response (Searle 1975).

2. Available at http://www.rulequest.com

3. On this, Lin and Pantel (2001) make a comment on manually generated paraphrases (vs. automatically extracted paraphrases): "It is difficult for humans to generate a di-

verse list of paraphrases, given a starting formulation and no context." Our data is in agreement with their observations indeed. Our paraphrase data is described in detail in Tomuro (2003).

Noriko Tomuro (tomuro@cs.depaul.edu) is an assistant professor at DePaul University's School of Computer Science, Telecommunications, and Information Systems. Her research interests include natural language processing and question-answering systems.

Steven Lytinen (lytinen@cs.depaul.edu) is a professor at DePaul University's School of Computer Science, Telecommunications, and Information Systems. His research areas are natural language processing and intelligent information retrieval.

Section Six

Advanced Methods for Question Processing and Answering

Section six introduces a number of exciting new methods for question processing and answering. The first chapter by Daniel Mahler (Cycorp) considers the use of graphical models to support holistic query expansion in the QUIRK system. The chapter focuses on relationship questions using the AQUAINT and CNS corpora. For example, a user can ask "What do Soviet Cosmonaut Valentina Tereshkova (Vladimirovna) and US Astronaut Sally Ride have in common?" and the QUIRK system responds "Connecting terms: first space shuttle woman" even when no document in the corpus mentions both women! The QUIRK system discovers connecting terms to expand the original query to find passages which mention the query terms together with the connecting terms then highlights their appearance in passages. Connecting terms should occur between query terms based on co-occurrence. A connecting terms feedback algorithm uses a graph-based method with terms as nodes and a "maximum spanning tree" to select connecting terms.

Experimentation with multiple algorithms for co-occurrence measures resulted in various tree topologies and revealed that deep trees tend to yield large sets of connecting terms that outweigh the original terms resulting in low weight link and thus less coherent units. In particular, shallow trees tend to be produced by the measures weight of evidence, quadratic information gain, relief, and relevance, while deep trees tend to be produced by information gain, stochastic complexity, and reduction of description length. The chapter reports that weight of evidence tends to outperform the other measures in its group because the small set of terms it produces contains terms that one would intuitively recognize as more relevant. After co-occurrence data is carefully computed, the system searches on both query terms and connecting terms. Redundancy in the AQUAINT data required duplicate elimination.

The system was evaluated in the AQUAINT relationship track evaluation pilot which consisted of 2 judges and 100 questions answers that were scored from 0 to 4 (bad to good). Assessment focused on content not form. Three systems participated in this evaluation pilot in addition to human answers. As the

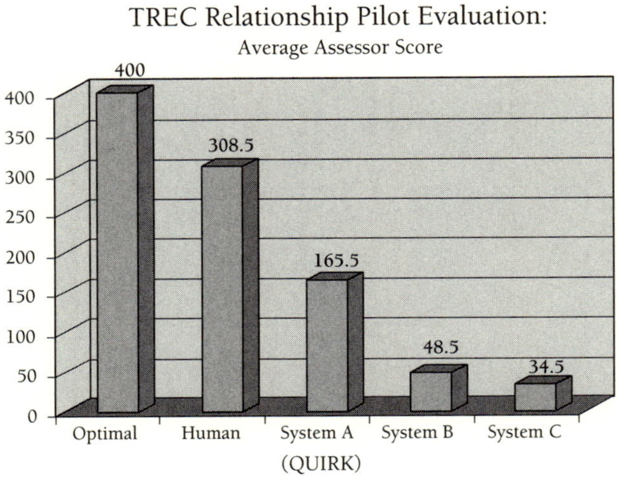

chart of averages on this page illustrates, QUIRK was the best performing system by the given criteria, achieving 54% of human performance. It is important to note that these results have not been scored or adjusted for length, a subject of current investigation. The chapter reports that while QUIRK was originally tuned to work on the AQUAINT corpus, it appears to work well on new corpora and unseen questions without recalibration.

The second chapter in this section by Boris Katz, Sue Felshin, Jimmy Lin, and Gregory Marton (MIT) describes a technique for turning the Web into a "virtual database" for question answering. As outlined in detail in this collection's introduction, natural language access to databases originated in the 1960s and 1970 in systems such as BASEBALL (Green et al. 1961) and Lunar (Woods et al. 1972). Although impressive in performance, these systems were domain specific and brittle. The authors report on START and Omnibase, two components of a system that understands natural language questions and responds with answers extracted on the fly from heterogeneous and semi-structured Web sources. Their approach exploits many sources such as the CIA World Factbook, with detailed information on countries of the world; biography.com, with 25,000 bios of famous people; and the Internet Movie Database, with filmography information on 100,000+ movies. Just ten Web sources, organized according to their data model, suffice to answer 27% of TREC-9 and 47% of TREC-10 questions from the QA Track (Lin, 2002).

A core element of their approach is a simple object-property-value model, as the subsequent table illustrates. Based on the observation that real-world question distribution qualitatively obeys Zipf's Law, i.e., a few question types

Question	Object	Property	Value
Who wrote the music for Star Wars?	Star Wars	composer	John Williams
How big is Costa Rica	Costa Rica	area	51,100 sq. km

account for a large fraction of all question instances, a relatively simple data model suffices to capture a large variety of English questions.

START parses English questions into embedded ternary expressions (T-expressions) of the form <subject relation object> (Katz 1988), where the subject and object can themselves be ternary expressions. Certain other constituents (adjectives, possessive nouns, prepositional phrases, etc.) are used to create additional T-expressions in which prepositions and several special words serve as relations. Additional grammatical features associated with a sentence (adverbs and their position, tense, auxiliaries, voice, negation, etc.) are recorded in a separate representational structure called a history. START also introduces structural transformational rules that make explicit the relationship between alternate realizations of verb arguments; these rules can be generalized to cover semantic verb classes to ensure broad coverage.

A large external lexicon helps START identify objects and the resource that they are associated with, for example, that "Gone with the Wind" is a movie from the Internet Movie Database. Omnibase contains a large collection of wrapper scripts tailored to specific Web resources, which are invoked from a uniform query language based on the object-property-value data model. These wrappers utilize regular expression pattern matching on textual landmarks of a webpage to extract the relevant information. As an example, the question "Who directed *Gone with the Wind?*" results in the query

(get imdb-movie "Gone with the Wind (1939)" DIRECTOR)

whose execution returns the result ("George Cukor" "Victor Fleming" "Sam Wood"). START repackages the result and displays the following answer:

"*Gone with the Wind* (1939) was directed by George Cukor, Victor Fleming, and Sam Wood.

Source: The Internet Movie Database"

Since the system came on line in December 1993, START has answered millions of questions from hundreds of thousands of users including questions about people, places, movies, dictionary definitions, etc., utilizing knowledge from over 100 Web resources. From January 2000 to December 2002, about a million questions were posed to START and Omnibase; of those, 67% were answered successfully. Of the questions posed, 10% contained unknown words or could not be successfully parsed; 22% could not be answered due to a lack of knowledge. A simplified version of Aranea was formally evaluated at the TREC-2002 QA track and was 71% accurate in answering previously unseen questions involving the object-property-value data model.

Custom versions of the system have been created for the Voyager 2 space probe (1989), a NASA open house (2001) for QA about Mars exploration, and a permanent exhibit at the MIT Museum. In addition, Ask Jeeves licensed certain technology pioneered by START.

In summary, the authors organize diverse heterogeneous and semi-structured data on the World Wide Web by creating an abstraction layer centered on the object-property-value model. START and Omnibase utilize a hybrid approach that integrates natural language processing and database techniques. The result is a system that provides access to a wealth of information freely available on the world wide web.

Whereas the previous chapter integrates language and database technology, the next chapter by Harris Wu (Univ. of Michigan), Dragomir R. Radev (Univ. of Michigan), and Weiguo Fan (Virginia Polytechnic Institute and State University) addresses the combination of QA and summarization to provide answer-focused summarization. An analysis of an Excite search engine corpus of 2.5 million user queries shows that only 8.4% of the queries are in the form of natural language questions. Of those natural language queries, 43.9% are factual questions that have short answers (e.g., "What is the country code for Belgium?"). The rest consist of nonfactual questions (e.g., how, why), are incorrect, or are unanswerable.

The authors distinguish between indicative and informative summaries, the latter which they exploit to answer questions. They describe this as a form of query-based passage retrieval. They first report a set of criteria and performance metrics to evaluate answer-focused summarization. Next they describe a proximity-based answer-focused summarization system, which complements existing search engines and other document retrieval systems. This summarization system is capable of analyzing and utilizing question types to provide better answer-focused summaries. Then they show, via experiments, how summarization provided by Google, one of the best search engines available, remains sub-optimal in question answering. Their answer-focused summarization system shows significant advantage in key performance metrics. Finally, they provide recommendations to search engines to improve their summarization for question answering. They also suggest some promising research directions and suggest that better answer-focused summarization may help bring Internet information systems to wireless and hand-held devices, where search cost is critical.

In their experiments, the authors focus on single-document summaries. Their answer evaluation stresses three measures: (1) accuracy (contains the answer), (2) economy (short answers preferred), and (3) support (evidence is provided to support the answer). They measure the first 2 categories considering whether a question is answered, the summary rank of the first answer, and the summary length in characters. They utilize mean reciprocal document rank (MRDR) and the TREC fixed number of extracted characters (50 or 250 bytes).

Their evaluation used the TREC-8 corpus which consists of 200 factual questions, most answers to which are definitive and short (less than 20 characters).

They first created a Google baseline, starting with a URL, title, description (rarely provided, only 203 of them were retrieved from 2000 hits), summary, and category. They removed 94 of 2000 hits from pages from TREC participant sites. They then measured performance on the number answers, average character length, and mean reciprocal of summary ranks (MRSR). Google MRSR summaries on 200 questions averaged .207. Point 2 (.2) means on average the answer to a question appears in the fifth summary provide by the system. A value of 1 means that a user on average can find the answers in the first summary they read. Seventy-three percent, or 200 hit lists, contained one or more answers.

They then performed three comparative experiments. In the first they evaluated proximity-based summarization. This approach quantifies the distance from the query words to answers in a document to support answer-focused summarization extraction. Their method looks for the optimal window size that maximizes the number of query words in the summary passage from the retrieved document. They trained on the first 100 TREC queries and tested on the second 100. At a window size of 4, 41 of 100 questions are answered (Google got 38).

In a second experiment they evaluated summarization where the question type is known. They manually classified TREQ 8 questions as person (56), place (36), name (29), number (23), date (22) and other (34). This approach learned window size based on the question type (e.g., place questions have an optimal window of 9, person questions 4, and number questions 2). In an evaluation, 46 questions were answered compared to 41 answered in experiment 1. This was 21% more than Google's, and 12% more than that of experiment 1. The MRSR on the evaluation set is 0.247, compared to experiment 1's 0.237 and Google's 0.228. In spite of the improved performance, complex questions were handled poorly by this method.

A final third experiment utilized summarization where the question type was guessed. A rule-based guesser looks at *wh*-words (e.g., "who" indicates person, "where" place) together with a long list of nouns and their answer type (e.g., answers for questions about population require numbers). Using this approach accuracy was 153 out of 200 TREC-8 questions or 76.5%. The AFS system only answers 43 questions when guessing question type as opposed to 46 when it is given the question type; however, this still outperforms the Google baseline.

In conclusion, the authors underscore the importance of different window sizes for different question types. They point out that even errorful question classification (a 23.5% error rate) improves QA performance. In the future they plan to improve query parsing and noun classification, provide support for the answer, and make tradeoffs between summary size, support, and accuracy. Finally, they are interested in looking at reciprocal word rank, or reciprocal character rank, to take into consideration how many words or characters a user has to read before reaching the answer to a question.

Whereas the previous two chapters explore the integration of different technologies (e.g., natural language, database, summarization), the next chapter by John Prager, Jennifer Chu-Carroll, and Krzysztof Czuba (IBM T. J. Watson Research Center) considers integrating heterogeneous components and systems using a multi-agent architecture. Their fundamental observation is that a human may answer a question to which she does not know the answer by a text search; by calculation; by look up in a dictionary, thesaurus, or other reference work; or some combination thereof. So too can a computer adopt different strategies or even try many strategies and combine answers from best. Indeed, exploiting answer redundancy and reinforcement from multiple agents, the authors demonstrate an improvement of up to 16.3% using the Mean Reciprocal Rank (MRR) metric and 11.9% using the confidence weight score (CWS) metric. Furthermore, the authors introduce two new methods, "QA-by-dossier" and "QA-by-dossier-with-constraints," where additional questions are asked to generate constraints on the answers to the original question. This approach can reduce the confidence of many wrong answers and reinforce many good ones, resulting in an increase in precision from .43 to .95 in one experiment.

The authors describe their PIQUANT system and consider the effects of black-box combination of multiple answering agents and knowledge sources. Their agent search strategies include:

Statistical—maximum entropy formalism plus Local Context Analysis.

Predictive—documents annotated a priori; Pattern-based-parse tree patterns which include a repository of question type specific patterns, such as a person's birthday, birthplace, cause of death; and so on. While currently manually created, future plans call for machine learning, e.g., dynamic predicate-argument patterns generated from the parse tree of the question.

Query by dossier—for people, it searches for their birthdate, birthplace, deathdate, profession, college attended, and so on. For organizations, it searches for their headquarters, CEO, and their line of business. For things, it provides a definition by invoking the Definition Agent. Future plans call for tailoring questions to subtypes of people, organizations, or things.

Query by dossier with constraints (QDC)-answers to related questions often constrain one another, e.g., when Mona Lisa was painted is constrained by the birth and death of the painter, Leonardo. Biographical data is constrained by life-cycle parameters, geographical data by 2-dimensional spatial geometry, and kinship data by reciprocal relationships. Currently the authors are looking at developing an ontology from which such questions and constraints can be derived.

Definition—Examine the superclasses (hypernyms) of the term in a source such as WordNet and evaluate candidates based on their co-occurrence with the term to be defined in the reference corpus.

Description–at a high level similar to that of Blair-Goldensohn et al.'s chapter in section 2.

PIQUANT exploits a variety of ways to search knowledge sources, including keyword search and semantic search of text corpora, as well as predicate look-up of structured sources like CYC and WordNet. After normalizing named entities from multiple agents, its answer resolution module sums multiple answers with confidence scores. Thus, similar answers from different agents reinforce one another.

PIQUANT was evaluated using an ablation study using the 500 questions from the TREC 10 QA track. Sixty of these were eliminated because they had no answer. In all but one system configuration, multi-agent systems outperformed their components. While the pattern agent did not add many new correct answers, it enabled the system to be more confident about previously found correct answers, resulting in a higher CWS.

In a separate evaluation of the constraint agent, 40 questions about celebrity marriages (e.g., "Who is married to who?") were tested. The authors introduced a new metric called the *risk-based score* (if the answer is correct, the overall score is increased, if not, decreased) on range 0-1. They also evaluated the people definition questions of TREC12. Using QDC, 78 incorrect and 18 correct nuggets were thrown out, giving a new precision of 0.95, a relative increase of 123%.

Related work by Burger et al. (2003) applied ensemble methods to combine the 67 runs submitted to the TREC 11 QA track; however the combined system did not work better than the top performing system. In contrast, using multiple agents the authors show a 16.3% and 11.9% relative improvement in MRR and CWS scores.

Chapter 15

Holistic Query Expansion Using Graphical Models

Daniel Mahler

15.1 Introduction

In this chapter I present a method for answering relationship questions, as posed for example in the spring of 2003 evaluation exercise of the AQUAINT[1] program, which has funded this research.

The goal of the exercise was to provide answers to questions requesting an account of the relationship between two or more entities. No restriction on the format of the answer was imposed, except that it should not consist of entire documents and that it should list document identifiers for the passages from which the answer was drawn or generated.

15.2 Relation Questions

An example question from the relationship exercise and the answer provided by our system, QUIRK, is presented in figure 15.1. What makes this question-answer pair interesting is the fact that no document in the target corpus mentions both Valentina Tereshkova and Sally Ride. This means that the passages that collectively elucidate the relationship between the two must be retrieved from the corpus by first finding terms (which I will call *connecting terms*) that are not present in the question but which describe (or are evocative of) the relationship between the terms in the question, in this case *first space shuttle* and *woman,* and then retrieving relevant passages for the original query expanded with these new terms.

Identifying such connecting terms from a corpus is the key aspect of the technique I present in this chapter. This technique differs in important respects from other well established query expansion techniques (Xu and Croft 1996, Mitra, Singhal, and Buckley 1998, Buckley, Salton, Allan, and Singha 1994, Kekäläinen and Järvelin) as the following examples are designed to

Question: What does Soviet Cosmonaut Valentina Tereshkova (Vladimirovna) and U.S. Astronaut Sally Ride have in common?

Connecting terms: **first space shuttle woman**

Answer: APW19990618.0223.11 In 1963, Soviet cosmonaut Valentina Tereshkova returned to Earth after spending nearly three days as the **first woman** in **space**.

APW19990115.0263.10 In 1978, NASA named 35 candidates to fly on the **space shuttle**, including Sally K. Ride, who became America's **first woman** in **space**, and Guion S. Bluford Jr., who became America's **first** black astronaut in **space**.

NYT19990723.0009.1 CAPE CANAVERAL, Fla. After a year of technical delays and two frustrating waits on the launching pad, the **space shuttle** Columbia blasted off from Cape Canaveral early Friday morning carrying the $1.5 billion Chandra X-ray Observatory, and vaulting its commander, Col. Eileen M. Collins of the Air Force into the ranks of aviation pioneers like Amelia Earhart and the Soviet cosmonaut Valentina Tereshkova, the **first woman** in **space**.

APW19981020.1367.6 June 18, 1983: Sally Ride becomes **first** American **woman** in **space**.

APW19990521.0292.6 Anger in **space**, by astronauts and cosmonauts, has been common since early in the manned **space** program.

APW19990525.0041.29 Former astronaut Sally K. Ride is 48.

Figure 15.1. A Relationship Question

show.[2] Ideal examples of connecting terms for pairs of query terms are: France, Germany → Europe country EU; Rushdie, Khomeini → fatwa, blasphemy; cats, dogs → pets domestic, mammals, chase, fight.

In contrast, based on our understanding of the algorithms, I would expect most other approaches to automatic query expansion to favor terms strongly related to *individual* query terms independently of other terms in the query. Hypothetical examples could be: France, Germany → French, Paris, German, Berlin; Rushdie, Khomeini → Salman, Ayatollah: cats, dogs Poodle, Retriever, Siamese, Manx, where *Paris* is only related to France and *Berlin* is only related to *Germany*. This style of expansion has the potential to lose the focus of the query. For example expanding a query as in dogs, training → Poodle, Retriever, Terrier, Setter, jogging, gym, weights; would be likely to cause a search engine to retrieve a mixture of documents about dog breeds and about sports training rather than documents on dog training, which is presumably the user's intent. I refer to this phenomenon as the *outweighing* or *overpowering* of the query by the expansion terms. Identifying *connecting terms,* such as: dogs, training obedience, sit, heel, leash, reward cannot always be achieved by considering the query terms in isolation.

15.2.1 Answer Presentation

The most effective presentation of answers to relationship questions is an issue in itself. Relationship and cause and effect questions differ significantly from the factoid questions used in TREC Q and A-track competitions, where the goal is to identify a single phrase that gives the answer. Often the relationship is not described in the corpus in a single concise phrase. Such a description may not be appropriate because of the subtlety/complexity of the relationship, as several questions in the sample in section 15.5 should illustrate. Even in cases where the connecting terms have been correctly identified, by themselves they usually do not constitute a useful answer, because, unless one already knows the answer, it is not obvious how the connecting terms account for the relationship between the query terms.[3] Even in patent cases such as Kennedy, Oswald $\rightarrow$ kill, if one were ignorant of modern history it would be impossible to rely on the connecting term *kill* to decide between the following interpretations: Kennedy killed Oswald; Oswald killed Kennedy; Kennedy and Oswald both killed someone; Kennedy and Oswald were both killed by someone.

Thus, I believe the most effective use of the discovered connecting terms is to expand the original query to find passages which mention the query terms together with the connecting terms. Such passages should then be presented to the user with the terms suitably highlighted, as in figure 15.1.

15.3 Identifying Connecting Terms

In this section I consider possible algorithms, which, given a corpus and a query, determine expansion terms that would match our *informal* notion of connecting terms. These algorithms then define a family of different *formal* notions of connecting terms. I adopt the standard statistical IR assumption that interterm relevance is reflected in the co-occurrence statistics over the corpus of interest. Applying this principle to the notion of connecting terms means that the connecting terms should lie *between* the query terms according to some co-occurrence based distance or similarity measure (see section 15.3.2) on terms (Tan, Kumar, and Srivastava 2000). This requires in turn defining what it means for a term C to be between two terms A and B with respect to the given measure. Thus, there are three parameters to making the original informal notion concrete: (1) the raw co-occurrence data itself; (2). the co-occurrence measure; (3) a notion of an *optimal connection,* for a given set of seed nodes in a weighted graph.[4]

Information Retrieval Engine (*E*)	Lemur
Number of documents retrieved (*N*)	25
Number of relevant sentences (*R*)	1/7 of all sentences in the *N* documents
Similarity measure (*M*)	overlap
Number of content words (*W*)	400
Similarity measure (*K*)	*weight of evidence* [9,7]
Algorithm for extracting	smallest connecting subgraph
connecting terms from graph (*C*)	of maximum spanning tree of G that contains $\{q_1,...,q_n\}$
Number of documents retrieved (*J*)	50

Table 15.1. Current Parameter Values for the QUIRK connecting terms Feedback Algorithm

Algorithm 1

(General form of the connecting terms expansion algorithm.)

For some choice of:

a probabilistic[5] information retrieval engine *E*;
a number *N* of documents to be retrieved;
a number of relevant sentences *R*;
a similarity measure *M*;
a number *W* of content words to consider;
a similarity measure *K*;
an algorithm *C* for retrieving nodes from a graph given a seed set of nodes;
a second number *J* of documents to be retrieved;

1. Compute query terms $\{q_1, ..., q_n\}$ from a query *Q*; in a Q and A exercise this may involve stripping question words and stop words.
2. Submit $\{q_1, ..., q_n\}$ to a search engine *E* and retrieve the top *N* documents;
3. Split documents into sentences and remove stop words from sentences;
4. Select the *R* sentences $\{s_1, ..., s_R\}$that are most relevant to *Q* by some measure of similarity *M* between $\{q_1, ..., q_n\}$and s_i;
5. Build word-sentence matrix for the *W* words $\{w_1, ..., w_W\}$ that occur in the greatest number of sentences in $\{s_1, ..., s_R\}$;
6. **Use similarity measure *K* to build a graph representation *G* of the pairwise similarity between any two w_i, w_j in $\{w_1, ..., w_W\}$;**
7. **Use method *C* to compute a set $\{c_1, ..., c_m\}$ of connecting terms for $\{q_1, ..., q_n\}$ from the graph *G*;**
8. Submit $\{q_1, ..., q_n\} \cup \{c_1. ... c_m\}$ to the search engine *E* and retrieve the top *J* documents;
9. Split documents into sentences and cluster them by agglomerative clustering;
10. Return a representative sentence from each cluster.

These parameters define a very large design space that results from instantiating the algorithm schema in algorithm 1. The steps that distinguish the connecting terms expansion algorithm from other forms of query expansion are highlighted.

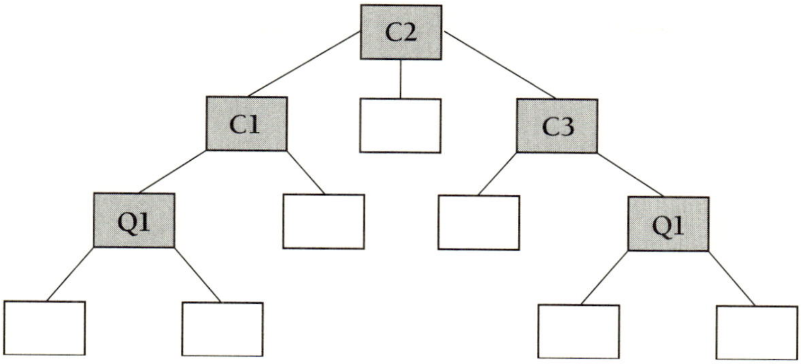

Figure 15.2. An Example of Connecting Terms Selection

Table 15.1 lists the particular values currently used by the QUIRK system. Below I discuss the choice for the values of the most significant parameters and alternatives that would be worth exploring.

15.3.1 The Definition of Connecting Node

In order to compute the list of connecting terms, cast the problem in terms of graphs. construct a graph *G* that has as nodes the union of the original query terms and a set of candidate expansion terms. The procedure by which the set of candidate expansion terms is selected is one of the three parameters of the connecting terms expansion algorithm schema and is explained in section 15.3.3. *G* is fully connected and the edge between nodes *A* and *B* is assigned as the similarity between *A* and *B*, as gleaned from the corpus co-occurrence statistics according to some measure (step 6 in algorithm 1). In the QUIRK system we define the connecting terms for a query as all the nodes in *G* that can be found on the smallest connected graph which (1) contains all query terms; and (2) is a subgraph of *G*'s maximum spanning tree (Sedgewick 1983).

The method for extracting this set corresponds to parameter C in step 7 of the connecting terms expansion algorithm schema.

Figure 15.2. is meant to depict the maximum spanning tree of some graph. The set of nodes highlighted in grey represents the smallest connected subgraph that contains *Q*1 and *Q*2. If *Q*1 and *Q*2 represent terms from a query (as *Tereshkova* and *Ride* might from the example in figure 15.1) then *C*1, *C*2, and *C*3 represent connecting terms for it, as **first**, **space**, and **woman** might be in the same example.

While the maximum spanning tree method proved to be satisfactory in the selection of connecting terms, one could readily think of plausible alternatives. Among them, other network algorithms such as *maxflow* and *mincut* algorithms (Sedgewick 1983), Bayesian Propagation as described in (Pearl 1998, Pearl 1994) or algorithms based on spreading activation such as Quillian (1968) and Charniak (1986). Choosing one of these other methods would result in a different definition of what it is for a node to be a connecting term for a query, and so in a different instantiation of the connecting terms expansion algorithm schema.

15.3.2 Co-Occurrence Measures

A second parameter of the connecting terms expansion algorithm schema is the particular choice of the similarity measure between two terms that appear in the corpus of interest (the K in step 6 of figure 15.1). Widely used *measures of dependence*[6] (Bargelt 2000) include χ^2, mutual information, correlation coefficient, cosine, Gini index and many others (see Hilderman and Hamilton 1999, Tan and Kumar 2000, and Tan, Kumar, and Srivastava 2002 for several insightful comparisons among them).

To experiment with a large number of such co-occurrence measures we have used Christian Borgelt's INES package (Bargelt 2000). This package implements over 20 such measures for which it can construct various graphical models such as optimal spanning trees. Experimenting with such a large number of measures we have observed that (1) measures tend to produce trees with characteristic shape types, with width versus depth being a salient dimension for differentiating them; and (2) deep and narrow trees tend to be inferior as a source of connecting terms because (a) deep trees yield large sets of connecting terms, (b) large sets of connecting terms can start to outweigh the original query terms and lead the IR engine astray; and (c) large, singly-connected graphs, from which the connecting terms are derived, are more likely to contain a low weight link and thus not be coherent units as desired.[7]

Shallow trees tend to be produced by the *measures weight of evidence, quadratic information gain, relief,* and *relevance,* while deep trees tend to be produced by *information gain, stochastic complexity,* and *reduction of description length.* In addition, we have found that *weight of evidence* (Michie 1998, Kononenko 1995), tends to outperform the other measures in its group because the small set of terms it produces contains terms that one would intuitively recognize as more relevant.

15.3.3 Selecting Initial Co-Occurrence Data

Because it is impractical to compute co-occurrence statistics for all terms in the corpus, our methods includes a step in which a selection of passages is retrieved over which such statistics are computed. This step is the most variable, and in some sense unsatisfactory aspect of our approach. The possible variations are too numerous to discuss in detail here. Here I simply state the choices we settled on after extensive experiments.

The co-occurrence data is selected from a small set of documents that match the original query sufficiently well as is done in pseudo-relevance feedback and local context analysis (Xu and Croft 1996). Currently we retrieve a fixed number of documents (25), but until recently we were setting the cutoff dynamically based on the differences amongst the scores[8] that the IR engine assigns to the top ranking documents. Further investigations would be needed to gather more empirical evidence on which strategy is best.

The retrieved documents are split into sentences, and a sentence-word matrix is constructed.[9] Only a top fraction of the sentences, as measured by their *overlap* (Manning and Schütze 1999) with the original query, is retained. Using sentences as the basis of co-occurrence is done because of the structure of news corpora, where documents tend to have tens of sentences, with most being irrelevant to the query. Having a finer grain of co-occurrence and discarding the irrelevant sentences from the documents leads to better connecting terms. This process may be inappropriate for a more focused corpus, such as the CNS corpus, which seems to average only about six sentences per document with highly focused documents.

Repetition counts are discarded and only presence/absence information is retained. This is done both because repetition within a single sentence is not significant, and because some dependence measures are designed for boolean data. Only terms that occur in a sufficient number of sentences and original query terms are retained for the computation of the connecting terms. This reduces dimensionality, helping prevent overfitting as well as speeding up computation.

15.3.4 Obtaining Final Answers

As discussed earlier returning the connecting terms by themselves is typically of limited use to a user. Instead I construct a new query, consisting of the original query terms and the connecting terms, with the original terms given greater weight. I retrieve a number of best matching sentences. Since the AQUAINT corpus contains large numbers of nearly identical passages, we have found it necessary to cluster the retrieved sentences using *overlap,* and return only one representative per cluster. This is designed to produce a set of sentences that between them contain all the query terms, without too much redundancy between the sentences.

15.4 Related Work

While our method bears superficial resemblance to local context analysis (Xu and Croft 1996), it seems conceptually closer to mining for indirect associations Tan, Kumar, and Srivastava2000).

Local context analysis expands queries with terms that are correlated to one or more query terms. However, the scoring formula does not appear to take the higher order dependency structure into account. In other words, given the query terms *dog* and *cat* local context analysis and pseudo relevance feedback are more likely to select terms that are strongly connected to a part of the query like *poodle, bone, siamese, mouse,* than terms that are moderately connected to all (or most) of the query like *veterinary, pet, animal*[10] which our method is designed to favor. This bias towards connecting terms is shared by Tan, Kumar, and Srivastava. (2000).[11] However, our approach can find linear chains of terms where each term is only correlated to its neighbors. This makes it at least in principle possible to trace a more complex relation between Alice and Emily like Alice lives next to Bob, Bob works with Cathy, Cathy carpools with Dick, Dick is Emily's cousin, provided the pairwise correlations exist in the corpus.

It also extends naturally to connecting more than two query terms since we actually work with trees. Tan, Kumar, and Srivastava (2000) only looked for one-step chains.

An experiment worth conducting would be to use our algorithm with Tan, Kumar, and Srivastava (2000)'s IS similarity measure,[12] which they show to have desirable properties for detecting associations.

There have also been other applications of graphical models to information retrieval (Callan, Croft, and Harding 1992, Tzeras and Hartmann 1993) as for example in the Inquery system (Callan, Croft, and Harding 1992). However, they are used at different levels of abstraction, with nodes representing entire documents and queries, rather than individual term occurrences.

15.5 Empirical Evaluation

Our system participated in the relationship track evaluation pilot conducted by the AQUAINT program.[13] Two assessors independently judged answers to 100 relationship questions, assigning to each answer a score between 0–4, inclusive. Zero was the low score: it meant that the response had no value at all. Four was the top score, and meant that the answer was completely satisfying. The other values had no specific meaning attached. The assessors were explicitly instructed to judge for content, not form, of the response. Apart from the three submissions to the pilot, the assessors were also given an answer set supplied by the human subjects who had created the questions. The assessors were unaware of the identities of the runs or even of the presence of a human-generated run. The following is a random sample of questions from the exercise:

1. In what country and by whom did Operation Turquoise take place?
2. What is the purpose in taking DHEA?
3. Why is the International Olympic Committee (IOC) concerned about human growth hormone?
4. What part did ITT (International Telephone and Telegraph) and Anaconda Copper play in the Chilean 1970 election?

Human	System A (QUIRK)	System B	System C
308.5	165.5	48.5	34.5

Table 15.2. Total Scores Averaged Over Assessors

Run	Assessor 1		Assessor 2	
	0	>0	0	>0
human	2	98	11	89
A (QUIRK)	22	78	45	55
B	76	24	79	21
C	78	22	87	13

Table 15.3. Zero Versus Nonzero Scores by the Assessors

5. What's the connection between the United States Navy and Puerto Rico's Vieques Island?
6. Who are the leaders of the Lebanese guerrilla organization Hezbollah?
7. What is the relationship between the West Nile Virus and the St. Louis encephalitis?
8. What caused the government to sue Microsoft?
9. What effect did introduction of the "iMac" computer have on the fortunes of Apple Corp.?
10. What is the connection between Jesse Ventura and Target Stores?
11. Why does Romania have a non-Slavic name?
12. What has been the relationship between Osama bin Laden and Sudan?
13. Was London's Millennium Dome successful as a tourist attraction?

In all results presented in the following figures our QUIRK system is system A. The total scores for the runs averaged between the two assessors are given in table 15.2.Table 15.3 gives the zero/non-zero score counts given by the two judges.

I must stress that these results must be interpreted against the background of an important design decision. While systems B and C tried to restrict their answers to either a single sentence or a short list of words describing the relationship[14] (comparable to our connecting terms), we decided, based on the reasoning in section 15.2.1, to display them in the context of complete sentences, as shown in figure 15.1. This accounts for the disparity in answer length, and makes it harder to draw conclusions from the scores. The developers of C confirmed our reasoning by performing their own evaluation, comparable to that in table 15.4, but also including a significantly higher scoring run of their system with answers presented in context (Run C-J). Their results of are presented in table 15.5.

Run	Min	Max	Median	Mean
humans	16	1007	151.5	200.0
A (QUIRK)	32	2844	757.0	832.1
B	4	401	48.5	86.8
C	2	863	15.0	33.2

Table 15.4. Answer Length Statistics Measured in Non-White-Space Characters

Run	0	>0
A (QUIRK)	39	61
B	80	20
C	78	22
C–J	59	41

Table 15.5. Team C's Reevaluation

15.6 Conclusion and Further Work

The system, originally tuned to work on the AQUAINT corpus, and tested on the 100 questions in the AQUAINT relationship pilot as discussed above, appears to work well on new corpora and unseen questions without recalibration. We use the same settings for querying the CNS abstracts data but with different questions, appropriate to this data ,hod as a part in other evaluations where we have observed it to be beneficial. Thus it appears at least that we have not overfitted the initial question set, which was quite diverse to begin with. This lends some further empirical support to the underlying ideas of our approach. However, many incidental decisions had to be made to turn these ideas into a working system. Most of these were arrived at by trial and error. More data on comparisons with other system is also desirable.

Acknowledgements

I would like to thank the other QUIRK members, Stefano Bertolo and Bjoern Aldag, for their feedback on the ideas leading to this approach and extensive editorial work on this chapter. I wish to acknowledge the support of the ARDA AQUAINT program, which has funded this research. I would also like to thank the anonymous reviewers for their constructive suggestions. Much credit is also due to the Open Source software community that has provided many critical components of our system: specific tools like Lemur and INES, as well as the ubiquitous infrastructure of Linux, GNU, Python, and Perl.

Notes

1. See http: //www.ic-arda.org/InfoExploit/aquaint/. Participants in this program have access to two corpora: a newswire corpus spanning 1996-2000 and a subset of the Center for Nonproliferation Studies abstracts. The AQUAINT evaluations are carried

out against these corpora. They are referred to as the AQUAINT and the CNS corpus respectively.

2. Unlike the example in figure 15.1, these examples are hypothetical and designed for pedagogical purposes. It is not claimed that any system exactly replicates any given example. They are offered in place of the actual output of the QUIRK system to avoid confusing the intuitions I wish to convey to the reader with the imperfections of our current system. For example, in figure 15.1, shuttle is actually returned by our system as a connecting term even if it is in fact irrelevant to the query.

3. This is an important point to which I return in section 15.5.

4. This would be a connected subgraph of the initial graph that contains all the seed nodes and optimizes some property, as a shortest path or a maximum spanning tree does. Any nodes in this subgraph, but not in the seed set, can be considered to be between the seed nodes in the initial graph.

5. A probabilistic retrieval model enables us to obtain good partial matches for a set of terms without having to construct complex boolean query expressions.

6. Sometimes also called measures of (im)purity (Kononenko 1995) or measures of interestingness (Hilderman and Hamilton 1999; Tan and Kumar 2000; Tan, Kumar, and Srivastava, 2002).

7. This is a generalized case of a chain being only as strong as its weakest link.

8. Kullback-Leibler (KL) divergence of the retrieved document from the query.

9. I effectively treat sentences as documents in their own right.

10. This example is hypothetical, intended to leverage the reader's intuitions about likely strength of associations. It would be an interesting research problem to actually define a protocol that would allow us to test these intuitions empirically and to use that protocol to test if there really is a significant difference between the technique I describe in this chapter and the other techniques to which I am comparing it.

11. I have become aware of this work only recently.

12. This measure is not among the measures provide by the Bayes net package we currently use. The experiment would thus require us to modify the internals of the INES package.

13. I thank Ellen Voorhees, who organized the relationship question evaluation at NIST, for giving me permission to use the evaluation data in this chapter.

14. Personal communications.

Daniel Mahler is a scientist at Cycorp Inc. in Austin, Texas.

Chapter 16

Viewing the Web as a Virtual Database for Question Answering

Boris Katz, Sue Felshin, Jimmy Lin, and Gregory Marton

1.1 Introduction

The vast amount of information available on the world wide web has given people potential access to more knowledge than they have ever had before. But much of this potential remains unrealized due to the lack of effective information access methods to help people separate useful knowledge from useless data.

Question answering has recently emerged as a technology that promises to provide more intuitive methods of information access. In contrast to the traditional information retrieval model of formulating queries and browsing resulting documents, a QA system accepts user information requests phrased in everyday language and responds with a concise answer. When asked "What country in Asia has the lowest infant mortality rate?" a computer system should be able to respond with something like "Singapore has the lowest infant mortality rate among countries in Asia (3.62 deaths per 1000 births)." Similarly, the computer should be able to return digital images of Monet's water lilies in response to "Show me some famous paintings by Monet."

In this chapter, we present a data model, called the *object-property-value model,* for organizing and integrating heterogeneous, semistructured, and structured resources. Because our data model naturally captures the semantic content of many real-world user questions, it serves as a powerful paradigm for building QA systems. We have implemented our ideas in START and Omnibase, two components of a web-based QA system.

Our data model can be illustrated through a simple scenario: suppose someone is asked a question like "Who was Abraham Lincoln married to?" He or she might locate a resource with the answer—say, a book on famous historical figures, or a web site about Presidents—find the section for Abraham Lincoln (figure 16.1), and look up information about his spouse. Millions of questions

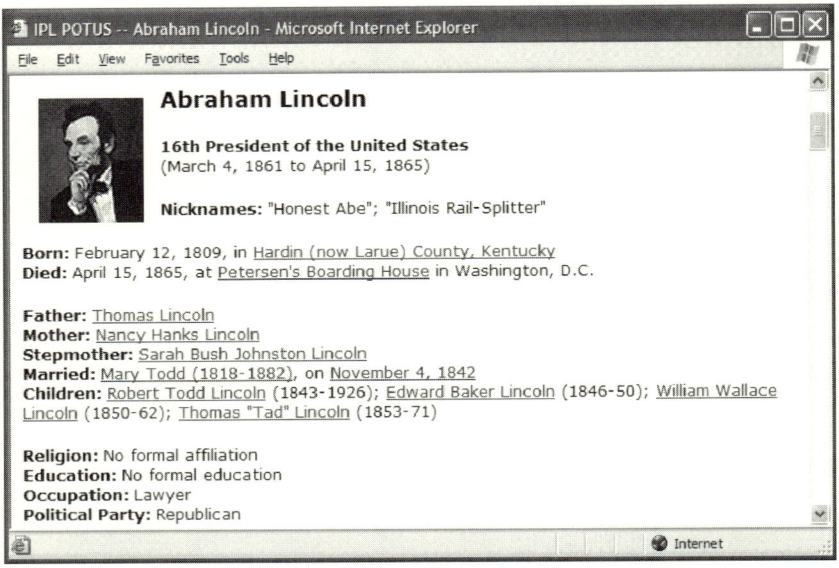

Figure 16.1. A Page from the Internet Public Library about an object (Abraham Lincoln), which contains values for many properties.

can be answered in this manner: by extracting an object (Abraham Lincoln) and a property (spouse) from the question, finding a data source (e.g., the Internet Public Library) for that type of object, looking up the object's web page, and extracting the value for the answer (Mary Todd). Our question answering system responds to natural language questions using exactly this procedure (figure 16.2).

The three main challenges in getting a computer to answer natural language questions are understanding the question, identifying where to find the information, and fetching the information itself. START (Katz 1988, Katz 1997) and Omnibase (Katz et al. 2002a) comprise our natural language QA system[1] developed to address these challenges. START is responsible for understanding user questions and translating them into structured object-property-value queries. Omnibase is a "virtual" database that provides a uniform interface to multiple web knowledge sources, and is capable of executing the structured queries generated by START.

16.2 The Web as a Database

The world wide web contains numerous resources that hold vast amounts of knowledge in relatively structured formats. For example, the World Factbook provides political, geographic, and economic information about every country in the world; Biography.com has collected profiles of over 25,000 famous peo-

Question	Object	Property	Value
Who wrote the music for *Star Wars?*	*Star Wars*	composer	John Williams
Who invented dynamite?	dynamite	inventor	Alfred Nobel
How big is Costa Rica?	Costa Rica	area	41,100 sq. km.
How many people live in Kiribati?	Kiribati	population	94,149
What languages are spoken in Guernsey?	Guernsey	languages	English, French
When did Sweden gain its independence?	Sweden	independence	June 6, 1523
Show me paintings by Monet.	Monet	works	[images]

Table 16.1. Sample Questions Captured by our Object-Property-Value Model

ple; the Internet Movie Database stores entries for hundreds of thousands of movies, including information about their cast, directors, and other properties. Many of these sources are part of the "deep" or "invisible" web, which cannot be accessed through normal hypertext navigation; such knowledge is stored in databases accessible only through specific search interfaces.

To effectively use these semistructured resources for question answering, the plethora of knowledge sources must be integrated under a common interface or query language. Our Omnibase system accomplishes just this by acting like a "virtual" database: the system presents a local and uniform view of content distributed across remote servers in heterogeneous formats. Diverse resources are captured using our object-property-value data model. Under this framework, data sources contain objects which have properties, and questions are translated into requests for the value of these properties. Omnibase serves as a mediator between a structured query interface and disparate resources. It is of course impossible to impose any uniform schema on the entire web. However, we believe that our object-property-value model is simple enough to capture the content of many web resources, and expressive enough to answer many types of natural language questions.

Natural language commonly employs an "of" relation or a possessive to express the relationship between an object and its property, e.g., "the director of La Strada" or "La Strada's director." Table 16.1 shows, however, that there are many alternative ways to ask for the value of an object's property. Often, properties can be encoded in the arguments of verbs, e.g., the subject of the verb *invent* is the value of the inventor property, and the direct object of the verb is the value of the invention property. Adjectives can similarly be interpreted as properties, e.g., "how big" is understood as requesting the area property of a particular country.

Clearly, many other possible types of queries do not fall into the object-property-value model, such as questions about the relation between two objects (e.g., "How can I get from Boston to New York?").[2] However, our experiments reveal that in practice questions of the object-property-value type occur

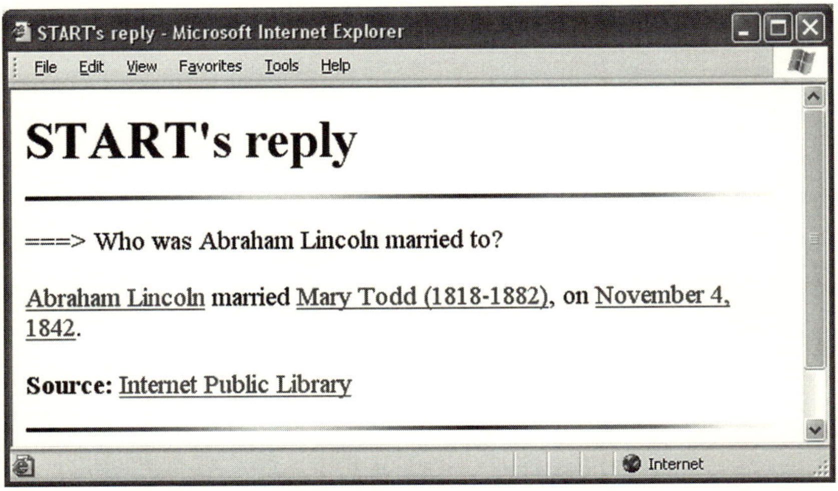

Figure 16.2. START Answering a Question Using Omnibase

quite frequently. For example, just ten web sources organized according to our data model suffice to answer 27% of TREC-9 and 47% of TREC-10 questions from the QA track (Lin 2002).

16.3 START and Omnibase

A schematic representation of the relationship between START and Omnibase is shown in figure 16.3. Conceptually, START is responsible for understanding the syntax and the semantics of user questions and then distilling the information requests into object-property-value queries. Omnibase is responsible for executing those queries and fetching answers from the world wide web and other sources. Omnibase serves as an abstraction layer over collections of heterogeneous semistructured data, providing START with a uniform query interface. The following sections describe in more detail how START and Omnibase interact to form two components of our question answering system.

16.3.1 Analyzing Natural Language

Given an English sentence containing various relative clauses, appositions, multiple levels of embedding, etc., the START system first breaks it up into smaller units, called kernel sentences (usually containing one verb). After separately analyzing each kernel sentence, START rearranges the elements of all parse trees it constructs into a set of embedded representational structures. These structures are made up of a number of fields corresponding to various syntactic constituents of a sentence, but the three most salient of them, the subject of a sentence, the object, and the relation between them, are singled

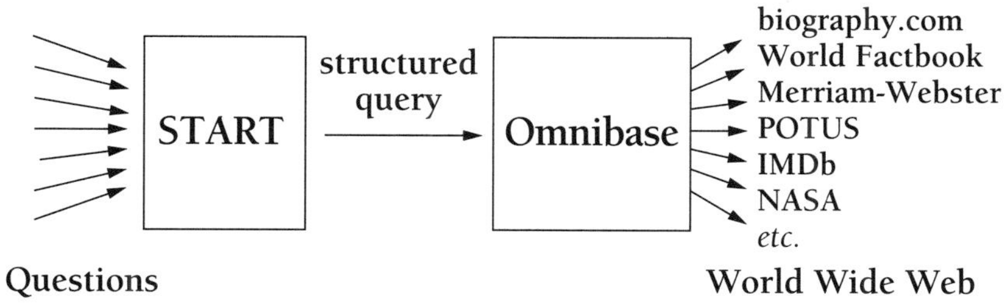

Figure 16.3. Overall architecture of START and Omnibase

out as playing a special role in indexing. These constituents are explicitly represented in a discrimination network for efficient retrieval. As a result, all sentences analyzed by START are indexed as ternary expressions (t-expressions), <subject relation object> (Katz 1988). Certain other constituents (adjectives, possessive nouns, prepositional phrases, etc.), are used to create additional t-expressions in which prepositions and several special words may serve as relations. Additional grammatical features associated with a sentence (adverbs and their position, tense, auxiliaries, voice, negation, etc.) are recorded in a separate representational structure called a history. When we index the t-expression in the knowledge base, we cross-reference its components and attach the history to it. One can thus think of the resulting entry in the knowledge base as a "digested summary" of the syntactic structure of an English sentence. In order to handle embedded sentences, START allows any t-expression to take another t-expression as its subject or object. Thus, the system can analyze and generate sentences with arbitrarily complex embedded structures.

Questions are requests for information from START's knowledge base. In order to answer a question, START must translate the question into a t-expression template which can be used to search the knowledge base for t-expressions containing information relevant to providing an answer.

The embedded ternary expressions used by START mimic the hierarchical organization of English sentences and parallel the representational characteristics of natural language. A language-based knowledge representation system has many advantages: it is very expressive and easy to use; it provides a uniform symbolic representation for parsing and generation; and it makes it possible to automatically create large knowledge bases from natural language texts. However, a representation mimicking the hierarchical organization of natural language syntax has one undesirable consequence: sentences differing in surface syntax but close in meaning are not considered similar by the system. For example, speakers of English would recognize that "The president surprised the country with his determination" and "The president's determination surprised the country" have the same meaning, despite differences in their syntactic structures. This poses a problem to any syntactically-based representation of language: due to different syntactic structures, a machine cannot automatically match a question stated one way with an answer formulated in another way.

To be able to handle such phenomena, commonly known as lexical alternations, a natural language system should be aware of the interactions between the syntactic and semantic properties of verbs. The *surprise* example above is just one example of the alternations phenomena that pervade natural language. In this instance, we want START to know that whenever *A* surprised *B* with *C*, then it is also true that *A*'s *C* surprised *B*. We do this by introducing structural transformational rules, called *s-rules* (Katz and Levin 1988), that make explicit the relationship between alternate realizations of verb arguments. Linguists have noticed that verbs which undergo the same alternations can be grouped into semantic classes (Levin, 1993); as a result, s-rules can be generalized to cover entire classes of verbs. Thus, a relatively small number of such rules suffice to capture a significant portion of the phenomena. In the example above, the verb *surprise* is a member of the *emotional reaction class*, whose members also include other verbs like *amaze, amuse, impress, scare, stun,* etc. Although s-rules must be manually constructed, a special component inside START allows the rules to be inferred from a set of English sentences which capture a specific instance of the rule. START analyzes these sentences, queries the user for additional information regarding elements of corresponding t-expressions, and then builds appropriately-generalized s-rules automatically.

16.3.2 Natural Language Annotations

Mediation between natural language questions and Omnibase queries is accomplished through a technology we developed called *natural language annotations* (Katz 1997), which are machine-parseable sentences and phrases that describe the content of various content segments. They serve as metadata describing the questions that a particular piece of knowledge can answer.

In the simplest mode of operation, annotations are attached to static content segments (e.g., a part of an HTML document, an image, etc.). The combination of natural language annotations and a content segment forms a simple *schema:*

Annotations:
Mars' two moons
Phobos and Deimos orbit Mars.

Content Segment:
[images] Mars has two small moons: Phobos and Deimos. Phobos (fear) and Deimos (panic) were named after the horses that pulled the chariot of the Greek war god Ares, the counterpart to the Roman war god Mars...

START parses the annotations and stores the parsed ternary expressions with pointers back to the original content segment. To answer a question, the user query is compared against the annotations stored in the knowledge base. Because this match occurs at the level of syntactic structure, linguistically sophisticated machinery such as synonymy, hyponymy, ontologies, and structural transformation rules are all brought to bear on the matching process. Linguistic techniques allow the system to achieve capabilities beyond simple keyword matching, for example, handling complex syntactic alternations (Katz and Levin 1988), recognizing active/passive variations, or dealing with such linguistic phenomena as dative movement. If a match is found between ternary expressions derived from annotations and those derived from the query, the corresponding segment is returned to the user as the answer. For example, the annotations above allow START to answer questions such as the following:

What satellites orbit Mars?
How many moons orbit Mars?
What are the names of Mars' moons?

An important feature of the annotation concept is that any information segment can be annotated: not only static content, but also procedures and-database queries. For example, one can annotate a procedure for calculating distances between two locations. In this case, the matching of a user question with an annotation triggers the extraction of relevant parameters, i.e., the name of the two locations. These extracted elements become dynamically instantiated parameters in the procedure attached to the natural language annotation. The execution of that procedure results in the computation of the answer. Similarly, START is connected to Omnibase through schemata annotated with natural language annotations.

16.3.3 Identifying Objects and Sources

Suppose a user asks "Who directed gone with the wind?" START cannot analyze this question without first knowing that *Gone with the Wind* can be treated as a single lexical item (otherwise, the question would make no more sense than, say, "Who hopped flown down the street?"). Omnibase serves as a large external lexicon that helps START identify the names of objects and the data sources they are associated with.

Knowledge about objects not only helps START understand the user question (which can now be read as "Who directed *x*?"), but also lets START know what data source contains the information; i.e., information about *x* is contained in a movie database. With this information, START can construct an Omnibase query that, when executed, will compute the answer to the user question.

16.3.4 Fetching Answers

Omnibase contains a large collection of wrapper scripts tailored to specific

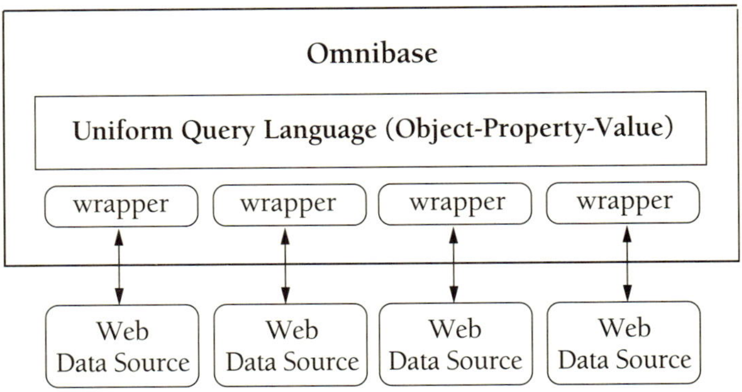

Figure 16.4. Organization of Omnibase

web resources and other data sources. With this framework, our system is able to abstract away the idiosyncrasies of each individual source and present START with a uniform query interface under the object-property-value model (figure 16.4).

For some sources, pages about individual objects exist as static HTML pages, but for other sources, pages are generated dynamically with a CGI script. Depending on the source, values of properties might be aligned in tables, in lists, or even in free text. Typically, values are extracted by performing regular-expression pattern matching on the source HTML page using Omnibase's built-in facilities for pattern matching.

Once again, consider the question "Who directed gone with the wind?" After *Gone with the Wind* is identified as the name of a movie from the Internet Movie Database, the question then matches a particular natural language annotation, resulting in a complete object-property-value query:

(get "imdb-movie" "Gone with the Wind (1939)" "DIRECTOR")

To execute the query, Omnibase looks up the data source and property to find the associated wrapper script and applies the script to the object in order to retrieve the property value for the object. The execution of the *imdb-movie* director script involves looking up a unique identifier for the movie (stored locally), fetching the correct page from the IMDb website, and matching a textual landmark on the page to find the director of the movie. As a result, the list of movie directors is returned:

("George Cukor" "Victor Fleming" "Sam Wood")

START then assembles the answer and presents it to the user either as a fragment of HTML or couched in natural language (see figure 16.5). By providing the right granularity of information to the user through natural language access, we can most effectively fulfill the user's information needs.

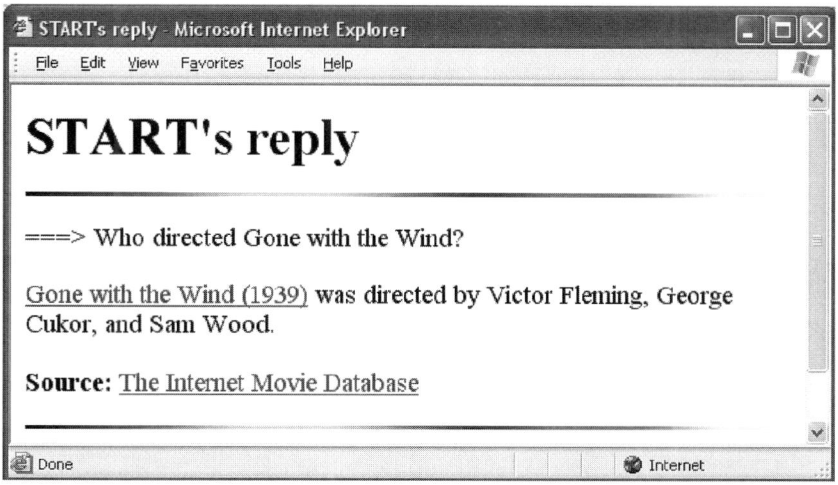

Figure 16.5. START's Answer to "Who Directed Gone With the Wind?"

16.3.5 Deployment and Evaluation

Since it came on-line in December 1993, START has engaged in exchanges with hundreds of thousands of users all over the world, supplying them with useful knowledge. Currently, over 100 web resources, many of them containing hundreds of thousands of individual pages, have been integrated into START and Omnibase.

At present, our system answers millions of natural language questions about places (e.g., cities, countries, lakes, coordinates, weather, maps, demographics, political and economic systems), movies (e.g., titles, actors, directors), people (e.g., birth dates, biographies), dictionary definitions, and much, much more. Because START performs sophisticated linguistic processing of questions to pinpoint the exact information need of a user, questions can be answered with remarkable precision.

In the period from January 2000, to December 2002, about a million questions were posed to START and Omnibase. Of those, approximately 67% were answered successfully by our system (table 16.2). The most common failure was the lack of knowledge: in those cases, START was successful in analyzing the user question, but the knowledge required to answer the question was simply not available to the system. Only in approximately 10% of the questions did START encounter unknown lexical items or fail to parse the sentence. Of all the questions successfully answered by our system, about 50% were handled by Omnibase.

We have also deployed a simplified version of our annotation-based approach to question answering in a system called Aranea, which was formally

	2000	2001	2002
Answered using Omnibase	85k (27.1%)	100k (37.6%)	129k (37.9%)
Answered with native KB	123k (39.3%)	74k (27.9%)	107k (31.5%)
Don't know	72k (22.9%)	65k (24.3%)	78k (22.8%)
Don't understand	19k (6.0%)	15k (5.5%)	14k (4.2%)
Unknown word	15k (4.8%)	12k (4.7%)	12k (3.6%)
Total	313k (100%)	266k (100%)	342k (100%)

	2000	2001	2002
Total Answered Successfully	208k (66.4%)	174k (65.5%)	237k (69.4%)
Answered using Omnibase	40.9%	57.4%	54.6%
Answered with native KB	59.1%	42.6%	45.4%

Table 16.2. Evaluation of START and Omnibase

The top table shows results of all types of system responses and the bottom table shows the performance contribution of Omnibase and START's native KB.

evaluated at the TREC-2002 question answering track. Our data model and annotation-based technique was able to achieve 71% accuracy in answering previously unseen questions (Lin and Katz 2003). Furthermore, similar techniques for structuring knowledge sources to answer frequently-occurring questions have been effectively used by other TREC systems (Chu-Carroll et al. 2002, Clarke et al. 2002).

In addition to the main START website, we have built domain-specific servers for a variety of custom applications. In September, 1989, the *Voyager 2* space probe concluded its grand tour of the solar system with a flyby of Neptune. In cooperation with researchers from the Jet Propulsion Laboratory (JPL), START was taught knowledge about *Voyager* and Neptune, and it successfully answered questions posed by members of the press during the encounter. In another collaboration with NASA, our system was on display at JPL's annual open house in May 2001. Guests of all ages were both informed and entertained by the system. Other custom applications of START include a permanent exhibit at the MIT Museum and a prototype in which the system was taught knowledge from a college-level biology textbook.

Finally, the viability of our annotation-based question-answering technique has also been demonstrated commercially. For example, Ask Jeeves, currently the web's second most popular search engine, has licensed certain technology pioneered by START (Katz and Winston 1994, 1995).

16.4 Related Work

The use of natural language interfaces to access databases can be traced back to the 1960s and 1970s in systems such as BASEBALL (Green et al. 1961), Lunar (Woods et al. 1972), and Lifer (Hendrix 1977); see Androutsopoulos et al. (1995) for a survey. In these systems, syntactic analysis of user questions was intertwined with the semantic interpretation process. The result was brittle, monolithic systems that were difficult to adapt to new domains. Furthermore, these early systems were applied to well-structured data originating from a single source, which severely limited the scope of possible applications. In contrast, START and Omnibase maintain strict separation of syntax and semantics through the object-property-value data model: START is capable of performing complex linguistic analysis, but distills results into a simple yet expressive semantic structure, i.e., a structured query to Omnibase.

The idea of applying database techniques to the world wide web is not new, either; see Florescu et al. (1998) for a survey. Many existing systems, e.g., Araneus (Atzeni et al. 1997), Ariadne (Knoblock et al. 2001), Information Manifold (Kirk et al. 1995), Lore (McHugh et al. 1997), Tsimmis (Hammer et al. 1997), and others, have attempted to integrate heterogeneous web sources under a common interface. Unfortunately, queries to such systems must be formulated in SQL, Datalog, or some similar formal language, which render them inaccessible to the average user. What makes START and Omnibase unique among database systems that integrate semistructured data is its use of the object-property-value data model and the natural language interface it facilitates. Because this model corresponds naturally to both user questions and online content, the data integration task becomes more intuitive. To our knowledge, the START-Omnibase combination is the first system to provide natural language access to heterogeneous and semistructured data.

16.5 Contributions

We have organized diverse heterogeneous and semistructured data on the world wide web by creating an abstraction layer centered around our object-property-value model. Because many natural language queries translate into this data model, we can capture their semantics in a simple yet expressive manner. Furthermore, since our data model is reflective of real-world user queries, broad knowledge coverage can be achieved with a reasonable amount of manual labor.

We have implemented our ideas in two components of a QA system. START understands users' natural language queries and translates them into object-property-value queries, which are subsequently executed by Omnibase. Our experience shows this to be a very intuitive division of labor that allows easy integration of both advanced natural language processing and database techniques. Together, START and Omnibase provide access to a wealth of information freely available on the world wide web. We believe that our techniques for structuring heterogeneous and semistructured data sources offer an effective strategy for tackling the information access challenge and that they will become an integral part of future QA systems.

Acknowledgments

This research was funded by DARPA under contract number F30602-00-1-0545. Additional funding was provided by the Oxygen Project.

Notes

1. http://www.ai.mit.edu/projects/infolab
2. START, however, is capable of handling such questions in a more ad-hoc fashion.

Boris Katz is a principal research scientist and head of the InfoLab group at the Computer Science and Artificial Intelligence Laboratory at the Massachusetts Institute of Technology.

Sue Felshin is a research scientist at the Computer Science and Artificial Intelligence Laboratory at the Massachusetts Institute of Technology.

Jimmy Lin is a graduate student at the Computer Science and Artificial Intelligence Laboratory at the Massachusetts Institute of Technology.

Gregory Marton is a graduate student studying natural language understanding at the InfoLab group at the Computer Science and Artificial Intelligence Laboratory at the Massachusetts Institute of Technology.

Chapter 17

Toward Answer-Focused Summarization Using Search Engines

Harris Wu, Dragomir R. Radev, and Weiguo Fan

17.1 Introduction

People use search engines to find answers to a variety of questions on the Internet. Sometimes users issue queries in the original form of a natural language question, such as "Who is the president of France?" An analysis of the Excite corpus of 2.5 million actual user queries shows that around 8.4% of the queries are in the form of natural language questions (Radev et al. 2001).

More often, users rewrite their natural language questions into keywords and try different combinations of keywords as queries on search engines. Obviously much information will be lost when a natural language question is reduced to a set of keywords. However, many users prefer to use keywords rather than natural language questions, because the search engines appear to be inefficient in accepting natural language questions as queries. In fact, search engines typically filter out stop-words such as "what" and "why" so a question would have been processed as a list of keywords even if it were submitted in a natural language question form.

After a search engine returns a set of hits related to the query, the user's next step is then to go through these documents in the hit list and find the answers to the original question. The search cost depends largely on how many document links a user has to click through, and the length of each document a user has to skim over.

Some search engines, such as Google and NorthernLight, provide a short summary for each document with query words highlighted. If a question has a short answer and if a user can find the answer in these summaries, the search cost can be largely reduced. In fact, many questions issued to search engines have short answers. Among the natural language questions on Excite, 43.9%

are factual questions that have short answers, e.g., "What is the country code for Belgium" (Radev et al. 2001). The rest of them consist of nonfactual ("How do I ..."), syntactically incorrect, or unanswerable questions.

Search costs would be greatly reduced if search engines could accept natural language questions and provide summaries that answer these questions. In this chapter, we will focus on this specific type of summarization, namely answer-rocused summarization (AFS), which summarizes documents to answer questions in a natural language question form. While traditional summaries aim to concisely state the main points of documents, answer-focused summaries try to extract information from documents to answer natural language questions.

Answer-focused summarization is not limited to search engines. The process of extracting answer-focused summaries from documents is a form of query-based passage retrieval (Callan 1994, Tombros and Sanderson 1992, White et al. 2001). The three most recent TREC conferences (1999 to 2001) (Voorhees 2002) included a popular track in which Q and A systems from more than 50 institutions competed. Simultaneously, the Document Understanding Conferences provide a forum for the evaluation and comparison of text summarization systems. As both recent roadmap papers on summarization (Baldwin et al. 2000) and question answering (Burger et al. 2000) indicate, the dual problems of information access, summarization and question answering, are bound to meet.

Here we provide some additional motivation showing how intricately related summarization and question answering are. We describe several experiments that indicate promising directions along which we can improve answer-focused summarization, and present a set of methods that significantly outperforms Google's summary generator in question answering. In this chapter: (1) we develop a set of criteria and performance metrics to evaluate answer-focused summarization; (2) we develop a proximity-based answer-focused summarization system, which complements existing search engines and other document retrieval systems (our summarization system is capable of analyzing and utilizing question types to provide better answer-focused summaries); (3) through experiments we find summarization provided by Google, one of the best search engines available, suboptimal in question answering (our summarization system shows significant advantage in key performance metrics); and (4) we provide recommendations to search engines to improve their summarization for question answering. We also suggest some promising research directions along which better answer-focused summarizations and information retrieval systems can be made. We suggest that better answer-focused summarization may help bring Internet information systems to wireless and hand-held devices, where search cost is critical.

17.2 Evaluating Answer-Focused Summaries

Not all answer-focused summaries are created equal. Ideally, a good answer-focused summary should satisfy three criteria in decreasing order of importance:

(1) *accuracy*—it should contain the answer to the user's question; (2) *economy*—it should be as short as possible; and (3) *support*—it should provide evidence that supports the answer.

We should note that support may contradict economy. For single-document summaries provided by search engines, users can go from a summary to the parent document to find support for the answer. In this chapter we will limit ourselves to single-document summaries and focus on the first two criteria. A future paper will be devoted to the support issue for extracted answers.

The TREC Q and A evaluation (up to the latest TREC-10) uses the mean reciprocal document rank (MRDR) metric to compare participating systems. MRDR is the mean of reciprocal ranks of the highest-ranked correct answers to a set of questions. For example, if the third answer presented by the system is the first correct one, the value of the reciprocal document rank will be $^1/_3$. If we treat the lists of answers in TREC evaluation as answer-focused summaries, the MRDR metrics address a combination of criterion 1 and criterion 2. In addition, The TREC evaluation addresses criterion 2 by stipulating a fixed number of characters (50 or 250) to be extracted by the systems. Given that most answers to the TREC evaluation corpus are rather short (less than 20 characters), a large percentage of the extracted characters do not contain answer words at all. Criterion 3, support, is not considered in the current TREC Q and A evaluation.

In this chapter, we will use three different metrics to evaluate the first two criteria, accuracy and economy, on answer-focused summaries of documents returned from search engine queries: (1) whether a question is answered; (2) summary rank of first answer; and (3) summary length in characters.

Summary rank depends on both the order of relevant documents returned by a system, and the quality of summarization. For example, if a search engine returns 10 documents and one summary per document, each 100 words long, then a hypothetical correct answer contained in the third summary would get a summary rank of 3. If the first two documents do not contain the answer at all, then the best possible summary rank is 3 because the summaries for the first two documents cannot possibly contain the answer. Summary rank is distinct from document rank used in TREC evaluation in that summaries may potentially come from multiple documents.

Figure 17.1 shows the summaries produced by Google for question 29 of TREC-8: "What is the brightest star visible from Earth?" The correct answer, "Sirius," also occurs in the summaries produced by Google. "Sirius" appears in the fourth hit, therefore, the summary rank of first answer is 4.

In the example above, it is clear by reading the summaries that somehow the Google's summarizer just misses the correct answer in the first two summaries by a small number of words. Obviously, a good summarization algorithm should catch these correct answers while, at the same time, should not produce extra-long summaries. In the following we will show from our experiments that there is a large potential for improvement in summaries provided

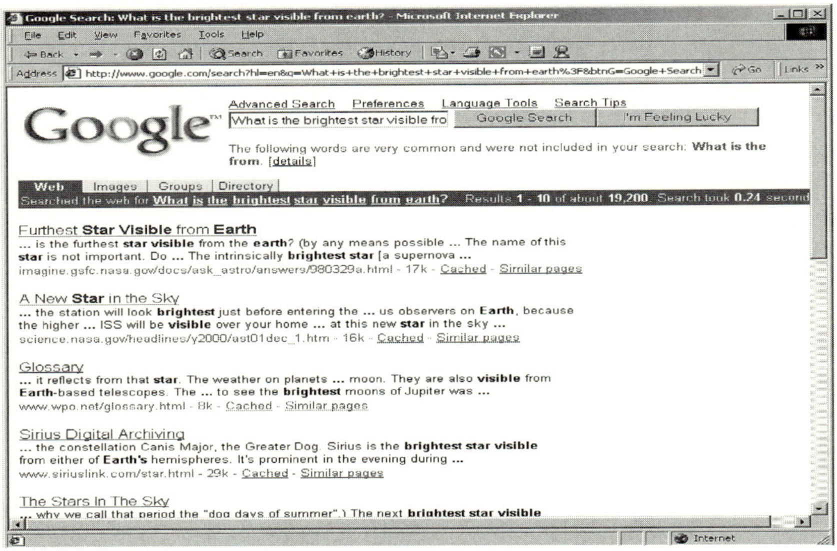

Figure 17.1. Summaries Provided by Google

by search engines for question answering. Furthermore, we will show that the information contained in a question itself, as simple as whether the question is a "who" or "where" question, can significantly contribute to the performance of summarization.

17.3 Experiments

In the following experiments we use the evaluation query corpus from the Q and A track in TREC-8, held in 1999. The TREC-8 Q and A track was the first large-scale evaluation of domain-independent QA systems (Vorhees and Tice 2000). The TREC-8 corpus consists of 200 factual questions and most answers to them are definitive and short (less than 20 characters). Thus the corpus suits our need for questions that can be answered by summaries. The size of the corpus allows us to split the corpus for training and evaluation purposes.

17.3.1 Baseline: Google

Google is one of the most popular search engines on the Internet. It has been shown that Google has the best performance in question answering among other search engines (Radev, et al. 2002b, Radev et al. 2001). Our baseline is based on Google's summaries.

First, we sent the 200 questions from TREC-8 (Voorhees and Tice 2000) to Google. We saved the first page of results for each question and parsed them to extract the different fields that Google produces: URL, title, description

TREC Questions	Answered	Avg Summary Length	MRSR
1-100	35/100	159	0.187
100-200	38/100	160	0.228
1-200	73/100	160	0.207

Table 17.1. Baseline Performance of Google's Summaries

(rarely provided, only 203 of them were retrieved from 2000 hits), summary, and category. Note that we did not have access to Google via an automated agent, so we had to query it manually.

Second, we removed from consideration hits originating in sites participating in TREC. Most of the time, such hits contain both the TREC question and its answer. Allowing these documents in the evaluation would have skewed the results. In total, 94 out of 2000 hits came from such places.

Third, we evaluate Google's summaries using the metrics for answer-focused summaries: number of questions answered, average character length of summaries, and mean reciprocal of summary ranks (MRSR). To illustrate MRSR, an MRSR value of 0.2 means that on average the answer to a question appears in the fifth summary provide by the system. Even when the order of documents returned remains the same, better quality of summaries will result in a higher MRSR. An MRSR value of close to 1 means that a user on average can find the answers in the first summary they read. Of course, MRSR is limited by the quality of document ranking provided by the search engine.

Overall, 73 of the 200 hit lists contained one or more answers. Table 17.1 gives the values of four metrics for Google's summaries.

17.3.2 Experiment 1: Proximity-Based Summary

This experiment is to test our proximity-based summarization system. Google's summarization algorithm is proprietary, and we do not have details of its implementation. Based on our observation of the summaries provided by Google, the algorithm seems to have used word proximity, relative word ordering, position in text, and a large indexed document database. Since we do not have a large document database, our summarization system uses a rather simple proximity-based extraction.

It has been observed that the distance from query words to answers in a document is relatively small (Prager et al. 2000). Here we try to quantify that distance and use it for AFS extraction. We follow the steps in the following list:

1. We identify all query words that appear in the documents on the hit list.
2. We extract short windows of size *wsize* around query words.
3. We put the windows in order so that the windows containing the biggest number of unique query keywords are placed in the front.
4. We concatenate as many short windows as possible to produce a summary

within *ssize* characters. The two variables, *wsize* and *ssize* are given as parameters. We run experiments with wsize from 1 to 20 at increment of 1, ssize from 100 to 400 at increment of 10.

The actual average passage size is below the summary size limit *ssize*. *ssize* = 200 generally provides summaries of average size below 160, which is comparable to Google's. We focus on finding the optimal window size for our proximity-based summary extraction. Using the first one hundred TREC-8 questions as training data and the metrics mentioned in last section, we find the best window size that has most questions answered given actual average passage size below Google's. We assume the number of questions answered is more important than the summary rank. In fact, in our experiments the results of two metrics turn out to be highly correlated to each other with correlation coefficient >0.9. The passage size *ssize* is more a constraint rather than a metric in the experiment. Note that for any given window size, larger *ssize* will always bring equal or better values on number of questions answered and summary ranks. Using the optimal window size from training and keeping the average passage size below Google's, we evaluate on the second one hundred questions in the corpus. The performance results are shown in table 17.2.

17.3.3 Experiment 2: Summarization With Question Type Known

This experiment is to test whether the knowledge of question types will help improve the performance of our proximity-based summary extraction.

In this experiment, we first manually classify each of the 200 TREC-8 questions into one of the following question types based on the answers they expect: person (56), place (36), name (29), number (23), date (22) and other (34). We use the same proximity-based extraction described in last section, to get the summary for each question, with different window size and passage size parameters. We find the best window size for each question type, using the first 100 TREC-8 questions as training data. Then we evaluate on the second 100 of the TREC-8 questions. Table 17.3 shows the performance results. In Table 17.3, "ansrd" stands for "answered," and "w" stands for *wsize*.

Using question type information, the performance of summary extraction has improved notably. On the training set, 47 questions are answered compared to 41 answered in experiment 1, which indicates that questions of different types tend to have different optimal window sizes. On the evaluation set, 46 questions are answered compared to 41 answered in experiment 1, and 38 answered by Google. The number of questions answered is 21% more than Google's, and 12% more than that of experiment 1. The MRSR on the evaluation set is 0.247, compared to experiment 1's 0.237 and Google's 0.228.

For person-type questions, the optimal window size from training data is 4, and the actual optimal window size in evaluation is 4 or 5. For number-type the actual optimal window size is 2 for both training and evaluation. The training seems to be very successful in these cases. Place-type questions seem to

	Eval on questions 1-100		Eval on questions 100-200	
wsize	#Answered	MRSR	#Answered	MRSR
1	23	.075	33	.167
2	38	.164	41	.243
3	38	.176	39	.242
4	43	.211	41	.237
5	37	.190	42	.231
6	37	.202	39	.243
7	37	.219	42	.243
8	39	.218	45	.226
9	39	.214	46	.232
10	38	.197	42	.248
11	38	.205	41	.225
12	37	.179	41	.226
13	37	.184	39	.215
14	36	.182	38	.195
15	38	.185	42	.202
16	37	.187	41	.205
17	38	.199	41	.207
18	37	.206	40	.199
19	33	.179	37	.188
20	34	.172	40	.189
Google	**35**	**.187**	**38**	**.228**

Table 17.2. Performance of Experiment 1, Proximity-Based Summary Extraction

have answers futher away from the query keywords, with optimal window size 11 learned from training, and actual optimal window size 9 in the evaluation.

In our experiment less than half of the date, number, and other questions are answered. These questions are indeed hard to answer. For example, "Why are electric cars less efficient in the north-east than in California?" or "How much could you rent a Volkswagen bug for in 1966?" Simple proximity-based summary extraction as described here does not handle these complex questions well.

17.3.4 Experiment 3: Summarization with Question Type Guessed

This experiment is to test whether imperfect knowledge of question types helps improve the summarization performance. If imperfect knowledge of question types still improves the summarization performance but just to a lesser degree, then it not only confirms our findings in experiment 2 but also suggests more effort in question preprocessing.

	Training optimum			Eval with training *wsize*		Actual optimal *wsize* in eval		
qtype	w	**#ansrd**	**MRSR**	**#ansrd**	**MRSR**	w	**#ansrd**	**MRSR**
person	4	14/34	.328	14/22	.370	4/5	15/22	.370
place	11	11/15	.218	15/21	.423	9	17/21	.462
name	7	14/19	.237	4/10	.114	10	5/10	.168
number	2	2/6	.056	5/17	.147	2	5/17	.147
date	18	3/10	.200	3/12	.139	4	5/12	.262
other	13	2/16	.133	5/18	.067	8/13	5/18	.136
all types		**47/100**	**.234**	**46/100**	**.247**		**52/100**	**.270**

Table 17.3. Performance of Experiment 2, With Question Type Known

In experiment 2, we assumed question types were known. In this experiment, we first develop a simple rule-based algorithm to automatically determine the question type. The algorithm recognizes question types for different "wh-" words; for example, "who" indicates a person question, and "where" indicates a place question. Also, the algorithm uses the ideas from the one described in Radev, et al. (2002a), which basically matches the informative noun in a question to a lexicon to determine the answer/question type. For example, for "what is the population of Japan?" the algorithm extracts the first noun after "what," which is "population," then looks into a lexicon to determine that "population" is a number. The lexicon is essentially a long, preconstructed list of nouns and their categories (person, number, etc). The algorithm's accuracy is 76.5% on TREC-8 corpus; that is, it correctly determines question type for 153 out of 200 TREC-8 questions. In this chapter we purposely refrain from improving the accuracy of this algorithm; rather we would like to see if, and how much, an imperfect question type determination can improve the AFS performance.

Similar to experiment 2, we use the first 100 TREC-8 questions as training data, and evaluate on the second 100 TREC-8 questions. We use our imperfect question type determination in both learning and evaluation. Performance results are shown in table 17.4.

With guessed question types, the performance is not as good as the performance with question types known, in both training and evaluation. On the evaluation set of questions, 43 questions are answered with question type guessed compared to 46 questions answered with question types known, and the MRSR is .238 with question type guessed compared to .247 with question type known. This indicates that the accuracy of question type recognition is important to the performance of the summarization. In general, preprocessing of questions should prove important to the performance of answer-focused summarization

However, the performance with question type guessed is still better than that of experiment 1. On the evaluation set of questions, 43 questions are an-

	Training optimum			Eval with training *wsize*		Actual optimal *wsize* in eval		
qtype	w	**#ansrd**	**MRSR**	**#ansrd**	**MRSR**	w	**#ansrd**	**MRSR**
person	4	14/34	.241	13/22	.228	5	17/22	.225
place	11	7/15	.377	15/21	.402	9	16/21	.437
name	2	9/19	.184	3/10	.167	10	4/10	.281
number	2	4/6	.041	4/17	.041	2	4/17	.041
date	18	3/10	.300	3/12	.097	4	5/12	.262
other	8	5/16	.174	5/18	.256	8	5/18	.265
all types		**43/100**	**.229**	**43/100**	**.238**		**51/100**	**.265**

Table 17.4. Experiment 3, Proximity-Based Summary Extraction With Question Type Guessed

swered compared to 41 answered in experiment 1, and 38 answered by Google. This indicates that even if the question type information is inaccurate to some degree, it still helps improve the answer-focused summarization.

Note that for the three most frequent question types, person, place, and number, the optimal window sizes learned from training happen to be the same as those in experiment 2, namely 4, 11, and 2 respectively. While it is a coincidence, it suggests that person and number questions may tend to have answers close to the question keywords, and place questions tend to have answers further away from the query keywords.

17.4 Discussion and Conclusion

Our work is related to query-biased summaries in information retrieval (Tombros and Sanderson 1998, White et al. 2001), where sentences ranked on the overlap with the query words are used to produce summaries for each search hit. However, answer-focused summarization is different from Tombros and Sanderson (1998) and White, Ruthven, and Jose (2001) in that AFS produces summaries in favor of getting answers to natural language questions. The Webclopedia project (Hovy et al. 2000), a web-based question answering system, is more similar to what we are doing although we focus on a sub-problem of theirs. Webclopedia first searches for documents related to a query, breaks the top documents returned into sentences, and builds answers from these sentences. In other words, Webclopedia may produce multiple answers from a relevant document and not every document returned is represented by an answer. But we assume the documents related to the question are already identified and ranked, and we extract one answer-focused summary from each document.

While the window size is often used in proximity-based search and summarization, to our knowledge, our study is the first to apply different window sizes for different question types. We showed that the window size could be optimized for different question types in providing answer-focused summaries. By discovery of this relationship between optimal window size and question type, we largely improved the performance of our proximity-based summary extraction mechanism. We developed a question type determination algorithm, and despite its prematureness (23.5% error rate), it still made a large contribution to the improvement of summary extraction. We also observed the pattern of optimal window sizes under different summary size constraints. Studying the pattern will help us make better decisions on summary sizes.

To improve the question type determination we can develop more complicated question parsers, or extend existing grammar parsers like CONTEX (Hermjakob and Mooney 1997). To accurately determine the question type, it is often helpful to classify nouns in a question as person, organization, location, etc. For this purpose we can use BBN's IdentiFinder (Bikel, Schwartz, and Weischedel 1999). It is also helpful to study refined question types, and the optimal window sizes for them. For this purpose we can use available categorization dictionaries based on WordNet (Fellbaum 1998). Further, there is a richness of information in the questions themselves beyond the simple question types we devised to improve our summary extraction. Query preprocessing such as stemming, expansion, term relationships, etc., has been studied for years. We believe Web search engines can greatly benefit from query preprocessing in providing answer-focused summaries.

One issue we did not address here is support for the answers. Providing the answer is only one part of the story, a user would only appreciate it if he or she can find sufficient contextual support and then accept the answer. We plan to do further study on how to provide efficient support in answer-focused summaries.

The summary size or the economics of summaries can be further studied. Summary size directly affects accuracy, which is whether a summary contains the answer, and the support, which certainly requires words other than just the answers. It is important to understand the tradeoff between summary size, support, and accuracy, to generate summaries for different user and application needs. One way to directly involve summary size in evaluation is to use reciprocal word rank, or reciprocal character rank, to take into consideration how many words or characters a user has to read before reaching the answer to a question.

Harris Wu is a doctoral student at the University of Michigan. His research interests focus on online knowledge management. Harris can be reached at harriswu@umich.edu.

Dragomir R. Radev is an assistant professor at the University of Michigan and leads the Computational Linguistics and Information Retrieval group. He has published more than 45 journal and conference papers and book chapters. Dragomir can be reached at radev@umich.edu.

Weiguo Fan is an assistant professor of information systems and computer science at Virginia Tech. His interests include information retrieval, text mining, web computing, and business intelligence. He can be reached at wfan@vt.edu.

Chapter 18

A Multiagent Approach to Using Redundancy and Reinforcement in Question Answering

John Prager, Jennifer Chu-Carroll, and Krzysztof Czuba

18.1 Introduction

As the field of question-answering evolves, we are learning that the one-size-fits-all approach of earlier systems is not the best way to tackle open-domain question answering with a broad set of question types. We believe that just as a human may answer a question to which he does not know the answer by a text search, by calculation, by look up in a dictionary, thesaurus, or other reference work, or some combination thereof, then so too can a computer adopt different strategies. Moreover, not only will the availability of different strategies allow for choosing the most appropriate one for the question in hand, but for many question types a selection of strategies can be tried together, with the answer(s) being selected from the pooled results.

This chapter explores our use of answer redundancy and reinforcement in question answering along two dimensions. First, we discuss our multiagent approach to question answering which utilizes multiple sources and strategies for answering questions. The benefits of redundancy within a single answering agent have been reported in Prager et al. (forthcoming). We have previously reported the use of structured knowledge sources on the overall performance of our QA system (Prager et al. 2001, Chu-Carroll et al. 2003b). Clarke et al. (2001) demonstrated the utility of redundancy by exploiting multiple answer sources (using the Web to reinforce answers found in the TREC corpus); however, they do not investigate utilizing multiple strategies. In Chu-Carroll et al. (2003a) we reported benefits from consulting multiple corpora, as well as results of a glass-box combination of two different answering agents; here we extend our earlier results to show the effects of a black-box combination of five answering agents. Second, we introduce a novel approach to question answer-

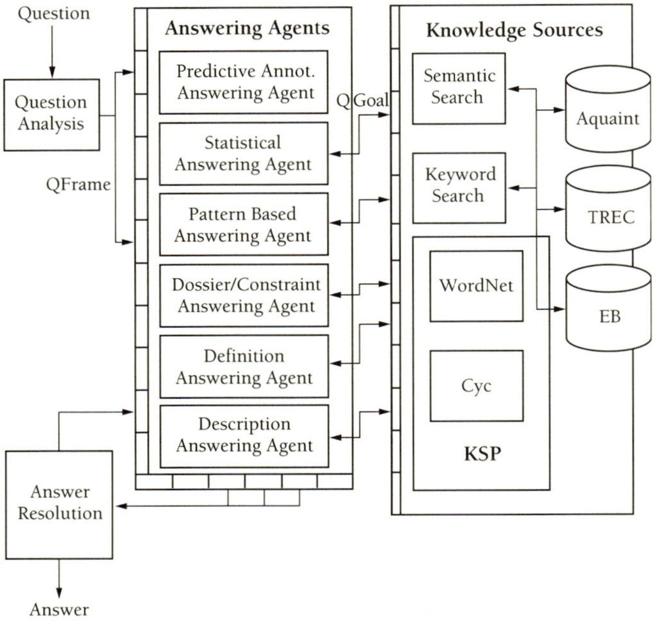

Figure 18.1. PIQUANT's Architecture

ing in the form of a constraint-based agent, which, while (currently) employing only a single strategy for answering questions, takes advantage of answer reinforcement by asking additional constraining questions. The answers to these constraining questions can then be used to support or refute answers proposed for the original question.

18.2 A Multiagent QA Architecture

To enable a multiagent approach to question answering, we developed a modular and extensible QA architecture as shown in figure 18-1. In this architecture, a question is first processed by the question analysis module, which is based on a deep parser and a feature structure unification-based rule matcher. The set of manually constructed rules allows the question analysis module to detect the required answer semantic type(s), the question type (such as definition, list, etc.), the normalized keywords from the question, and a simple semantic form (single predicate with arguments) to represent the question meaning when one can be built. This information is represented in a QFrame, which is a set of question features used to activate one or more answering agents. Based on the QFrame, each agent generates its own requests to a variety of knowledge sources. This may include performing search against a text corpus and extracting answers from the resulting passages, or querying a structured knowledge source, such as WordNet (Miller, 1995) or Cyc (Lenat 1995). The (intermediate) results from the individual agents are then passed on to the Answer Resolution component, which combines and reconciles the set of results and either produces the system's final answers or feeds the intermediate results back to the answering agents for further processing.

Our system currently employs several answering agents, as shown in figure 18-1. Some agents are general purpose, such as the Predictive Annotation Agent (Prager et al. 2000) and the Statistical Agent (Ittycheriah et al. 2001), while others are designed to handle specific question types. Note that given a question, one or more answering agents will be activated, allowing the system to take into account the redundancy factor (Clarke et al. 2001) for answer reinforcement.

18.3 Answering Agents

In this section, we describe our various agents, and focus on two kinds of evaluation experiments, one of which is an ablation study on the impact of adopting multiple strategies in question answering, and the other a pair of evaluations of the performance of our constraint agent.

18.3.1 Predictive Annotation Agent

The Predictive Annotation Agent (Prager et al. 2000, to appear), takes as input the QFrame produced by the question analysis module. It issues a query to the search engine based on the answer type and the question keywords, and receives answer passages which are then processed by an answer selection module to locate and rank candidate answers. The key feature of predictive annotation is that before the text corpora are indexed, they are processed by our semantic annotator, which recognizes approximately 100 semantic types. The identified semantic labels are then indexed along with the text. The search engine query contains the answer type, thus guaranteeing that each returned passage contains at least one candidate answer of the right type. Answer selection evaluates candidate answers according to a number of text-based features. The output of answer selection is a ranked list of answer candidates with confidences.

18.3.2 Statistical Agent

This agent is based on a statistical approach to question answering (Ittycheriah et al. 2001). Because of the specific approach, it does not use the information in the QFrame as the answer type assignment is statistically modeled. The agent models the "correctness" of an answer to a question using a maximum entropy formalism (Berger et al. 1996). At runtime, the question is first analyzed by the answer type model, which selects one of 31 possible answer types for use by the answer selection model. Simultaneously, the question is expanded using local context analysis (Xu and Croft 1996) with an encyclopedia, and the top 1000 documents are retrieved by the search engine. From these documents, the top 100 passages are chosen based on lexical and syntactic features. From the passages, candidate answers are extracted and ranked using the answer selection model. The top candidate answers are returned, each with an associated confidence score.

18.3.3 Definition Agent

The Definition Agent (Prager et al 2001) is used to answer definitional questions, such as "What is X?" and "Who is X?" whose answer type typically cannot be determined from the question itself. The agent employs an ontology provided by an external, structured resource such as WordNet to look up candidate answers by examining the superclasses (hypernyms) of the term to be defined. These candidates are evaluated using a collocation method based on the reference corpus, thus allowing the system to determine the most natural granularity level for the answer. The reference corpus is then consulted to select passages that define the term in question as the preferred answer.

18.3.4 Description Agent

The Description Agent (Prager et al. forthcoming) targets a subset of questions handled by the Definition Agent. However, instead of using an external knowledge source for answers as in the Definition Agent, the Description Agent attempts to identify answers that satisfy predetermined syntactic constructs used commonly for definitions, including appositions, pre- and post-modifiers, and relative clauses. This approach is at a high level similar to that of Blair-Goldensohn et al., in chapter 4. The Description Agent first retrieves passages containing the term to be defined from the reference corpus. Descriptive constructs related to the question term are then dynamically annotated and the answer selection component evaluates and ranks all such identified descriptions.

18.3.5 Pattern Agent

The Pattern Agent (Czuba et al., forthcoming) addresses question types unsuitable for a general purpose strategy because of the potentially low precision or an unknown answer type. It extends approaches such as Soubbotin et al. (2002) and Hermjakob et al. (2002) by basing patterns on the deeper representation of parse trees. It leverages a broad-coverage parser based on the English Slot Grammar (McCord 1990) formalism to create parse trees for answer passages on which pattern matching is performed. Its patterns are parse tree fragments representing contexts in which an answer is likely to be found. The agent utilizes patterns from two sources. The first is a repository of question type specific patterns, such as a person's birthday, birthplace, cause of death, etc., which were manually created.[1] These question semantic types are usually parameterized with an argument, such as *birthday(Robert Frost)* for "When was Robert Frost born?" The repository contains a set of patterns that match the parse trees for the typical contexts in which someone's birthday can occur in text and these patterns are retrieved based on the predicate (birthday). They are then instantiated with the argument (Robert Frost) and passed on to the matcher.

The second source is dynamic patterns generated from the parse tree of the question. They are useful for questions for which the predicate-argument structure is clear enough to allow for precise matching. For instance, for "What does Knight Ridder publish?" since the question is a simple transitive verb construct, a pattern that matches clauses whose subject is "Knight Ridder," and whose main verb is "publish" is generated. The content of the obligatory object slot in the parse tree is considered to be an answer candidate.

18.3.6 Dossier Agent

The Dossier Agent addresses definitional questions using a new approach called QA-by-Dossier by issuing auxiliary questions intended to build a profile/dossier on the question subject. For people, it asks for their birthdate, birthplace, deathdate, profession, college attended, and so on. For organizations, it asks for their headquarters, CEO, and their line of business. For things, it provides a definition by invoking the Definition Agent described in section 18.3.3.

Currently these auxiliary questions are manually constructed. We are developing an ontology of interesting properties, which not only will provide a source of these questions, but also of follow-up questions determined by first-round answers. For example, depending on a person's profession, it will ask what they wrote, performed in, explored, invented, etc. We currently ask these questions by default for all people, on the assumption that inappropriate questions will generate low confidence answers which will be rejected.

18.3.7 Constraint Agent

The constraint agent employs a novel approach to improving QA precision by building upon QA-by-Dossier. QA-by-Dossier-with-Constraints (QDC) exploits answer reinforcement and is based on the idea that answers to related questions often constrain one another and thus allow a system to more confidently select the correct answer to each. We illustrate this idea by way of the example, "When did Leonardo paint the Mona Lisa?" Columns 2 and 3 in table 18-1 show the Predictive Annotation Agent's top answers to this question, with associated scores in the range 0-1.

	Score	Painting Date	Score	Born	Score	Died
1	.64	2000	.66	1452	.99	1519
2	.43	1988	.12	1519	.98	1989
3	.34	1911	.04	1920	.96	1452
4	.31	1503	.04	1987	.60	1988
5	.31	1490	.04	1501	.60	1990

Table 18.1. Answers for "When did Leonardo paint the Mona Lisa?" "When was Leonardo born?" and "When did Leonardo die?"

The correct answer is "1503," which is in fourth place with a low score. Using QDC, we ask two related questions "When was Leonardo born?" and "When did Leonardo die?" The answers to these auxiliary questions are shown in columns 4-7 in table 18-1.

Given common knowledge about a person's life cycle, the best proposed dates consistent with one another are that Leonardo was born in 1452, died in 1519, and painted the Mona Lisa in 1503. This example illustrates how the use of auxiliary questions helps constrain answers to the original question, and promotes correct answers with initial low confidence scores. Note that by using QDC, not only have we correctly answered the original question, but we have built a simple "dossier" on Leonardo, with three important dates in his life-cycle.

Applying QA-by-Dossier. To automatically apply QA-by-Dossier (with or without constraints) during question answering, several problems need to be addressed. First, we must develop criteria for invocation for the process. Second, we must identify question types suitable for this approach, and, for each question type, develop auxiliary questions and constraints among the answers. Third, for each question type, we must determine how the results of applying constraints should be utilized.

The first problem is addressed by a cursory examination of the scores associated with answers to the original question. The process is invoked when either the top score or the difference between the top two scores is below a threshold. The second issue is currently addressed by manually constructing auxiliary questions and general, reusable constraints among answers for select questions. For instance, biographical data is constrained by life-cycle parameters, geographical data by 2-d spatial geometry, and kinship data by reciprocal relationships. As mentioned earlier, we are currently investigating developing an ontology from which such questions and constraints can be derived. The third issue concerns the (general) problem of when more than one combination of answers satisfies our constraints. In that case we combine the first-round scores of the individual answers to provide a score for the dossier. There are several ways to do this, and we found experimentally that it does not appear critical exactly how this is done. In the examples in the evaluation we mention one particular combination algorithm.

18.4 Answer Resolution

Our earlier experiments showed that although the greatest improvement in performance was obtained by combining agents at multiple levels (after question analysis, passage retrieval, and answer selection), near optimal results can be achieved by treating each agent as a black box and performing answer resolution only on the ranked candidate answers. Thus, in this work, we investigate combining candidate answers from multiple answering agents and examine how answer redundancy and reinforcement result in overall performance improvement.

PIQUANT's current Answer Resolution component takes as input the top n (=5) answers for a question from each agent, with their associated confidence scores, and selects the overall best answer(s). It first determines semantic equivalence of answers using named entity normalization to equate proper names (e.g., "Clinton," "Bill Clinton," and "President Clinton") (Byrd and Ravin 1999). Semantically equivalent answers are then combined using a simple voting procedure where each instance of an answer votes with a weight equal to its confidence score, and the weights of equivalent answers are summed. The answers are sorted based on the combined score, and the top answer(s) selected as the system's final answer(s). In this fashion, answer resolution exploits answer redundancy and reinforcement by allowing equivalent answers proposed by different agents to provide support for one another. In the next section, we describe experiments conducted to measure performance improvement using this multiagent question-answering paradigm.

18.5 Impact of Answering Redundancy and Reinforcement

We describe two sets of experiments intended to evaluate the impact of answer redundancy and reinforcement on overall system performance. One is an ablation study for evaluating the effectiveness of employing multiple agents for QA, and the other is designed to assess the contributions of the dossier and constraint agents.

18.5.1 Experimental Results—Ablation Study

For our ablation study, we selected a test set of 500 questions from the TREC 10 QA track (Voorhees 2002). We eliminated questions for which there is no known answer in the reference corpus, which resulted in 440 questions in the final test set.

To evaluate the impact of individual answering agents on a multiagent QA system, we combined each specialized agent with the Predictive Annotation Agent and evaluated the combined performance of all available agents. We then compared the combined performance with the best performing agent.

	# Q's	#Q's all agents	Subclass MRR	Overall MRR	Subclass CWS	Overall CWS
Predictive Annotation (PA)	304	304	0.445	0.307	0.600	0.510
Description (DS)	94	94	0.254	0.054	0.230	0.119
Definition (DF)	133	133	0.402	0.121	0.464	0.278
Pattern (PT)	16	16	0.812	0.029	0.779	0.118
Statistical (ST)	440	440	0.424	0.423	0.540	0.539
PA+DS	396	2	0.399	0.358	0.530	0.509
PA+DF	400	37	0.435	0.395	0.556	0.538
PA+PT	304	16	0.449	0.310	0.624	0.527
PA+DS+DF	421	2	0.430	0.410	0.542	0.533
PA+DS+DF+PT	421	0	0.434	0.414	0.572	0.562
All	440	0	0.493	0.492	0.604	0.603
Improvement over ST				16.3%		11.9%

Table 18.2. Ablation Study Results

For each run, the MRR (Voorhees, 2000) of the top 5 answers was computed. Furthermore, the top answer for each question was selected for each question and all answers were sorted based on the overall confidence scores and evaluated using the CWS metric (Voorhees, 2003).

Table 18-2 summarizes the results of our ablation study. For each run, we show (1) the number of questions for which answers were returned, (2) the number of questions for which an answer was returned by all agents involved, (3) the MRR/CWS for the questions attempted, and (4) the MRR/CWS computed over the whole test set. The last row in table 18-2 shows the relative improvement of our full multiagent system over the Statistical Agent, the best "overall" agent.

Table 18-2 shows that the Predictive Annotation Agent answers a large subset of questions, while the Statistical Agent answers all questions. The description and Definition Agents, both address primarily definition questions, are triggered in rough one third of the questions. The Pattern Agent achieves the highest precision of all our agents; however, it was applicable in only a small number of questions.

Our results show that in all but one case, multiagent systems outperformed their components. The Predictive Annotation and Description agents answered nearly disjoint sets of questions, and their combined MRR (PA+DS) was nearly the sum of the component MRRs. The Definition Agent also provided fairly substantial gain over the Predictive Annotation Agent alone (PA+DF) using both metrics. Although the high-precision Pattern Agent, which answered a subset of questions addressed by the Predictive Annotation Agent, yielded only a small improvement in MRR (PA+PT versus PA, and PA+DS+DF+PT versus PA+DS+DF), the corresponding gain in CWS is much greater. This indicates that while the Pattern Agent did not add many new correct answers, it enabled the system to be more confident about previously

	No. Correct	CWS	Risk-Based Score
Baseline	32 (80%)	0.95	0.698
QDC	36 (90%)	0.98	0.900

Table 18.3. Results of Performance Evaluation of QA-by-Dossier-with-Constraints

found correct answers, resulting in a higher CWS. The Predictive Annotation Agent and all specialized agents (PA+DS+DF+PT) again outperformed the pair-wise combination. Finally, the addition of a second general purpose agent (ST) yielded the overall best performance, achieving a 16.3% relative improvement in MRR and 11.9% in CWS over the performance of the Statistical Agent.

18.5.2 Experimental Results—Constraint Agent

We performed two evaluations of the constraint agent. The first involved 40 questions about celebrity marriages. The original question was "Who is *X* married to?" and for the auxiliary question, we asked the same of the candidate answers. The constraint was simply that the second-round answer be the same as the person in the original question. Thus, for each person *X*, we asked "Who is *X* married to" and collected the top 5 answers $\{X_i\}$. For baseline performance we examined the top answer X_1. We then generated 5 auxiliary questions and collected 5 answers for each, $\{X_{ij}\}$. We then assigned each X_i the average of the supported score of the sum of the scores of the X_{ij} that matched *X*, and the original score of X_i. The X_i with the greatest resulting score was output as the QDC answer.

We compare the baseline versus QDC answers using three metrics. The first is percent-correct. The second is the CWS. Unfortunately, at relatively high accuracy and ranking ability, CWS fails to make necessary distinctions (Chu-Carroll et al. 2003c). Thus we introduce a third metric called the "risk-based score," where an answer score *p* (in the range 0–1) is treated as a bet: if the answer is correct, the overall score is increased by p; otherwise, it is decreased by p. The resulting totals are normalized into the range 0–1. The risk-based score is intuitively appealing, has a basis in both gambling and multiple-choice test scoring, and overcomes many deficiencies of the CWS.

Table 18-3 shows that by using QDC, a few more questions were answered correctly, but the risk-based score shows a dramatic improvement. This is because a principal contribution of QDC is to provide more accurate confidence scores. As with the Pattern Agent performance discussed in section 18.5.1, we expect that a major contribution of QDC when used with other agents will be to improve the system's overall confidence in its answers, and to improve the other measures by promoting the correct answer to the top.

The second evaluation was based on the people definition questions of TREC12 ("Who was X?"). We evaluate an auxiliary question "What compositions did X have?" The system was asked to return as many answers or nuggets

	Total	No. Correct	No. Incorrect	Precision	Recall (see text)	F
Baseline	140	60	80	0.43	1.0	.60
QDC	44	42	2	0.95	.70	.81

Table 18.4. Results of Performance Evaluation of QA-by-Dossier-with-Constraints

as possible, based on developed rejection criteria. For each C_i returned by the auxiliary question, we asked the reciprocal constraining question "Who had C_i?" and looked at the top 5 answers. We boosted the original subject *X*'s score by the confidence of the reciprocal answer that was equal to *X*, if it existed. Row 1 in Table 18-4 shows the evaluation of the plain Dossier Agent, which correctly found 60 nuggets out of 140, a precision of 0.43. Using QDC, 78 incorrect and 18 correct nuggets were thrown out, giving a new precision of 0.95 — a relative increase of 123%. We cannot calculate absolute recall figures because we don't have a list of all possible correct nuggets; if we consider the baseline recall to be 1.0 (because in this set-up, QDC cannot introduce new answers), the resulting recall is .70. This gives a change of balanced *F*-measure from .60 to .81.

18.6 Related Work

A number of researchers have investigated federated systems for identifying answers to questions. For example, Clarke et al. (2003) and Lin et al. (2003) employ techniques for utilizing both unstructured text and structured databases for QA. However, their approaches differ from ours in that they enforce an order between the two strategies by locating answers in structured databases first and falling back to unstructured text when the former fails, while we explore multiple options in parallel and combine the results from all answering agents.

The multiagent approach to question answering most similar to ours is that by Burger et al. (2003). They applied ensemble methods to combine the 67 runs submitted to the TREC 11 QA track, using an unweighted centroid method for selecting among the 67 proposed answers for each question. However, their combined system did not outperform the top scoring system. Furthermore, their experiments focused on exploiting a large number of general purpose answering agents, while we studied the impact of several specialized agents on overall system performance.

The precision-oriented approach of QA-by-Dossier-with-Constraints can be contrasted with the work of Weischedel et al. in chapter 5, who use a general IR query and then IE techniques to find information nuggets, and that of Blair-Goldensohn et al. in chapter 4, who search for instances of a set of general definitional predicates. These latter approaches stand to be more recall-oriented; a combination experiment would be a very interesting exercise.

18.5 Conclusions

We have described two approaches we are exploring simultaneously to improve the performance of our QA system. We use a variety of agents with different intrinsic coverage and precision to tackle more question types than any individual agent can handle well. Where the agents' coverage overlap, we use redundancy to adjust answers and their confidences. In addition, we developed a constraint-based agent, which uses answers to auxiliary questions to greatly increase the confidence of mutually reinforcing answers. Using multiple agents we have shown a 16.3% and 11.9% relative improvement in MRR and CWS scores, respectively. Our experiments show that while the major benefit of some agents is that they contribute more correct answers, others reinforce existing correct answers and thus improve confidence scores. The Constraint Agent is not yet fully integrated, but a separate evaluation showed very promising results, including a relative increase in precision of 123% .

Acknowledgments

We would like to thank Dave Ferrucci and Chris Welty for helpful discussions, and Abe Ittycheriah and Salim Roukos for making their system available for experimentation. This work was supported in part by the Advanced Research and Development Activity (ARDA)'s Advanced Question Answering for Intelligence (AQUAINT) Program under contract number MDA904-01-C-0988.

Note

1. In future work, we plan to investigate automatic acquisition of these patterns.

John Prager is a researcher at the IBM T. J. Watson Research Center in Yorktown Heights, New York.

Jennifer Chu-Carroll is a researcher at the IBM T. J. Watson Research Center in Yorktown Heights, New York.

Krzysztof Czuba is a researcher at the IBM T. J. Watson Research Center in Yorktown Heights, New York.

Section Seven

Knowledge and Inference-Enabled Question Answering

Future QA systems must deal not only with factoid questions which might be readily retrieved and redundantly available on the web, but also must address more sophisticated classes of questions such as how, why, and what-if. This final section addresses knowledge and inference, which are essential to answering more complex questions, inferring answers, and providing explanations and justifications.

The first chapter in this section addresses deductive question answering from multiple resources. Richard Waldinger, Douglas E. Appelt, John Fry, David J. Israel, Peter Jarvis, David Martin, Susanne Riehemann, Mark E. Stickel, and Mabry Tyson (SRI International), Jerry Hobbs, (USC-ISI), and Jennifer L. Dungan, (NASA Ames) present their question answering through reasoning and knowledge (QUARK) system, which consults multiple sources (e.g., databases, unstructured text, the web) and infers answers (text or visualizations) from information they provide, especially geographic questions. QUARK employs an automated deduction system with an axiomatic application-domain theory as the central integrator. It extracts answers from proofs. For example, answering a question such as "Could Mohammed Atta have met with an Iraqi agent?" requires extraction, temporal, and geospatial reasoning.

In QUARK, the question is parsed and translated into a logical form by Gemini, a broad-coverage English parser. Next a logical form is submitted to the automated deduction system, SNARK, a general-purpose theorem prover that incorporates resolution (for general deductive reasoning), paramodulation (for reasoning about equality), and temporal and spatial reasoning. SNARK transforms the query and decomposes it into subqueries. Knowledge resource capabilities are specified by axioms in the application domain theory, which serve to advertise the corresponding resource, so it can be invoked as appropriate while the proof search is underway. Resources are linked to the theory by a procedural-attachment mechanism, which allows the theorem prover to behave as if knowledge possessed by the resource were represented axiomatically in the theory. These knowledge resources include the Alexandria

Digital Library Gazetteer (a geographical dictionary with six million entries), the CIA World Factbook, a variety of NASA data sources, the ASCS Semantic Web search engine, the TextPro Information Extraction Engine, geographical computation agents, and visualization agents (e.g., NIMA's Geospatial Engine and Generic Mapping Tools for maps, and TerraVision's flight-simulator-like three-dimensional view of a selected region). Their system accepts assertions by the user.

Deductive question answering has roots in early work in deductive question answering and program synthesis (Green 1969). Cyc (Lenat and Guha 1994) also uses theorem proving as a part of the question-answering process. And LCC (Moldovan et al. 2003) has been using a theorem prover to incorporate inference into the information-extraction process.

The authors' future plans include exploring dialogue, providing answer explanation/justification, and creating a schema of related questions. They are also interested in drawing conclusions from data (e.g., finding sums and maxima, computing averages, and performing other computations and statistical inferences) and generating new tables, charts, and similar visualizations of numerical data to enrich the range of possible answers.

The second chapter by Farah Benamara and Patrick Saint Dizier (Institut de Recherches en Informatique de Toulouse) considers relaxation for cooperative QA. The authors argue that providing advanced reasoning for QA to infer answers or provide explanations and justifications requires multiple knowledge bases (e.g., both domain and common sense) and multiple forms of reasoning. Reasoning is essential to respond to unanticipated questions, to react when there are no answers in known data sources (e.g., consider constraint relaxation), to identify and explain false presuppositions or various types of misunderstandings found in questions (e.g., cf McCoy's 1985 research in misclassification and misattribution), to generate summaries, or to provide conditional responses. Intelligent and cooperative responses can include: (1) providing answer explanations, (2) returning intensional responses and answer summarization (e.g., "which students have good marks?" → "All do"), (3) generalizing queries using neighborhood information (e.g., query relaxation, abstraction), (4) comparing answers that have similar questions, and (5) information fusion. This chapter deals with the first three, with a focus on the third.

The authors explore cooperative QA in a limited tourism domain dealing with accommodation and transportation. The authors describe their system WEBCOOP, which incorporates information extraction, retrieval, language generation, and cooperative rules to provide cooperative QA. Their work is motivated by a corpus analysis of human question answer pairs (in French) found on tourism web sites. In spite of diverse human responses, they were able to organize, model, and implement stereotyped versions.

Their response strategy to problematic user queries first explains user misconceptions; then it employs "intensional description techniques" and "intelli-

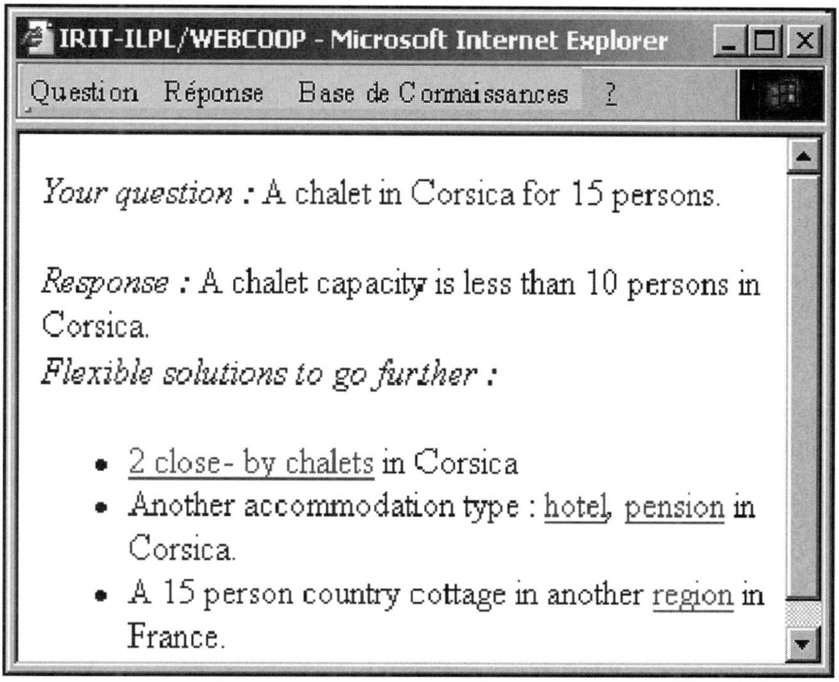

gent relaxation procedures" plus "dedicated cooperative rules" to attempt to cooperatively satisfy the user's information need. For example, if a user asks to rent a 15 person chalet in Corsica (shown in the figure on this page), the system can say it is not possible because only 10 people can be in a chalet, but then relaxes the cardinality (e.g., try 2 instead of one chalet), the type of accommodation (to a hotel or pension), or the region to find a satisfying solution.

WEBCOOP can detect both misconceptions (the query violates an integrity constraint) and false presuppositions (the query has an empty set of solutions). The relaxation technique is based on a generic proximity relation that refers to inherent properties of objects, a conceptual ontology, and lexical semantics relations. As exemplified above, proximity can be in terms of cardinality (e.g., quantity, location, time), ontological type (e.g., propose siblings, parent), or constants (e.g., fixed times). In our example query "give me (chalets)1 in (Corsica region)2 (for 15 persons)3, the relaxation order can be performed in syntactic order (from 3 to 1) or pragmatic order (e.g., relax most specific first, from 1 to 3).

Unlike Inference Web, which is addressed in the next chapter, WEBCOOP does not provide the user with access to the inference steps, such as axioms, derived rules, or all activated nodes within the domain ontology, during the reasoning process. The authors argue their approach is more cooperative. In summary, they propose several kinds of minimally and conceptually accurate relaxations and show that, for each type of relaxation, a general and underspecified natural language pattern can be defined that translates the relaxation into accessible terms.

The final chapter in this last section, and the last one in this book, is appropriately about trust. No question answerer, machine nor human, is valued unless its responses can be trusted. Deborah McGuinness and Paulo Pinheiro da Silva (Stanford) explore this issue in one of the most uncontrolled information repositories, the world wide web.

While a bastion of information and knowledge, there is no information provenance on the web. In many of today's QA systems it is often unclear what sources answers came from, their frequency of update, the reliability of source, what information was looked up versus derived, and so on. The authors point out that knowledge provenance for answers includes both source metadata information and knowledge process information. Their explanation strategy is to provide initial self-contained explanations and then automated support for follow-up questions. They argue that source metadata information for answers is the most important (e.g., author names, authoritativeness, currency, consistency). Also important, however, is explanation of information manipulation (e.g., by reasoners, extractors, summarizers) or query expansion explanation where one can expose equivalence and subclass relationships from the ontology. Effective explanation has its roots in the MYCIN medical system explanation (Shortliffe 1976) and explainable expert systems (Swartout et al. 1991) although these prior efforts were not as distributed as the web.

The authors exercise their approach in the KSL Wine Agent (www.ksl.stanford.edu/people/dlm/webont/wineAgent). If choosing wine for a pasta dish, a user can ask why the agent suggested a red wine (because of the red sauce) or where the information came from (the DAML wines ontology) or where the specific wine recommendation came from (the wines ontology or a match from an online website). A portable proof specification is written in the web markup language DAML+OIL/OWL. Their inference web provides proof browsing and explanation generation services with support for provenance summaries and abstracted derivation information. Explanations can be limited English descriptions, metadata provenance information, and multi-step proof presentations. Their proof lens capability provides a user configurable view into a proof diagram linking inference steps. The authors describe explanation needs gathered from multiple relevant government programs (e.g., HPKB, RKF, DAML, AQUAINT, NIMD) and the World Wide Web Consortium. Inference web aims to provide increased trust for question answering systems by providing proofs and explanations of answers in an interoperable manner aimed at distributed heterogeneous environments such as the web.

Chapter 19

Deductive Question Answering from Multiple Resources

Richard Waldinger, Douglas E. Appelt, Jennifer L. Dungan, John Fry, Jerry Hobbs, David J. Israel, Peter Jarvis, David Martin, Susanne Riehemann, Mark E. Stickel, and Mabry Tyson

19.1 Introduction

Much question-answering research is restricted to finding a single information resource that contains the answer to a question in a form that is a simple rephrasing of the question itself. The present work explores the possibility of constructing answers that are not known by any one source, but that rather must be inferred from information supplied by many sources. We are using an automated deduction system, with an axiomatic application-domain theory, as the central integrator.

Our research prototype, called QUARK (question answering through reasoning and knowledge—its geographical version is called GeoLogica [Waldinger et al. 2003]), has the following structure: The question is parsed and translated into a logical form by Gemini, a broad-coverage English parser. The logical form is phrased as a conjecture and submitted to the automated deduction system SNARK, a general-purpose theorem prover with special capabilities for temporal and spatial reasoning. SNARK is equipped with an application-domain theory that provides knowledge as to how the question can be decomposed. The capabilities of each knowledge resource are specified by axioms in this theory; these axioms serve to advertise the corresponding resource, so it can be invoked as appropriate while the proof search is underway. Each resource is linked to the theory by a procedural-attachment mechanism, which allows the theorem prover to behave as if knowledge possessed by the resource were represented axiomatically in the theory.

QUARK's approach is domain-independent; we can adapt it to a new subject by changing the application-domain theory and the resources. The application we have experimented with most is geographical question answering.

Among the resources we have linked are an information-extraction engine, TextPro; the Alexandria Digital Library (ADL) Gazetteer, a geographical dictionary with 6 million entries; the CIA World Factbook; the ASCS Semantic Web search engine; and a variety of NASA data sources. Answers can contain text, maps, or visualizations of satellite image data.

For example, the question "Could Mohammed Atta have met with an Iraqi agent?" was answered positively by consulting TextPro (to determine, from online text sources, that Atta went to Ruzyne, Czech Republic, on a certain day in 2000 and that the Iraqi agent al-Ani was with the Iraqi embassy to the Czech Republic in 2000); date and temporal reasoning to verify that the two times do overlap; an axiom from the application-domain theory to determine that embassies are in capitals; the CIA World Factbook (via the Semantic Web search engine ASCS) to establish that the capital of the Czech Republic is Prague; the ADL Gazetteer to find the latitudes and longitudes of Prague and Ruzyne; and a geographical computation web page from Northern Arizona University to determine that the distance between those two latitude-longitude (lat/long) pairs is less than seven miles, close enough to permit a visit. Further questioning causes the display of maps and satellite images of Ruzyne, illustrating its proximity to Prague. (In fact, the reality of this meeting is hotly disputed, but the point is that we can reproduce the reasoning that uncovers the possibility.)

In this chapter, we introduce the central notion behind QUARK, the extraction of answers from mathematical proofs. We describe the individual components of QUARK and illustrate its behavior on some typical questions. We then discuss possibilities for the future development of QUARK.

Because of limited space, we have omitted detailed examples of the performance of QUARK.[1]

19.2 Extracting Answers from Proofs

Questions are presented to QUARK in English, but they are translated by the parser Gemini into a logical form, which we can write

```
Q[?z], answer ?z.
```

(Our convention is that variables are prefixed by question marks.) This is viewed as a conjecture that an entity *?z* exists for which *Q[?z]* is true; this is the conjecture that is submitted to the theorem prover SNARK. The understanding is that we would like to find an expression *?z* for which *Q[?z]* follows from the axioms of the application-domain theory; if we succeed, *?z* is our answer. In general, we prove the existence of an entity that satisfies the conditions of our query, and we extract an answer, an expression that stands for such an entity, from the proof.

It is common that a query will have many different possible answers.

SNARK will find one answer at a time, but can be reinvoked to find other proofs, some of which will yield different answers.

19.2.1 The Application-Domain Theory

The application-domain theory provides the meanings for the symbols that appear in the query and in the answer, describes the relationships between the various concepts, advertises the capabilities of the information sources, and serves as a repository of knowledge in its own right. For example, in the example concerning Mohammed Atta mentioned in the introduction, the text specified that the agent al-Ani was located at the Iraqi embassy to the Czech Republic, but did not say where that embassy was. We relied on a piece of background knowledge that states that the embassy to a country is in the capital of that country. This was represented by the axiom

```
in(embassy(?country1, ?country2),
   capital(?country2)).
```

Here the term *embassy(?country1, ?country2)* is the embassy of *?country1 to ?country2*. Our convention is that *?country1* and *?country2* are variables of sort *country;* during a proof they can only be instantiated to entities that are countries. The sort mechanism of SNARK is not merely a convenient abbreviation: it can reduce the size of the search space of a proof by restricting the sorts of entities to which a variable may be instantiated.

19.2.2 Representation of Places

Part of the effort of designing an application-domain theory is to find good ways of representing the important entities of the theory. In developing a geospatial theory for geographical reasoning, we were faced with the need to find a systematic way of naming places. While we could always represent a city name, such as Springfield, Illinois, United States by a long constant name

```
Springfield-Illinois-United-States,
```

the theorem prover has no mechanism for looking inside the names of constants. SNARK would behave no differently if the city were called F17. Instead, we use a systematic naming convention, in which countries are represented by their own names (e.g., United-States), subdivisions of countries are represented by terms such as

```
feature(state, Illinois, United-States),
```

and subdivisions of subdivisions are represented by even more deeply nested terms, such as

```
feature(city, Springfield,
      feature(state, Illinois,
                 United States)).
```

In general, we use expressions of form

```
feature(<type>, <name-indicator>, <region>)
```

to stand for the subregion of *<region>* whose geographical classification is *<type>* and whose internal name is *<name-indicator>*. These names are far more informative than long constant symbols. Axioms in the theory can tell us that the term above is of geographical classification *<type>*, is called *<name-indicator>*, and is a subregion of *<region>*.

The internal naming scheme we use for representing places and other entities is not meant for use by the users of QUARK, nor is it accepted by any of the external sources we consult for information. The axiomatic theory allows us to couple conventional names, which are strings, with the internal terms. For instance, the city of Springfield, Illinois, is represented conventionally by the string

```
"Springfield, Illinois, United States"
```

The geospatial theory defines a relation "name" that relates the conventional string with its internal name. Thus,

```
name("Springfield, Illinois, United States",
      feature(city, Springfield,
              feature(state, Illinois,
                      United States)))
```

is true in the geospatial theory. Given either representation, the theory contains enough information to construct the other. This loose coupling allows us to deal with places that have multiple names and with names that refer to more than one place.

19.3 Procedural Attachment

While some of the knowledge of QUARK resides in its application-domain theory, the theory functions largely as a catalogue, index, and coordinator of external knowledge resources, sometimes called agents. Selected symbols of the theory are linked to these resources by the procedural-attachment mechanism. When one of these symbols takes a part in the proof search, the corresponding agent is invoked; the proof search resumes when the agent returns an answer.

19.3.1 The Mechanism

Procedural attachment was originally introduced to allow the more efficient representation of procedures in an axiomatic theory. For example, in a theory that involves numerical computation, it is possible to represent a function such as addition by a set of axioms that define it, but computation of the value of a term such as *plus(2, 2)* would then be cumbersome. If we procedurally attach the symbol *plus* to an arithmetic procedure, the procedure would invoke the addition function and return the value *4*.

While we also use procedural attachment for efficiency, we get other benefits by linking to external knowledge sources, where it would be impossible to represent the same knowledge axiomatically. For example, the ADL Gazetteer not only contains information about 6 million place names but also is continually being extended and changed. Other symbols may be linked to sensors or other sources that are in constant flux.

The Gazetteer is linked to several expressions in our geospatial theory, including the expression

```
adl-region-bounding-box(?region-name, ?type-name,
                        ?lat1, ?lat2, ?long1, ?long2).
```

Here, if *?region-name* is the name of a place whose geographical category is named *?type-name,* the four numbers *?lat1, ?lat2, ?long1, ?long2* stand for the bounding box of the place in question, i.e., the north and south latitudes and the east and west longitudes that enclose it.

The expression is linked to the Gazetteer in such a way that the first two argument variables, *?region1* and *?type,* are regarded as inputs, and the rest are regarded as outputs. This means that if the region and its type are instantiated, the Gazetteer will be invoked to find values for the latitudes and longitudes of the bounding box. For example, if, during the course of a proof, the expression

```
adl-region-bounding-box("Zimbabwe", "country"
                        ?lat1, ?lat2, ?long1, ?long2)
```

appears, the Gazetteer will be invoked and the four output variables will be instantiated:

```
adl-region-bounding-box("Zimbabwe", "country",
                        "-15.22","-22.93","33.65","25.11").
```

Henceforth, SNARK will behave as if the above formula were included in the theory as an axiom. This means that in proving a theorem, SNARK will act as if the six million lat/long pairs and bounding boxes provided by the Gazetteer were included in the geospatial theory.

19.3.2 Axioms that Advertise the Capabilities of Agents

One of the chief virtues of using an axiomatic theory to coordinate multiple agents is that we can exploit axioms to advertise the capabilities of an agent. This means that, when we introduce a new agent into the system, we provide one or more axioms that express what that agent can do. This ensures that the agent is invoked when appropriate, even if (as is usually the case) none of the other agents know about the new one. Whenever a new subquery is formulated, those agents that are capable of answering it step forward, invoked not by name but as a by-product of the theorem-proving process.

For example, let us look at the axiom that advertises the ability of the ADL Gazetteer to find the bounding box of a country:

```
region-to-bounding-box(?country) =
bounding-box(?lat1, ?lat2, ?long2, ?long2)
```

```
    <=
  name(?region-name, ?country) &
  adl-region-bounding-box(
     ?region-name, "country", ?lat1, ?lat2, ?long1, ?long2).
```

In other words, to find the bounding box of a country, first find a name-string for the country, *?region-name;* then call the ADL Gazetteer to find the corresponding four numbers that constitute the bounding box.

Finding bounding boxes of countries is simple because there are no two countries with the same name. Finding bounding boxes of subregions of countries is more difficult, because different subregions of different countries may have the same name, and we must be careful not to find the wrong one. Another, more complicated axiom advertises the capabilities of the ADL Gazetteer to find states, cities, lakes, and other subregions.

One problem that we face in creating interoperability for multiple disparate agents is that they do not adhere to uniform conventions in notation. For example, for agents that deal with latitudes and longitudes, some adopt a decimal notation, while others employ the older notation of degrees, minutes, and seconds. Of those that use decimal notation, some will write "32S" while others prefer "-32" for the latitude 32 degrees south of the Equator. Some of the least glamorous but most important agents are those that convert from one notation to another. These are also invoked by procedural attachment and are summoned by providing axioms that advertise their capabilities.

19.4 Components of QUARK

In this section we will describe the components of QUARK in roughly the order in which they come into play in answering a question.

19.4.1 Gemini

Questions to QUARK are translated into a logical form by Gemini (Dowding et al. 1993), a mature, robust parsing and interpretation system that has been used by several projects at SRI, Stanford, NASA, and elsewhere over the past ten years. Although we currently only use Gemini to parse questions, in the future we may use it to parse information supplied by the user in dialogue and text from other source material. Gemini may also be used to generate text to present and explain answers to questions.

A broad-coverage English grammar and lexicon for QUARK was compiled from several earlier projects. The open-ended nature of QUARK queries required a much larger vocabulary than previous Gemini projects. More than 50,000 new items were added to the lexicon, including 6000 adjectives and 35,000 nouns from WordNet, and 400 geographical terms from the ADL Gazetteer and NASA sources.

Gemini also has a capability for guessing the part of speech of an out-of-vocabulary word and temporarily adding that word to the lexicon. This has proved necessary for dealing with the large number of place names, personal names, and specialized vocabulary that occur in QUARK questions ("Mohammed Atta," "ATGW-3LR missile") that cannot be catalogued in advance.

19.4.2 SNARK

Theorem provers have traditionally excelled at mathematical reasoning, which requires finding non-obvious proofs over theories defined by relatively small sets of axioms. In contrast, SNARK has been developed for applications in artificial intelligence and software engineering, which require straightforward reasoning on theories defined by large axiom sets.

SNARK (Stickel et al. 2000) is a first-order logic theorem prover with resolution (for general deductive reasoning) and paramodulation (for reasoning about equality), implemented in Common Lisp. It has a sort mechanism, which allows all expressions to be categorized according to a hierarchical sort structure. It is particularly well suited for question-answering applications for several reasons: it has strategic controls that allow us to tailor it to exhibit high performance in selected application domains; it has a mechanism for extracting answers from proofs; it has a procedural-attachment mechanism; and it has built-in procedures for reasoning efficiently about space and time.

SNARK is used in NASA's system Amphion (Lowry et al. 1994), for automatic software composition, and in the Kestrel Institute's software development environment, SPECWARE (Kestrel Institute 2002), as well as in several SRI projects.

19.5 Agents

In this section we describe some of the agents invoked by SNARK's procedural-attachment mechanism.

19.5.1 ADL Gazetteer

The ADL Gazetteer (Hill et al. 1999) is a dictionary of about six million place names. For each place, it provides a latitude and longitude or bounding box; a geographical type; a map; a list of super-regions, i.e., regions that include the place; and a list of variant names and spellings. Given a name and a type, it can find places of the appropriate type with that name. It is capable of searching within a bounding box, so it will find only places that are within the box. If the name is not specified, it can find all places of the appropriate type; e.g., it can find all the lakes or airports within a given bounding box. The server is located at UC Santa Barbara.

19.5.2 CIA World Factbook

The CIA World Factbook (CIA 2002) is an almanac of the world's countries, including geographic, economic, political, and military information about each. We consult the Factbook for such information as bordering countries, principal subdivisions, capital cities, and religious makeup. The Factbook's information complements that provided by the ADL Gazetteer; it does not provide bounding boxes or detailed information about cities, for instance.

19.5.3 ASCS Search Engine

The Agent Semantic Communications Service (ASCS; Pease et al. 2002a), developed by Teknowledge, is a search engine that collects and indexes all pages on the Semantic Web that are annotated with markup from the DARPA Agent Markup Language (DAML). Although we have extracted some information from the CIA World Factbook directly, most of the knowledge we get from the Factbook is obtained through ASCS because DAMLized versions of the Factbook have been produced.

19.5.4 TextPro Information Extraction Engine

TextPro (Appelt and Martin 1999) can preprocess selected text documents and extract relational information, which is then stored in a database. This information can be queried as the proof is in progress. Presently information is being extracted from documents on weapons of mass destruction, terrorism, and related topics provided to the AQUAINT program by the Center for Nonproliferation Studies.

19.5.5 Geographical Computation Agents

QUARK consults a number of agents that perform geographical computations, such as find the distance between two given lat/long pairs, or find the lat/long pair that is a given distance north of a given lat/long pair. These include a website at the Northern Arizona University and some internal agents.

19.5.6 Visualization Agents

QUARK invokes a number of providers of maps and satellite image terrain visualization systems. NIMA's Geospatial Engine and Generic Mapping Tools supply maps for a given region; the agent can select features to highlight or provide points or vectors to be superimposed on the map. Satellite imagery is provided by USGS's Landsat Project and the NASA Goddard Distributed Active Archive. TerraVision (Reddy et al. 1999) presents a flight-simulator-like three-dimensional view of a selected region; the user can navigate around the selected region using a mouse as a controller.

19.6 Related Work

This work has its roots in early work in deductive question answering and program synthesis, including that of Green (1969) and Manna and Waldinger (1980). The large knowledge base Cyc (Lenat and Guha 1994) uses theorem proving as a part of the question-answering process. Teknowledge has been building a public upper-level ontology for general world knowledge (Pease et al. 2002b). LCC (Moldovan et al. 2003) has been using a theorem prover to incorporate inference into the information-extraction process. The approach of using procedural attachment from a theorem prover to coordinate multiple agents is relatively new; see Infomaster (Genesereth et al. 1997) and Ariadne (Knoblock and Minton 1998), for example. Fonseca et al. (2002) are developing a geographical ontology, with vocabulary but as yet no axioms. Hobbs et al. (2003) are building an axiomatic geographic theory and ontology within the DAML framework. The SWEET ontology (Raskin 2003) is specifically for the earth sciences. These should all be valuable resources for us.

19.7 Future Research

Up to now we have been developing QUARK's ability to answer individual questions. In our future research, we will begin to have QUARK engage in a dialogue with its user, in which the user can provide background information as well as questions, and in which new questions can ask for modifications of previous questions or elaboration on the answers. Already QUARK can accept assertions made by its user, which are translated by Gemini into logic and stored temporarily in a local knowledge base, to be invoked in answering future questions. Certain questions will be taken to represent a schema of related questions (e.g., "Who is John X?" may mean to find John X's role, John X's background, a picture of John X, and other personal information).

We will also extend QUARK's ability to explain and justify its answers. Currently it can produce a textual or visual presentation of its answer and a list of facts on which it was based, including quotations of source material. It can also produce the proof from which the answer was extracted, but most users will not be inclined to read it. Gemini, however, has the ability to generate coherent text from logical expressions, which we have not yet exploited in QUARK. As a first step, it may be useful to present the text corresponding to the ground axioms from which the answer was derived.

Evaluation mechanisms which require dealing with only a single source of information are inappropriate to QUARK. Devising a mechanism for evaluating QUARK progress is part of our planned research.

The theorem prover SNARK has well developed capabilities for reasoning about space and time, which we have not exploited much yet in QUARK. It includes time and date arithmetic and an implementation of the Allen Temporal Interval Calculus for reasoning about time; we plan to use this for detecting and reasoning about environmental change, itineraries, and other objects that have a temporal as well as a spatial dimension. Eventually we should be able to produce animations as well as static visualizations. SNARK also has an implementation of the RCC8 calculus for reasoning about regions in space; use of this procedure makes it unnecessary to state certain axioms, like the transitivity of the subregion relation, that have an explosive effect on the size of the search space of the proof.

We plan to develop QUARK's abilities to draw conclusions from data (e.g., finding sums and maxima, computing averages, and performing other computations and statistical inferences). It should be able to produce new tables, charts, and similar visualizations of numerical data.

Note

1. These may be found at www.ai.sri.com/pubs/full. php?id=986

Acknowledgements

This work has been supported by the ARDA AQUAINT program, the DARPA DAML program, and the NASA Intelligent Systems program.

Richard Waldinger is a principal scientist at the Artificial Intelligence Center of SRI International, Menlo Park, California. His home page is www.ai.sri.com/people/waldinger.

Douglas E. Appelt is a senior computer scientist at the Artificial Intelligence Center of SRI International, Menlo Park, California.

Jennifer L. Dungan (Jennifer.L.Dungan@nasa.gov) is a research scientist with NASA's Ames Research Center in Mountain View, California, specializing in geospatial information from remotely sensed data of the Earth's land surface.*John Fry* is a research linguist at SRI International in Menlo Park, California.

Jerry R. Hobbs is a research professor at the University of Southern California's Information Sciences Institute, specializing in research in natural language understanding and knowledge representation.

David J. Israel is the director of the Natural Language Program in the Artificial Intelligence Center, SRI International.

Peter Jarvis is a computer scientist at SRI International specializing in computational intelligence. He can be reached at Peter.Jarvis@sri.com.

David Martin is a senior computer scientist in the Artificial Intelligence Center at SRI International. His research interests include natural language understanding, software agents and the semantic web. He can be reached at www.ai.sri.com/~martin.

Susanne Riehemann is a research linguist at SRI International in Menlo Park, California.

Mark E. Stickel is a principal scientist in the Artificial Intelligence Center of SRI International. He specializes in automated deduction and can be reached at www.ai.sri.com/~stickel.

Mabry Tyson is a senior computer scientist at the Artificial Intelligence Center of SRI International, Menlo Park, California.

Chapter 20

Advanced Relaxation for Cooperative Question Answering

Farah Benamara and Patrick Saint Dizier

20.1 Introduction

Advanced reasoning for QA systems, as described in a recent roadmap (http://www-nlpir.nist.gov/projects/duc/papers/qa.Roadmap-paper_v2.doc), raises new challenges, since answers are not only directly extracted from written texts or structured databases but also constructed via several forms of reasoning in order to generate answer explanations and justifications. These systems require the integration of reasoning components operating over a variety of knowledge bases, encoding common sense knowledge as well as knowledge specific to a variety of domains by means, for example, of conceptual ontologies. These kinds of QA systems can be viewed as an enhancement, rather than a rival to retrieval based approaches. Integrating knowledge representation and reasoning mechanisms allow, for example, to respond to unanticipated questions and to resolve situations in which no answer is found in the data sources. Cooperative answering systems are typically designed to deal with such situations by providing useful and informative answers. These systems can, for instance, identify and explain false presuppositions or various types of misunderstandings found in questions. Constraints relaxation in questions occurs when the system cannot find any response. Intensional responses are provided instead of a large unstructured set of extensional answers. Cooperative answering systems can also provide summaries or conditional responses. An overview of these aspects is given in Gaasterland et al. (1994).

WEBCOOP is a logic based QA system that integrates knowledge representation and advanced reasoning procedures to generate intelligent and cooperative responses to natural language (NL) queries on the web. To evaluate the cost of the procedures involved, the project is developed, in a first stage, on a relatively limited domain that includes a number of aspects of tourism (accommodation and transportation). Our approach requires the development of a knowledge extractor from web pages (similar to a knowledge extractor operating on passages resulting from an IR component) and the elaboration of a robust and accurate question parser. In WEBCOOP, responses provided to users are built in web style by integrating natural language generation (NLG) techniques with hypertexts in order to produce dynamic responses (Dale et al. 1998). NL responses are produced from semantic forms constructed from reasoning processes. During these processes, the system has to decide, via cooperative rules, what is relevant and then to organize it in a way that allows for the realization of coherent and informative responses.

In WEBCOOP, responses are structured in two parts: (1) the production of explanations that report user misconceptions, and then (2) the production of flexible solutions that reflect the cooperative know how of the system. This component is the most original. It is based on intensional description techniques and on intelligent relaxation procedures going beyond classical generalization methods elaborated in AI. This component also includes additional dedicated cooperative rules that make a thorough use of the domain ontology and of general knowledge.

To have a more accurate perception of how cooperativity is realized in human-human communication, we collected corpora of question answer pairs found in numerous web sites dedicated to tourism. We first noted that human responses are much more diverse than any machine could produce in the near future. Nevertheless, it is possible to normalize these forms to more stereotyped utterances that a machine can produce. Next, we noted the large number of situations where constraint relaxations are used, and their large variety (Benamara et al. 2003c). This chapter presents an attempt to organize them, to provide a homogeneous model and an implementation of both the reasoning and the natural language generation aspects. First we present related work on the use of inferences in QA systems, and then a description of the current main aspects of WEBCOOP. Then, the advanced relaxation processes and their related NLG issues are presented. The chapter ends by suggesting how to evaluate these types of QA systems.

20.2 Inferences in QA Systems

In the first generation of QA systems, which were designed to answer NL questions from structured databases, only a few QA tasks were claimed to need inference. In fact, inference complemented the extensional processes of relational database querying (SQL). In today's QA systems, where answers can be found in free texts or unstructured data (like the web), inference can enhance Open Domain QA systems capabilities and improve the quality and the accuracy of their answers (Burger et al. 2000). This has been illustrated in the TREC 2002 QA task where the top system was produced by the LCC team

(Moldovan et al. 2003) and also by the emergence of the inference web (IW), which aims at explaining reasoning paths used to retrieve answers (McGuinness et al. 2003). Inference allows enhanced or extended QA services by providing intelligent and cooperative answers. There are many ways for a query to be answered intelligently, including: (1) providing answer explanations, (2) returning intensional responses and answer summarization, (3) generalizing queries using neighborhood information, (4) comparing answers that have similar questions, and (5) realizing information fusion when answers are inferred from multiple data sources, etc. In this section, we deal with items (1), (2) and (3). For a general panorama of inference uses for QA tasks, see Webber et al. (2002).

20.2.1 Answers Explaining a Query Failure

This situation generally occurs when a user has a false or unclear understanding of what he is asking for. For example, a direct answer to the question: "Which train should I take to go from Paris to Algiers?" should be "no," while a cooperative and informative answer should be: "there cannot be any train between Paris and Algiers because of the sea." Inference is needed to detect in a question false presuppositions or misconceptions that conflict with the system knowledge base (false presuppositions occur with respect to the database contents; misconceptions usually occur with respect to the database semantics). Several techniques were developed for recognizing presupposition failure and for generating answer explanations. Let us cite the work carried out by Gaasterland et al. (1994) that detects user misconceptions using logical inference and integrity constraints of the database, and the WhyNot tool (Chalupsky et al. 2002), which generates plausible partial proofs that approximate the correct proof that answer a query that fails.

20.2.2 Query Rewriting Using Neighborhood Information

Query rewriting using neighborhood Information is often useful to provide neighborhood information to a query. For example, if the question: "Give me chalets in Corsica region?" has an empty or a too small set of solutions, the query scope can be extended to provide bungalows or country cottages in Corsica instead of just chalets. One way to increase the yield of potential answers is, for example, to find, within concept hierarchies (such as ontologies), a set of most appropriate concepts which are conceptually close to the relaxed concept in the initial query. A number of techniques were developed within the AI community to address the query relaxation problem. For example, Gaasterland et al. (1994) modify the query either to provide more information to the user, or to repair the query if it fails, and Minock et al. (1996) employ, within their COBASE system, an abstraction/refinement method for providing related answers to the original query.

20.2.3 Intensional Answer Descriptions

A query can be answered by generalization and summarization of the answer set when this set is too large, making answer underlying implications much more clear. For example, the query: "Which students have good marks in computer science?" can be answered intelligently in several ways: (1) "100% of the graduate students, 25% of the senior students", or (2) "all of the graduate students and the undergraduate students are the following...." To realize this task, inference is needed, e.g., for cleaning answers when they partly overlap, for determining whether an answer is more specific than another one and for organizing mutually consistent answers. Gal (1988) uses heuristics that apply to sets of integrity constraints to produce synthetic responses, i.e., by summarizing, sorting explanations or by focusing on a particular one. In the remainder of this chapter, we focus on the query rewriting task (20.2.2).

20.3 WEBCOOP, a Cooperative QA System on the Web

Similarly to standard web search engines, WEBCOOP is not settled within a dialogue perspective and does not include any user model. WEBCOOP is a comprehensive QA system, going from question processing to natural language answer generation using advanced reasoning procedures. In the 90s, in a number of cooperative answering systems, most of the efforts were concentrated on fundamental reasoning procedures, while in standard QA systems (as those evaluated in the TREC QA track), the focus is on language syntax and semantics issues to improve question analysis and answer extraction, however with little reasoning. In most of these latter systems, there is no NL generation. Furthermore, we claim that responses should make explicit in some way the underlying explanation and justification mechanisms that led to the answer. Answer explanation strategy in WEBCOOP is organized as follows: first a short message explains the reasons of a query failure (integrity constraint violation or no solution), then, by means of underspecified NL patterns, the crucial steps of the inference procedures are given. This strategy is inspired from our corpora analysis (Benamara et al. 2003c), where answer justifications are brief and accurate. We believe this is sufficient to understand responses. This is why, unlike inference web, WEBCOOP does not give the user all the inference steps such as axioms, derived rules, or all activated nodes within the domain ontology during the reasoning process. We think this latter approach, that resembles expert systems of the past decade, is not very cooperative.

20.3.1 WEBCOOP General Architecture

The general architecture of the system is illustrated in figure 20.1. In WEBCOOP, user questions may range from keywords to comprehensive natural language expressions. Their parse produces a semantic logical representation

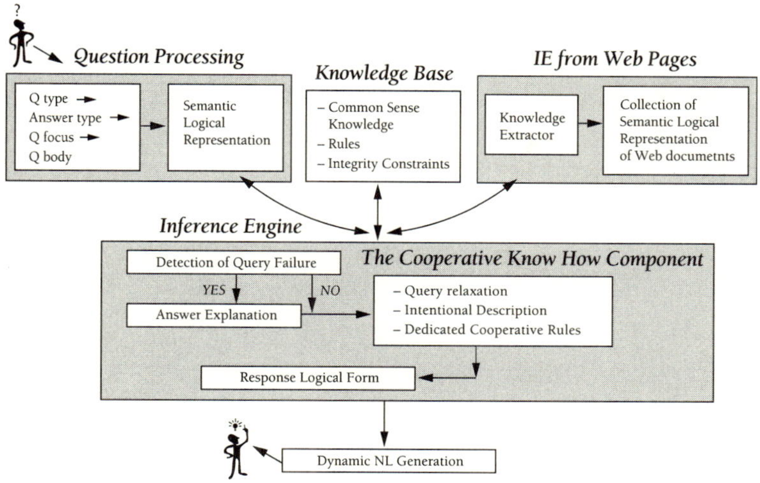

Figure 20.1. WEBCOOP Architecture

that includes the question conceptual category, the question focus, and the question contents. Our approach requires two, very classical, levels of knowledge representation: general purpose knowledge, specified by hand; and domain knowledge, acquired via knowledge extraction procedures from web pages. Knowledge is represented by means of rules and integrity constraints and by means of an ontology where nodes are concepts with properties. A uniform framework is used, based on a simplified version of the Lexical Conceptual Structure (LCS), (Jackendoff 1990). The question analysis and the knowledge extraction processes are presented in Benamara et al. (2003b).

20.3.2 WEBCOOP: a Two Level Structure for Responses

Responses are structured in two parts. The first part contains explanation elements in natural language. It is a first level of cooperativity that reports user misconceptions in relation with the domain knowledge. The second part is the most important and the most original. It reflects the know-how of the cooperative system, going beyond the cooperative statements given in the first part. It is based on intensional description techniques and on intelligent relaxation procedures going beyond classical generalization methods used in AI. This component also includes additional dedicated cooperative rules that make a thorough use of the domain ontology and of general knowledge. Responses provided to users are built in web style, by integrating natural language generation (NLG) techniques with hypertext links to produce "dynamic" responses. Hyperlinks are dynamically created at generation time. This leaves the high-level planning tasks inher-

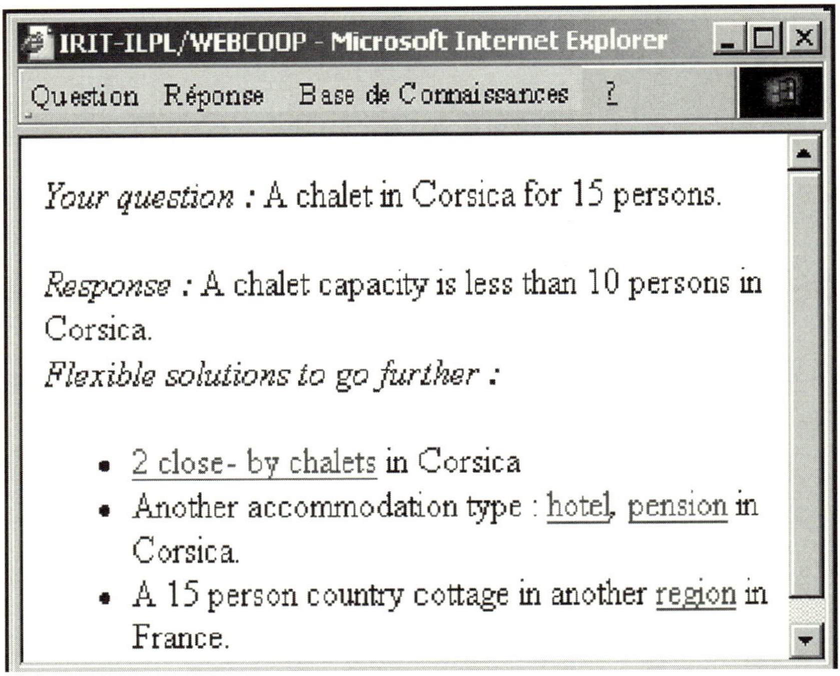

Figure 20.2. Message Regarding a Chalet in Corsica

ent to NLG up to the user and improves readability and information access. The standard generation difficulties (lexicalisation, aggregation, argumentation) remain crucial to generate cooperative responses, but their web-style greatly reduces the overall complexity. The know-how component also allows for the dynamic determination of those text fragments to be defined as hypertext links, from which the user can get more information. To better characterize our problem, we collected a corpus of question answer pairs in French that reflects different cooperative behaviors. The example below is extracted from this corpus. For the sake of readability, it is translated into English.

An Example: Suppose one wishes to rent a 15 person chalet in Corsica and (1) observations made on the related web pages, or (2) a constraint or a regulation indicates that the maximum capacity of a chalet in Corsica is 10 persons. The first part of the response relates the detection of a false presupposition or the violation of an integrity constraint for respectively cases (1) and (2). This entails the production of the following message (see figure 20-2), which is generated by a process that evaluates the question logical formula against the knowledge base: A chalet capacity is less than 10 persons in Corsica.

In a second step, the know-how component of the cooperative system generates a set of flexible solutions as shown in figure 20.2, since the first part of the response is informative but not really productive for the user. The three flexible solutions proposed emerge from know-how cooperative rules based on relaxation procedures designed to be minimal and conceptually relevant. The first flexible solution is based on a cardinality relaxation, while in the last two solutions, relaxation operates gradually on concepts such as the type of accommodation (hotel or pension) or the region (possibly a close-by region, with similar characteristics), via the domain model and the ontology. Dynamically created links are underlined. The user can then, at will, get more precise information, dynamically generated from the data base of indexed web pages.

20.4 Query Relaxation in WEBCOOP

The cooperative know how component has potentially a large number of capabilities and facets. We focus here on a basic, but frequently used, reasoning schema: query rewriting that pairs accurate relaxation techniques with ontological knowledge. Instead of considering a direct ancestor for the relaxed element in the query, our contribution focuses on the taking into account of more subtle forms of constraint relaxation, such as considering sister nodes under constraints or more remote nodes sharing a significant number of properties with the concept to be relaxed. The reasoning aspects of the relaxation and the related main natural language generation aspects are presented here.

20.4.1 Prerequisites to the Relaxation Process

(a) The Knowledge Base Elaboration. We designed a hand crafted ontology of the tourism domain, where nodes are concepts, decorated by means of attributes which describe concept properties or any other relevant information. Since descriptions are hierarchically organized, properties are inherited, if there is no conflict. We define over this ontology a metrics $M(C,C')$ that expresses the ontological distance between two concepts C and C'. Considering the form of our ontology, we are, at the moment, experimenting with different kinds of metrics. The simplest one is to consider the sum of the distance in the ontology between the two concepts C and C' in terms of the number of arcs traversed *NbArc* and the inverse proportion of shared properties, w.r.t the total number of properties on these nodes. This metrics can be written as:

$$M(C,C') = NbArc(C,C') + \frac{Card(prop(C) \cup prop(C'))}{Card(prop(C) \cap prop(C'))}$$

(b) The Misconception Report. NL query parsing produces a logical formula of the following general form : $Q = Q_1(X_{11},...,X_{1m}) \wedge ...... \wedge Q_n(X_{n1}, ...,X_{nl})$ where $\overline{X}_i = (X_{i1},...,X_{ik})$ is the tuple of arguments of the subquery Q_i. Arguments can be variables, constants, or semantic fields of the lexical conceptual structure. The subqueries $Q_i(\overline{X}_i)$ are positive literals of the knowledge base. We have

now to check if the query is coherent with the knowledge base. If it is not, either an integrity constraint has been violated by the user (misconception), or the query has an empty set of solutions (false presupposition). In both cases, the system has to identify the subqueries and the set of rules and integrity constraints which are at the origin of the query failure, in order to be able to provide explanations. To reach this goal, we use a complete and a sound method, based on the positive hyper resolution, defined in Chang et al. (1973), that detects all possible reasons of a query failure, focusing on the literals of the query.

20.4.2 The Relaxation Schema

The relaxation mechanisms of the know how component proceed gradually on each of the subqueries at the origin of the failure. They are modeled as a rewriting system, managed by a supervisor which includes an iterative process running until a flexible solution is found that leads to a nonempty and coherent solution. The relaxation strategy returns the most immediate relaxations once the original query is exhausted and leaves it up to the user to select the relaxation direction. This can be very useful to correct user misconceptions and to help him navigate the database of extracted web pages.

The relaxation technique is based on a generic proximity relation that refers to inherent properties of objects, a conceptual ontology and lexical semantics relations. It is applied to different ontological or technical domains such as, fares, capacity (example in section 20.3.2), type of transportation. The notion of proximity is implemented by the predicate *near(CD, V, Y, Result)* where *CD* is a type in a conceptual domain, *V* is the resource on which the relaxation operates and *Y* is a resource resulting from the relaxation, of the same type as *V*. *Result,* which contains the sorted set of results according to the criteria associated with the conceptual category. The general relaxation schema is modeled by means of rewriting rules. Its general form is: *Relax(Type, QPredicates-To-Relax, Rest-QPredicates, Results)*$\rightarrow$ *NewQuery(Results)*, where *Type* realizes several generic types of relaxations as shown below, *QPredicates-To-Relax* is the conjunction of subqueries Q_i on which the relaxation operates (the reason of the query failure), *Rest-Qpredicates* is the remainder of the query and *Results* contains the set of coherent and flexible solutions resulting from the relaxation process, after evaluation of the relaxed query against the knowledge base. Among different cases of query relaxation we have investigated, here are three which are very frequently used:

(a) Relaxation based on cardinality addresses the case of a question where the quantity of the resource does not meet the cardinality constraints specified in the question. The query logical formula is : $Q = C(X) \wedge F(X,NB) \wedge R$, where *C* is a concept with *X* the focused resource, *F(X,NB)* is the conjunction of predicates of *Q* that contains occurrences of *X*, *NB*, the desired quantity of *X*, and *R* is the remainder of the query. The relaxation duplicates the sequence $C(X) \wedge$

F(X,NB) N times to introduce several instances of the object *X* until the desired quantity (*NB*) of *X* is reached. The relaxation rule is (for $N = 2$):

$Relax(Cardinality, C(X) \wedge F(X,NB), R, Results) \rightarrow C(X1) \wedge C(X2) \wedge F(X1, NB1) \wedge F(X2, NB2) \wedge X1 \neq X2 \wedge (NB1 + NB2 \geq NB) \wedge R \wedge near(CD, X1, X2, Results).$

The conceptual domain *CD* in the proximity relation *near* can be, for example, *localization* (geographical proximity) if the type physical localization can be derived from the ontological type of *X;* or *temporal* for a temporal duration or the simultaneity of events. Let us consider again the example of section 20.3.2, if the maximum chalet capacity in Corsica is 10 persons, the query:

$Q = chalet(X) \wedge region(corsica) \wedge in(place, X, corsica) \wedge capacity(X,15)$

is relaxed into:

$chalet(X1) \wedge in(place, X1, corsica) \wedge capacity(X1, NB1) \wedge chalet(X2) \wedge in(place, X2, corsica) \wedge capacity(X2, NB2) \wedge region(corsica) \wedge X1 \neq X2 \wedge (NB1 + NB2 \geq 15) \wedge near(localization, X1, X2, Results)$

which searches for two close-by chalets in the Corsica region for 15 persons. To evaluate proximity of the two chalets, near consults the set of facts chalets in the database of extracted web pages.

(b) Relaxation on the ontological type of the focus provides minimal and gradual relaxation on the ontological type of the question focus which is generally at the origin of the failure. The question general form is: $Q = C(X) \wedge R$, where *C* is the type of the resource denoted by the variable *X*, and *R* the remainder of the query. The general relaxation schema is:

$relaxation(\text{Onto-Type}, C(X), R, Result) \rightarrow NewQuery(Result),$

where, depending on *Onto-Type*, we have one of the following two cases:

Case b.1: The set $S = \{C'_1, ..., C'_n\}$ of sisters of the relaxed concept *C* can be used to meet the question requirements. This is the case in the example in section 20.3.2, where a hotel or a pension is proposed instead of a chalet, which has a too small capacity. This case occurs mainly when the set **S** is not empty and when there is a subset $S' \subseteq S$ where the distance computed by $M(C,C')$ is small for every sister concept C' in S' (section 4.1). The relaxation schema is the following:

$\forall (C' \in S')\ Relaxation(Sister\text{-}Node, C(X), R, C'(X)) \rightarrow C'(X) \wedge R.$

Case b.2: If the set **S** of sister nodes of the concept *C* is empty or if the distance computed by $M(C,C')$ is large, for every C' in **S**, then a mother node *Mnode* of *C* is considered. Two cases may occur:

(1). if the ontological distance *M(C, Mnode)* between the relaxed concept *C* and its direct ancestor *Mnode* is small, the relaxation process is a generalization and the general rewriting rule is:

$Relaxation(Generalization, C(X), R, Mnode(X)) \rightarrow Mnode(X) \wedge R.$

(2). if the ontological distance *M(C, Mnode)* between the relaxed concept *C* and its direct ancestor *Mnode* is large, then the relaxation process searches for a more remote concept C' in the ontology which shares a maximum of properties with *C*. Then, when searching for responses in the indexed web pages, the system looks for texts satisfying $C'(X) \wedge R$ and containing some or possibly all the properties of C not present in C'. This is implemented by the predicate:

similarto(C, C', *prop*($C - C'$)).

The general rewriting rule is:

Relaxation(*Similarity*, $C(X)$, R, $C'(X) \wedge$ *prop*$(C - C')) \rightarrow$
$C'(X) \wedge R \wedge$ *similarto*(C, C', *prop*(C-C')).

For example, if one is looking for village de vacances en Bretagne (holiday village in Brittany), and there is none in Brittany, a hotel-restaurant can be proposed (subset of the properties of holiday village: accommodation and meals) with sport activities, children day-care, etc., close-by, (i.e., specified in the hotel restaurant web pages, but not attached to the hotel-restaurant resource).

(c) *Relaxation on constants* may occur when the origin of the query failure is a constant. The query logical form is $Q = C(cst) \wedge R$, where *cst* is a constant of type C. The relaxation process replaces in Q the constant *cst* by a variable *Var* which denotes the same kind of resource with a set of potential values close to cst. If the number of solutions is small, they can be enumerated, otherwise a hyperlink is generated. The relaxation schema is then:

Relaxation(*Constant*, *C*(*cst*), *R*, *Result*) $\rightarrow$ *C*(*Var*) $\wedge$ *near*(*CD*, *cst*, *Var*, *Result*) $\wedge$ *R*,

where *CD* can be for example a localization if the type physical localization can be derived from the ontological type of *cst*, or *temporal* (flights between 8PM and 9PM are proposed if there is no flight at 8:30 PM.). For example, if there is no commercial airport in Albi, the query:

$Q =$ *flight*(*ID*, *paris*, *albi*) $\wedge$ *city*(*albi*) $\wedge$ *city*(*paris*),

is relaxed into:

$Q =$ *flight*(ID, *paris*, *Var*) $\wedge$ *city*(*Var*) $\wedge$ *city*(*paris*) $\wedge$ *near*(*place*, *albi*, *Var*, *Results*),

i.e., searching for the nearest cities to Albi served from Paris, which can be ordered by increasing distance from Albi.

This relaxation can also occur when the question focus is a free variable which is constrained in a relational predicate by means of a constant. The query logical representation is: $Q = C(X) \wedge P(X,\overline{Y}) \wedge R$, where P is a predicate that constrains the variable X of type C and $\overline{Y}$ a tuple of variables that exclude X. We relax X w.r.t. the constraints that hold on it, namely $P(X, \overline{Y})$. For example, the query "give me country cottages in the north of France" can be relaxed into "give me country cottages in the center of France" assuming that it is the closest region that has solutions.

20.4.3 The Relaxation Control Strategies

A supervisor manages the calls to the different relaxation procedures. Each relaxation type runs iteratively until a solution is found. This avoids the problem of having to guess the user's intent. The relaxation process returns all the possible answers related to the detected conflict without sorting them. The use of the proximity relation near and the ontological metrics M guarantee that the

***Cardinality** ➔ *N* lexicalisation(C(X), plural) proximity(C(X) R
Example : 2 *séjours consécutifs d'une semaine en Tunisie (Two Consecutive one-week stays in Tunisia).*
***Ontological Type**
– **Sister Node** ➔ *Un(e) autre* lexicalisation(Mnode(X)) : lexicalisation(sister(C)) R.
Example : *Un autre type d'hébergement touristique : hôtels, pensions, en Corse pour 15 personnes.*
(another type of touristic accommodation: hotels, pensions, in Corsica for 15 persons).
– **Generalisation** ➔ *Seulment:* lexicalisation(Mnode(X) R.
– **Similarity** ➔ *lexicalixation(C'),* R *et les éléments suivants a proximité:* lexicalisation (prop(C)).
***Constant (CST)** ➔ *Un(e) autre* lexicalisation(C) *proche de* CST, R. If CST is the question of focus

Figure 20.3. Basic Generation Patterns for the Relaxation Schemas

nearest and the most appropriate set of solutions that meet the question requirements is found. Then, important display strategy problems have to be solved, such as choosing the relevant display order of the relaxed answers and presenting to the user a manageable number of flexible responses. This can be done, for example, by adding a priori preferences to query literals. Different directions are under investigation considering the following criteria: (1) syntactic criteria, for instance, the inverse reading order of the question: give me (chalets)[1] in (Corsica region)[2] (for 15 persons),[3] we can choose to relax first 3, then 2, and finally 1, or (2) pragmatic criteria if we consider that the most precise information is the most reliable. In the above example, we would then relax first 1, then 2, and finally 3.

20.4.4 Natural Language Responses Involving Relaxation

NLG techniques can make explicit in some way the explanation and the justification mechanisms that led to the answer. In Benamara et al. (2003a), we show that using hypertext links avoids, to a large extent, managing the general structure of the response, and leaves open navigation possibilities for the user. For each type of relaxation, a general and somewhat underspecified natural language pattern can be defined that translates the relaxation in accessible terms. Underspecified elements depend on the question, on local semantic factors and on the type of solution elaborated. Their generation relies on ontological knowledge, general linguistic knowledge and lexicalisation and aggregation functions. Patterns have been defined from a number of question-response pairs found in the tourist domain on the web. Responses have been normalized without losing their accuracy in order to get stereotyped response forms usable in NL generation frameworks. A large portion of the pattern is presented as a hyperlink to the user as illustrated in the example of section 20.3.2. Let $C(X)$ the predicate being relaxed in the query and let lexicalisation(C) the function that generates the adequate NL fragment expressing the concept C. The set of possible lexicalisations for a given concept is defined in the domain ontology. The figure below examplifies some of these generation patterns for French, for each of the three types of relaxation introduced in section 20.4.2. Underlined portions are generated as hyperlinks.

20.5 Conclusion and Future Directions

In this chapter, we propose a logic-based QA system that integrates knowledge representation and advanced reasoning procedures to generate intelligent responses to NL queries on the web. We focus on a specific reasoning procedure that pairs accurate relaxation techniques with ontological knowledge. We propose several kinds of minimally and conceptually accurate relaxations and show that, for each type of relaxation, a general and underspecified natural language pattern can be defined that translates the relaxation in accessible terms.

The relaxation mechanisms of the know how component are implemented in Prolog via meta-interpretation. We use a case based implementation method. First, we collected a set of question examples then ranked them by increasing order of complexity (such as complex WH questions (Diekema et al. 2003)). We concentrated our implementation around these examples. Then, we evaluated the results at two levels: (1) the quality of the services offered to a user by comparing our results to human answers in frequently asked question corpora, and (2) the re-usability to other corpus examples. We evaluated each kind of relaxation separately first and the overall functioning of the system via the supervisor. In the future, we plan to use what Barr and Klavans (Barr et al. 2001) call component performance evaluation which consists of assessing the performance of system components and determining their impact on the overall system performance.

This project has obviously several future directions among which we plan to (1) develop new cooperative know-how strategies and their related logical expressions and implementations, (2) specify different strategies for generating intensional responses in the know how component, for example when the number of direct responses is very large, and (3) investigate advanced natural language generation issues in order to elaborate specific explanation schemas for each kind of cooperative responses that WEBCOOP proposes.

Farah Benamara is a Ph.D. student at Toulouse III university. Her interest is in advanced question answering systems and natural language processing. She can be reached at benamara@irit.fr

Patrick Saint-Dizier is research director at CNRS at IRIT-Toulouse. His main interests include computational linguistics, lexical semantics and logic for language. He can be reached by email at stdizier@irit.fr

Chapter 21

Trusting Answers from Web Applications

Deborah L. McGuinness and Paulo Pinheiro da Silva

21.1 Introduction

Inference web (IW) (McGuinness and Pinheiro da Silva 2003) aims to enable applications that can generate portable and distributed explanations for any of their answers. IW addresses needs that arise with systems performing reasoning and retrieval tasks in heterogeneous environments such as the web. Users (humans and computer agents) need to decide when to trust answers from varied sources. Our belief is that the key to trust is understanding, and explanations of information provenance and derivation history can be used to provide that understanding. In the simplest case, users may retrieve information from individual or multiple sources and they may need provenance information (e.g., source identification, recency, authoritativeness, credibility, etc.) before they may decide to trust an answer. Users may also obtain information from systems that manipulate data and derive information that was implicit rather than explicit. Users may need access to information in the proof trace before they can understand and trust the implicit information. Since proof traces are long and complex, users may also need the proof transformed (or abstracted) into an explanation. Since users may obtain information from hybrid and distributed systems, they may need help integrating answers and solutions. As web usage grows, broader and more distributed information services become available, thus increasing the need for explanations that are portable, sharable, and reusable.

The IW provides an answer to the problem of trusting information from QA systems on the web. We introduce the notion of knowledge provenance and show how IW provides provenance information, thereby increasing users' trust in answers. We describe the IW using the KSL Wine Agent example. We also present a block diagram of the IW architecture as viewed by a user. Through this example and using IW components, we describe explanation needs in typical web agents. We put our work in context by stating our contributions and relations to other work.

21.2 Question Answering with Explanations

An explanation is any statement that improves the understanding of an answer. Answers typically have multiple explanations, each one possibly exposing different aspects of the answer. This section introduces knowledge provenance and our explanation strategy.

21.2.1 Knowledge Provenance for Answers

Knowledge provenance includes *source metadata information,* which is a description of the origin of a piece of knowledge, and *knowledge process information,* which is a description of the reasoning process used to generate the answer. We exploit this distinction in our explanation strategies since users and applications have varying needs with respect to explanations of the two classes.

We have used the phrase *knowledge provenance* instead of data provenance intentionally. Data provenance (Buneman et al. 2001, Cui et al. 2000) may be viewed as the analog to knowledge provenance aimed at the database community. That community's definition typically includes both a description of the origin of the information and the process by which it arrived in the database. Knowledge provenance is essentially the same except it includes proof-like information about the process by which knowledge arrives in the knowledge base. The typical process by which knowledge arrives in a knowledge base may include extensive reasoning such as complicated theorem proving to generate deductive closure information while the typical process by which data arrives in a database may not include as much extensive reasoning. Thus, there may be different challenges and a different emphasis for knowledge provenance work in comparison to data provenance work.

21.2.2 Explanation Strategies

Many types of explanations may need to be available if users are to understand answers from distributed web applications. Our strategy is to provide simple initial self-contained explanations and provide automated support for follow-up questions. The user may then ask only about additional information in which they are interested and not be overwhelmed with extraneous details. The initial question and the follow-up questions may involve source metadata information or knowledge process information or a combination of both.

Information retrieval techniques for the web, such as document ranking, are widely used in QA environments. The presentation of some source metadata along with the answers as performed by many search engines can be viewed as an explanation strategy. Our past experience explaining knowledge representation systems has shown that source metadata information for answers is the most important explanation feature for many users and, in many cases, it meets most of their explanation needs. For example, users may need to know the author names, authoritativeness, currency, consistency, etc., of sources in order to trust answers depending upon them. However, source metadata may not be enough for explaining retrieved answers. Users may be interested, for example, in understanding the process of selecting answers. Also, if users are using QA systems that have manipulated information (by reasoners, extractors, heterogeneous agents, etc.), then it would be expected that users would need some kind of understanding of the manipulations and their rationale before they could trust the answers. In this case, some description of how the answer selection was made, as described in JAVELIN (Nyberg et al. 2002), may be a useful way of presenting knowledge process information.

Standard information retrieval techniques may be augmented for question answering by using background knowledge. Query expansion techniques such as Verity's Topic Sets may be used to retrieve additional relevant answers. Query terms are expanded by related terms in the topic set and thus additional answers may be retrieved that would have been missed otherwise. Explanations that show why answers were retrieved, including the terms that were used in the query expansion, provide an additional source of explanations. QA systems that use background ontologies, such as FindUR (McGuinness 1998) use equivalence and subclass relationships for query expansion. Explanations that expose the equivalence/subclass relationships are used to support those answers.

As QA environments are supported with more structured information, such as ontologies and annotated documents, they may be able to provide additional answers or more precise answers for questions. The process of explaining derived answers may become much more complex than explaining retrieved answers. In fact, any particular reasoning path to an answer may have many reasoning steps, each one applying one of the available rules implemented by the inference engine used to derive the answers. IW provides a number of options for explaining the deductive path used in these cases.

21.3 KSL Wine Agent: A Case Study

We will use the KSL Wine Agent[1] as motivation and as a pedagogical tool for explaining how IW can be used. The KSL Wine Agent is a prototype implementation of the wine agent described in Smith et al. (2003). It is also an extension of the description logic tutorial (McGuinness et al. 1994, Brachman et al. 1991). It allows a user to choose a meal course (such as pasta with red sauce) and ask for a description of the suggested wine to drink (such as a dry, red, medium bodied, moderate-flavored wine, a suggested variety such as zinfandel, or a specific suggestion such as Marietta Zinfandel). In its web setting, it can also connect to a few wine sites and check for matching, available wines. Before a user chooses to buy the wine suggested, they may also ask for information such as why the agent suggested a red wine (because of the red sauce) or where the information came from (the DAML wines ontology) or where the specific wine recommendation came from (the wines ontology or a match from the online web site).

A user might use a search engine interface or a structured query language (e.g., DQL[2]) for retrieving information such as "zinfandels from Napa Valley'" or "wine recommended for serving with a spicy red meat meal'." A user might ask for an explanation of why the particular wines were recommended as well as why any particular property of the wine was recommended (like flavor, body, color, etc.). The user may also want information concerning whose recommendations these were (a wine store trying to move its inventory, a wine writer, etc.). In the next section we demonstrate the KSL Wine Agent's use of IW's explanations.

21.4 Inference Web Support for Question Answering

The portable proof specification (Pinheiro da Silva and McGuinness 2003) written in the web markup language DAML+OIL (Connolly et al., 2001) is used by IW to provide interoperability. We describe how portable proofs along with proof-based tools and proof metadata can support explanations in QA environments using the IW.

21.4.1 Using the Inference Web

Figure 21.1 presents a diagrammatic representation on how a QA environment can use the IW. The dashed circle represents a generic QA environment. The lightning symbol represents an inference or search engine embedded in the QA environment used for deriving/retrieving answers. To use the IW, the engine needs to generate proofs in the IW portable proof format. Once the engine generates a proof, it calls the IW explainer passing the URI of the proof fragment at the end of the proof. Using tactics in the IW registry, the explainer abstracts the proof into an explanation. It then calls the browser and passes in the URI of the fragment at the end of the explanation. The browser can then present explanations in varying formats (e.g., figures 21.2 through 4). IW also provides automatic, context-dependent follow-up question support. In addition, it always provides access to either an incremental or complete view of the proof trace.

21.4.2 Explaining Answers

The IW aims to present explanations that help users to identify whether they

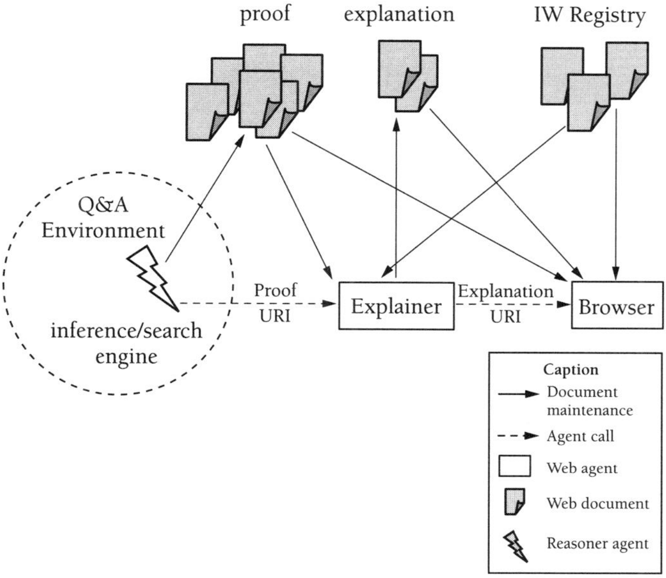

Figure 21.1. Using the Inference Web

should trust answers in a limited number of interactions with the IW browser. Users may view different forms of explanations: limited English descriptions, metadata provenance information, and multi-step proof presentations.

Simple Initial Explanations. Default initial explanations in the IW are very short and are presented in a simple English format as in figure 22.2. In this case, one can imagine a scenario where a user is interested in knowing why the Wine Agent suggested a white wine to go along with the meal that is called "Tony's Specialty." We learn that Tony's specialty is a crab dish that is also a seafood dish. Later if we asked more follow-up questions, we would discover that the wine ontology suggests white wines with seafood dishes.

The IW browser is used to render all the explanations presented in this chapter. When interacting with the browser, users may select from a number of styles and sentence formats for displaying explanations. Initially, the browser includes the "English," "Proof," and "Dag" styles and the restricted "English" and "KIF" sentence formats for rendering explanations (and their associated proofs). We also expect that some applications may implement their own customized display modes using the IW API. The browser implements a lens metaphor responsible for rendering a fixed number of levels of inference steps according to the lens magnitude setting. This is used to limit the information presented. Any portion of the explanation can be probed for follow-up infor-

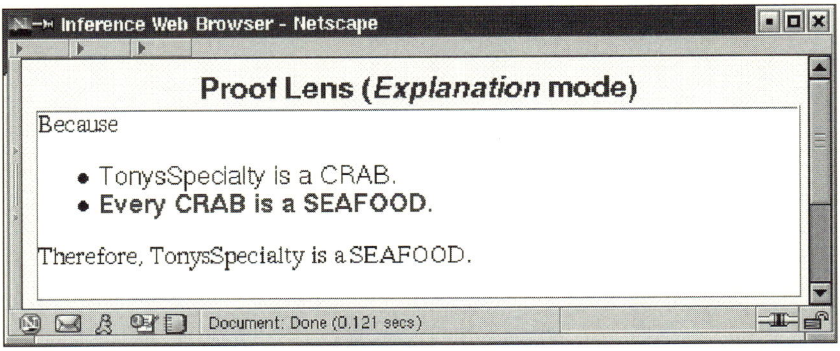

Figure 21.2. An Explanation in Limited English Format

mation. Thus, users can obtain additional information only on the portions of the explanation in which they are interested.

The explanation in figure 21.2 presents a small part of the knowledge provenance since it shows just the last inference step of what is already a simplification of a proof dumped by an inference engine. We believe that one of the keys to presentation of justifications is breaking proofs into separable pieces. Each explanation fragment stands alone in that it does not require the rest of the proof to be understandable, yet it is probable so that any term or sentence in it can be queried as to what its definition is, what meta information is known about it, or how it was derived.

A Source-Oriented Explanation. If users rely on embedded inference/search engines but do not understand answers, they may ask the browser for the sources metadata information used in the answer. Figure 21.3 presents the source metadata information for *TonysSpecialty* is a *SEAFOOD* dish. IW displays the current sentence, the assertions used in the proof, and the metadata about the knowledge bases containing the assertions. Figure 21.3 shows three sentences that were all from the WINE-TEST ontology authored by the KSL team.

In practical scenarios such as those used on the ARDA AQUAINT[3] and NIMD[4] projects, presentation of the source metadata information can be a large list of axioms and sources, since a typical scenario can include hundreds of axioms from multiple ontologies. Moreover, these ontologies and knowledge bases may be the result of analyzing, summarizing, and compiling information described in multiple documents. Thus, all the original documents and the analysts and subject matter experts involved in the process of compiling these documents also become sources of ontologies.

A Process-Oriented Explanation. When users obtain answers from hybrid reasoning environments, explanations of integrated QA systems may be required. If these new environments have been built by “plugging” in a number of special purpose reasoners, end users may need to know the inference rules used along with the sentences they were used on. The order of application of these rules

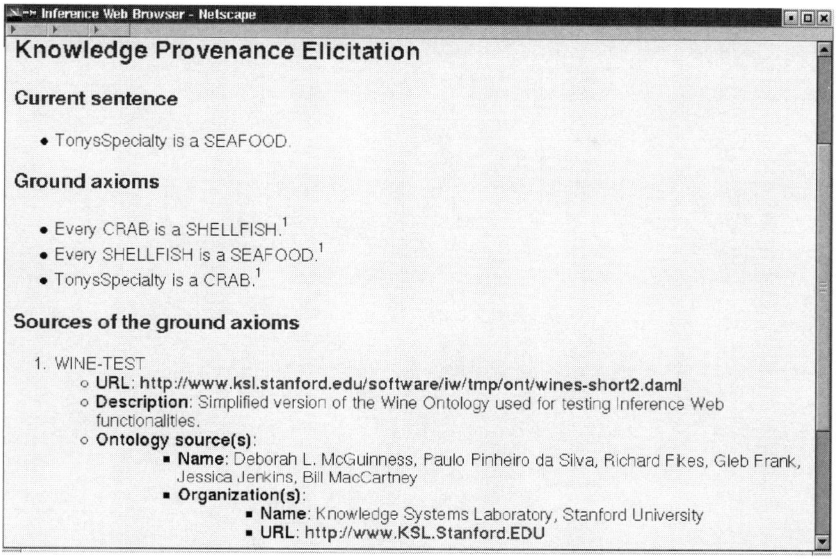

Figure 21.3. Presenting Source Metadata Information

may also be of interest. Figure 21.4 presents an approach to explaining knowledge process information. There, for example, the class transitivity inference rule was used to derive that every CRAB dish is a SEAFOOD dish from the premises. CRAB is a subclass of SHELLFISH, and SHELLFISH is a subclass of SEAFOOD.

Since the contents in figures 21.2 and 21.4 are explanation fragments, automatic support for follow-up questions is important. Every element in the viewing lens can trigger a browser action. For example, the selection of an antecedent re-focuses the lens on an antecedent's inference step. Thus, context-appropriate follow-up questions are generated for the user.

21.5 Contributions and Future Work

Two example IW-supported semantic web agents are the KSL Wine Agent and the DAML Query Service (www.ksl.stanford.edu/projects/dql/). They use Stanford's JTP theorem prover that produces portable proofs. The IW registry is populated with JTP information: one *InferenceEngine* entry for the reasoner itself, nine entries for its primitive inference rules, one entry for its set of DAML axioms, and 56 entries for the axioms. With the registration of a few web agents we provided operational specifications and implementations of web agents enhanced with portable explanations.

If either of these applications wanted to use another reasoner (other than the ones already registered in IW), the inference engine entry would need to be made for the new reasoner along with its core inference rule entries. If the

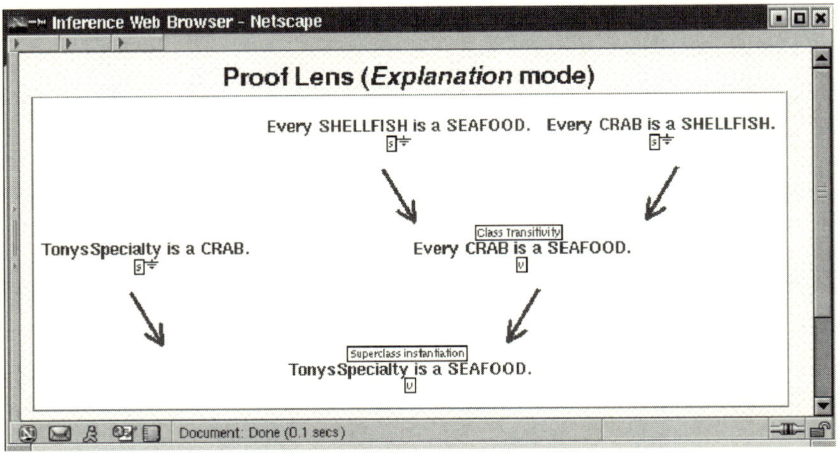

Figure 21.4. A Graphical Explanation

new reasoner was similar to a reasoner already registered, one might find that it was using many of the same core inference rule entries and thus those could be reused. For example, we registered the inference rules published for OTTER, and later when we registered SNARK, we reused a number of the previously registered core inference rules. We have registered JTP completely and have provided registration of a few other sets of inference rules for some published reasoning systems like OTTER. We have also provided supporting mechanisms for assisting reasoner authors in registering their reasoning agents so as to minimize their efforts in utilizing the IW.

Beyond explaining a single system, IW attempts to incorporate "best in class" explanations and provide a way of combining and presenting proofs that are available. It does not take one stance on the form of the explanation since it allows engines to dump single or multiple explanations of any information manipulation producing answers. It provides the user with flexibility in viewing fragments of single or multiple explanations in multiple formats. IW simply requires inference rule registration and portable proof format. It uses a set of user preference settings for choosing the presentation format. Default settings are provided according to usage choices, and users may modify the choices. In the future, user modeling could be exploited to determine a user-specific and context dependent set of preferences automatically for the user.

The IW Registry contains information that may be used in any IW proof. As a side effect of IW use, the Registry provides a collection of ontologies, source information, and query answering tools that may be useful for web agents. Today the registry contains limited information about authoritativeness and credibility assessments of the registered ontologies, but we expect over time that this information will grow and may be a resource for others in evaluating source information. Additionally, IW can collect statistics about how many question answering systems are relying on different ontological sources and thereby provide some empirical information about use and reuse of ontologies, potentially providing more information about the credibility of sources.

The foundation of the portable proof specification allows us to connect to other reasoners with minimal impact on implementations. It is the key to working portably in distributed heterogeneous environments. We are exploring other reasoning paradigms including more procedural components found in the KM reasoner.[5] We are also soliciting input from broader communities that may need non-monotonic reasoning or probabilistic reasoning and checking the portable proof specification for its flexibility.

We are currently extending SRI's SNARK[5] theorem prover to produce portable proofs and simultaneously populating the IW registry with SNARK information. Also, we are in the process of discussing the registration of the W3C's CWM[6] theorem prover reasoner in the IW. Future work includes the registration of more inference engines, work on database support for scaling, and. specialized support for why-not questions expanding upon Chalupsky and Russ (2002) and McGuinness (1996). We are also looking at additional support for proof browsing and pruning. We have also initiated conversations with the verification community in order to provide a portable proof and registry format that meets their needs as well as the needs of the applications that require explanation.

21.6 Related Work

Recognition of the importance of explanation components for reasoning systems has existed in a number of fields for many years. Expert system research, e.g., MYCIN (Shortliffe 1976) and the explainable expert system (Swartout et al. 1991) recognized the need for systems that understood their reasoning processes and could generate explanations in a language understandable to its users. That work lays a critical foundation on generating explanations and interoperating with reasoning applications but lacks the focus on distributed environments and explanation fragments

IW builds on the learnings of explanation in description logics (e.g., Borgida et al.. (1999), McGuinness (1996), and McGuinness and Borgida (1995)) that provide a logical infrastructure for separating pieces of logical proofs and automatically generating follow-questions based on the logical format. That work focuses on explanation fragments but lacks the focus on distributed environments. IW also attempts to integrate learnings from the theorem proving community on proof presentation (e.g., Boyer et al. (1995), Felty and Miller (1987)) and explanation (e.g., Huang (1994)). IW is distinguished from previous work with its focus on distributed environments, stand-alone proof fragments, and knowledge provenance, potentially for extracted and merged knowledge bases.

IW builds on experience designing query components for frame-like Systems (Borgida and McGuinness 1996, Fikes et al. 2002, McGuinness 1996) to generate requirements. This foundational works typically focus on answers and only secondarily on information supporting the understanding of the answers. During requirements gathering, we also obtained input from DARPA programs (the High Performance Knowledge Base program,[7] Rapid Knowledge Formation Program,[8] and the DARPA Agent Markup Language Program,[9] and more recently, the ARDA AQUAINT and NIMD programs). We also gathered requirements from work on the usability of knowledge representation systems (e.g., McGuinness and Patel-Schneider [2003]) and ontology environments (e.g., Das et al. [2002]). We have also gathered needs from the World Wide Web Consortium (W3C) efforts on CWM[10] and the related reasoner effort on Euler.[11] Finally, we gathered knowledge provenance requirements from the programs above and from work on data provenance from the database community (e.g., Buneman et al. (2001)).

21.7 Conclusion

QA environments can use the IW for explaining their answers. We identified the support for provenance information, reasoning information, explanation generation, distributed proofs, and proof presentation as requirements for explanations in the web. We described the major components of IW-the portable proof specification based on the emerging web language-DAML (soon to be updated to OWL) supporting proofs and their explanations, the registry, the explainer, and the browser. We described how IW features provide infrastructure for the identified requirements for web explanations. We facilitated use in a distributed environment by providing IW tools for registering and manipulating proofs, proof fragments, and metadata about inference engines, rules, and sources. We also facilitated interoperability by specifying the portable proof format and providing tools for manipulating proofs and fragments. We have implemented the IW approach for two web agents based on JTP and are in discussions with additional reasoner authors to include more reasoning engines. We have presented the work at government sponsored program meetings (RKF, DAML, AQUAINT, and NIMD) to gather input from other reasoner authors/users and have obtained feedback and interest.

Acknowledgments

Many people have provided valuable input to our work. Thanks in particular to KSL colleagues including Richard Fikes, Jessica Jenkins, Gleb Frank, Eric Hsu, Sheila McIlraith, Rob McCool, and Yulin Li for input on JTP, our specification or applications. Also thanks go to a number of colleagues in some government programs who provided input including Hans Chalupsky, Peter Clark, Ken Forbus, Ken Murray, and Steve Reed. All errors, of course are our own.

Notes

1. www.ksl.stanford.edu/people/dlm/webont/winteAgent/
2. www.daml.org/2002/08/dql/
3. www.ic-arda.org/InfoExploit/aquaint/
4. www.ic-arda.org/Novel_Intel-ligence/
5. www.cs.utexas.edu/users/mfkb/km.html
6. www.ai.sri.com/~stickel/ snark.html
7. reliant.teknowledge.com/HPKB/
8 reliant.teknowledge.com/RKF/
9 www.daml.org
10. www.w3.org/2000/10/swap/doc/cwm.html
11. www.agfa.com/w3c/euler/.

Deborah McGuinness is the associate director and a senior research scientist at the Knowledge Systems Labortory at Stanford Univerity. She specializes in explanation, ontologies, representation and reasoning, and the semantic web. Her web page with contact information is at www.ksl.stanford.edu/people/dlm .

Paulo Pinheiro da Silva is a postdoctoral fellow in the the Knowledge Systems Laboratory at Stanford University.

Glossary

AAAI	American Association of Artificial Intelligence
ACE	Automated Content Extraction (www.itl.nist.gov/iad/894.01/ tests/ace)
ACL	Association for Computational Linguistics
ACM	Association for Computing Machinery
ADL	Alexandria Digital Library
AECMA	European Association of Aerospace Industries
AFS	Answer-Focused Summarization
AIDE	Advanced Interactive Discovery Environment for Engineering Education
AMAI	Annals of Mathematics and Artificial Intelligence
AMIA	American Medical Informatics Association
AMM	Aircraft Maintenance Manual
ANLP	Conference on Applied Natural Language Processing
API	Application Programming Interface
AQUAINT	Advanced Question Answering for Intelligence Program (www.ic-arda.org/InfoExploit/aquaint)
ARDA	Advanced Research and Development Activity in Information Technology (www.ic-arda.org)
ASCII	American Standard Code for Information Interchange
ASCS	Agent Semantic Communication Service
ASR	Automatic Speech Recognition
AT&T	American Telephone and Telegraph
ATA	Air Transport Association
ATRANS	Abstract Transfer (from Conceptual Dependency Theory)
AWB	Alembic Workbench

BBN	Bolt, Beranek and Newman
BLEU	BiLingual Evaluation Understudy
CADE	Conference on Automated Deduction
CAE	Collection Analysis Engine
CAS	Common Analysis System
CBR	Case-based Reasoning
CGI	Common Gateway Interface
CIA	Central Intelligence Agency
CIKM	International Conference on Information and Knowledge Management
CLEF	Cross-Language Evaluation Forum
CLiViR	Common Linguistic-Visual Representation
CMU	Carnegie Mellon University
CNS	Center for Nonproliferation Studies, Monterey, California
COLING	International Conference on Computational Linguistics
CPM	Collection Processing Manager
CUNY	City University of New York
CWM	Closed World Machine (www.w3.org/2000/10/swap/doc/ cwm.html)
CWS	Confidence Weighted Score
DAML	DARPA Agent Markup Language Program (www.daml.org)
DARPA	Defense Advanced Research Projects Agency
DB	Database
DEXA	International Conference on Database and Expert Systems Applications
DIA	Defense Intelligence Agency
DISEQuA	Dutch Italian Spanish English Questions and Answers
DQL	DAML Query Language (www.daml.org/2002/08/dql)
DUC	Document Understanding Conferences (duc.nist.gov)
EACL	European Association for Computational Linguistics
ECAI	European Conference on Artificial Intelligence
EDT	Entity Detection and Tracking
EELD	Evidence Extraction and Link Discovery Program
EES	Explainable Expert Systems
EIS	Enterprise Information System

EMNLP	Conference on Empirical Methods in Natural Language Processing
ESPN	Entertainment Sports Network
FAQ	Frequently Asked Question
FOIS	International Conference on Formal Ontology in Information Systems
GATE	General Architecture for Text Engineering
GNU	GNU's not UNIX
HITIQA	High-Quality Interactive Question-Answering
HLT	Human Language Technology
HMM	Hidden Markov Model
HPKB	High Performance Knowledge Base program (reliant.teknowledge. com/HPKB)
HTML	HyperText Markup Language
IAAI	Innovative Applications of Artificial Intelligence Conference
IBM	International Business Machines
IDF	Inverse Document Frequency
ICDE	Proceedings of International Conference on Data Engineering
IE	Information Extraction
IEEE	Institute of Electrical and Electronics Engineers
IJCAI	International Joint Conference on Artificial Intelligence
IJCIS	International Journal on Cooperative Information Systems
IMDb	Internet Movie Database
IR	Information Retrieval
IRIT	Institut de Recherches en Informatique de Toulouse
ISWC	International Semantic Web Conference
IW	Inference Web
JAVELIN	Justification-based Answer Valuation through Language Interpretation
JPL	Jet Propulsion Laboratory
JTP	JAVA Theorem Prover (ksl.stanford.edu/software/jtp)
KB	knowledge base
KIF	Knowledge Interchange Format
KSA	Knowledge Source Adapter
KSL	Knowledge Systems Lab (at Stanford)

KSS	Kanisa Site Search
L2L	Language-to-Logic
LCC	Language Computer Corporation
LCS	Lexical Conceptual Structure
LDC	Linguistic Data Consortium
LIMSI-CNRS	Laboratoire d'Informatique pour la Mécanique et les Sciences de l'Ingénieur - Centre National de la Richerche Scientifique
LNAI	Springer Lecture Notes in Artificial Intelligence
LNCS	Springer Lecture Notes in Computer Science
LREC	International Conference on Language Resources and Evaluation
MIT	Massachusetts Institute of Technology
MLF	Minimal Logical Forms
MPQA	Multi-Perspective Question-Answering
MRDR	Mean Reciprocal Document Rank
MRR	Mean Reciprocal Rank
MRSR	Mean Reciprocal of Summary Ranks
MUC	Message Understanding Conference
MWT	MultiWord Terms
NAACL	North American Chapter of the Association for Computational Linguistics
NAFTA	North American Free Trade Agreement
NASA	National Aeronautics and Space Administration
NASD	www.nasd.com
NE	named entity
NIMA	National Imagery and Mapping Agency
NIMD	Novel Intelligence from Massive Data Program (www.ic-arda.org/Novel_Intelligence)
NIST	National Institute of Standards and Technology
NLDB	International Conference on Applications of Natural Language to Information Systems (www.nldb.org)
NLG	Natural Language Generation
NLP	Natural Language Processing
NRO	National Reconnaissance Organization
NRRC	Northeast Regional Research Center (nrrc.mitre.org)

NSA	National Security Agency
NSD	Non-Specific Definitional
OCR	Optical Character Recognition
OIL	Ontology Inference Layer (www.ontoknowledge.org/oil)
OWL	Ontology Web Language
PDM	Perceptual Data Mining
PIQUANT	Practical Intelligent Question ANswering Technology
PIRCS	Probabilistic Indexing Retrieval—Components—System Propbank Proposition Bank (www.cis.upenn.edu/~ace)
QA	Question Answering
QANDA	(MITRE's) Question and Answering system
QDC	Query by Dossier w/Constraints
Q-to-A	Question to Answer (matching)
Q-to-Q	Question to Question (matching)
QUARK	Question Answering through Reasoning and Knowledge
RDBMS	Relational Database Management System
RDF	Resource Description Framework (www.w3.org/RDF)
RIAO	Recherche d'Informations Assistee par Ordinateur
RIDIT	Rectangularly DIstributed Trait
RKF	Rapid Knowledge Formation Program (reliant.teknowledge. com/RKF)
RLV	Reusable Launch Vehicle
RQL	Revue Québécoise de Linguistique
SAP	Systems, Applications, and Products (in data processing) [from the German Systeme, Anwendungen und Produkte (in der Datenverarbeitung)]
SDO	Searchable Data Object
SEC	Securities and Exchange Commission
SGML	Standard Generalized Markup Language
SIGDAT	ACL Special Interest Group for Linguistic Data and Corpus-based Approaches to NLP
SIGDIAL	ACL Special Interest Group on Discourse and Dialogue
SIGIR	ACM Special Interest Group in Information Retrieval
SIGMOD	ACM Special Interest Group on Management of Data
SITI	The Swedish Research Institute for Information Technology

SMU	Southern Methodist University
SNARK	SRI's New Automated Reasoning Kit
SQL	Standard Query Language
START	SynTactic Analysis using Reversible Transformations
SWEET	Semantic Web for Earth and Environment Terminology
TAE	Text Analysis Engine
TCP/IP	Transmission Control Protocol/Internet Protocol
TDT	Topic Detection and Tracking
TERQAS	Time and Event Recognition for Question Answering Systems
T-expressions	Ternary expressions
TIA	Terminologie et Intelligence Artificielle
TIDES	Translingual Information Detection Extraction and Summarization
TIMEBANK	Time bank of gold standard of temporally annotated documents
TimeML	Time Markup Language
TIMEX	Time Expression
TIPSTER	DARPA funded text and information processing program (Not an acronym)
TPS	Thermal Protection System
TREC	Text REtrieval Conference
TREEBANK	www.cis.upenn.edu/~treebank/home.html
UIMA	Unstructured Information Management Architecture
UPS	United Parcel Service
URL	Uniform Resource Locators
USC/ISI	University of Southern California Information Sciences Institute
USGS	United States Geological Survey
USPTO	US Patent and Trade Office
W3C	World Wide Web Consortium
WEBCOOP	A Cooperative Question-Answering System on the Web
WIPO	World Intellectual Property Organization
WWW	World Wide Web
XML	eXtensible Markup Language

Bibliography

Agichtein, E.; and Gravano, L. 2000. Snowball: Extracting Relations from Large Plain-Text Collections. In Proceedings of the Fifth ACM International Conference on Digital Libraries. New York: Association for Computing Machinery.

Air Transport Association of America, Inc. 1997. *ATA Common Support Data Dictionary for the Air Transport Industries.* Washington, D.C.: Air Transport Association of America.

Allen, J. 1983. Maintaining Knowledge About Temporal Intervals. *Communications of the ACM.* 26(11): 832–843.

Allen, J. F. 1984. Towards a General Theory of Action and Time. *Artificial Intelligence* 23(2): 123–154.

Allen, J. F. and Hayes, P. J. 1989. Moments and Points in an Interval-Based Temporal Logic. *Computational Intelligence* 5(4): 225–238.

Allen, J. F.; and Ferguson, G. 1997. Actions and Events in Interval Temporal Logic. In *Spatial and Temporal Reasoning*, 205–268, ed. Oliveiro Stock. Dordrecht, The Netherlands: Kluwer Academic Publishers.

Allen, J. F.; and Kautz, H. A. 1985. A Model of Naive Temporal Reasoning. In *Formal Theories of the Commonsense World,* 251–268, ed. Jerry R. Hobbs and Robert C. Moore, Norwood, N.J.: Ablex Publishing.

Androutsopoulos, I.; Ritchie, G. D.; and Thanisch, P. 1995. Natural Language Interfaces to Databases—An Introduction. *Natural Language Engineering* 1(1): 29-81.

Angel, M. 1999. System and Method for Document Management Based on a Plurality of Knowledge Taxonomies. World Intellectual Property Organization Application WO 00/77690. Geneva, Switzerland.

Appelt, D. E.; Martin, D. L. 1999. Named Entity Recognition in Speech: Approach and Results Using the TextPro System. Gaithersburg, Md: National Institute of Standards and Technology. (www.nist.gov/speech/publications/darpa99/html/ie30/ie30.htm)

Aslandogan, Y., and Yu, C. 1999. Techniques and Systems for Image and Video Retrieval. *IEEE Transactions on Knowledge and Data Engineering.* 11(1): 56–63.

Atzeni, P.; Mecca, G.; and Merialdo, P. 1997. Semistructured and Structured Data in the Web: Going Back and Forth. Paper at the SIGMOD '97 Workshop on Management of Semistructured Data. Tucson, Ariz., May 11.

Banfield, A. 1982. *Unspeakable Sentences.* Boston: Routledge and Kegan Paul.

Barr, V.; and Klavans, J. 2001. Verification and Validation of Language Processing Systems: Is It Evaluation? Paper presented at the Association for Computational Linguistics (ACL) Workshop on Evaluation Methodologies for Language and Dialogue Systems. Toulouse, France, July 6–7.

Barzilay, R.; McKeown, K. R.; and Elhadad, M. 1999. Information Fusion in the Context of Multi-Document Summarization. In *Proceedings of the Thirty-Seventh Annual Meeting of the Association for Computational Lingusitics*, 550–557. San Francisco: Morgan Kaufmann Publishers.

Belnap, N. D. 1963. An Analysis of Questions: Preliminary Report. Scientific Report TM-1287. The Rand Corporation, Santa Monica, Calif.

Belnap, N. D.; and Steel, T. B. 1976. *The Logic of Questions and Answers.* New Haven, Conn: Yale University Press.

Benamara, F.; and Saint Dizier, P. 2003a. Dynamic Generation of Cooperative Natural Language Responses. Paper presented at the Ninth European Workshop on Natural Language Generation, Eleventh Conference of the European Chapter of the Association for Computational Linguistics, Budapest, Hungary, 12–17 April.

Benamara, F.; and Saint Dizier, P. 2003b. WEBCOOP: A Cooperative Question-Answering System on the Web, Paper presented at the Eleventh Conference of the European Chapter of the Association for Computational Linguistics, Budapest, Hungary, 12–17 April.

Benamara, F.;and Saint Dizier, P. 2003c. Construction de Réponses Coopératives: Du Corpus à la Modélisation Informatique (Construction of Co-operative Answers: Corpus with Data-processing Modeling). Revue Québécoise de Linguistique RQL (Special Issue: TALN, Corpus et Web).

Berger A.; V.; Pietra, V.; Della and Pietra, S. Della. 1996. A Maximum Entropy Approach to Natural Language Processing *Computational Linguistics* 22(1): 39–71.

Berger, A.; and Mittal, V. 2000. Query-relevant Summarization Using FAQs. Paper presented at the Thirty-Eighth Annual Meeting of the Association for Computational Linguistics (ACL-2000), Hong Kong, October 1–8.

Berger, A.; Caruana, R.; Cohn, D.; Freitag, D.and V. Mittal. 2000. Bridging the Lexical Chasm: Statistical Approaches to Answer-finding. Paper presented at the Twenty-third annual International ACM SIGIR Conference on Research and Development in Information Retrieval. Athens, Greece, July 24–28.

Bikel, D., Schwartz, R., and Weischedel, R. 1999. An Algorithm that Learns What's in a Name. *Machine Learning* 34(1–3): 211–231.

Blair-Goldensohn, S.; McKeown, K. R.; and Schlaikjer, A. H. 2003. DefScriber: A Hybrid System for Definitional QA (Demonstration). In Proceedings of the Twenty-Sixth ACM Special Interest Group on Information Retrieval. New York: Association for Computing Machinery.

Bobrow, D.; Kaplan, R.; Kay, M.; Norman, D.; Thompson, H.; and Winograd, T. 1977. GUS: A Frame Driven Dialog System. *Artificial Intelligence* 8(2): 155–173.

Bopp, R. E.; and Smith, L. C. 2001. *Reference and Information Services: An Introduction.* Third Edition. Englewood, Colo.: Libraries Unlimited.

Borchardt, G. C. 1992. Understanding Causal Descriptions of Physical Systems. In *Proceedings of the Tenth National Conference on Artificial Intelligence,* 2–8. Menlo Park, Calif.: AAAI Press.

Borgelt, C. 2000. Data Mining with Graphical Models. Ph.D. dissertation, Dept. of Computer Science, Otto-von-Guericke-University of Magdeburg, Magdeburg, Germany.

Borgida, A.; and McGuinness, D. L. 1996. Asking Queries about Frames. In *Proceedings of Fifth International Conference on the Principles of Knowledge Representation and Reasoning*. San Francisco: Morgan Kaufmann, Publishers.

Borgida, A.; Franconi, E.; Horrocks, I.; McGuinness, D. L.; and Patel-Schneider, P. F. 1999. Explaining ALC Subsumption. Paper presented at the International Workshop on Description Logics (DL'99), Linköping, Sweden, July 30 - Aug. 1.

Boyer, R.; Kaufmann, M.; and Moore, J. 1995. The Boyer-Moore Theorem Prover and Its Interactive Enhancements. *Computers and Mathematics with Applications* 29(2): 27–62.

Brachman, R. J.; Borgida, A.; McGuinness, D. L.; Patel-Schneider, P. F.; and Resnick, L. A. 1991. Living with CLASSIC: When and How to Use a KL-ONE-Like Language. In Principles of Semantic Networks: Explorations in the Representation of Knowledge, 401–456, ed, J. Sowa. San Mateo, Calif.: Morgan Kaufmann, Publishers.

Brill, E.; and Resnik, P. 1994. A Rule-Based Approach to Prepositional Phrase Attachment Disambiguation. In Proceedings of the Fifteenth International Conference on Computational Linguistics (COLING 94), Vol. 2, 998–1004, Kyoto, Japan. Stanford, Calif.: International Committee on Computational Linguistics.

Buckley, C.; Salton, G.; Allan, J.; and Singha, A. 1994. Automatic Query Expansion using SMART: TREC 3. In Overview of the Third Text Retrieval Conference (TREC-3). NIST Special Publication 500-225, 69–80. Gaithersburg, Md.: National Institute of Standards and Technology.

Buckley, Chris. 1985. Implementation of the SMART Information Retrieval System. Technical Report TR85-686, May, Department of Computer Science, Cornell University, Ithaca, N.Y.

Buneman, P.; Khanna, S.; and Tan, W. C. 2001. Why and Where: A Characterization of Data Provenance. In *Proceedings of Eighth International Conference on Database Theory (ICDT 2001), Lecture Notes in Computer Science,* 316–330. Berlin: Springer-Verlag.

Burger J.; Cardie C.; Chaudhi V.; Gaizauskas, R.; Harabagiu, S.; Israel, D.; Jacquemin, C.; Lin, C.-Y.; Maiorano, S.; Miller, G.; Moldovan, D.; Ogden, B.; Prager, Riloff, E.; Singhal, A.; Shrihari, R.; Strzalkowski, T.; Voorhees, E.; and Weishedel, R. 2000. Issues,Tasks and Program Structures to Roadmap Research in Question Answering. Technical Report, NIST. Gaithersburg, Md.: National Institute of Standards and Technology.

Burger, J. D.; Ferro, L.; Greiff, W.; Henderson, J.; Light, M.; and Mardis, S. 2003. MITRE's Qanda at TREC-11. In Proceedings of the Eleventh Text Retrieval Conference (TREC 11). NIST Special Publication SP 500-251, ed. E. M. Voorhees and D. K. Harman. Gaithersburg, Md.: National Institute of Standards and Technology.

Burger, J.; Cardie, C.; Chaudhri, V.; Gaizauskas, R.; Harabagiu, S.; Israel, D.; Jacquemin, C.; Lin, C.-Y.; Maiorano, S.; Miller, G., Moldovan, D.; Ogden, B.; Prager, J.; Riloff, E.; Singha, A.; Shrihari, R.; Strzalkowski, T.; Voorhees, E.; and Weischedel, R. 2002. Issues, Tasks, and Program Structures to Roadmap Research in Question and Answering. Gaithersburg, Md: National Institute of Standards and Technology. (www-nlpir.nist.gov/Projects/Duc/Papers/Qa.Roadmap-Paper_v2.doc.)

Burke, R.; Hammond, K.; Kulyukin, V.; Lytinen, S.; Tomuro, N. and Schoenberg, S. 1997. Question Answering from Frequently-Asked Question Files: Experiences with the FAQ Finder System. *AI Magazine* 18(2): 57–66.

Byrd, R.; and Ravin, Y. 1999. Identifying and Extracting Relations in Text, Paper presented at the Fourth International Conference on Applications of Natural Languages to Information Systems. Klagenfurt, Austria, June 17-19.

Callan, James P.; Croft, W. Bruce; and Harding, Stephen M. 1992. The INQUERY Retrieval System. In *Proceedings of the Third International Conference on Database and Expert Systems Applications (DEXA-92),* 78–83. Berlin: Springer-Verlag.

Carbonell, J. G.; and Goldstein, J. 1998. The Use of MMR, Diversity-Based Reranking for Reordering Documents and Producing Summaries. In Proceedings of the Twenty-first ACM International Conference on Research and Development in Information Retrieval. New York: Association for Computing Machinery.

Central Intelligence Agency, U.S. Government. 2002. The World Factbook. Washington, D.C.: Government Printing Office (http://www.cia.gov/cia/publications/factbook/)

Chalupsky, H.; and Russ, T. 2002. WhyNot. Debugging Failed Queries in Large Knowledge Bases. In *Proceedings of the Fourteenth Conference on Innovative Applications of Artificial Intelligence Conference (IAAI-02),* 870–877. Menlo Park, Calif.: AAAI Press.

Chang, C. L.; and Lee, R. C. T. 1973. *Symbolic Logic and Mechanical Theorem Proving.* Boston: Academic Press.

Chang, J.; Lau, R.; and McCandless, M. 2000. Information Access Method. World Intellectual Property Organization Application WO 01/84374. Geneva, Switzerland.

Chang, S. K.; Shi, Q.; and Yan, C. 1987. Iconic Indexing By 2-D String. *IEEE Transactions on Pattern Analysis and Machine Intelligence.* 9(3): 413–428.

Chen, J. Y.; Taskiran, C.; Albiol, A.; Delp, E. J.; and Bouman, C. A. 1999. ViBE: A Video Indexing and Browsing Environment. In Proceedings of the International Society for Optical Engineering Conference on Multimedia Storage and Archiving Systems IV, Vol. 3846, 148–164. Bellingham, Wash.: SPIE.

Chinchor, N.; Brown, E.; Ferro, L.; and Robinson, P. 1999. *Named Entity Recognition Task Definition,* Boston, Mass., The MITRE Corporation, 1999.

Chinchor, N.; Hirschman, L.; and Lewis, D. 1993. Evaluating Message Understanding Systems: An Analysis of the Third Message Understanding Conference (MUC-3). *Computational Linguistics* 19(3): 409–449.

Chu-Carroll, J.; Czuba, K.; Prager, J.; and Ittycheriah, A. 2003. In Question Answering, Two Heads Are Better Than One. Paper Presented at the Human Language Technology Conference (HLT-NAACL 2003), Edmonton, Canada, May 30.

Chu-Carroll, J.; Ferrucci, D.; Prager, J.; and Welty, C. 2003. Hybridization in Question Answering Systems. In New Directions in Question Answering: Papers from the 2003 AAAI Spring Symposium. AAAI Tech. Rep. SS-03-07, American Association for Artificial Intelligence, Menlo Park, Calif.

Chu-Carroll, J.; Prager, J.; Welty, C.; Czuba, K.; and Ferrucci, D. 2003. A Multi-Strategy Multi-Source Approach to Question Answering. In The Twelfth Text Retrieval Conference (TREC 2003), ed. E. M. Voorhees and D. K. Harman. NIST Special Publication 500-255. Gaithersburg, Md.: National Institute of Standards and Technology.

Clark, P.; Thompson, J.; and Porter, B. A Knowledge-Based Approach to Question-Answering. In Question Answering Systems: Papers from the 1999 Fall Symposium, 43–51.Technical Report FS-98-04, American Association for Artificial Intelligence, Menlo Park, Calif.

Clarke, C.; Cormack, G.; Kemkes, G.; Laszlo, M.; Lynam, T.; Terra, E.; and Tilker, P. 2002. Statistical Selection of Exact Answers (MultiText Experiments for TREC 2002). In Proceedings of the Eleventh Text Retrieval Evaluation Conference (TREC 2002) NIST Special Publication 500-251. Gaithersburg, Md.: National Institute of Standards and Technology.

Clarke, C.; Cormack, G.; Kisman, D.; and Lynam, R. 2001. Question Answering by Passage Selection. In The Tenth Text Retrieval Conference (TREC 2001), ed. E. M. Voorhees and D. K. Harman. NIST Special Publication 500-250. Gaithersburg, Md.: National Institute of Standards and Technology.

Clarke, C.L.A.; Cormack, G. V. and Lynam, T. R. Sept. 2001. Exploiting Redundancy in Question Answering. In Proceedings of the Twenty-Fourth ACM SIGIR Conference on Research and Development in Information Retrieval, 358–365. New York: Association for Computing Machinery.

Cohen, W. 1995. Fast Effective Rule Induction. In *Proceedings of the Twelfth International Conference on Machine Learning,* 115–123. San Francisco: Morgan Kaufmann.

Collins, M. 1997. Three Generative, Lexicalised Models for Statistical Parsing. In Proceedings of the Thirty-Fifth Annual Meeting of the Association for Computational Linguistics, 16–23. Morristown, N.J.: Association for Computational Linguistics.

Connolly, D.; van Harmelen, F.; Horrocks, I.; McGuinness, D. L.; Patel-Schneider, P. F.; and Stein, L. A. 2001. DAML+OIL (March 2001) Reference Description, Technical Report Note 18, World Wide Web Consortium (W3C), Massachusetts Institute of Technology, Cambridge, Mass.

Cooper, E.; and Hammond, K. 1997. The OnPoint System: A Meta-Search Engine that Answers Natural Language Questions, Technical Report, Department of Computer Science, University of Chicago, Chicago, Ill.

Copestake, A.; Flickinger, D.; and Sag, I. A. 1997. Minimal Recursion Semantics: An Introduction. Technical Report, Center for the Study of Language and Information (CLSI), Stanford University, Stanford, Calif.

Cui, Y.; Widow, J.; and Wiener, J. L. 2000. Tracing the Lineage of View Data in a Warehousing Environment. ACM Transactions on Database Systems 25(2): 179–227.

Cunningham, H.; Maynard, D.; Bontcheva, K., Tablan, V.; and Wilks, Y. 2000 Experience of Using GATE for NLP R&D. Paper presented at the COLING 2000 Workshop on Using Toolsets and Architectures to Build NLP Systems, Centre Universitaire, Luxembourg, 5 August.

Cunningham, H.; Maynard, D.; Bontcheva, K.; and Tablan, V. 2002. GATE: A Framework and Graphical Development Environment for Robust NLP Tools and Applications. In Proceedings of the Fortieth Annual Meeting of the Association for Computational Linguistics. Morristown, N.J.: Association for Computational Linguistics.

Dahlgren, K. 1998. *Naive Semantics for Natural Language Understanding.* Dordrecht, The Netherlands: Kluwer Academic Publishers.

Dahlgren, K.; and Stabler E. 1998. Natural Language Understanding System. U.S. Patent 5794050. Washington, D.C.: Government Printing Office.

Dale, R.; Oberlander, J.; Milosavljevic, M.; Knott, A. 1998. Integrating Natural Language Generation and Hypertext to Produce Dynamic Documents. *Interacting with Computers* 11(2): 109–135.

Dar, S.; Entin, G.; Geva, S.; and Palmon, E. 1998. DTL's DataSpot: Database Exploration Using Plain Language. In *Proceedings of the Twenty-Fourth International Conference on Very Large Data Bases* (VLDB-24). San Francisco: Morgan Kaufmann.

Das, A.; Wu, W.; and McGuinness, D. L. 2002. Industrial Strength Ontology Management. In *The Emerging Semantic Web,* ed. I. Cruz, S. Decker, J. Euzenat, and D. McGuinnes, eds. Amsterdam: IOS Press.

Day, Y. F.; Dagtas, S.; Iino, M.; Khokhar, A.; and Ghafoor, A. 1995. Object-Oriented Conceptual Modeling of Video Data. In Proceedings of the Eleventh International Conference on Data Engineering (ICDE), 401–408. New York: Institute of Electrical and Electronics Engineers (IEEE).

Degerstedt, L. and Jönsson, A.. 2001. A Method for Systematic Implementation of Dialogue Management. Paper presented at the IJCAI Workshop on Knowledge and Reasoning in Practical Dialogue Systems, Seattle, Wash, Aug. 5.

Dias, G.; Guilloré, S.; and Lopes, J. G. P. 1999. Multilingual Aspects of Multiword Lexical Units. Paper presented at the Workshop on Language Technologies of the Thirty-second Annual Meeting of the Societas Linguistica Europea, Ljubljana, Slovenia, July, 11–21.

Diekema, A.; Liu, X.; Chen, J.; Wang, H.; McCracken, N.; Yilmazel, O.; and Liddy, E. D. 2001. Question Answering: CNLP at the TREC-9 Question Answering Track. In Proceedings of the Ninth Text Retrieval Conference (TREC-9), NIST Special Publication 500-249. Gaithersburg, Md.: National Institute of Standards and Technology.

Dorr, B. 1992. The Use of Lexical Semantics In Interlingual Machine Translation. *Machine Translation* 7(3): 135–193.

Dowdall, J.; Hess, M.; Kahusk, N.; Kaljurand, K.; Koit, M.; Rinaldi, F.; and Vider, K. 2002. Technical Terminology as a Critical Resource. Paper presented at the Third International Conference on Language Resources and Evaluation (LREC). Palacio De Congreso De Canarias, Canary Islands, Spain, May 28.

Dowding, J.; Gawron, J. M.; Appelt, D.; Bear, J.; Cherny, L.; Moore, R.; and Moran, D. 1993. GEMINI: A Natural Language System for Spoken-Language Understanding. In Proceedings of the Thirty-First Annual Meeting of the Association for Computational Linguistics, 54–61. Morristown, N.J.: Association for Computational Linguistics.

Dumais, S.; Banko, M.; Brill, E.; Lin, J.; and Ng, A. 2002. Web Question Answering: Is More Always Better? In Proceedings of the Twenty-Fifth Annual International ACM SIGIR Conference on Research and Development in Information Retrieval, 291–298. New York: ACM Press.

Egenhofer M.; and Franzosa R. 1991. Point-Set Topological Spatial Relations. *International Journal of Geographic Information Systems*. 5(2): 161–174.

European Association of Aerospace Industries. (AECMA) 2001. AECMA Simplified English, AECMA Document PSC-85-16598. A Guide for the Preparation of Aircraft Maintenance Documentation in the International Aerospace Maintenance Language. Issue 1, Revision 2. Brussels, Belgium: European Association of Aerospace Industries.

Fellbaum, C., ed. 1998. *WordNet: An Electronic Lexical Database. Language, Speech, and Communication.* Cambridge, Mass.: The MIT Press.

Felty, A. and Miller, D. 1987. Proof Explanation and Revision, Technical Report MSCIS8817, University of Pennsylvania, Philadelphia, Penn.

Ferret, O.; Grau, B.; Hurault-Plantet, M.; Illouz, G.; Jacquemin, C.; Masson, N.; and Lecuyer, P. 2001. Qalc—The Question Answering System of LIMSI-CNRS. In The Ninth Text Retrieval Conference (TREC 9). NIST Special Publication 500-249, ed. E. M. Voorhees and D. K. Harman. Gaithersburg, Md.: National Institute of Standards and Technology.

Ferro, L.; Mani, I., Sundheim, B. and Wilson, G. 2001. TIDES Temporal Annotation Guidelines. Version 1. 0. 2 MITRE Technical Report, MTR 01W0000041, Cambridge, Mass.

Ferrucci, D.; and Lally, A. 2003. Accelerating Corporate Research in the Development, Application and Deployment of Human Language Technologies. Paper Presented At the Workshop on the Software Engineering and Architecture of Language Technology Systems (SEALTS), Human Language Technology Conference (HLT-NAACL 2003), Edmonton, Canada, May 30.

Fikes, R.; Hayes, P.; and Horrocks, I. 2002. DAML Query Language (DQL) Abstract Specification, Technical Report, W3C. World Wide Web Consortium (W3C), Massachusetts Institute of Technology, Cambridge, Mass.

Filatova, E.; and Hovy, E. 2001. Assigning Time-Stamps to Event-Clauses Paper presented at the ACL-2001 Workshop on Temporal and Spatial Information Processing, ACL-2001. Toulose, France, 6–11 July.

Fleiss, J. L. 1981. *Statistical Methods for Rates and Proportions.* New York: John Wiley.

Florescu, D.; Levy A.; and Mendelzon, A. 1998. Database Techniques for the World-Wide Web: A Survey. SIGMOD Record 27(3): 59–74.

Flycht-Eriksson, A.; and Jönsson, A. 2003. Some Empirical Findings on Dialogue Management and Domain Ontologies in Dialogue Systems—Implications from an Evaluation of BirdQuest. Paper presented at the Fourth SIGdial Workshop on Discourse and Dialogue, Sapporo, Japan, July 5–6.

Foley, M.; and Rothenberg, M. 2003. Why Panther May Tear Up Longhorn. *Microsoft Watch* May 15.

Fonseca, F.; Egenhofer, M.; Davis, C.; and Câmara, G. 2001. Semantic Granularity in Ontology-Driven Geographic Information Systems. *AMAI Annals of Mathematics and Artificial Intelligence,* Special Issue on Spatial and Temporal Granularity 36(1-2): 121–151.

Gaasterland, T.; Godfrey, P.; Minker, J. 1994. An Overview of Cooperative Answering. In *Papers in Nonstandard Queries and Nonstandard Answers, Studies in Logic and Computation,* ed R, Demolombe and T. Imielinski, 1–40. Oxford: Clarendon Press.

Gaizauskas, R.; and Setzer, A., eds. 2002. Annotation Standards for Temporal Information in Natural Language. Paper presented at the Third International Conference on Language Resources and Evaluation (LREC). Palacio De Congreso De Canarias, Canary Islands, Spain, May 28.

Gal, A. 1988. Cooperative Responses in Deductive Databases, Ph.D. dissertation, University of Maryland, Department of Computer Science, College Park, Md.

Galitsky, B.; and Grudin, M. 2001. System, Method, and Computer Program Product for Responding to Natural Language Queries. U.S. Patent App. 20010053968. Washington, D.C.: Government Printing Office.

Genesereth, M.; Keller, A. M.; and Duschka, O. M. 1997. Infomaster: an Information Integration System. *SIGMOD Record* (ACM Special Interest Group on Management of Data. 26(2): 539–542.

Gifford, R.; Anderson, E.; Kirkbride, L.; and Evans, J. Computer-Aided Customer Support System with Bubble-Up. U.S. Patent 5,301,314. Washington, D.C. Government Printing Office.

Green, B.; Wolf, A.; Chomsky, C.; and Laughery, K. 1961. BASEBALL: An Automatic Question Answerer. In *Readings In Natural Language Processing,* ed. Barbara Grosz, Karen Sparck Jones, and Bonnie L. Webber. San Mateo, Calif.: Morgan Kaufmann Publishers.

Green, C. 1969. Application of Theorem Proving to Problem Solving. In Proceedings of the First International Joint Conference on Artificial Intelligence. Los Altos, Calif.: William Kaufmann, Inc.

Green, C. 1969. Theorem-Proving by Resolution as a Basis for Question Answering Systems. In *Machine Intelligence 4,* 183–205, ed. B. Meltzer and D. Michie. Edinburgh: Edinburgh University Press.

Grinstein, G. G.; Levkowitz, H.; Pickett, R. M.; Smith, S. 1993. Visualization Alternatives: Non-Pixel Based Images. In Proceedings of the Society for Imaging Science and Technology's Forty-Sixth Annual Conference, 287–289. Springfield, Va.: Society for Imaging Science and Technology.

Grishman, R. 1996. TIPSTER Architecture Design Document V.2.2. Gaithersburg, Md: National Institute of Standards and Technology (www.itl.nist.gov/iaui/894.02/related_projects/tipster/).

Grishman, R. 1997. *Information Extraction: Techniques and Challenges Information Extraction: International Summer School on Information Extraction: A Multidisciplinary Approach to an Emerging Information Technology,* ed. Maria Teresa Pazienza. Berlin: Springer-Verlag.

Grosz, B.; and Sidner, C. 1986. Attention, Intentions, and the Structure of Discourse. *Computational Linguistics* 12(3): 175–204.

Gruber, T. R. 1993. A Translation Approach to Portable Ontology Specification. *Knowledge Acquisition* 5(2): 199–220.

Hamilton, J. 2000. Natural Language Processing System. World Intellectual Property Organization Application WO 01/35189 A2, Geneva, Switzerland.

Hammer, J.; Garcia-Molina, H.; Cho, J.; Aranha R.; and Crespo, A. 1997. Extracting Semistructured Information from the Web. Paper presented at the Workshop on Management of Semistructured Data. Tucson, Ariz., May 13–15.

Hamon, T.; and Nazarenko, A. 2001. Detection of Synonymy Links Between Terms: Experiment and Results. In *Recent Advances in Computational Terminology*, 185–208, ed. D. Bourigault C. Jacquemin, and M–C. L'Homme. Amsterdam: John Benjamins Publishing Company.

Harabagiu, S.; Moldovan, D.; Pasca, M.; Surdeanu, Mihalcea, R.; M.; Girju, R.; Rus, V.; Lacatusu, F.; Moraréscu, P.; and Bunescu, R. 2001.. Answering Complex, List and Context Questions with LCC's Question-Answering Server. In The Tenth Text Retrieval Conference (TREC 2001), 355-361, ed. E. M. Voorhees and D. K. Harman. NIST Special Publication 500-250. Gaithersburg, Md.: National Institute of Standards and Technology.

Harabagiu, S.; Moldovan, D.; Pasca, M.; Mihalcea, R.; Surdeanu, M.; Bunescu, R.; Girju, R.; Rus, V.; and Moraréscu, P. 2001. Falcon: Boosting Knowledge for Answer Engines. In the Ninth Text Retrieval Conference (TREC 9). NIST Special Publication 500-249, ed. E. M. Voorhees and D. K. Harman. Gaithersburg, Md.: National Institute of Standards and Technology.

Harabagiu, S.; Pasca, M.; and Maiorano, S. 2000. Experiments with Open-Domain Textual Question Answering. Paper presented at the Eighteenth International Conference on Computational Linguistics, Saarbrücken, Germany, July 31–August 4.

Hardy, H.;. Shimizu, N.; Strzalkowski, T.; Ting, L.; Wise, B.; and Zhang, X. 2002. Cross-Document Summarization by Concept Classification. In Proceedings of the Twenty-fifth Annual International ACM SIGIR Conference on Research and Development in Information Retrieval (SIGIR-2002). New York: Association for Computing Machinery.

Harris, L. 2001. Distributed Search System and Method, U.S. Patent Application 20020059204. Washington, D.C.: Government Printing Office.

Harrison, T., Barrett, M., Reddi, S., Lowe, J., Chevsky, G. 2003. Natural Language Query Processing. U.S. Patent Application 20030069880. Washington, D.C.: Government Printing Office.

Hatzivassiloglou, V., Klavans, J. L., and Eskin, E. 1999. Detecting Text Similarity Over Short Passages: Exploring Linguistic Feature Combinations Via Machine Learning. In Proceedings of the 1999 SIGDAT Conference on Empirical Methods in Natural Language Processing, 203–212. Morristown, N.J.: Association for Computational Linguistics.

Hearst, M. 1997. Texttiling: Segmenting Text into Multi-Paragraph Subtopic Passages. *Computational Linguistics* 23(1): 33–64.

Hendrix, G. G. 1977. Human Engineering for Applied Natural Language Processing. In Proceedings of the Fifth International Joint Conference on Artificial Intelligence, 183–191. Los Altos, Calif.: William Kaufmann, Inc.

Hermjakob, U.; Abdessamad, E.; and Marcu, D. 2002. Natural Language Based Reformulation Resource and Web Exploitation for Question Answering. In Proceedings of the Eleventh Text Retrieval Evaluation Conference (TREC 2002) NIST Special Publication 500-251, 734–742. Gaithersburg, Md.: National Institute of Standards and Technology.

Hess, M.; Dowdall, J.; and Rinaldi, F. 2002. The Challenge of Technical Text. Paper presented at theWorkshop on Question Answering: Strategy and Resources, Third International Conference on Language Resources and Evaluation (LREC). Palacio De Congreso De Canarias, Canary Islands, Spain, May 28.

Hilderman, R. J. and Hamilton, H. J. 1999. Heuristic Measures of Interestingness. In *Principles of Data Mining and Knowledge Discovery: First European Symposium* (PKDD '97) Lecture Notes in Artificial Intelligence, 232–241. Berlin: Springer Verlag.

Hill, L. J.; Frew, J.; and Zheng, Q. 1999. Geographic Names: The Implementation of a Gazetteer in a Georeferenced Digital Library. *D-Lib Magazine* 5(1)

Hirschman, L.; and Gaizauskas, R. 2001. Natural Language Question Answering: The View from Here. Natural Language Engineering 7(4): 275–300.

Hobbs, J. 1979. Coherence and Coreference. *Cognitive Science* 3(1): 67–90.

Hobbs, J. 2002. An DAML Ontology of Time. Unpublished paper. (www.cs.rochester.edu/~ferguson/daml/daml-time-nov2002.txt)

Hobbs, J. R. 1985. Ontological Promiscuity. In Proceedings of the Association for Computational Linguistics, 61 69. Somerset, NJ.: Association for Computational Linguistics

Hovy, E. H. 1993. Automated Discourse Generation Using Discourse Structure Relations. *Artificial Intelligence Journal* 63(1–2): 341–385.

Hovy, E. H.; Gerber, L.; Hermjakob, U.; Junk, M.; and Lin, C-Y. 2001. Question Answering in Webclopedia. In The Ninth Text Retrieval Conference (TREC 9). NIST Special Publication 500-249, ed. E. M. Voorhees and D. K. Harman. Gaithersburg, Md.: National Institute of Standards and Technology.

Hovy, E.; Gerber, L.; Hermjakob, U.; Lin, C.; and Ravichandran, D. 2001. Toward Semantics-Based Answer Pinpointing. Paper presented at the DARPA Human Language Technologies (HLT-2001) Workshop, San Diego, Calif., March.

Huang, X. 1994. Reconstructing Proofs at the Assertion Level. In Proceedings of the Twelfth International Conference on Automated Deduction (CADE-94), Lecture Notes in Computer Science 814, 738–752, Berlin: Springer-Verlag.

Humphreys, Gaizauskas; Azzam, R., S.; Huyck, C.; Mitchell, B.; Cunningham, H; and Wilks, Y. 1998. Description of the LaSIE-II System as Used for MUC-7. In Proceedings of the Seventh Message Understanding Conference (MUC-7). Gaithersburg, Md.: National Institute of Standards and Technology.

Ingria, R., and Pustejovsky, J. 2002. TimeML Specification 1.0. Technical report, Brandeis University, Dept. of Computer Science, Waltham, Massachusetts. (www.cs.brandeis.edu/~jamesp/arda/time/documentation/TimeML-Draft3.0.9.html)

Ittycheriah A.; Franz, M.; Zhu, Wei-Jing and Ratnaparki, A. 2001. Question Answering Using Maximum Entropy Components. Paper presented at the Second Meeting of the North American Chapter of the Association for Computational Linguistics, Pittsburgh, Penn., June 2–7.

Ittycheriah, A.; Franz, M.; Zhu, W.-J.; Ratnaparkhi, A.; and Mammone, R. J. 2001. IBM's Statistical Question Answering System. In Proceedings of the Eighth Text Retrieval Conference (TREC 8), E. Voorhees and D. K. Harman, Eds. NIST Special Publication 500-246. Gaithersburg, MD: National Institute of Standards and Technology.

Jackendoff, R. 1983. *Semantics and Cognition.* Cambridge, Mass.: The MIT Press.

Jackendoff, R. 1990. *Semantic Structures.* Cambridge, Mass.: The MIT Press.

Kageura, K. 2002. *The Dynamics of Terminology: A Descriptive Theory of Term Formation and Terminological Growth.* Terminology and Lexicography, Research and Practice 5. Amsterdam: John Benjamins Publishing.

Katz, B. 1988. Using English for Indexing and Retrieving. In Proceedings of the Recherche d'Information Assistée par Ordinateur (RIAO) 1988 Conference on User-oriented Content-based Text and Image Handling. Paris: Le Centre de Hautes Etudes Internationales d'Informatique Documentaire.

Katz, B. 1997. Annotating the World Wide Web Using Natural Language. In Proceedings of the Recherche d'Information Assistée par Ordinateur (RIAO). Paris: Le Centre de Hautes Etudes Internationales d'Informatique Documentaire.

Katz, B.; and Levin, B. 1988. Exploiting Lexical Regularities in Designing Natural Language Systems. In Proceedings of the Eleventh International Conference on Computational Lingusitics. Budapest, Hungary: John von Neumann Society for Computing Sciences.

Katz, B.; and Winston, P. 1994. Method and Apparatus for Generating and Utilizing Annotations to Facilitate Computer Text Retrieval. U.S. Patent 5,309,359. Washington, D.C.: Government Printing Office.

Katz, B.; and Winston, P. 1995. Method and Apparatus for Utilizing Annotations to Facilitate Computer Retrieval of Database Material. U.S. Patent 5,404,295. Washington, D.C.: Government Printing Office.

Katz, B.; Felshin, S.; Yuret, D.; Ibrahim, A.; Lin, J.; Marton, G.; McFarland, A. J.; and Temelkuran, B. 2002. Omnibase: Uniform Access To Heterogeneous Data for Question Answering. Paper presented at the Eighth International Conference on Applications of Natural Language to Information Systems, Burg (Spreewald), Germany, June 23–25.

Katz, B.; Lin, J.; and Felshin, S. 2001. Gathering Knowledge for a Question Answering System from Heterogeneous Information Sources. Paper presented at the Association for Computational Linguistics 2001 Workshop on Human Language Technology and Knowledge Management, Toulouse, France, July 7.

Kekäläinen, J. and Järvelin, K. 1998. The Impact of Query Structure and Query Expansion on Retrieval. In Proceedings of the Twenty-First Annual International ACM SIGIR Conference on Research and Development in Information Retrieval. New York: Association for Computing Machinery.

Kestrel Institute. 2003. The Specware System. Palo Alto, Calif.: Kestrel. (www.kestrel.edu/HTML/prototypes/specware.html)

Kirk, T.; Levy A.; Sagiv, Y.; and Srivastava, D. 1995. The Information Manifold. Technical Report, AT&T Bell Laboratories, Murray Hill, N.J.

Klavans, J.; and Muresan, S. 2000. DEFINDER: Rule-Based Methods for the Extraction of Medical Terminology and Their Associated Definitions from On-Line Text. Paper presented at the American Medical Informatics Association 2000 Annual Symposium, November 4–8, Los Angeles, Calif.

Knoblock, C. A.; and Minton, S. 1998. The Ariadne Approach to Web-Based Information Integration. *IEEE Intelligent Systems* 13(5): 17-20.

Knoblock, C.; Minton, S.; Ambite, J. L.; Ashish, N.; Muslea, I.; Philpot, A.; and Tejada, S. 2001. The Ariadne Approach to Web-based Information Integration. *International Journal on Cooperative Information Systems (IJCIS)* Special Issue on Intelligent Information Agents: Theory and Applications, 10(1/2):145-169.

Kolodner, J. L. 1993. *Case-based Reasoning.* San Francisco: Morgan Kaufmann Publishers.

Kononenko, I. 1995. On Biases in Estimating Multi-valued Attributes. In *Proceedings of the Fourteenth International Joint Conference on Artificial Intelligence,* 1034–1040. San Francisco: Morgan Kaufmann Publishers.

Krippendorf, K. 1980. *Content Analysis: An Introduction To Its Methodology.* Beverly Hill, Calif.: Sage Publications.

Kupiec, J. 1996. Method for Extracting from a Text Corpus Answers to Questions Stated in Natural Language By Using Linguistic Analysis and Hypothesis Generation. U.S. Patent 5,519,608. Washington, D.C.: Government Printing Office.

Kwok, K.; Grunfeld, L.; Dinstl, N.; and Chan, M. 2001. TREC-9 Cross Language, Web and Question-Answering Track Experiments Using PIRCS. In The Ninth Text Retrieval Conference (TREC 9). NIST Special Publication 500-249, ed. E. M. Voorhees and D. K. Harman. Gaithersburg, Md.: National Institute of Standards and Technology.

Lappin, S. and Leass, H. J. 1994. An Algorithm for Pronominal Anaphora Resolution. *Computational Linguistics* 20(4): 535–561.

Laprun, C.; Fiscus, J.; Garofalo, J.; and Pajot, S. 2002. A Practical Introduction to ATLAS. Paper presented at the Third International Conference on Language Resources and Evaluation (LREC). Palacio De Congreso De Canarias, Canary Islands, Spain, May 28.

Lau, R.; Flammia, G.; Pao, C.; and Zue, V. 1997. WebGalaxy: Beyond Point and Click – a Conversational Interface To a Browser. Paper presented at the Sixth International World Wide Web Conference, Santa Clara, Calif., April 7–11. (www.raylau.com/webgalaxy/).

Lehnert, W. 1977. The Process of Question Answering. Ph.D. Dissertation, Dept. of Computer Science, Yale University. Research Report 88, New Haven, Conn.

Lehnert, W;. and Sundheim, B. 1991. A Performance Evaluation of Text Analysis Technologies. *AI Magazine* 12(3): 81–94.

Lenat, D. B. 1995. "Cyc: A Large-Scale Investment in Knowledge Infrastructure. *Communications of the ACM* 38(11): 33–38.

Lenat, D. B.; and Guha, R. V. 1994. Enabling Agents to Work Together. *Communications of the ACM* 37(7): 126 -142.

Lenz, M.;, Huebner, A.; Kunze, M. 1998. Question Answering with Textual CBR. In Flexible Query Answering Systems, Lecture Notes in Artificial Intelligence 1495, ed. : T. Andreasen, H. Christiansen, and H. L. Larsen. Berlin: Springer Verlag.

Levin, B. 1993. *English Verb Classes and Alternations.* Chicago: University of Chicago Press.

Liddy, E. D. 2002. Why Are People Asking These Questions? A Call for Bringing Situation Into Question-Answering Evaluation. Paper presented at the Workshop on Question Answering-Strategy, Third International Conference on Language Resources and Evaluation (LREC). Palacio De Congreso De Canarias, Canary Islands, Spain, May 28.

Light, M.; Ittycheriah, A.; Latto, A, and McCracken, N. 2003. Reuse in Question Answering: A Preliminary Study. In New Directions in Question Answering: Papers from the 2003 AAAI Spring Symposium. AAAI Tech. Rep. SS-03-07, American Association for Artificial Intelligence, Menlo Park, Calif.

Lin, C-Y.; and Hovy, E. 2002. Automated Multi-Document Summarization in NeATS. Paper presented at the Human Language Technology Conference. San Diego, Calif., 24–27 March.

Lin, C-Y.; and Hovy, E. 2003. Automatic Evaluation of Summaries Using N-Gram Co-Occurrence Statistics. Paper Presented At the Human Language Technology Conference (HLT-NAACL 2003), Edmonton, Canada, May 30.

Lin, D. and Pantel, P. 2001. Discovery of Inference Rules for Question Answering. *Natural Language Engineering* 7(4): 343—360.

Lin, J. 2002. The Web as a Resource for Question Answering: Perspectives and Challenges. Paper presented at the Third International Conference on Language Resources and Evaluation (LREC). Palacio De Congreso De Canarias, Canary Islands, Spain, May 28.

Lin, J. and Katz, B. 2003. Question Answering from the Web Using Knowledge Annotation and Knowledge Mining Techniques. In Proceedings of the 2003 ACM CIKM International Conference on Information and Knowledge Management,. 116-123. New York: Association for Computing Machinery.

Lin, J.; Fernandes, A.; Katz, B.; Marton, G.; and Tellex, S. 2003. Extracting Answers from the Web Using Knowledge Annotation and Knowledge Mining Techniques. In Proceedings of the Eleventh Text Retrieval Evaluation Conference (TREC 2002) NIST Special Publication 500-251. Gaithersburg, Md.: National Institute of Standards and Technology.

Linguistic Data Consortium. 2002. ACE Phase 2: Information for LDC Annotators. University of Pennsylvania, Philadelphia, Penn. (www.ldc.upenn.edu/Projects/ACE2/.)

Lowe, J. 2000.What's in Store for Question Answering ? Invited talk presented at the Joint SIGDAT Conference on Empirical Methods in Natural Language Processing and Very Large Corpora (EMNLP/VLC-2000), Hong Kong, Oct. 7–8.

Lowry, M.; Philpot, A.; Pressburger, T.; Underwood, I.; Waldinger, R.; and Stickel, M. Amphion: Automatic Programming for the NAIF Toolkit. NASA Science Information Systems Newsletter 31(February): 22–25.

Lynch, C. A. 2001. When Documents Deceive: Trust and Provenance as New Factors for Information Retrieval in a Tangled Web. *Journal of the American Society for Information Science and Technology* 52(1): 12–17.

Lytinen, S.; and Tomuro, N. 2002. The Use of Question Types to Match Questions in Faqfinder. In Mining Answers from Texts and Knowledge Bases: Papers from the 2002 AAAI Spring Symposium, ed. S. Harabagiu and V. Chaudhri. Tech. Rep. SS-02-06, American Association for Artificial Intelligence, Menlo Park, Calif.

Lytinen, S.; Tomuro, N.; and Repede, T. 2000. The Use of Wordnet Sense Tagging in Faqfinder. In Artificial Intelligence for Web Search: Papers from the AAAI Workshop. Technical Report WS-00-01, American Association for Artificial Intelligence, Menlo Park, Calif.

Magnini, B.; Romagnoli, S.; Vallin, A.; Herrera, J.; Penas, A.; Peinado, V.; Verdejo, F.; and De Rijke, M. 2003. Multiple Language Question Answering Track At Third Workshop of the Cross-Language Evaluation Forum. In *Cross-Language Information Retrieval and Evaluation,* ed. C. Peters, M. Braschler, J. Gonzalo, and M. Kluck. Berlin: Springer-Verlag.

Mahesh, K. and Nirenburg, S.. 1995. A Situated Ontology for Practical NLP. Paper presented at the IJCAI '95 Workshop on Basic Ontological Issues in Knowledge Sharing, Montreal, Canada, August 20.

Mani, I.; and Bloedorn, E. 1997. Multi-Document Summarization by Graph Search and Matching. In *Proceedings of the Fifteenth National Conference on Artificial Intelligence,* 622–628. Menlo Park, Calif.: AAAI Press.

Mani, I.; and Wilson, G. 2000. Robust Temporal Processing of News, In Proceedings of the Thirty-Eighth Annual Meeting of the Association for Computational Linguistics (ACL'2000). Somerset, NJ.: Association for Computational Linguistics

Mann, W. C.; and Thompson, S. A. 1988. Rhetorical Structure Theory: Toward a Functional Theory of Text Organization. *Text* 8(3):243–281.

Manna, Z.; and Waldinger, R. 1980. A Deductive Approach to Program Synthesis. ACM Transactions on Programming Languages and Systems 2(2): 90–121.

Manning, C. D. and Schütze,. H. 1999. Foundations of Statistical Natural Language Processing. Cambridge, Mass.: The MIT Press.

Marcu, D. 1997. Rhetorical Parsing of Natural Language Texts. In Proceedings of the Thirty-Fifth Annual Meeting of the Association for Computational Linguistics and the Eighth Conference of the European Chapter of the Association for Computational Linguistics, 96–103. Morristown, N.J.: Association for Computational Linguistics.

Marcus, M.; Santorini, B.; and Marcinkiewicz, M. 1994. Building a Large Annotated Corpus of English: The Penn Treebank. *Computational Linguistics* 19(2):313–330.

Mardis, S.; and Burger, J. 2002. Qanda and the Catalyst Architecture. In Mining Answers from Text and Knowledge Bases: Papers from the AAAI Spring Symposium. AAAI Technical Report SS-02-06, American Association for Artificial Intelligence, Menlo Park, Calif.

Maybury, M. 2002. Toward a Question Answering Roadmap. Paper Presented at the Workshop on QA Resources and Evaluation, Third International Conference on Language Resources and Evaluation (LREC). Palacio De Congreso De Canarias, Canary Islands, Spain, May 28.(www.mitre.org/work/tech_papers/tech_papers_02/maybury_toward/maybury_toward_qa.pdf)

Maybury, M. T.; Day, D.; Prange, J.; Pusteyovsky, J.; and Wiebe, J., eds. 2003. New Directions in Question Answering: Papers from the 2003 AAAI Spring Symposium. AAAI Tech. Rep. SS-03-07, American Association for Artificial Intelligence, Menlo Park, Calif.

Maybury, M. T.; Sparck Jones, K.; Voorhees, E.; Harabagiu, S.; Liddy, L.; and Prange, J., eds. 2002. Workshop on Strategy and Resources for Question Answering in Conjunction with the Third International Conference on Language Resources and Evaluation (LREC). Palacio De Congreso De Canarias, Canary Islands, Spain, Tuesday May 28. (www.lrec-conf.org/lrec2002/lrec/wksh/questionanswering.html.)

McCord, M. C. 1990. Slot Grammar: A System for Simpler Construction of Practical Natural Language Grammars. In *International Symposium on Natural Language and Logic,* ed. R. Studer. Berlin: Springer-Verlag.

McCoy, K. F. 1985. Correcting Object-Related Misconceptions. Ph.D. diss, University of Pennsylvania, Department of Computer and Information Science, Technical Report MS-CIS-85-57, Philadelphia, Penn.

McDermott, D.; Borden, J.; Burstein, M.; Smith, D.; and Waldinger R. 2001. A Proposal for Encoding Logic in RDF/DAML. Unpublished paper available at ftp.cs.yale.edu/pub/ mcdermott /papers/noworry.ps.gz

McGuinness, D. L. 1996. Explaining Reasoning in Description Logics Ph.D. thesis, Rutgers University, Newark, N.J.

McGuinness, D. L. 1998. Ontological Issues for Knowledge-Enhanced Search. In N. Guarino (ed.), Proceedings of the First International Conference on Formal Ontology in Information Systems (FOIS'98), 302-316. Amsterdam: IOS Press.

McGuinness, D. L. and Pinheiro da Silva, P. 2003. Infrastructure for Web Explanations. In *Proceedings of the Second International Semantic Web Conference (ISWC2003)*. Berlin: Springer-Verlag.

McGuinness, D. L.; Abrahams, M. K.; Resnick, L. A.; Patel-Schneider, P. F.; Thomason, R.; Cavalli-Sforza, V.; and Conati, C. 1994. CLASSIC Knowledge Representation System Tutorial, Technical report, Artificial Intelligence Principles Research Department, AT&T Labs Research. Technical Report, AT&T Bell Laboratories, Murray Hill, N.J.

McGuinness, D. L.; and Borgida, A. 1995. Explaining Subsumption in Description Logics. In Proceedings of the Fourteenth International Joint Conference on Artificial Intelligence, 816–821. San Francisco: Morgan Kaufmann, Publishers.

McGuinness, D. L.; and Patel-Schneider, P. 2003. The Description Logic Handbook: Theory, Implementation, and Applications. In *Description Logic Provers to Knowledge Representation Systems,* 265–281, ed. D. McGuinness and P. Patel-Schneider. Cambridge: Cambridge University Press.

McHugh, J.; Abiteboul, S.; Goldman, R.; Quass, D.; and Widom, J. 1997. Lore: A Database Management System for Semistructured Data. Technical Report, Stanford University Database Group, Stanford, Calif.

McKeown, K. R. 1985. *Text Generation.* New York: Cambridge Univ. Press.

McKeown, K.; and Blair-Goldensohn, S. 2003. Generating Definitional Descriptions, Paper presented at the Advannced Question Answering for Intelligence (AQUAINT) Eighteen-Month Workshop, San Diego, Calif., June 10–12.

Mekikian, G.; and Yuret, D. 2001. Answering Natural Language Queries, World Intellectual Property Organization Application WO 01/88662 A2, Geneva, Switzerland.

Michie, D. 1988. Personal Models of Rationality. *Journal of Statistical Planning and Inference* 21.

Miller, D.; Leek, T.; and Schwartz, R. 1999. A Hidden Markov Model Information Retrieval System. In Proceedings of the Twenty-Second Annual International ACM SIGIR Conference on Research and Development in Information Retrieval, 214–221. New York: Association for Computing Machinery Special Interest Group on Information Retrieval.

Miller, G. 1990. WordNet: An Online Lexical Database. *International Journal of Lexicography* 3(4): 235–244.

Miller, G. 1995. WordNet: A Lexical Database for English *Communications of the ACM* 38(11): 39–41.

Miller, S.; Bratus, S.; Ramshaw, L.; Weischedel, R.; and Zamanian, A. 2001. FactBrowser Demonstration. Paper presented at the Human Language Technology Conference, San Diego, Calif., March 19–21.

Miller, S.;. Fox, H.; Ramshaw, L.; and Weischedel, R. 2000. A Novel Use of Statistical Parsing to Extract Information from Text. In Proceedings of the North American Association for Computational Linguistics. Somerset, NJ.: Association for Computational Linguistics.

Minock, M.; Chu, W.; Yang, H.; Chiang, K.; Chow, G. and Larson, C. 1996. CoBase: A Scalable and Extensible Cooperative Information System. *Journal of Intelligent Information Systems* 6(2/3): 223–259.

Mitra, M.; Singhal, A.; and Buckley, C. 1998. Improving Automatic Query expansion. Paper presented at the Twenty-First Annual International ACM-SIGIR Conference on Research and Development in Information Retrieval, 206–214. New York: Association for Computing Machinery.

Moldovan, D.; Clark, C.; Harabagiu, S.; and Maiorano, S. 2003. COGEX: A Logic Prover for Question Answering. Paper presented at the North American Chapter of the Association for Computational Linguistics, Human Language Technology Conference (HTL-NAACL), Edmonton, Canada, May 27–June 1.

Moldovan, G.; Harabagiu, D.; Girju S.; R.; Morarescu, P.; Lacatusu, F.; A.; Novischi, Badulescu, A.; and Bolohan, O. 2002. LCC Tools for Question Answering. In Proceedings of the Eleventh Text Retrieval Evaluation Conference (TREC 2002) NIST Special Publication 500-251. Gaithersburg, Md.: National Institute of Standards and Technology.

Mollá, D. 2001. Ontologically Promiscuous Flat Logical Forms for NLP. In Proceedings of the Fourth International Workshop on Computational Semantics (IWCS-4), 249–256. Dortrecht, The Netherlands: Kluwer Academic Publishers.

Mollá, D.; Schwitter, R.; Hess, M.; and Fournier, R. 2000. ExtrAns, An Answer Extraction System. *Journal T. A. L.* Special Issue on Information Retrieval Oriented Natural Language Processing 41(2): 495–522.

Moore, J. D.; and Paris, C. L. 1992. Planning Text for Advisory Dialogues: Capturing Intentional and Rhetorical Information. *Computational Linguistics* 19(4): 651–695.

Nyberg, E.; Mitamura, T.; Carbonell, J.; Callan, J.; Collins-Thompson, K.; Czuba, K.; Duggan, M.; Hiyakumoto, L.; Hu, N.; Huang, Y.; Ko, J.; Lita, L.; Murtagh, S.; Pedro, V.; and Svoboda, D. 2003. The Javelin Question-Answering System at TREC 2002. In The Eleventh Text Retrieval Conference (TREC 11). NIST Special Publication SP 500-251, ed. E. M. Voorhees and D. K. Harman. Gaithersburg, Md.: National Institute of Standards and Technology.

O'Neil, J. and Pustejovsky, J. 2001. Method and System for Query Reformulation for Searching of Information. U.S. Patent Application 20020147578. Washington, D.C.: Government Printing Office.

Palmon, E. 1998. Associative Search Method for Heterogeneous Databases with an Integration Mechanism Configured to Combine Schema-Free Data Models Such as a Hyperbase, U.S. Patent 5740421. Washington, D.C.: Government Printing Office.

Papineni, K.; Roukos, S.; Ward, R. T.; and Zhu, W. J. 2002. BLEU: A Method for Automatic Evaluation of Machine Translation. In Proceedings of the Fortieth Annual Meeting of the Association for Computational Linguistics. Somerset, NJ.: Association for Computational Linguistics.

Parsons, T. 1990. *Events in the Semantics of English: A Study in Subatomic Semantics*. Cambridge, Mass.: The MIT Press.

Passonneau, R. and Litman, D. 1993. Intention-Based Segmentation: Human Reliability and Correlation with Linguistic Clues. In Proceedings of the Thirty-First Annual Meeting of the Association for Computational Linguistics (ACL-93), 148–155. Somerset, NJ.: Association for Computational Linguistics

Pearl, J. 1994. *Probabilistic Reasoning in Intelligent Systems: Networks of Plausible Inference,* Second Edition. San Mateo, Calif.: Morgan Kaufmann, Publishers.

Pearl, J. 1998. Graphical Models for Probabilistic and Causal Reasoning. In *Handbook of Defeasible Reasoning and Uncertainty Management Systems,* Volume 1: Quantified Representation of Uncertainty and Imprecision, ed. Dov M. Gabbay and Philippe Smets, 367–389. Dordrecht, The Netherlands: Kluwer Academic Publishers.

Pease, A.; Li, J.; and Barbee, C. 2002a. DAML Agent Semantic Communications Service (ASCS). Teknowledge Inc., Palo Alto, Calif. (oak.teknowledge.com:8080/daml/damlquery.jsp)

Pease, A.; Niles, I.; and Li, J. 2002b. The Suggested Upper Merged Ontology: A Large Ontology for the Semantic Web and its Applications. In Ontologies and the Semantic Web: Papers from the AAAI Workshop, ed. Adam Pease. Tech. Rep. WS-02-11, American Association for Artificial Intelligence, Menlo Park, Calif.

Phillips, E. 1999. If It Works, It's Not AI : A Commercial Look At Artificial Intelligence Startups. Masters Thesis, Massachusetts Institute of Technology, Dept. of Computer Science, Cambridge, Mass.

Pinheiro da Silva, P.; and McGuinness, D. L. 2003. Combinable Proof Fragments for the Web, Technical Report KSL-03-04, Stanford University, Stanford, Calif.

Prager, J. M.; Brown, E. W.; Coden, A. and Radev, D. 2000. Question-Answering by Predictive Annotation. In Proceedings of the ACM SIGIR Conference on Information Retrieval (SIGIR 2000), 184–191. New York: Association for Computing Machinery.

Prager, J. M.; Chu-Carroll, J.; Brown, E. W. and Czuba, K. Forthcoming. Question Answering by Predictive Annotation. in *Advances in Open-Domain Question-Answering* ed. T. Strzalkowski and S. Harabagiu, eds. Dortrecht, The Netherlands: Kluwer.

Prager, J. M.; Radev, D. R. and Czuba, K. March 2001. Answering What-Is Questions by Virtual Annotation. Paper presented at the DARPA Human Language Technologies (HLT-2001) Workshop, San Diego, Calif., March.

Prager, J.; Brown, E.; Radev, D. R.; and Czuba, K. 2001. One Search Engine or Two for Question-Answering. In The Ninth Text Retrieval Conference (TREC 9). NIST Special Publication 500-249, ed. E. M. Voorhees and D. K. Harman. Gaithersburg, Md.: National Institute of Standards and Technology.

Prager, John, Radev, Dragomir R., and Czuba, Krzysztof. 2001. Answering What-Is Questions By Virtual Annotation. Paper presented at the Human Language Technology Conference, Demonstrations Section, San Diego, Calif., March 18–21.

Pustejovsky, J,, and Ingria. R. 2000. Answering Verbal Questions Using a Natural Language System. U.S. Patent Application 20010039493. Washington, D.C.: Government Printing Office.

Pustejovsky, J. 1993. Type Coercion and Lexical Selection, In *Semantics and the Lexicon,* ed. J. Pustejovsky. Dordrecht, the Netherlands: Kluwer Academic Publishers.

Pustejovsky, J. 1995. *The Generative Lexicon.* Cambridge, Mass: The MIT Press.

Pustejovsky, J.; and Gauizauskas, R. 2004. *Time and Event Recognition in Natural Language*. Amsterdam: John Benjamins Publishers.

Pustejovsky, J.; Clippinger J.; and Ingria, R. 1999. A Natural Knowledge Acquisition Method. World Intellectual Property Organization Patent Application WO 00/33216, Geneva, Switzerland.

Pustejovsky, J.; Ingria, R.; Gaizauskas, R.; Sauri, R.; and Setzer, A. 2002. Annotation Guideline To TimeML 1.0. Technical report, TERQAS report, Brandeis University, Dept. of Computer Science, Waltham, Massachusetts.

Quillian, M. R. 1968. Semantic Memory. In Semantic Information Processing, ed M. Minsky, editor, 227–270. Cambridge, Mass.: The MIT Press.

Quinlan, R. 1994. C4.5: Programs for Machine Learning. San Francisco: Morgan Kaufman, Publishers.

Quirk, R.; Greenbaum, S.; Leech, G.; and Svartvik, J. 1985. *A Comprehensive Grammar of the English Language*. New York: Longman.

Radev, D. R.; and McKeown, K. R. 1998. Generating Natural Language Summaries from Multiple On-Line Sources. *Computational Linguistics* 24(3): 469–500.

Radev, D. R.; Jing, H.; and Budzikowska, M. 2000. Centroid-Based Summarization of Multiple Documents. Paper presented at the ANLP/NAACL Workshop on Summarization, Seattle, Wash., April 30.

Radev, D.; and McKeown, K. 1997. Building a Generation Knowledge Source Using Internet-Accessible Newswire. In Proceedings of the *Fifth Conference on Applied Natural Language Processing*, 221–228. San Francisco: Morgan Kaufmann Publishers.

Ramshaw, L.; Boschee, E.; Bratus, S.; Miller, S.; Stone, R.; Weischedel, R.; and Zamanian, A. 2001. Experiments in Multi-Modal Automatic Content Extraction. Paper presented at the Human Language Technology Conference, San Diego, Calif., March 18–21.

Rashid, R. 2003. Remarks by Dr. Richard Rashid, Senior Vice President, Microsoft Research, Microsoft Research "Valley Road Show" April 16, 2003. Redmond, Wash., Microsoft Research (www.microsoft.com/presspass/exec/rick/04-16svalley.asp)

Raskin, J. 2003. Semantic Web for Earth and Environmental Terminology (SWEET). Paper presented at the Earth Science Technology Conference, Adelphi, Md., June 24–26.

Reddy, M.; LeClerc, Y. G.; Iverson, L.; and Bletter, N. 1999. TerraVision II: Visualizing Massive Terrain Databases in VRML. *IEEE Computer Graphics And Applications* (Special Issue on VRML). 19(2): 30-38.

Reiter, E.; and Dale, R. 2000. *Building Natural Language Generation Systems*. New York: Cambridge Univ. Press.

Rinaldi, F.; Dowdall, J.; Hess, M.; and Mollá, D. 2003a. Exploiting Paraphrases in a Question Answering System. Paper presented at the Association for Computational Linguistics 2003 Workshop on Paraphrases (IWP2003), Sapporo, Japan.

Rinaldi, F.; Dowdall, J.; Hess, M.; Kaljurand, K.; and Karlsson, M. 2003b. The Role of Technical Terminology in Question Answering. Paper presented at the Terminologie et Intelligence Artificielle TIA-2003 Conference, Strasbourg, France, 31 March–1 April.

Rinaldi, F.; Dowdall, J.; Hess, M.; Mollá, D.; and Schwitter, R. 2002. Towards Answer Extraction: An Application To Technical Domains. Paper presented at the ECAI2002, European Conference on Artificial Intelligence, Lyon, France, 21–26 July.

Robertson, Stephen E.; Walker, Steve; and Hancock-Beaulieu, Micheline. 2000. Experimentation as a Way of Life: Okapi At TREC. *Information Processing and Management* 36(1): 95–108.

Ross, C. S.; Nilsen, K.; and Dewdney, P. 2002. *Conducting the Reference Interview.* New York: Neal-Schuman Publishers.

Sager, J. C. 1990. *A Practical Course in Terminology Processing.* Amsterdam: John Benjamins.

Sager, J. C.; and L'Homme, M. C. 1994. A Model for Definition of Concepts. *Terminology* 1(2): 351–374.

Salton, G. 1971. *The SMART Retrieval System: Experiments in Automatic Document Processing.* Engelwood Cliffs, N.J.: Prentice-Hall.

Salton, G.; and McGill, M. 1983. *Introduction to Modern Information Retrieval.* New York: McGraw-Hill.

Sarner, M.; and Carberry, S. 1988. A New Strategy for Providing Definitions in Task Oriented Dialogues. In *Proceedings of the Twelfth International Conference on Computational Linguistics (COLING-88),* Vol. 1. San Francisco: Morgan Kaufmann Publishers.

Schank, R. 1973. Identification of conceptualizations underlying natural language. In Computer Models of Thought and Language, ed. R. Schank and K. Colby. San Francisco: W. H. Freeman.

Schapire, R. E.; and Singer, Y. 2000. BoosTexter: A Boosting-Based System for Text Categorization. *Machine Learning* 39(2/3): 135–168.

Schiffman, B.; Mani, I.; and Concepcion, K. Producing Biographical Summaries: Combining Linguistic Knowledge with Corpus Statistics. In *Proceedings of the Thirty-Ninth Annual Meeting of the Association for Computational Linguistics and the Tenth Conference of the European Chapter of the Association for Computational Linguistics.* San Francisco: Morgan Kaufmann Publishers.

Schilder, F.; and Habel, C. 2001. From Temporal Expressions to Temporal Information: Semantic Tagging of News Messages, Paper presented at the the ACL-2001 Workshop on Temporal and Spatial Information Processing, (ACL-2001). Toulose, France, 6–11 July.

Searle, J. 1975. Indirect Speech Acts. In Syntax and Semantics 3, Speech Acts, ed. P. Cole and J. Morgan. Boston: Academic Press.

Sedgewick, R. 1983. *Algorithms.* Reading, Mass.: Addison Wesley.

Seneff, S. 1992. TINA: A Natural Language System for Spoken Language Applications. *Computational Linguistics.* 18(1): 61–86.

Seneff, S.; Hurley, E.; Lau, R.; Pao, C.; Schmid, P.; and Zue, V. Galaxy-II: A Reference Architecture for Conversational System Development. Paper presented at the Fifth International Conference on Spoken Language Processing, Incorporating the Seventh Australian International Speech Science and Technology Conference, Sydney Australia, 30 November–4 December.

Setzer, Andrea. 2001. Temporal Information in Newswire Articles: An Annotation Scheme and Corpus Study, Ph.D. Dissertation, Dept. of Computer Science, University of Sheffield. Sheffield, England.

Shortliffe, E. H. 1976. *Computer-Based Medical Consultations: MYCIN.* Amsterdam: Elsevier North-Holland.

Sleator, D. D. and Temperley, D. 1993. Parsing English with a Link Grammar. In Proceedings of the Third International Workshop on Parsing Technologies, 277–292. Morristown, N.J.: Association for Computational Linguistics.

Smeaton, A.; and Qigley, I. 1996. Experiments on Using Semantic Distances Between Words in Image Caption Retrieval. In Proceedings of the Nineteenth Annual International ACM SIGIR Conference on Research and Development in Information Retrieval. New York: ACM Press, 174–180.

Smeaton, A.; Over, P.; and Taban, R. 2001. The TREC-2001 Video Track Report. In The Ninth Text Retrieval Conference (TREC 9). NIST Special Publication 500-249, eds. E. M. Voorhees and D. K. Harman. Gaithersburg, Md.: National Institute of Standards and Technology.

Smith J.; Srinivasan S.; Amir A.; Basu S.; Iyengar, G.; Lin, C. Y.; Naphade, M.; Ponceleon, D.; and Tseng, B. 2001. Integrating Features, Models, and Semantics for TREC Video Retrieval. In The Ninth Text Retrieval Conference (TREC 9). NIST Special Publication 500-249, eds. E. M. Voorhees and D. K. Harman. Gaithersburg, Md.: National Institute of Standards and Technology.

Smith, M.; Welty, C, and McGuinness, D. L. 2003, OWL Web Ontology Language Guide. World Wide Web Consortium Candidate Recommendation. World Wide Web Consortium (W3C), Massachusetts Institute of Technology, Cambridge, Mass.

Sneider, E. 1999. Automated FAQ Answering: Continued Experience with Shallow Language Understanding. In Question Answering Systems: Papers from the 1999 Fall Symposium.Technical Report FS-98-04, American Association for Artificial Intelligence, Menlo Park, Calif.

Soubbotin M. M.; and Soubbotin, S. M. 2002. Use of Patterns for Detection of Likely Answer Strings: A Systematic Approach. In Proceedings of the Eleventh Text Retrieval Evaluation Conference (TREC 2002) NIST Special Publication 500-251, 134–143. Gaithersburg, Md.: National Institute of Standards and Technology.

Srihari, R.; and Li, W. 2001. Information Extraction Supported Question Answering. In The Ninth Text Retrieval Conference (TREC 9). NIST Special Publication 500-249, ed.s E. M. Voorhees and D. K. Harman. Gaithersburg, Md.: National Institute of Standards and Technology.

Staav, R.; and Fransson, T. 1991. *Nordens Fåglar.* Stockhom: Norstedt.

Stauffer, C. 2002. Perceptual Data Mining. Ph.D. fissertation, Computer Science Dept., Massachusetts Institute of Technology, Cambridge, Mass.

Stauffer, C.; and Grimson, W. E. L. 2000. Learning Patterns of Activity Using Real-Time Tracking. *IEEE Transactions on Pattern Analysis and Machine Intelligence* 22(8): 747–757.

Stickel, M. E.; Waldinger, R. J.; Chaudhri, V. K. 2000. A Guide to SNARK. Technical Report, SRI International, Menlo Park, Calif.

Sundheim, Beth.1995. Proceedings of the Sixth Message Understanding Conference (MUC-6). Advanced Research Projects Agency Information Technology Office, Columbia, MD. San Francisco: Morgan Kaufmann Publishers.

Swartout, W.; Paris, C.; and Moore, J. 1991. Design for Explainable Expert Systems. *IEEE Intelligent Systems* 6(3): 58–64.

Swartz, N. 1997. Definitions, Dictionaries, and Meanings. Notes, Dept. of Philosophy, Simon Fraser University, Burnaby, B. C., Canada.

Tan, P.; and Kumar, V. 2000. Interestingness Measures for Association Patterns: A Perspective. Technical Report, University of Minnesota, Dept. of Computer Science and Engineering, Minneapolis, Minn.

Tan, P.; Kumar, V.; and Srivastava, J. 2000. Indirect Association: Mining Higher Order Dependencies in Data. In *Principles of Data Mining and Knowledge Discovery: First European Symposium* (PKDD '97) Lecture Notes in Artificial Intelligence, 632-637. Berlin: Springer Verlag.

Tan, P.; Kumar, V.; and Srivastava, J. 2002. Selecting the Right Interestingness Measure for Association Patterns. In Proceedings of the Eighth ACM SIGKDD International Conference on Knowledge Discovery and Data Mining. New York: Association for Computing Machinery.

Tang, Rong; Ng, K. B.; Strzalkowski, Tomek; and Kantor, Paul. 2003. Automatic Prediction of Information Quality in News Documents. Paper Presented at the Human Language Technology Conference (HLT-NAACL 2003), Edmonton, Canada, May 27–June 1.

Tomuro, N. 2003. Interrogative Reformulation Patterns and Acquisition of Question Paraphrases. Paper presented at the Second International Workshop on Paraphrasing (IWP-03), Sapporo, Japan, July 11.

Tomuro, N.; and Lytinen, S. 2001. Selecting Features for Paraphrasing Question Sentences. Paper presented at the Workshop on Automatic Paraphrasing, Sixth Natural Language Processing Pacific Rim Symposium (NLPRS-2001) Tokyo, Nov. 27–30.

Traub, K.; Beckerle, M.; and Ziering, E. 2000. Automatically Determining a Response to an Inquiry Using Structured Information. World Intellectual Property Organization Application WO 01/65412 A2, Geneva, Switzerland.

Tzeras, K.; and Hartmann, S. 1993. Automatic Indexing Based on Bayesian Inference Networks. In Robert Korfhage, Edie Rasmussen, and Peter Willett, editors, Proceedings of the Sixteenth ACM SIGIR International Conference on Research and Development in Information Retrieval, 22-34. New York: Association for Computing Machinery.

Ulicny, B. 2003. Putting Your Customers' Questions To Work. In New Directions in Question Answering: Papers from the 2003 AAAI Spring Symposium. AAAI Tech. Rep. SS-03-07, American Association for Artificial Intelligence, Menlo Park, Calif.

Ulicny, B., Jensen. J., and Allen, B. 1996. Method and Apparatus for Natural Language Querying and Semantic Searching of An Information Database. World Intellectual Property Organization Patent Application WO 98/25217, Geneva, Switzerland.

Voohees, E. M. 2003. Evaluating Answers to Definition Questions. Paper Presented at the Human Language Technology Conference (HLT-NAACL 2003), Edmonton, Canada, May 27–June 1.

Voorhees, E. M. 1999. The TREC-8 Question Answering Track Report. In Proceedings of the Eighth Text Retrieval Conference (TREC 8), 77–82. NIST Special Publication 500-246. Gaithersburg, Md.: National Institute of Standards and Technology.

Voorhees, E. M. 2000. Overview of the TREC-9 Question Answering Track. In Proceedings of the Ninth Text Retrieval Conference (TREC 9). NIST Special Publication. 500-249. Gaithersburg, Md.: National Institute of Standards and Technology.

Voorhees, E. M. 2001. The TREC Question Answering Track. *Natural Language Engineering* 7(4):361–378.

Voorhees, E. M. 2002. Overview of the TREC 2002 Question Answering Track. In Proceedings of the Eleventh Text Retrieval Evaluation Conference (TREC 2002) NIST Special Publication 500-251. Gaithersburg, Md.: National Institute of Standards and Technology.

Voorhees, E. M. 2003. Evaluating Answers to Definition Questions. Paper Presented At the Human Language Technology Conference (HLT-NAACL 2003), Edmonton, Canada, May 27–June 1.

Voorhees, E. M.; and Harman, D. K. 2000. Overview of the Ninth Text Retrieval Conference TREC-9. In Proceedings of the Ninth Text Retrieval Conference (TREC-9). NIST Special Publication 500-249. Gaithersburg, Md.: National Institute of Standards and Technology.

Voorhees, E. M.; and Harman, D. K., eds. 2001. Proceedings of the Ninth Text Retrieval Conference (TREC-9). NIST Special Publication 500-249. Gaithersburg, Md.: National Institute of Standards and Technology.

Voorhees, E. M.; and Harman, D. K., eds. 2002. Proceedings of the Eleventh Text Retrieval Conference (TREC-11). NIST Special Publication SP 500-251. Gaithersburg, Md.: National Institute of Standards and Technology.

Voorhees, E. M.; and Tice, D. M. 1999. The TREC-8 Question Answering Track Evaluation. In Proceedings of the Eighth Text Retrieval Evaluation Conference (TREC-8) NIST Special Publication 500-246. Gaithersburg, Md.: National Institute of Standards and Technology.

Wactlar, H.; Hauptmann, A.; Christel, M.; Houghton R.; and Olligschlaeger, A. 2000. Complementary Video and Audio Analysis for Broadcast News Archives. *Communications of the ACM* 32(2): 42–47.

Waldinger, R.; Jarvis, P.; and Dungan, J. 2003. Pointing to Places in a Deductive Geospatial Theory. Paper presented at the Workshop on Analysis of Geographical References, Human Language Technology Conference, Edmonton, Canada, May 27-June 1.

Warthen, D. 2000, Grammar Template Query System. World Intellectual Property Organization Application, WO 00/57302, Geneva, Switzerland.

Webber, B.; Gardent, C.; Bos, J. 2002. Position Statement: Inference in Question Answering. Paper presented at the Third International Conference on Language Resources and Evaluation (LREC). Palacio De Congreso De Canarias, Canary Islands, Spain, May 28.

Wiebe, J. 1994. Tracking Point of View in Narrative. *Computational Linguistics* 20(2): 233–287.

Wiebe, J.; Breck, E.; Buckley, C.; Cardie, C.; Davis, P.; Fraser, B.; Litman, D.; Pierce, D.; Riloff, E.; Wilson, T.; Day, D.; and Maybury, M. 2003. Recognizing and Organizing Opinions Expressed in the World Press. In New Directions in Question Answering: Papers from the 2003 AAAI Spring Symposium. AAAI Tech. Rep. SS-03-07, American Association for Artificial Intelligence, Menlo Park, Calif.

Wilson, T.; and Wiebe, J. 2003. Annotating Opinions in the World Press. Paper presented at the Fourth Workshop on Discourse and Dialogue (SIGDIAL 2003), Sapporo Japan, 5–6 July.

Winograd, T. 1972. *Understanding Natural Language.* Boston: Academic Press.

Woods, W. 1997. Conceptual Indexing: A Better Way to Organize Knowledge. Technical Report TR-97-61, Sun Microsystems Laboratories, Mountain View, Calif.

Woods, W. A.; Kaplan, R. M.; and Nash-Webber, B. L. 1972. The Lunar Sciences Natural Language Information System: Final Report. Technical Report 2378, BBN Technologies, Cambridge, Mass.

Xu, J.; and Croft, W. B. 1996. Query Expansion Using Local and Global Document Analysis. In Proceedings of the Nineteenth Annual International ACM SIGIR Conference on Research and Development in Information Retrieval, 4-11. New York: Association for Computing Machinery.

Yangarber, R.; and Grishman, R. 1997. Customization of Information Extraction Systems. Paper Presented at the International Workshop on Lexically Driven Information Extraction, Frascati, Italy, July 16.

Yoshitaka, A.; and Ichikawa, T. 1999. A Survey on Content-Based Retrieval for Multimedia Databases. *IEEE Transactions on Knowledge and Data Engineering* 11(1): 81–93.

Zukerman, I.; and Horvitz, E. 2001. Using Machine Learning Techniques to Interpret WH-Questions. In Proceedings of the Thirty-Ninth Annual Meeting of the Association for Computational Linguistics. Morristown, N.J.: Association for Computational Linguistics.

Index